WHOLENESS
AND
HOLINESS

WHOLENESS
AND
HOLINESS

Readings In The
Psychology/Theology
Of Mental Health

H. NEWTON MALONY

EDITOR

Baker Book House

Grand Rapids, Michigan 49506

Copyright 1983 by
Baker Book House Company

ISBN: 0-8010-6147-4

Printed in the United States of America

Contents

Methods of Therapy 257

Contributors

Jay E. Adams, formerly Professor of Counseling, Westminster Theological Seminary, Philadelphia, Pennsylvania.

Allen E. Bergin, Professor of Psychology, Director of the Center for the Study of Values, Brigham Young University, Provo, Utah.

John D. Carter, Professor of Psychology, Rosemead Graduate School of Professional Psychology, Biola University, La Mirada, California.

Robert W. Duke, Professor of Preaching, Lancaster Theological Seminary, Lancaster, Pennsylvania.

John G. Finch, Consulting Psychologist in private practice, Gig Harbor, Washington.

Konstantin Geocaris, formerly Chief of Psychiatric Services, Hillcrest Medical Center, Tulsa, Oklahoma.

Seward Hiltner, Professor Emeritus of Theology and Personality, Princeton Theological Seminary, Princeton, New Jersey.

Richard D. Kahoe, Psychologist, Christian Haven Homes, President, Manna Forty, Wheatfield, Missouri.

H. Newton Malony, Professor of Psychology, Director of Programs in the Integration of Psychology and Theology, Graduate School of Psychology, Fuller Theological Seminary, Pasadena, California.

Robert E. Morosco, Associate Professor of Biblical Studies and Theology, Biola University, La Mirada, California.

S. Bruce Narramore, Dean, Rosemead Graduate School of Professional Psychology, Biola University, La Mirada, California.

Thomas C. Oden, Henry Anson Butts Professor of Theology, Drew University, Madison, New Jersey.

H. L. Parsons, formerly Professor of Philosophy, University of Tennessee, Knoxville, Tennessee.

Frank C. Peters, President and Vice-chancellor Emeritus, Wilfrid Laurier University, Ottawa, Ontario.

David E. Roberts, Marcellus Hartley Professor of the Philosophy of Religion, Union Theological Seminary, New York, New York (deceased).

William R. Rogers, President, Professor of the Psychology of Religion, Guilford College, Greensboro, North Carolina.

Roger L. Shinn, Reinhold Niebuhr Professor of Social Ethics, Union Theological Seminary, New York, New York.

Samuel Southard, Professor of Pastoral Care, Fuller Theological Seminary, Pasadena, California.

Bernard Spilka, Professor of Psychology, University of Denver, Denver, Colorado.

Walter E. Stuermann, Professor of Philosophy, University of Tulsa, Tulsa, Oklahoma (deceased).

Paul J. Tillich, University Professor, Harvard University, Cambridge, Massachusetts (deceased).

Glenn E. Whitlock, Professor of Psychology Emeritus, University of Redlands, Redlands, California.

William P. Wilson, Professor of Psychiatry, Duke University Medical Center, Durham, North Carolina.

Valerie Worthen, Marriage and Family Counselor, Bellevue, Washington.

Preface

Books of readings are like diving boards. Their purpose is to attract persons to walk out on them and to plunge into the issues with vigor and enthusiasm. I hope this collection of essays does just that, i.e., evokes an interest in "wholeness and holiness" and provokes an involvement which will take the reader far beyond the thoughts expressed here.

My interest in the relationship between religious faith and mental health can be traced to four events in my life—all seed experiences which grew into lifelong pursuits.

The first was a friendship with Dr. Roy A. Burkhart, late pastor of First Community Church, Columbus, Ohio, who in the early 1950s was thought to be one of the ten most outstanding ministers in the United States. He was a pastor. He was a psychologist. His ministry tied psychology and theology together in a marvelous manner. He was the first to inspire me to consider such a double vocation.

The second was a two-year stint as chaplain of Davidson County Hospital, Nashville, Tennessee, during the early years of my graduate training in clinical psychology. It was here that I came face to face with tortured mixtures of illness and faith. At the same time I led worship services each Sunday in the hospital chapel in a desperate attempt to combine salvation with health. Looking back, I think I received more than I gave. The experience convinced me the answers were not simple.

The third experience came at the end of my graduate training when I served an internship at Topeka State Hospital, Topeka, Kansas. This time I functioned as a psychologist, not as a chaplain. However, for the first time I observed case conferences in which chaplains were expected to participate as full-fledged mental health professionals. They were always asked to give a "religious diagnosis." The influence of the Menninger Foundation was pervasive at Topeka. Paul Pruyser, among others, had long attempted to relate religion and healing. As a result of this experience, I became inspired to combine more seriously my clinical psychology and my Christian faith.

The last event which intensified my interest in wholeness and holi-

ness was my appointment in the late 1960s to teach in the Graduate
School of Psychology of Fuller Theological Seminary. Although I was
interested in combining faith with clinical practice before, I certainly
was challenged with this task after I arrived in Pasadena. That is what
the whole school is about! The goal is high; the achievements have
been moderate. My designation as "Director of Programs in the Integration of Psychology and Theology" some years later did not make
the task any easier, although it definitely made it more focused. I am
deeply dedicated to the task of studying the "psychology/theology of
mental health." It is not only a professional, but also a personal
commitment.

So these are the events which led to this book of readings which are
intended to provide a "jumping off place" for others who want to
become involved. I have tried to bring together seminal articles of the
last twenty-five years. Of course, such a collection is itself a selection.
It is not exhaustive, even though I feel it is representative. Breadth of
approach rather than depth of treatment was my aim. A variety of
positions is presented.

The articles are grouped into both theoretical and practical sections. While not intending to be an apology for any one conceptual
approach or counseling technique, nevertheless, they confine themselves to ideas emergent out of the interaction of Western psychology
and the Christian faith.

The underlying assumption of the organization of the readings is
that practice must be grounded in principles. Thus sections on the
human predicament, the experience of living, and the meaning of health
precede those on the process of healing and methods of therapy. The
relationships of faith to counseling are far more complex than some
have assumed. The sequence of these readings is meant to engage the
student in a meaningful dialogue with the subtle but important relationships between basic assumptions and professional intervention.
While not meant to inhibit people-helpers in their work, these readings
are intended to awaken and cultivate a sophisticated understanding
of these issues that will preclude premature or easy solutions.

Each section includes an introduction and also contains a summary
which poses questions for dialogue and suggests additional readings.
The introduction includes a précis of the section theme, a brief quote
from each article in the section, and a statement about what the reader
may expect to find in the articles. In addition, preceding each article
is an abstract written by the author(s) or by me. At the beginning of
the book I have included a general introduction, which delineates the

overarching theme of the collection. It provides the framework for the other materials to follow.

This book can be read with profit by an individual studying alone. The framework for a fruitful education experience is here if one will but follow the outline. Practicing mental health professionals may want to follow this format.

However, the book's prime intent is to provide a basic structure for an advanced undergraduate or a graduate level seminar in religion and mental health. There is ample material here for class discussion and serious reflection. The dialogue questions can be used as essay exams and the additional readings will provide ready leads for more intensive reflection.

I hope this contribution accomplishes its intended goals and, at the same time, assists many in being "workmen that need not be ashamed, rightly dividing the word of truth" (II Tim. 2:15b).

I express thanks to my secretary, Mindy Tallent, and to my academic colleagues—all of whom have made this venture possible and productive.

Pasadena, California
Advent, 1982

Introduction

"Mental health is a moving target." So said the late Margaret Mead, well-known anthropologist. Unlike stationary bullseyes mounted on bales of hay at rifle ranges, mental health is more like ducks that pop up unexpectedly on conveyor belts at circus shooting galleries. She meant something more than "mental health differs from culture to culture"—a fact she knew only too well! She was stating that health of mind varies from time to time and situation to situation. Mental health can mean getting rid of anxiety for one person and the fulfillment of a life goal for another. To apply the same criteria to everyone is a mistake. Thus, to "hit" mental health, it is necessary continually to readjust one's sights and shift one's weapon. There is no one definition that will satisfy all conditions.

Mead's noteworthy comment draws attention to important distinctions between terms such as *health, wholeness, salvation,* and *holiness*— prime concerns in this book of readings. Often these terms have been treated as easily defined synonyms (i.e., stationary targets) when, in fact, they have different meanings due to a variety of circumstances (i.e., moving targets). Considering some of these differences and interrelationships will provide a foundation for understanding the selection of articles included in this volume.

Positive and Negative Definitions of Health and Salvation

Many definitions of health have been proposed, as Marie Jahoda noted in her seminal volume, *Current Concepts of Positive Mental Health*

15

(1958). Health has often been defined as the absence of disease. For example, a person might say in answer to the question, "How are you?" "I'm healthy, thank you. I haven't caught a cold all winter long." Or one might say, "My stomach was upset for two weeks after I went to Mexico, but I'm healthy now." These are what Jahoda would term negative definitions of health just as the absence of depression, anxiety, and/or lethargy might be termed negative definitions of mental health.

A negative definition could also be given to salvation, used here as a label for the religious counterpart of health. Al Elby, a man whose religious experience is reported in a volume, *Ways People Meet God: Today's Religious Experience* (Malony, 1978, 11-12), defined salvation merely as no longer cursing, smoking, or drinking—bad habits he once had. On the other hand, the prophet Amos gave a resounding negative definition of salvation:

> For three transgressions of Israel,
>   and for four, I will not revoke the punishment;
> because they sell the righteous for silver,
>   and the needy for a pair of shoes—
> they that trample the head of the poor into the dust of the earth,
>   and turn aside the way of the afflicted (2:6-7a, RSV).

He was not satisfied with this negative definition of salvation. After expressing dissatisfaction with Israel because of her sins, Amos went on:

> I hate, I despise your feasts,
>   and I take no delight in your solemn assemblies.
> Even though you offer me your burnt offerings and cereal offerings,
> I will not accept them, . . .
> Take away from me the noise of your songs;
>   to the melody of your harps I will not listen.
> But let justice roll down like waters,
>   and righteousness like an ever-flowing stream (5:21-24, RSV).

Two aspects of this proclamation indicate Amos affirmed something more than merely a negative view of salvation.

First, his comments about feasts, assemblies, offerings, and songs refer to a normal, rather than a negative, definition of salvation. What the average person does is normal. From this point of view, convention or custom determines the meaning of salvation. For example, many persons would answer the question "Are you saved?" by replying, "I go to church every week; I give to the United Fund; I put money in the Salvation Army basket at Christmas; I am a good person." These are acts which are expected of religious persons. "Going to church . . ." is the equivalent of Amos's assemblies, songs, etc.

Normal understandings of physical or mental health are similar to normal definitions of salvation. Health is often understood in terms of adjustment to one's culture. Many parents will say that their children are healthy because they are normal—not too thin, not too heavy; not too bright, not too dumb; not too strong, not too weak. Fitting in to the average in terms of being well and of having good self-esteem "most of the time" are characteristics of normal health. They indicate one has adjusted to the environment and is doing what is expected.

However, Amos goes beyond the normal definition of salvation by implying that simply adjusting to convention and custom is not enough. God "despises" worship services and "will not listen" to singing, as if to say that this is not full salvation. Amos suggests that salvation is something more than going to church on Sunday. Salvation is being righteous and being just! These are accomplishments over and beyond stopping doing the bad (a negative definition) or fitting in to what good people do (a normal definition). This doing of a new thing could be called a positive definition of salvation. Paul speaks of this:

> Therefore, if any one is in Christ, he is a new creation; the old has passed away, behold, the new has come (II Cor. 5:17, RSV).

The "new" in Paul's statement is something more than a negative or normal view of salvation. In Paul's mind salvation includes the appearance of something that had not been there before: a character that reflects a change for the better.

This positive definition of salvation is most clear in Paul's admonition to the Christians at Rome:

> "I appeal to you therefore, brethren, by the mercies of God, to present your bodies as a living sacrifice, holy and acceptable to God, which is your spiritual worship. Do not be conformed to this world but be transformed by the renewal of your mind, that you may prove what is the will of God, what is good and acceptable and perfect" (Rom. 12:1-2, RSV).

Paul clearly redefines worship (normal salvation) in a way that moves it toward change rather than conventional morality. He calls for the Romans themselves to become living sacrifices rather than simply bringing their sacrifices to the temple. In the next sentence Paul makes it even more clear: the Romans are to be transformed rather than conformed. Conformity would be normal salvation. Transformation would be positive salvation!

The Christian faith has termed positive spiritual health "holiness" or "sanctification." The ideal to which both Amos and Paul called persons was that of living completely under the direction and will of God Almighty. This is what it meant to be holy. "Consecrate yourselves therefore, and be holy; for I am the LORD your God" (Lev. 20:7, RSV). The New Testament portrayal of this positive dimension of salvation is in terms of the ideal of perfection. Jesus speaks of this in comparing Christian living to the conventional behavior of tax collectors and Gentiles. He states, "You, therefore, must be perfect, as your heavenly Father is perfect" (Matt. 5:48).

What is true for salvation can also be seen in regard to mental health. Jahoda's whole book addresses positive definitions of mental health. She lists six characteristics of those whose mental health goes beyond adjusting to their environment and desisting from bad habits:

1. *Accurate perception of reality* which includes seeing what is really there in spite of pressures from the environment to distort;

2. *Mastery of the situation* which includes a sense of control and success in love, work, and play;

3. *Autonomy* which includes a sense of independence, self-determination, acceptance or rejection of influence, and the ability to surrender or commit oneself if one so desires;

4. *Having a positive attitude toward oneself* which includes acceptance, awareness, identity, and lack of self-consciousness;

5. *Personal integration* which includes an adequate balance of inner forces and a philosophy of life;

6. *Self-actualization* which includes a sense that one is growing and developing toward self-realization and long-range goals which one has set for oneself.

These are all achievements which result from efforts to excel in accomplishments. This is what it means to have positive mental health. These attainments are all positives; not negatives or normals.

Physical, as well as mental, health has its positive dimension. Athletes who train their bodies to perform exceptional feats are good examples. Jack LaLanne, who leads early-morning TV watchers in strenuous exercise routines, exhibits strength and vitality far in excess of what one would expect for a sixty-year-old man. He and his followers illustrate this way of understanding health. They are "weller than well." The concern in our culture for diet and exercise further reflects this positive understanding of health. Persons are no longer satisfied merely with not being sick. They want to keep fit and vigorous well into the retirement years. Health means to develop one's body, to keep it finely tuned, and to excel in alertness and physical performance. These are positive achievements of an ideal! Thus to be healthy or whole implies more than not being sick or being just as healthy as one's neighbors.

So, health and salvation can be defined in a variety of ways. Negative, normal, and positive understandings exist along a continuum. At one extreme health and salvation are described as the absence of sickness or sin while at the other extreme they are described as the achievement of certain abilities or virtues. These relationships are diagrammed in Figure 1.

The next question is, "Where do the concepts of wholeness and holiness fit within such a model?" Initially, it would seem as if these terms would apply solely to the positive end of the continuum since their dictionary definitions include words such as complete, unimpaired, intact, sound, perfect, pious, sinless, and saintly. All these words imply a state in which parts are working together harmoniously and goals are being achieved. Wholeness and holiness appear to be concepts which have an absolute rather than a relative meaning. Furthermore, these terms seem to imply the presence of the good rather than simply the absence of the bad.

This initial impression may well be true but there is a sense in which these ideal states of wholeness and holiness need always to be interpreted in process dimensions which include time, place, and person. Wholeness may be one thing for a Midwest high-school athlete and another thing for a poverty-level South American teenager, or a paraplegic Vietnam veteran, or a Seattle retiree. Holiness may be one thing for a Moscow Baptist and another thing for a South African Episcopalian, or a Four-Square Pentecostal, or a Boston Christian Scientist. On the one hand, it would seem untenable, if not unjust, to apply absolute criteria for either wholeness or holiness to those for whom such goals would be impossible or make no sense. God's will is always a demand to be holy in a given place and at a given time. On the other hand, it would seem perfectly appropriate to hold up standards of health and salvation which transcend culture and experience. From this point of view, holiness should be holiness anywhere and anytime. The complexity of the issues is great.

What is needed is a model for the healing and the redemptive processes which will encompass the multiplicity of these variables yet

Figure 1

Definitions of Health and Salvation

NEGATIVE	NORMAL	POSITIVE
absence	adjustment	achievement

retain the essence of wholeness and holiness as ideal states to be attained. It is hoped the proposals to follow will meet these criteria.

A Role/Process/State Theory of Healing and Redemption

A role theory perspective on these issues is grounded in the dictum that life or living is understood as "the effort to maintain a mutually interdependent relationship with one's environment over an extended period of time." The role(s) one plays are attempts to establish these interdependent relationships. When one is successful, we can say that life is organized. This is health. When one is not successful, we can say that life is disorganized. This is sickness. When one has reestablished a relationship with his/her environment, we can say that life is reorganized. This is healing.

These ideas refer to points in time as well as periods of time. That is, they refer to states and to processes. One may have attained a given role status at a given time yet be in the process of maintaining or achieving a new role status at the same time. For example, a person could say, "I'm over the flu and will return to work tomorrow. But, I want to get back to jogging next week in preparation for the 10K run which will be held next month." Or one could say with Paul,

> Not that I have already obtained this or am already perfect; but I press on to make it my own, because Christ Jesus has made me his own. Brethren, I do not consider that I have made it my own; but one thing I do, forgetting what lies behind and straining forward to what lies ahead, I press on toward the goal for the prize of the upward call of God in Christ Jesus (Phil. 3:12-14, RSV).

The environmental dimension should be added to the model in order to clarify the application of this theory to religion. Persons live in relation to several environments, not just one, and they must achieve an interdependent role with each of them. The example given above of the individual who was returning to work after being sick illustrates at least two of these environments: the physical (his/her body) and the situational (his/her work).

T. R. Sarbin in an important article on the nature of social identity (1970) offered descriptions of five life environments to which persons must adapt if they would survive. In his descriptions there is an idealistic as well as a transcendental environment which accords a place to religious issues alongside physical and social issues.

1. *Physical*: the inner biological state and the outer natural conditions in which one lives;

2. *Situational*: the cultural setting of work, play, and action in which one lives;

3. *Interpersonal*: the human beings with whom one interacts as family, friends, and acquaintances;

4. *Idealistic*: the goals, ambitions, standards, and values one adopts for one's life;

5. *Transcendental*: the supernatural transempirical reality to which one relates and in terms of which one finds ultimate meaning to life and death.

The uniqueness of Sarbin's list lies in its inclusion of the idealistic and transcendental environments. This suggests that working out relationships with the valuative and religious dimensions is not an option but a necessity. If health be defined in terms of establishing a mutually satisfying relationship with all of these environments, then there is warrant for saying that wholeness and holiness, health and salvation are interdependent. The term *whole person* applies to this idea. To be whole means to be conscious of and adequate in all, not just some, of life's environments.

However, Sarbin's concept of role is equally important for our discussion. Role is that set of thoughts, words, feelings, and actions adopted by a person in interacting with a given environment so that the person experiences satisfaction and status. This satisfaction and status is termed *identity*. Identity provides meaning to life. Persons strive for identity and are not content until they find it.

Sarbin calls this sense of identity the psychological environment. He suggests that the psychological environment is the overarching perception one has of one's functioning in all the other environments. The relationships among these environments is diagrammed in Figure 2.

Figure 2

Interrelationships Among Life Environments

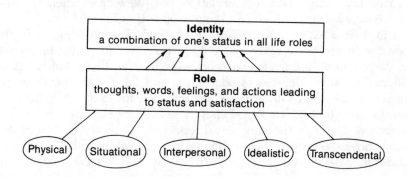

Several comments could be made about this model.

First, if organization is synonymous with health, then being organized could be understood as having an identity in all of life's environments, not just some of them.

Second, attaining and maintaining those identities is by no means a task that is achieved totally at any one time; it is uneven and it varies from time to time and environment to environment.

Third, identities which may be satisfying and fulfilling for one person may not be satisfying and fulfilling for another.

Fourth, a person may have achieved a certain state yet be actively involved in achieving another because she/he is not satisfied with her/himself.

All of these comments would seem to relativize the meaning of wholeness and holiness in the sense that the achievement of any absolute standards of these characteristics may be much more complex than was previously imagined. In what sense, then, can one retain an understanding of wholeness and holiness as overarching ideals to be attained alongside these incontrovertible truths about the differences in their meaning from person to person and time to time?

A Reevaluation of Wholeness and Holiness

The thesis of this section is that wholeness and holiness can have both absolute and relative meanings. However, this perspective requires the kind of interpretation which is possible only through a careful examination of some aspects of the Christian gospel.

Before elaborating on this thesis, it is important to recall the proposal to consider health and salvation as both a state and a process. This proposal relates integrally to attempts to find identity by assuming roles in relation to various life environments. At any one time identity is the composite of the status one has attained through the process of playing roles. And as previously noted, status can result in negative (absence), normal (average), or positive (achievement) meanings. Two examples will clarify these propositions.

A Lutheran pastor with no major physical problems and in fairly good condition for his sixty years of age resigned his pulpit to open a marriage counseling center with his wife. Both of them had recently obtained masters' degrees in counseling and desired to specialize in this service as well as have more personal time for each other. Several months later he had a routine chest x ray before elective surgery on his foot. A cancer of the lung was discovered. He received chemotheraphy and experienced no problems for several months. Then his condition deteriorated and he spent six weeks in treatment at the hospital, after which the cancer went into remission again. But the remission did not last and he entered the hospital in a weakened condition. Shortly before his death he told a visitor, "It has been a good life and I am ready to die. What is remarkable to me is that the faith I had in good times has been sufficient for me. I trust God and feel I am his child now just as much as I did when I was not sick."

This story illustrates several of the propositions about health and salvation. At one point health was defined in a negative way in that the pastor was not sick and in a normal way in that he was in as good condition as most men his age. At another time it was defined in a negative way in that the cancer went into remission. Healing was understood not as a return to former functioning but rather as a stopping of a malignant process. In another sense health was defined in a positive way in that he and his wife set out to attain a new status as counselors. His adjustment to several life environments can be seen in the way that he attempted to find a role to play with his wife (interpersonal), his weakening body (physical), and with God (transcendental).

Another example is that of a young woman who graduated in business administration from a large Midwestern university. She was an adventuresome sort who spent the next eight years in a variety of pursuits: helping build a school at a mission in Mexico, fishing in Alaska, repairing boats in San Francisco Bay, cooking for an anthropological expedition, training guides for the Spokane world's fair, and being a hostess in a VIP lounge near a metropolitan airport. While in Alaska she met a summer fisherman with whom she fell in love. They married and moved to the southeastern United States. Presently she is a free-lance public relations consultant and he is the representative for an Alaskan fishing company. Much of her work takes her to distant cities but she and her husband get together every three or four weeks. While growing up she was a faithful Catholic but does not see herself as religious at present. She is in her early thirties and in excellent physical condition, having recently run a 6.2 mile race in record time.

This story, too, illustrates several of the propositions about health and salvation. Her concern for proper diet and for physical training reflects a positive definition of health in the sense that she is not satisfied with just being normal. Her movement from job to job indicates an attempt to find a fulfilling role in relation to the situation life environment of work. Her marriage is one aspect of her effort to find a satisfying role in relation to the interpersonal life environment. The continuing readjustment of her marriage and her work with that of her husband reflects the process dimension of health. It would seem as if the transcendent life environment is not being considered at present or has been relegated to an area of less importance.

In what sense do these two stories relate to the evaluation of wholeness and holiness? If nothing else, they illustrate the complexity of health and salvation issues. But is there a way in which either the Lutheran pastor or the young public relations consultant could be considered holy or whole?

If the physical and the spiritual could be separated, it might be said that the Lutheran pastor was holy and the public relations consultant was whole. She certainly was in good physical shape and he certainly had made his peace with the transcendent. Yet this would be too limited a view since wholeness, at least, has been understood to refer to a fulfilling adjustment to all of life environments, not just the physical.

This leads into another issue: "Must one be fulfilled in all life environments to be judged whole?" If this is true, then neither the Lutheran pastor nor the public relations consultant could be considered whole. This interpretation would make wholeness completely unattainable except at that time in early adulthood when one's body was potentially at its peak. The problem with this position is that finding one's identity in several of the other life environments cannot be satisfactorily done without more years of experience than young adulthood allows. So the answer would seem to be, "No, wholeness cannot be defined as satisfactory status in all of life environments at one time." Some allowance must be made for uneven development.

Another question is, "How should the roles one plays in relation to various life environments be related? Are they additive? interactive? multiplicative?" Is it the sum, the meshing, or the product of one's status in these areas that determines wholeness or holiness?

From one point of view the answer is additive. This perspective suggests that wholeness or holiness is the sum of the role satisfaction a person has in each of the roles that she/he plays. If it were possible to rate the status one had from the role one played in each of the life environments along a continuum from 1 to 10 (inadequate to ideal), then one could add these up and obtain a measure of health or salvation. A person with a score of forty-five would be more whole than a person with a score of thirty-one. This would imply that no one environment was more important than another and that all were weighted equally.

From another point of view the answer is interactive. This perspective suggests that wholeness or holiness is a result of the meshing of the roles one has achieved in relation to the several life environments. The assumption behind this position is that the whole is more than the sum of the parts. One's identity at a given time may be due to the unique pattern of interactions among the roles. One woman spoke of this as the "tip theory." She said on some days she tipped in the direction of wholeness, while on other days she did not. The tip of a given day depended on her general assessment of the overall status she had that day as a result of the interaction of the roles she was playing.

In my judgment, the optimal answer is multiplicative in the sense that, while the physical, situational, interpersonal, and idealistic life environments are strategic, the transcendental life environment is of prime importance. It should be weighted more heavily than the others and it functions as the multiplier in the wholeness/holiness formula. While adequate adjustment in this area does not obliterate the necessity for attending to the other life environments, this dimension of life is so crucial that unless one adopts a fulfilling role in regard to it, there can be no genuine wholeness.

The formula for wholeness and holiness, therefore, might look something like this: transcendent identity **times** physical identity **plus** situational identity **plus** interpersonal identity **plus** idealistic identity. Who one is in relation to the transcendent environment is so crucial that it multiplies the effect of one's identity in all other areas of life.

Furthermore, from the viewpoint of Christian faith, there is a sense in which satisfying status in the transcendent life environment is less an achievement and more an acceptance. This is not true of one's identity in any other life environment. Identity in these areas is attained or achieved, status can be found and it can be lost. This is not true in the transcendent life environment. Many Scripture texts attest to this truth. For example:

> But God, who is rich in mercy, out of the great love with which he loved us, even when we were dead through our trespasses, made us alive together with Christ (by grace you have been saved), and raised us up with him, and made us sit with him in the heavenly places in Christ Jesus, that in the coming ages he might show the immeasurable riches of his grace in kindness toward us in Christ Jesus. For by grace you have been saved through faith; and this is not your own doing, it is the gift of God—not because of works, lest any man should boast. For we are his workmanship, created in Christ Jesus for good works, which God prepared beforehand, that we should walk in them (Eph. 2:4-10, rsv).

In a strange manner, while holiness is a demand, at the same time it is a gift!

The gist of these ideas is that the status persons seek in the transcendent life environment is not something that they have to achieve or attain by work and study but something that they can accept through trust and faith. This is the distinction between ascribed and achieved status. As I have noted elsewhere (Collins and Malony, 1981), this status as "forgiven child of the living God" is given freely by God out of His love. This role is there for the receiving and one does not have to work long or hard for it. It is the only status which is not subject to change. All the other conditions of life demand that persons remain vigilant and on guard. This status is given to human beings in spite of their sin and whether or not they deserve it. It provides a basis where they can confidently ask God, "What is your will for my life?" and know that He will provide a way for His will to be done!

Firm status in the transcendent area provides a foundation for achievement in all other dimensions. These dimensions are put in perspective; they are not diminished and their importance is not discounted. One is now aware that full achievement in these life environments is often illusory and transitory and, in the final analysis, satisfactory identity can be had without such achievements.

Although this may sound like an exaggeration, it may not be. As Paul Tillich noted in *The Courage to Be* (1952), all anxiety about one's status in relation to one's body, one's fellows/sisters, one's house, one's work, and one's play is probably grounded in basic anxiety about who one is, why one is here, and in what one can hope. If this be true, as I think it is, then to settle one's quest for status in relation to the transcendent environment by accepting the role as "forgiven sinner: redeemed servant" is to establish a firm foundation on which all the rest of life can be lived.

Furthermore, accepting such a Christian identity transvalues the meaning of status in the other life environments so that giving becomes as important as receiving and justice becomes as important as possessing. This brings us back to the type of holiness described by Amos and James. It is not that one's identity as a child of God is dependent on these good deeds but that when one comes to know who one is in the eyes of God, then one will be busy doing good, or as Jesus said:

> Let your light so shine before men, that they may see your good works and give glory to your Father who is in heaven (Matt. 5:16, RSV).

For this relationship between wholeness and holiness, I would suggest the term *holy wholeness*. In this sense the Lutheran pastor was whole while the young public relations consultant was not—no matter how healthy she was in a physical sense! It may be true that we should also coin the term *whole holiness* to stand for the type of life that has settled the question of status in the transcendent environment and then turns with vitality and vigor to finding a satisfying role in the other environments. Accepting Christian identity does not imply denial of the physical or social worlds. Quite to the contrary, Christians are to work in the world for the sake of their fellow/sister human beings. In that sense, the public relations consultant has the potential of being holy while the Lutheran pastor does not. She still has time for invested involvement in the world while, alas, his days are numbered.

My firm conviction is that these ideas about wholeness and holiness are good psychology and good theology. The Christian faith is complementary, not contradictory, to the concepts of identity, role, and status which have been presented here. Furthermore, I believe that the model presented above allows for a combining of the absolute and relative meanings of wholeness and holiness. It acknowledges that both wholeness and holiness are goals to which persons aspire. They are a process of attainment as well as a state of achievement.

This essay has presented a model for relating wholeness and holiness as a prelude to a discussion of these issues by several theologians and psychologists. While their presentations are not elaborations of these ideas, they, nevertheless, will not contradict them in any significant manner. By a considering of these issues, I hope the reading of these presentations will be enlivened and the discussion of the psychology/theology of mental health will be enriched. For, as Margaret Mead suggested, mental health is, indeed, a moving target!

References

Collins, G. R., and Malony, H. N. 1981. *Psychology and theology: Prospects for integration*. Nashville: Abingdon.

Jahoda, M. 1958. *Current concepts of positive mental health*. New York: Basic Books.

Malony, H. N. 1978. The Christian church: An organization to develop. *Theology News and Notes*, 10:21-23.

————. 1978. *Ways people meet God*. Nashville: Tidings.

Sarbin, T. R. 1970. A role theory perspective for community psychology: The structure of social identity. In *Community psychology and mental health: Perspectives and challenges*, edited by D. Adelson and B. L. Kalis. Scranton, Pa.: Chandler. pp. 89-113.

Tillich, P. 1952. *The courage to be*. New Haven, Conn.: Yale University.

The Human Predicament

*P**redicament* is a strong word. Many in Western society would prefer the term *opportunity* or *experience*. However, those who counsel troubled persons will readily affirm that being alive is, indeed, a predicament or dilemma. I use the term in a sense similar to the existentialists who have asserted that meaning in life *must* be discovered and affirmed. Finding a purpose for living is not easy. It is the univeral human predicament.

Central to this dilemma is the question of human nature. The answer to "who *really* are we?" is the search for underlying structure or essence. Counseling should be grounded in a view of human nature or else it will flounder in a morass of haphazard problem solving. This section provides readings which depict understandings of human nature from both psychological and theological points of view.

Shinn's essay, "The Story of Man and the Image of Man," is a theological statement emphasizing a view of humans based on God's acts as reported in the Bible and as seen in Jesus. As he states, "The second image of Christian faith is the image of God-in-action and man-in-action in Jesus Christ. Through Him we discover what it is to know God and neighbor and self."

Whitlock's article, "The Structure of Personality in Hebrew Psychology," is subtitled "The Implications of the Hebrew View of Man for Psychology of Religion." He traces Hebrew meanings of words such as *body, flesh, spirit,* and *soul,* and states, "In relationship to God, man stands in a situation similar to the patient in psychotherapy. Spiritual holiness or emotional wholeness can be achieved only when the total

29

self is involved. . . . Neither . . . can be achieved through man's own efforts. The flesh *(basar)* is powerless to act. It is the spirit *(ruach)* of God which enables man to become a whole person."

Stuermann and Geocaris's essay compares John Calvin's and Sigmund Freud's "Image of Man." They state, "The opening words of Calvin's *Institutes* proclaim that true and substantial wisdom consists principally of two parts, the knowledge of God and the *knowledge of ourselves.* Freud's psychoanalytic technique represents a search for knowledge of the self. . . . According to both of them, a man's assessment of his nature determines his behavior."

Spilka writes as a psychologist in his article, "Images of Man and Dimensions of Personal Religion: Values for an Empirical Psychology of Religion." In detailing the past distinctions between reductionistic and humanistic tendencies, he states, ". . . there are strong trends within psychology to resurrect man *in toto* from a misplaced emphasis on him as a compound of variables and fractionated processes. Current humanistic-psychological versions of man *qua* man are basically similar to the views of man held in Western theology."

The reader should expect to find in these four essays ample material to stimulate him/her to explore more broadly the basic presumptions about human nature which he/she utilizes in dealing with others in both casual and professional relationships.

Secular views tell us something but not everything about human beings. Sacred images of persons deal with the mystery, the pathos, and the hope of existence. From Jesus Christ come two new views of God-in-action and man-in-action. From this we gain new divine, neighbor, and self understandings. There is mystery in selfhood, tragedy in human life, and salvation from a living God.

The Story of Man and the Image of Man

Roger L. Shinn

Part of the marvel of human personality is its rich diversity. As Shakespeare's Marc Antony wondered at the "infinite variety" of Cleopatra, we may wonder at our many glimpses of human nature in ordinary experience. Swift pictures of people flash upon us. With more or less success we fuse these impressions into coherent images.

I recall, for example, a coed who sat in my class some years ago. At a campus dance one night I watched her, a picture of blonde gracefulness. Poised, confident, friendly, she whirled among the dancers. A few days later I saw her slouched over a blue book, struggling with questions I had inflicted on her. Face and posture were a study in defeat. I wondered—only momentarily, I admit—what right I had to destroy the radiance of a few days before. I wondered for a longer time how one person could produce two images, so vastly different. I pondered how the coed resolved her own self-images coming out of these two situations.

Then I wondered how I resolved my many self-images—images of a self-in-triumph and a self-in-frustration, of a generous and a jealous

Reprinted from the March-April 1958 issue of the journal, *Religious Education*, by permission of the publisher, The Religious Education Association, 409 Prospect St., New Haven, CT 06510. Membership or subscription available for $25.00 per year.

self, of a self loved by family and friends and a self misunderstood and made lonely by these same people. By this time I was thoroughly baffled.

That bafflement is a warning. When we consider images of man, we dare not make the arrogant assumption that religion has "figured out" this man and produced the one right image. And, when sacred and secular images clash, we dare not reason that one or the other must be rejected out of hand. It is foolish to assert that the men who run rats through mazes can tell us *nothing* about how human beings function—as foolish as to claim that they have the clue to human love and fidelity and worship. Likewise it is absurd to say that the opening chapters of Genesis or the traditional doctrines of the church tell us everything worth knowing, or tell us nothing at all, about the human person.

Our image of man must come from glimpses of men—of self and of others. And this self, glimpsed and glimpsing, cannot fuse the glimpses into any complete, consistent composite. Revelation offers its own glimpses and modifies other glimpses, but does not transmit a completed, sufficient image.

The planners of this National Convention of the Religious Education Association have wisely refused to make secularism a whipping boy. They have distinguished between that *secular* which rightly designates affairs of the world and which the sacred should seek to embrace and that other *secular* which denies or excludes the sacred. The trouble is that these two *seculars*, so important to distinguish, are constantly mingled in our culture. Hence the secularism which opposes religion has something to say to religious people. Quite possibly we would not come to this meeting—Jews, Roman Catholics, Protestants, ready to learn from each other—had we not been educated and chastened by the secularism of the Enlightenment, a secularism which denies the truth of most of what we are saying to each other. It is not enough to answer that we should have learned from our faiths what we have learned from secularism. Of course we should have—and should have learned it more profoundly than secularism could teach it. But usually we and our forefathers *did not*. God has taught us through those who deny Him, as well as through His prophets and apostles.

Nevertheless, it is our responsibility to affirm what He has taught us against those who deny it. Hence every generation needs to describe the sacred image of man against the background of its particular contemporary culture.

Any sacred image of man takes account of what George Santayana called "the mystery and pathos of existence." The opposite of the sacred is not so much the evil and immoral as it is the irreverent. It is normal for men to respond with wonder and awe to the marvels of other persons, of themselves, of this universe that is their home—and of the hidden source of all that is. Although this reverence can be stifled by human contrivances and indoctrination, it persistently reemerges.

The mystery of life and the universe does not simply overwhelm and terrify the human race. Man recognizes that this mystery has given him his being, that he is somehow akin to it. Although it threatens and destroys him, it lures him to see past its hostility to its hidden kinship. It draws him to trust it. Hence every sacred view of man expresses, not only his reverence before mystery and his pain before pathos, but his hope for salvation. The sacred means promise, healing, redemption.

All this can be traced in a vast variety of human experiences and in the history of many religions. The sacred images of man are formed in startling diversity. But all of them include in some way the three elements of *mystery, tragedy,* and *salvation.*

When we look at the distinctive image of man in the Hebrew-Christian Scriptures, we see characteristically an image-in-action. Selfhood is selfhood-in-activity. Therefore the appropriate form of description is narrative. The Bible has no books or chapters which give formal description of human nature. Later theologians and philosophers may attempt to abstract from the biblical narratives such analyses; they have a right to do so, but they had better recognize the peril in such attempts. Even those abstractions which are most faithful to the scriptural accounts are misleading just because the Scriptures are not abstract. Even if formal concepts use the very stuff of the Bible, the result is strange because the biblical images are not static or formal.

The Bible tells about man by telling the epic story of man. Out of this story—packed with movement and activity, with conflict and triumph and defeat, with deeds of fidelity and rebellion—come tumbling the brilliant metaphors and vivid images which have entered the language of faith. Dust of the ground . . . breath of life . . . a living soul . . . in the image of God . . . dust and ashes . . . but little lower than God . . . mortal man . . . eternity in their hearts . . . a faithless generation . . . my people . . . a new covenant . . . generation of vipers . . . hypocrites . . . betrayers and murderers . . . saints in Caesar's household . . . a royal priesthood. . . .

So the words might continue, page after page. But all get their meaning from the relation of man to God, a relation wrought out and constantly renewed in activity. The images of man come out of the life of a people. God, who created all that is, created this people and bade them be faithful. When they distrusted God and rebelled against Him,

He approached them and offered to win them back. He renewed covenant with Noah, with Abraham, with Moses. Through the prophets (Hosea, Jeremiah, Ezekiel, Second Isaiah) He promised a new covenant of forgiveness, a redemption. In the fullness of time He sent His Son to be born of a woman, to do for man what man could not do for himself.

So from Jesus Christ came two new images, fulfillments of old images, definitive images for the Christian. But again these are not static images, frozen concepts. Jesus of Nazareth, who directed men's faith not to Himself but to the Father who sent Him, nevertheless has given us the image of God-in-action. And this Jesus has given us the image of man-in-action—not, indeed, of ourselves as we act but of ourselves restored by God's grace to the family of God.

No wonder this image of man appears somewhat bizarre among its competitors. It cannot be catalogued alongside a Freudian or Jungian concept, the theories of idealistic or materialistic metaphysics, the economic man or culture man of academic discourse. To be sure, able theologians have worked out Christian doctrines of man, have carried their doctrines into the intellectual arenas, and have slugged it out (frequently with notable success) against the opposition. But the most formidable champions of the Christian doctrine of man have been the first to admit that their statements are inadequate, for the formulations arise out of the living relation between God and man, and that relation can never be imprisoned in the formulas.

But if there is this difficulty in forming a Christian concept of man, the source of difficulty is nevertheless a source of insight for religious education, the interest which has brought us here. As many churches are discovering, the nature of Christian education in its own right offers a way through the old warfare of slogans (Bible-centered versus pupil-centered, doctrine versus religious experience). If the Hebrew-Christian images of God and man gain their meaning in the midst of the life of a historical community aware of its relation to God, then those images will live in this community. To introduce the child or adult into a covenant community obviously requires concern for its traditions and habits, its symbols, its writings and doctrines, its continuing experiences both in its own life and in its relations with the world. To work all this out is, of course, far more than to state it in a sentence.

If I have warned sufficiently against the danger of turning an image-in-action into a concept, perhaps I may now examine some concepts that we may draw from biblical faith. For conceptualization is useful if we remember that it is derivative, not primary.

Freedom is one Christian concept. Christian faith tells of a self whose birthright and destiny is freedom, but who finds himself in bondage. When men cultivate a self-image of freedom, they often attack the Christian image for its emphasis on bondage. Any vigorous, red-blooded American, they argue, will get out and accomplish things for himself, not lament his fate. But just now it is more common to attack the Christian image from the side of determinism. The psychological and social sciences frequently offer a deterministic image of man. Practical experience shows the obvious bondage of people to bewildering economic forces, to the random workings of selective service, to international conflicts that are so far beyond any individual's control that many a person turns fatalist.

In this context Christians can describe their image of man. They can enter into conversation with Freudians and behaviorists, with economists and sociologists. In these conversations they can expect to learn, to gain in self-discovery. But they can expect also to contribute illumination to others, for they believe in the truth of the Christian self-image.

The Christian image-in-action goes on to describe God's act of redemption and His gift of freedom. By His deed in Christ, God brings freedom to those who respond in faith. He breaks the grip of fate and sin—of the principalities and powers at large and of the pride and distrust that enslave man from within. Man is granted this new freedom as he participates in the death and resurrection of Christ—as he dies to sin and rises to life. From Paul through Augustine and Martin Luther until today, Christians have proclaimed this freedom.

But Christian freedom is neither the lonely rebellion of an atheistic existentialist nor the self-will of the rugged individualist. It is freedom-in-community. In prayer it addresses "the God whose service is perfect freedom."

Again this image of man can be compared with secular images. It differs from David Riesman's image of the autonomous man, who maturely chooses his goals; for though it recognizes choice, it starts from Christ's words: "You did not choose me, but I chose you." Likewise it differs from the totalitarian image of the man who surrenders to the capricious promises and threats of a dictator, for its meaning is emancipation.

Such comparisons have their value for purposes of explanation and clarification. But they should not be expected to make secularists into Christians. The entry into faith is trustful response to God's grace in the community which lives by the sacred images.

Here, then, we see how the Christian image of man's slavery and freedom involves the three elements of every sacred image: mystery,

tragedy, and salvation. Freedom is *mystery*, never reducible to formula. Bondage is *tragedy*. God's gift of restored freedom in sonship is
salvation.

The weakness of the secular images, as the Christian sees them, is
not that they produce criminals and juvenile delinquents. Plenty of
secularists are active in good causes and nice to their families and
their dogs. The secular image, however, usually stifles reverence before
mystery. Then it turns tragedy either into a success story or into frustration without hope. Living by a stunted self-image, a man becomes
less than a self.

Part of the mystery of human freedom concerns the self-in-relation.
Christ's two great commandments (quoted from Deuteronomy and
Leviticus) sets the self in a three-way relation—with God, neighbor,
and itself. From Augustine until today Christian thinkers—recently
with the powerful help of the Jewish scholar, Martin Buber—have
elaborated this theme.

It is not enough to say that the self lives in these three relations.
More important, this self discovers itself, becomes itself, in these relations. Secular social studies have shown how the emergence of selfhood
depends on social relations. Psychological studies have shown how the
self-revelation and the self-concept participate in the very making of
the self. Long before these discoveries, the biblical image of a self-in-
action was clearly that of a self-in-relations. The self is not a thing, not
even (despite some errors of Christian thinkers) a chunk of some meta-
physical substance. It is a historical self, a self born for its time and
society, able in its freedom to resist that society but not to forsake it.
And it lives in relation to God, becoming what it is as it responds to
God in faithfulness or rejection. Orthodoxy has always said that man
cannot know himself except as he knows God—and himself in relation
to God.

We must grant, of course, that man resembles a thing in some
respects. Counting ten people is not much different from counting ten
automobiles. But the physical laws and the analytic processes that
describe automobiles do not adequately describe persons. It was George
Bernard Shaw, I think, who gave a doctor in his play this line: "The
soul is an organ which in my anatomical research I have not come
across." The doctor was less cynical, more Christian than he thought.
For the soul is the self-in-action, the self-in-freedom, the self-in-relation. It is no thing. No autopsy will discover it.

The sacred image refuses to make of man a thing. When secularism
makes God a thing (or a no-thing), it soon unwittingly turns man and

his neighbors into things. In the process it falsifies the God-image, the neighbor-image, and the self-image.

1. *The God-image.* Secularism does not always deny God. It may simply conceive Him as a thing, as a bargaining power. The primitive religions which seek by incantations and offerings to maneuver God into granting favors are already well on the way to secularism. When modern religious practitioners describe their neat devices for securing from God gifts of confidence and prosperity, they are actually reverting to the ancient formula of *do ut des* (I give, in order that you will give). They have destroyed the three elements of the sacred: mystery, tragedy, and salvation.

Once the God-image becomes a thing-image, it makes rather little difference to go on and deny God's reality. Reverence before holiness is gone. Now man, whether in churchly secularism or worldly secularism, must do without the sacred.

One result is the trivializing of life. To make God a thing is to make the self a thing. This self can still pursue goals of comfort and respectability, but it can no longer respond to the divine. T. S. Eliot describes the end of such selves in his poignant verse:

> And the wind shall say: "Here were decent godless people:
> Their only monument the asphalt road
> And a thousand lost golf balls."[1]

More often, because men cannot endure such triviality, they turn to false gods. They worship these deities of blood and soil, of class and ideology, of economic gain and social prestige. Such gods can demand utter devotion, promise infinite satisfactions. But they bring man neither judgment nor salvation.

Or again, man without God may sink into despair. Such despair may be a romantic cry for attention. When a famous and prosperous novelist says, "I have no thesis except that people get a very raw deal from life," we have a right to wonder whether he is not cultivating the bravado of the sentimental "tough guy." But when an Albert Camus raises his agonized cries for integrity in an empty world, he shows the depth of honest pain. He apprehends the mystery of life without salvation. One wonders whether he is not closer to the sacred than those modern clerical medicine men who think they can purvey salvation without mystery and tragedy.

2. *The neighbor-image.* When man loses the sense of sacred mystery, he sees his neighbor as a thing. The profound personal meeting of self with self gives way to the maneuvering of objects. David Riesman

1. Choruses from *The Rock*, pt. 3.

describes a common situation: "Social mobility . . . depends less on what one is and what one does than on what others think of one—and how competent one is in manipulating others and being oneself manipulated."[2]

Such manipulation is not usually vicious in aim. It may be a somewhat jovial procedure, a business of "you scratch my back, I'll scratch yours." Each of the manipulators may feel better if, while using the other as a means, he also helps the other get what he wants. But in the mutual tactics genuine personal concern gets slaughtered.

The American vernacular shows the increasing tendency to transfer the language of mechanics and impersonal techniques to discourse about people. We "contact" people, practice "social engineering," cultivate the "know-how" for handling group relations.

This issue requires careful definition. It is too easy to make a romantic protest against techniques, when all of us know that good technique is a help to any process of education or group organization. The subtle but decisive issue is whether the techniques facilitate free personal relations or deny freedom by making people less than persons even with their approval.

3. *The self-image.* Riesman, in the sentence I have quoted, points out that success requires skill not only in manipulating but also in being manipulated. Thus the self-image becomes a thing-image. And the self seeks to exercise its know-how on itself.

Inevitably the result is confusing. What is the relation between the manipulating self and the manipulated self? The difficulty of this question, of course, lies deep in human nature. Men have always wondered about the relation of the self to itself. How can the self repent of its own deeds and motives? How can it accept or reject itself? The secular image of man simply shifts these old questions into a different form, which is more puzzling only because secularism had denied the marvelous quality of selfhood. Instead of sacred mystery evoking reverence, we have confusion evoking bewilderment. D. W. Brogan describes this self-image with only moderate satire:

> That life is not reducible to formulas, that there are bound to be sorrows and disillusionments even for the best prepared, for the new elect who have had the right eugenic ancestry, the proper education, the necessary contacts—these ideas are heresy in modern America. The man who has cured himself of B. O. and halitosis, has learned French to surprise the waiter, and the saxophone to amuse the company, may, as Heywood Broun said, find that people still avoid him because they do not like him.[3]

2. *The Lonely Crowd,* Doubleday, Anchor ed., p. 63.
3. *The American Character,* Vintage ed., p. 83.

The rash of self-improvement books among the best-sellers shows the craving for devices for self-manipulation. Self-improvement, to be sure, has its virtues; it is a form of the perennial craving of man for fuller life. But when the self becomes a thing, the sacramental participation in death and resurrection gives way to a technique for improving the self by denying its personal selfhood. Only a responsible self can make decisions, can respond to God and to fellow men with trust and commitment.

I have aimed to avoid the popular pastime of blaming all the world's evils on secularism. The secularist rightly claims that he is often ethical and public-spirited, whereas religion has often been cruel and fanatical.

Christian faith, which has for centuries spoken profoundly of human sin, cannot suddenly blame sin on the twentieth century. But sin today (like good works today) takes forms characteristic of contemporary culture. It threatens to make man less than man, to reduce him from person to object, to deny his selfhood. When mystery, tragedy, and salvation depart, the grandeur of selfhood goes too. When man ceases to live by a sacred self-image, he gives up his profoundest privilege and destiny.

And that surrender is portentous. Man, who is always a dangerous creature, loses none of his weapons when he becomes less than man.

Gian-Carlo Menotti in his opera, *The Consul*, tells a story of the totalitarian dehumanization of man. John Sorel, the hero of a struggle for freedom, has fled his country for safety. His wife Magda knows that he will return to her and their child, unless she can join him. She tries to see the Consul who can permit her to join her husband in a neighboring land, but she gets only as far as the secretary.

> Magda: I must see my John, and you, only you, can help me. May I speak to the Consul?
> Secretary: I give you these papers, this is how to begin. Your name is a number, your story is a case, your need a request, your hopes will be filed. Come back next week.
> M: And you will explain to the Consul?
> S: But what is there to explain?
> M: Explain that John is a hero ... Explain that the web of my life has worn down to one single thread, that the hands of the clock glitter like knives. Explain to the Consul, explain!
> S: But what is there to explain?
> M: Explain that John is a hero, explain that he's my John! Explain to the Consul, explain! Tell him my name, tell him my story, tell him my need!
> As frustration mounts on frustration, Magda finally cries out!

If to men, not to God, we now must pray, tell me Secretary, tell me,
who are these men?
If to them, not to God, we now must pray, tell me, Secretary, tell me!
Who are these dark archangels?

The parable concerns not only the workings of dictatorships. It tells
us of an image of man. Well-meaning people have sought to free us
from supernatural hopes and fears, that we might more intelligently
enjoy human goals in this world. In destroying the sacred image of
man, they have unwittingly made human beings something less than
selves.

In contemporary culture the sacred image must learn to live with
secular images, which have their glimpses of truth. But without arrogance, faith can assert the power and truth of its image of man. Behind
the confusion of our times, it can point to the genuine *mystery* of selfhood. Behind frustrations and despair it can point to the authentic
tragedy in human life. Behind the schemes of manipulation, which
have proved all too feeble to deal with the dark archangels of our day,
it can point to the gift of *salvation* from a living God.

The sacred image of Christian faith is the image of God-in-action
and man-in-action in Jesus Christ. Through Him we discover what it
is to know God and neighbor and self.

All psychology includes a view of humans; all theology includes a psychology. The Old Testament provides a foundational anthropology for the Christian faith which must be understood by contemporary psychology. Hebrew understandings of "flesh," of "spirit," and of "soul" are discussed. However, these are not separate parts but components of a whole. The unity of the person is the essential Hebrew concept.

The Structure of Personality in Hebrew Psychology

The Implications of the Hebrew View of Man for Psychology of Religion

Glenn E. Whitlock

The foundation for any clinical approach to psychology lies in the understanding of the nature of man, and any theological formulation about man's nature must be founded upon an adequate psychology. Hence it is necessary for the student of psychology and religion to study the nature of man in the early Old Testament writings. Since the Christian faith is rooted in the Hebrew tradition, it is of primary importance to discover the conception of personality in Hebrew thought. The foundation for a psychology of religion which has anything to say about the nature of man within the context of the Christian faith is necessarily grounded in this tradition.

The nature of man in the early writings of the Old Testament is presented with vivid realism and absolute honesty. The Hebrew view of man is essentially derived through an empirical approach. It is the understanding of primitive man rather than intellectual man. It is essentially a clinical rather than a philosophical understanding.

Originally published in *Interpretation*, vol. 14 (January 1960), pp. 3–13. Reprinted by permission.

The Hebrew has no word for "body" in the same sense that the Greek *sōma* is used. The word which is used in speaking of the nature of man as creature is *basar*, which is usually translated "flesh." This word *basar* is used in referring to all living creatures. When God is speaking to Noah about destroying all living creatures He says, "destroy all flesh [*basar*]" (Gen. 6:17). The usage of this word indicates the nature of man as creature. Man does not, as a creature, differ greatly from the "beasts of the field." He breathes the same air; he reproduces his kind; he eats and sleeps for the renewal of strength. Hence the nature of man as creature is accepted. Man has biological urges as a creature. His nature is limited in his very creation; the creatureliness of man is the will of the Creator.

A further implication of the use of the word *flesh (basar)* indicates that there is no ethical judgment upon flesh as such. Flesh refers simply to man as creature. Referring to the muscular part of the body in distinction from other parts, such as the skin, bones, blood, etc., the Hebrew came to use *flesh* to indicate the living creature in general. Therefore, when *flesh* refers to man as creature, it does not indicate that in its essence flesh is evil. There does not seem to be any use of flesh in the ethical sense as Paul uses the Greek word *sarx*. To the Hebrew, flesh does not corrupt the spirit in the Greek sense. Flesh as such does not imply moral defect. Hence, man can accept his creatureliness without fear of any corrupting influence. There is no need for an ascetic rejection of the flesh as evil.

Although there is no hostility against the flesh as a corrupting influence, there is a recognition of the limitation of its power. The term *flesh* is often used as opposed to God and His power, indicating the frailty of flesh. The power of God cannot be identified with the weakness of man. "Then the LORD said, 'My spirit shall not abide in man forever, for he is flesh'" (Gen. 6:3). The weakness of man in comparison with the power of God is brought out in the chronicler's account of Sennacherib's invasion of Judah. King Hezekiah reassures the people and tells them to be strong and of good courage, for they have on their side a greater power than the Assyrian. "With him is an arm of flesh, but with us is the LORD our God, to help us and to fight our battles" (II Chron. 32:8). Isaiah says that men are flesh in contrast with God, who is spirit. "The Egyptians are men, and not God; and their horses are flesh, and not spirit" (31:3). A. B. Davidson indicates that Isaiah's point here is not to indicate what the horses are composed of, but what they are able to accomplish.[1] It is not a question of essence, but

1. *The Theology of the Old Testament* (New York: Charles Scribner's Sons, 1936), p. 190.

of power. Hence flesh (*basar*) does not indicate anything about the essence of man, but of his power. Flesh is limited, powerless. It is God who has power to move man. Hence, the Hebrews did not place their ultimate faith in man, but in God. The God in whom the Hebrews placed their faith was the God who acts through men and events. They are not concerned with God as "being" or essence, but only with the activity of God.

The Hebrew understanding of the flesh and the power of God indicates their understanding of the nature of man. It is an empirical or clinical insight. There is a finiteness, a limitation which is inherent in the very structure of man; it is an element in the ontological structure of man. Hence any experience which enables man to be victorious over the enemy can come only from God. The structure of man is so constituted that he is limited; he is unable to save himself. It is only the power of God which saves man from destruction. The early Hebrew writers were chiefly concerned with God's power as it saved their people from enemy armies, and as God's power enabled them to overcome these armies when they were on the offense. Nevertheless, this understanding of the inherent limitation of the flesh seems to indicate a conviction that man cannot save himself in any sphere. Man is saved only through the power of God. Hence any saving experience of religious or psychotherapeutic insight which enables a person genuinely to realign his sense of values would indicate the power of God working through this limited nature of man.

The Hebrew word *ruach* is translated in various ways, but it is usually used in the sense of "spirit." In some of its uses it refers to the breath of the mouth: "For behold, I will bring a flood of waters upon the earth, to destroy all flesh in which is the breath [*ruach*] of life from under heaven . . ." (Gen. 6:17). This breath is the sign of life in the creature.

Ruach is also translated as "breath" in the sense of breath of air, or of air in motion, or a wind. In the account of the flood it is reported, "And God made a wind [*ruach*] blow over the earth, and the waters subsided" (Gen. 8:1).

These meanings of *ruach* indicate that it is something from God. It is the gift of life in creation. It is that which makes the clod of dust into a living person. It is *ruach* that is breathed into man so that he may become a living person. It is that which exerts power over man. Furthermore, the wide range of meaning indicates something else. The various aspects of *ruach* indicate that it is not a substance as such, but rather a power. It is a power by which God gives life to man, and through which he continues to sustain the life of his creation. It is a power by which man is moved in various ways as he lives out his life;

but it is always a power rather than a substance. This power from God has a sense of direction. It is both teleological and creative in that it gives life to the clod of dust. This power is what makes for wholeness of man; it is that which makes for wholeness of the person.

Comparing the early with the later uses of *ruach* indicates the development of the word from the more primitive usage as "breath"—the sign of life—to the vital principle of life itself. Therefore, *ruach* becomes not merely the sign of life, but the principle of life itself. It comes to be used in much the same sense as the Greek *pneuma*, when it is used in reference to the vital force (spirit) which animates the body. Therefore Isaiah says, "O Lord, by these things men live, and in all these is the life of my spirit [*ruach*]. Oh, restore me to health and make me live" (38:16).

The meaning of *ruach* which indicates the vital principle of life develops into that which means the unseen spiritual element in man. In this meaning it comes to indicate the spirit or rational mind of man. In the first place it indicates the spirit of man as evidenced in the senses, affections, and emotions. When Rahab told the two spies from Joshua how the people of Jericho felt when they learned of the power of the Lord, she said, "And as soon as we heard it, our hearts melted, and there was no courage [*ruach*] left in any man, because of you; for the LORD your God is he who is God in heaven above and on the earth beneath" (Josh. 2:11). This power (*ruach*) of God is courage in this sense. Hence, this courage is the "courage to be" (Tillich) which man receives from God. It is courage (*ruach*) which man needs to realize the potentialities of being a person rather than a clod of earth.

Secondly, *ruach* is used as spirit referring to a mode of thinking and acting. Sometimes it is used as a spirit or disposition common to many. Hosea relates, "For a spirit [*ruach*] of harlotry has led them astray, and they have left their God to play the harlot" (4:12). Such a passage indicates that *ruach* refers to a power from God which restrains the person from acting. Moreover, it may indicate that when man uses God's gift for his own egocentric needs, the *ruach* becomes harlotrous. Hence, even the *ruach* from God can be prostituted to man's egocentric needs. A passage in Isaiah reads, "And a spirit [*ruach*] of justice to him who sits in judgment, and strength to those who turn back the battle at the gate" (28:6). In this sense the *ruach* of God enables the person to act. It is a spirit which is divinely given to man, and which is poured upon him from heaven.

Thirdly, *ruach* is used to indicate will and counsel. Hence it means to stir up anyone's spirit to anything. There is also some indication that *ruach* may be used to indicate the self-assertion of the person.

"So the God of Israel stirred up the spirit [ruach] of Pul, king of Assyria, and the spirit [ruach] of Tiglath-pilneser, king of Assyria, and he carried them away" (I Chron. 5:26). Furthermore, it may be used as meaning to put an intention into anyone. When the servants of King Hezekiah came to Isaiah, he gave the following message to them for the king: "Behold, I will put a spirit [ruach] in him, so that he shall hear a rumor and return to his own land; and I will cause him to fall by the sword in his own land" (II Kings 19:7). Ruach is also used to mean mind or will which impels a person. "Then all the congregation of the people of Israel departed from the presence of Moses. And they came, everyone whose heart stirred him, and everyone whose spirit [ruach] moved him, and brought the LORD's offering to be used for the tent of meeting" (Exod. 35:20–21). It is also used to refer to that which arises in the mind, and which occupies the mind, such as in the case of any counsel. When David gave Solomon the plans for the temple, the Chronicler relates that the plan came through the spirit. "Then David gave Solomon his son the plan of the vestibule of the temple . . . and the plan of all that he had in mind [ruach] for the courts of the house of the LORD" (I Chron. 28:11–12).

In the fourth place, ruach is used as spirit in the sense that it is applied to the intellect. Isaiah relates, "And those who err in spirit [ruach] will come to understanding, and those who murmur will accept instruction" (29:24). Hence it would seem to indicate that ruach may refer to intellect in the sense of insight or self-understanding.

The use of ruach in the Old Testament does not indicate the essence of God, but His power. When ruach is given to man it is not understood in the sense of a faculty psychology in which a particular faculty is given to man by God. It is not a faculty residing in man. Rather it is to be understood in a functional sense. When the various concepts of ruach appear, they appear in action. It is the functioning of the total organism as it appears in the courage, self-control, bitterness of spirit, etc., of the individual or group. It is behavioristic in the broadest sense, but it is definitely not a stimulus-response psychology.

Ruach is from God. It is the power through which man receives life and through which God continues to move in the lives of men. Regardless of whether or not ruach refers to the breath of life, or to the principle of life itself, or to the spirit of man, it is a gift of God which is known as it functions in the lives of men. The function of ruach is known through the emotions, the actions, the will, and the intellect of men. Therefore, it is inherent in the very nature of the universe that the power of God works through the emotions, actions, will, and intellect of man. Hence, it is the ruach of God which enables man to make

an about-face in a religious conversion or to gain insight by psychotherapeutic relationship. Hence, man has the responsibility to act, but
it is the *ruach* of God which *enables* him to act.

The next important psychological term is *nephesh*, which is translated variously. It is often used in reference to the soul, or that through
which the person lives. Hence, it means the vital principle of life itself,
without which the person dies. "And as her soul [*nephesh*] was departing (for she died) . . ." (Gen. 35:18). In another instance, Elijah prayed,
"O LORD my God, let this child's soul [*nephesh*] come into him again"
(I Kings 17:21). In another passage the idea is expressed of the life
(*nephesh*) being poured out, or ebbing away, in the sense of departing
with the blood. "As their life [*nephesh*] is poured out on their mother's
bosom" (Lam. 2:12). Hence, in some senses it is used in a similar way
as *ruach*, and there is no clear distinction between the two terms.

Nephesh refers to either the loss or the preservation of life. In the
sense of saving lives, there is the passage in the Second Book of Kings,
they "fled for their lives [*nephesh*]" (7:7). It is also used in the sense of
looking out for one's self. "Therefore take good heed to yourselves
[*nephesh*] . . ." (Deut. 4:15).

Nephesh is also used in many expressions which belong to the sus-
taining of life by food and drink, or to the withholding of these
necessities of life. There is the passage in Isaiah, "As when a hungry
man dreams he is eating and wakes with his hunger unsatisfied" (29:8).

Nephesh is used in reference to the mind as the seat of the senses,
affections, and various emotions. It is used to refer to love. "And his
soul [*nephesh*] was drawn to Dinah the daughter of Jacob" (Gen. 34:3).
It refers to fear in the passage in Isaiah, "Therefore, the armed men
of Moab cry aloud; his soul [*nephesh*] trembles" (15:4). In regard to
hatred, Isaiah relates the word of the Lord, "Your new moons and your
appointed feasts my soul [*nephesh*] hates" (1:14). In regard to sensa-
tions in general, it is related in Exodus, "You shall not oppress a
stranger; you know the heart [*nephesh*] of a stranger, for you were
strangers in the land of Egypt" (23:9).

More rarely *nephesh* is used in referring to the soul as it wills and
purposes. David says to his son, "And you, Solomon my son, know the
God of your father, and serve him with a whole heart and with a
willing mind" (I Chron. 28:9). *Nephesh* is also used in reference to the
soul in its understanding and the function of thinking. When Jonathan
is talking to David, he says, "Whatever you say, I will do for you"
(I Sam. 20:4).

Concretely, *nephesh* refers to that in which there is a soul or mind.
A passage in Joshua relates, "And Joshua took Makkedah on that day,
and smote it and its king with the edge of the sword; he utterly

destroyed every person [*nephesh*] in it, he left none remaining" (10:28). It is also used in a somewhat different sense in referring to the animal essence of life with which every living creature must be endued. In one of the creation stories, it is related, "Then the LORD God formed man of dust from the ground, and breathed into his nostrils the breath of life; and man became a living being [*nephesh*]" (Gen. 2:7).

With a suffix, *nephesh* is sometimes used as "I myself," or "Thou thyself." In one passage it is related, "I have yearned for thee in the night, with all my heart I seek thee" (Isa. 26:9). In the example, *nephesh* refers to the total person with a special emphasis.

Hence, for the most part, *nephesh* refers to the concrete individual. It is that to which the personality of the individual belongs; or it is that which bears the individual personality. The *ruach* is the power or energy which moves the individual, but it is the *nephesh* which exhibits the power or energy. *Nephesh* does not refer to a thing in itself. It is not a faculty of the mind, but the total person. It is a symbol for the identification of the whole life of a man, especially in its affective and nonbodily form. *Nephesh* refers to both biological and psychic life. When the *ruach* is breathed into the man, biologically he becomes a living person (*nephesh*). When emotions are expressed in a man's psychic life, they are centered in the personality or will (*nephesh*).

Therefore, *nephesh* is not a soul in the Greek sense where a distinct dualism is required. Rather it indicates the total life of a man. There is no indication of a sharp dichotomy between body (*basar*) and soul (*nephesh*). The use of *nephesh* to refer to the total person in his biological and psychic life indicates a concept of organismic unity which has its counterpart in dynamic psychology and psychiatry.

As he faced the basic problems of the nature and origin of man, the Hebrew maintained the fundamental unity of the person. In contrast with the more highly developed philosophical view of the Greeks, the Hebrews believed that man was essentially a unity. He was able to function with his body, his spirit, or his mind as he reacted to the various aspects of his environment; but he was a unitary organism. No fundamental dualism was recognized. It is true that man was created from matter (dust of the earth) and from spirit (*ruach* of God); but once he was created, he was a unitary organism. Plato had made a clear-cut distinction between mind and matter. Although Aristotle had recognized that they were interdependent, he still insisted that mind and matter were unlike. Even Descartes, who marks the actual beginning of modern psychology, held to a dualism, although he recognized an interaction between mind and body. But the early Hebrew recognized that in man's psychological responses, his glands and other biological organs were involved. The Old Testament writers often refer to the bowels, kidneys, liver, and bones. Hence, the Hebrew viewpoint of man as a unitary organism is basically a clinical understanding. The modern development of psychosomatic medicine is a recognition of the unity of the human organism in medical science. The organismic approach is also evident in contemporary psychology and psychiatry.

This understanding of the unity of man has theological implications. The human person is a totality. It is not the body or the mind which acts, but it is the total person. It is the total "I" who confronts God. It is the total self which is responsible to God. The "I" cannot escape the reality of this confrontation by saying, "My body has seduced my mind." In relationship to God, man stands in a situation similar to the patient in psychotherapy. He is responsible for bringing his total self into involvement. Spiritual holiness or emotional wholeness can be achieved only when the total self is involved. Neither holiness nor wholeness will be secured if the self remains segmented, and either the soma or psyche is withdrawn from involvement in confrontation. Furthermore, neither holiness nor wholeness can be achieved through man's own efforts. The flesh (*basar*) is powerless to act. It is the spirit (*ruach*) of God who enables man to become a whole person (*nephesh*).

This understanding of man also has implications for the nature of sin and repentance. Sin is enacted by the total person. In a dualism, evil resides in either the body or mind, depending upon the nature of the evil. But to the Hebrew, evil resides in the total person. It is the whole man who sins. Therefore, in repentance a dualist "repents" for the sin either of his body or of his mind, as the case may be. In any event, the dualist evades taking sin seriously. It is a repentance for separate mind-acts or body-acts. However, in the Hebrew concept of repentance, the person repents not for the separate acts which he has committed, but for being the kind of person (the totality of his person) in which such sinful acts could originate and be committed. Hence, in modern psychology and psychiatry, emotional wholeness is achieved not by treating separate symptoms, but in treating the total person in whom the symptoms reside.

Evidence for unity in the nature of man is also taught in the story of creation. The stories in Genesis (1:27, 2:7) teach that man is created by God and is dependent upon Him. Furthermore, God created man in His own image. It is difficult to discover just what is meant by the Priestly and Yahwist writers when they refer to the "image of God." Undoubtedly the phrase is a symbolic expression which is impossible to define accurately. However, the manner in which the writers describe the creation of man gives us at least some important clues. Since man is the only creature created in the image of God, he is a special creation with a special relationship to God. Man has a position above the animals because he is placed in charge over them (Gen. 1:26–30); and by naming them he gains control over them (Gen. 2:19). Man is also created with an ethical responsibility to choose between good and evil, since he has that choice to make in the garden (Gen. 2:15–17, 3:1–7).

Indeed, man is accepted as creature in earthy language and yet he has a high position in Hebrew thought. The psalmist expresses the paradox of the nature of man in superb poetry.

> When I look at thy heavens, the work of thy fingers,
>   the moon and the stars which thou hast established;
> what is man that thou art mindful of him,
>   and the son of man that thou dost care for him?
> Yet thou hast made him little less than God,
>   and dost crown him with glory and honor.
> Thou has given him dominion over the works of thy hands;
>   thou has put all things under his feet. . . .   Psalm 8:3–6

To the Hebrews, man has stature which can only be described as being a "little less than God." And yet, man is such that the writer wonders why God pays any attention to him at all.

The predicament of man is the paradox that he not only acknowledges his dependence upon God as his Creator, but he also revolts against his creatureliness. Man was created "in the image of God"; but he cannot be God. In the fall, the serpent tempted Eve by saying, "You will not die. For God knows that when you eat of it, your eyes will be opened, and you will be like God, knowing good and evil" (Gen. 3:4–5). Adam revolts, refusing to accept his creatureliness. He perceives that he has a special relationship with God, and that he is dominant over all the animals. But man asserts himself not only over the beasts, but over man as well. In *The Nature and Destiny of Man*, Reinhold Niebuhr indicates that sin is occasioned precisely by the fact that man pretends to be more than he is.[2] In his egocentricity, man tends to assert himself as an end in himself rather than to recognize himself as a part of a greater whole. He asserts himself both over and against his fellows and God. Hence, he tends to separate himself both from the community in which he becomes a person, and from God who is the "ground of his being."

The life of man is an organic whole. His total interests belong together. His spiritual, social, physical, economic, political, or so-called secular interests are simply different aspects of man's relationship to

2. (New York: Charles Scribner's Sons, 1942), vol. 1, p. 16.

a complex world. Hence, man's problem is not only his relatedness to himself, but also his relatedness to his world.

Hebrew man cannot be considered in isolation any more than modern man can be studied in isolation from his culture. Indeed, the early Hebrew was much more closely related to the community than is modern man. G. Ernest Wright suggests in *The Challenge of Israel's Faith* that according to the Hebrew psychology, the greatest curse which can befall a man is that he be alone.[3] When Hosea is describing the misery of his people, he compares them to the "wild ass wandering alone" (8:9). Just as the natural place for the wild ass is in the herd, the normal place for a man is in the community. The happy man is the man who is able to live in peace with his fellows.

According to the Hebrews, man was a unitary organism related inextricably with other persons in community. Hence, there were ethical obligations for the man living in community which were enunciated by the prophets. Since the Hebrews accepted a covenanted relationship with God, the eighth-century prophets usually presented their appeals for ethical behavior to the nation rather than to the individual. Amos thundered against the nation, and exhorted the people to do justly in their social and institutional life. "Thus says the LORD: 'For three transgressions of Israel, and for four, I will not revoke the punishment; because they sell the righteous for silver, and the needy for a pair of shoes . . .'" (2:6). In this way Amos illustrates the prophetic view that the ethics of the individual are related inextricably with the community.

There is a strong emphasis in contemporary theology and psychology to study and to treat man in his social context. Group psychotherapy is one recent methodology which utilizes this insight in the treatment of emotional disturbance. Some of the recent developments in the various church-school curricula also reflect this emphasis.

In the effort to develop an adequate psychology of religion, it is necessary to examine the roots of Christian thought in the Hebrew view of man. Studying the structure of personality in Hebrew psychology may help ministers and teachers in the church to understand the situation in which modern man finds himself, and to help the church to examine how it can meet this predicament.

The *primary* function of the church in the area of psychology of religion is not to concern itself with the psychological services which will provide self-understanding. The primary vocation of the church is to understand the nature of the person in relationship to both God

3. (Chicago: University of Chicago, 1944), p. 75.

and his fellows, as well as his relationship to himself. Psychology of religion is concerned with a dimension that is unexplored in psychology. It is primarily a dimension of depth, since it is the nature of the righteous and loving God which sets man's nature in its true perspective. The depth of man's misery and the height of his grandeur is evident only within the perspective of a psychology of religion which studies the creature in relationship to the Creator.

In Hebrew psychology, the weakness of the flesh (creature) is set off in contrast to the power of God. In this context, the person is shorn of any undue confidence in self. The Hebrew would assume that selfhood could not be achieved through will power. The courage to realize the potentialities of being a whole person comes from God. Indeed, it is the spirit (*ruach*) of God who enables the person to act in any way whatsoever. It is God's spirit who moves the total person to achieve any degree of intellectual insight or emotional self-understanding. It is the spirit of God who enables the individual to become a whole person in relatedness with other persons in community.

Freud abolished the distinctions between mental health and illness and made us aware of the depths of personality—including a human proclivity toward evil. Calvin lifted up the conflict between good and evil in human nature and offered a view of salvation based on the power of God. Faith (Calvin) is compared and contrasted with insight/redecision (Freud).

The Image of Man

The Perspectives of Calvin and Freud

Walter E. Stuermann and Konstantin Geocaris

Both Calvin and Freud recognized the importance of man's image of himself. The opening words of Calvin's *Institutes* proclaim that true and substantial wisdom consists principally of two parts, the knowledge of God and *the knowledge of ourselves*. Freud's psychoanalytic techniques represent a search for a *knowledge of the self* in its biological and psychological dimensions and in its connections with the wider world. According to both of them, a man's assessment of his nature determines his behavior and, in the long run, his cultural environment. Each of these inquirers was also very sensitive to the shadowed movements within the depths of the psyche and to the connections between those movements and man's image of himself. Separated in time by a handful of centuries and by the tension between a scientific and a theological perspective, these two investigators nevertheless shared some significant judgments about human nature and conduct. Freud's image of man and Calvin's image of man are strikingly similar in several respects. The points at which they agree are ones of some consequence for the contemporary human situation.

Originally published in *Interpretation*, vol. 14 (January 1960), pp. 28–42. Reprinted by permission.

Jerome Bruner rightly contended that an age's image of man finds expression in the social, ethical, and political dimensions of society:

> The view that one takes affects profoundly one's standard of dignity and the humanly possible. And it is in the light of such a standard that we establish our laws, set our aspirations for learning, and judge the fitness of men's acts. Those who govern, then, must perforce be jealous guardians of man's ideas about man for the structure of government rests upon an uneasy consensus about human nature and human wants. Man has a deep and emotional investment in his image of himself. If we have learned anything in the last century of psychology, it is that man has powerful and exquisite capacities for defending himself against violation of his cherished self-image.[1]

Freud's image of man was the result of his startling discoveries about the human mind. These disclosures are producing a revolution in thought of a magnitude comparable to those which attended the discoveries and theories of Copernicus and Darwin. Just as those earlier revolutions in the world *about* man and the world *of* man shattered certain human concepts, the Freudian revolution in the world *within* man has had similar crashing consequences and has forced a transformation of the image of man. The first blows in this revolution were struck in 1899 when the psychoanalyst published his famous *Interpretation of Dreams*. The consternation produced in a cultural context fashioned by Victorian mores and morality was immense. Nevertheless, Freud tenaciously stood his ground alone, saying, "Today you may be critical of my findings, but tonight you will dream by these principles."

Bruner says, "Freud's contribution lies in the continuities of which he made us aware." On this score his work is more comprehensive than that of Darwin, for the continuities to which the psychoanalyst called attention included not only the totality of man's psychological and biological experience but also myth, anthropology, sociology, religion, the occult, art, and literature. Furthermore, his work helped to erase the sharp lines of division between mental health and mental illness and between man and society. Our present concern is with what Freud sensed in the depths of the human psyche, for it is at this point that he and the Swiss Reformer appear to agree in a striking manner. Each of them devoted attention to how the hidden work within man, in its creative and destructive dimensions, exhibited itself in overt conduct.

1. "Freud and the Image of Man," *Freud and the Twentieth Century*, ed. Benjamin Nelson (New York: Meridian Books, 1957), p. 278.

With his own peculiar emphases, Calvin brought to expression certain themes set forth in or read into the biblical literature. Those ideas of biblical ancestry fashioned his image of man. Let us look for a moment at one of those themes.

The biblical stories which bring to expression the conflict between the destructive and creative forces in nature and life are among the richer treasures of the Judeo-Christian literature. They deserve our careful attention, whatever accretions they may have acquired through the course of the centuries. Following hard on the heels of the contrast between chaos and order, darkness and light, in Genesis 1, we find the ingenious "myth" concerning Adam (mankind) and Eve (life). The interpretation of the myth points to two things about Adam: first, he is created in the image of God (Gen. 1:26; 2:7); second, by a rebellious and self-destructive act he fell from his paradisiacal state (Gen. 3:6). We must overlook other fascinating and revealing aspects of this story. In brief, as it carries the freight of Christian themes, the myth says that man is ambivalent—side by side there lurk beneath his skin both creative and destructive impulses.[2] Within the human person are found the roots of what we deem orderly, good, pleasing, and exhilarating. We find there also—seated just as firmly in the ground of being—the roots of what we judge to be chaotic, evil, painful, and depressing. Man is neither by nature simply good nor by nature simply evil.

This biblical view of man stands in clear contrast to those optimistic perspectives which, in effect, say that man is created in a divine image and suffered no fall and which exalt in an anomalous fashion man's rationality and goodness (this tendency appears, for example, in Plato, Aristotle, Rousseau, Kant, and, in a curious way, Marx[3]). It also stands

2. Freud, *Civilization and Its Discontents* (London: Hogarth, 1946), pp. 99–100: "I can remember my own defensive attitude when the idea of an instinct of destruction first made its appearance in psychoanalytical literature and how long it took until I became accessible to it. That others should have shown the same resistance, and still show it, surprises me less. Those who love fairy-tales do not like it when people speak of the innate tendencies in mankind towards aggression, destruction, and, in addition, cruelty. For God has made them in his own image, with his own perfections; no one wants to be reminded how hard it is to reconcile the undeniable existence . . . of evil with his omnipotence and supreme goodness." In this paper we argue that the biblical writers and Calvin did not close their eyes to the dark side of human nature but rather gave expression to it in mythological form. They stand with Freud on this point, not against him. It might be interesting to inquire why Freud did not sense that they were making a common cause with him. We contend that he had no real appreciation of the themes of anxiety and dread set forth in the symbols of the Judeo-Christian tradition, adept as he was at interpreting other kinds of symbols.

3. *Civilization and Its Discontents*, pp. 87–89, gives Freud's opinion that Marxism is "psychologically . . . founded on an untenable illusion." Cf. also *New Introductory Lectures on Psychoanalysis* (New York: W. W. Norton, 1933), pp. 95–96.

over against those extreme pessimisms which see in human life nothing except what is "nasty, brutish, and short" (the bias exhibited, for example, in Hobbes, Machiavelli, Schopenhauer,[4] and Leopardi). The symbols of the image and of the fall set forth the inescapable conflict of God and Satan, or, as we shall see, in Freud's terms of Eros and Death. This theme finds other expressions in the biblical saga and discovers its culmination in the crucifixion and resurrection. We can invest time here in only a few additional clues. Note, for example, that some biblical writers at least give a frank confession of faults and of unworthy impulses in their most celebrated heroes, despite their disposition to idealize the champions of faith. So it is with Abraham, the father of faith, with Moses, the authoritative lawgiver, and even with great King David, the prototype of the Messiah. Notwithstanding the trend toward idealization among biblical writers, generally they did not so far lose touch with the blood and thunder of life that they deified the ancients. In a recent article, Donald C. Hodges has called attention to the recurring themes of parricide and fratricide in the biblical texts, indicating the dual orientations (love and hate) toward the father and the brother and their respective surrogates.[5] Even the story of the temptation of Jesus Christ appears to display the theme to which we call attention. Here was an inner struggle—in one who is interpreted as the incarnation of the divine—between "angelic" powers and "demonic" powers, between Eros and Death. Paul and other Christian writers testify to an urgent warfare within the believer, to a crucial contest between the powers of life and of death. Finally, this theme of strife comes nicely to expression in the climactic event in the biblical scene: the indissoluble connection between crucifixion and resurrection. In the Christian perspective on life, there is no crucifixion without resurrection, no resurrection without crucifixion—Eros and Thanatos are immortal but inseparable adversaries. We are not talking, of course, about historical events, but rather about the logic of life in general. It is not insignificant that Jesus Christ is sometimes termed Adam, the second Adam. The point is that the contest between the creative and destructive components in the person, between life instincts and death instincts, is displayed in the "first" men, in other men, and also in the "last" man (for, according to the theologians, Jesus Christ is in a sense the "last" man).

The image of man entertained by Calvin emerged from a context containing ideas like these. This Calvinistic image is analogous to that

---

4. At several points we find Freud admitting that certain ideas he exploits were earlier expressed in Schopenhauer's writings.

5. "Fratricide and Fraternity," *Journal of Religion* 38, no. 4 (October, 1958).

found in Freud's writings, we shall be contending. The two inquirers agree in maintaining that beneath what we know to be ourselves there is a hidden work going on which determines our thought and overt behavior. We discover both of them certifying to the ambivalent nature of the human creature. Furthermore, each contends that there are rooted in human nature innate forces, destructive as well as constructive. Let us now attend more carefully to the details of the psychoanalyst's and the theologian's image of man.

In his early years, Freud (1856–1939) was influenced by the nature philosophy of nineteenth-century Europe. When he became interested in biology and physiology, his keen powers of observation and inference permitted him to contribute significantly to these disciplines. Economic necessities forced him to take belatedly a medical degree and to practice neurology. After his colleague, Josef Breuer, apparently cured a young woman of hysteria through the use of hypnosis, Freud turned his attention to the study of neuroses and hypnosis. Breuer soon abandoned the new technique, but Freud pushed the inquiries forward. The results were psychoanalysis and new theories in metapsychology. The psychoanalyst was a prolific writer as well as an ingenious investigator. His works fill twenty-four volumes and once he won the Goethe Prize for literature.

Many thinkers before Freud had suggested the existence of an unconscious psychic domain. In his *Confessions*, St. Augustine pondered how a remembrance could at the same time be outside memory (as when we vainly strive to recollect it) and yet within it (for otherwise we could not recognize it when we remembered it). Others who had made contributions to the development of this concept were Leibnitz, Schelling, Schopenhauer, Nietzsche, and Eduard von Hartmann. A similar situation prevailed with respect to the doctrine of instinctual movements within man. It remained for Freud, however, to propose in rather concrete and scientific form the idea of a dynamic unconscious energy system and to advance the idea that human nature was a scene of conflicting forces, both conscious and unconscious. His theorizing was supplemented and in a measure warranted by scientific evidences which proceeded from clinical work.

Freud's findings were based on hypnotic productions, dreams, and free associations. As his work progressed, the latter two kinds of phenomena took on more significance for him than the first, which was his heritage from Josef Breuer and Jean Charcot. Prior to the psychoanalyst's pioneer work, dreams—mental excreta, so to speak—were generally considered worthy of the attention of a charlatan only. At one time, we must remember, the urine was similarly ignored by medical men; but now the analysis of it tells us much about the state of health of the body. According to Freud, dreams were products of the mind, the analysis of which would provide an understanding of the human psyche. They were, he said, the royal road to the unconscious. Other phenomena also told stories about the human mind and its maneuvers—such as slips of the tongue, and the forgetting of a friend's name. Nothing in the individual's psychological life was an accident. Freud was, therefore, an absolute determinist with respect to psychological events.

According to Freud's description, the psyche exhibited three functional areas—the id, the ego, and the superego. Each had its specific functions and relations to the others. The id, which is entirely unconscious, is the primitive powerhouse from which originate the instinctual energy drives. It is illogical, timeless, and chaotically scrambled. Side by side with those recent perceptions which have entered it unnoticed by the conscious mind, it contains all of our forgotten memories. The ego, which begins its development at birth, includes our conscious thought processes, our conscious feelings, and our available knowledge and memory. It is a mediator between the demands of our instinctual drives, which arise in the id, and the requirements of external reality as represented in the environment. The forces within the id build up tension and seek release as expeditiously as possible in accord with the pleasure principle. In the interest of self-preservation, the ego must, however, juggle things, delay, plan, and scheme for the "right expression." The ego functions, not according to the pleasure principle, but according to the reality principle. The superego is largely unconscious, but it has in the conscious realm a representative, which is roughly synonymous with what we call conscience. This part of the human personality begins to develop in the third or fourth year when the child makes identification with his parents and takes into himself, so to speak, an inhibiting force on his own behavior. The ego—that part of the person which he knows to be his "self"—must always serve three masters: the id, the superego, and external reality. Furthermore, it functions as their mediator. A mediator is required where there is conflict or estrangement. According to Freud's analysis, the human being is a constant scene of conflict.

In addition to the themes of determinism, depth and complexity of the psyche, and conflict, heavy emphasis is placed by Freud on man's instinctual life. The instinctual energies arising in the id are parried by the ego, which seeks to modify the aim, delay the satisfaction, or even to suppress and/or repress an unacceptable impulse. It is such repression or stalemated conflict between conscious and unconscious which is the basic stuff of which neurotic symptoms are ultimately made. To the extent to which communal living and the use of authorities require the subjugation or modification of instinctual energies, any civilization is itself a generalized form of a neurosis. This is, of course, not necessarily bad. The civilized situation may be deemed satisfying and excellent, though we recognize that etiologically it is the result of the thwarting of primitive tendencies, especially the sexual and aggressive instincts. At this point we may comment that all too often Freud's terms are read as words of deprecation, whereas he intended nothing of the sort.

Finally, we may mention another important contribution of Freud to the image of man: his theory of sexuality. He emphasized that there were clear manifestations of sexual activity many years before the period of adolescence. Furthermore, he contended that the growing interest of the child in the outside world is a part of his sexuality, that is, his pleasure-seeking interest. The interest which the child invests in things outside of himself is love drawn from the great reservoir of affection which at an earlier stage he invested entirely in himself. In this sense, sexuality or love expresses itself in unselfish ways. The achievement of maturity is consequently interpreted as a partial conquest of narcissism. For Freud, sexuality is the very substance of the creative instinct and finds its expression in various ways in the earliest stages of the development of the organism. As psychoanalytic investigations continued, it became clear that alongside of the creative instincts of love there existed also negative or destructive tendencies. These aggressive impulses had as their emotional representative hate. When they are properly directed the aggressive instincts have great utility in the world, but they must be invested in objects suitable for carrying out their destructive aims—ignorance, pain, disease, and the like. Hates which are directed too strongly against one we love result in disaster. Karl Menninger has written of the many forms of self-destructiveness in his book, *Man against Himself*, indicating that suicide is only one form of it. In the matter of instincts, Freud was a dualist. From the beginning of the development of the psyche, a conflict ensues between Eros, the creative sexual drives, and Thanatos, the destructive drives. Between the two there is only conflict, but life can continue only so long as Eros is in the ascendancy. Consequently, death is not something which appears at the last moment of life, but it is a power which continually operates in life. We should perhaps note that the psychoanalyst did not restrict the death instinct to man's psychological life. On the contrary, he suggested that it is operative throughout the whole of living nature.[6]

6. A recent criticism of Freud's dualism can be found in Franz Alexander's "Unexplored Areas in Psychoanalytic Theory and Treatment," *Behavioral Science* 3, no. 4 (October, 1958), pp. 293–316.

As his devotion to therapy suggests, Freud sensed the possibility of salvation so far as man's life was concerned. This hope he expressed with his characteristic aptness, saying, "Where id was, let there ego be." He looked long and deep into man and saw there much that was dark and unlovely. Yet the view was not such as to lead him to abandon all hope. Addressing the American Psychoanalytic Association on the hundredth anniversary of Freud's birth, Karl Menninger said,

> Freud was a great optimist. He struggled to control too great an expectation from man or life. He strove to be as honest as it is possible to be, but had he lacked faith and hope he could not have gone on, he could not have borne his great sufferings and withstood the impact of his discoveries. . . . It is a reflection of Freud's basic faith and optimism as much as of his courage that he could face the destructive essence of human personality and assign it a basic role in our existence. Perhaps it was the bravest thing he ever did, and even in his discouragement over the outlook for civilization, he did not fail to add that reason and love can neutralize hate. . . . The clinical axiom, "You can live if you can love," came thus not only from the New Testament but from the new psychology, and not only from religion but from medical science.[7]

Freud's own words from *Civilization and Its Discontents* bear witness to the faith and hope which infused his work. They sound more relevant for the 1950s than for the 1930s in which he wrote them:

> The fateful question of the human species seems to me to be whether and to what extent the cultural process developed in it will succeed in mastering the derangements of communal life caused by the human instinct of aggression and self-destruction. In this connection perhaps the phase through which we are at this moment passing deserves special interest. Men have brought their powers of subduing the forces of nature to such a pitch that by using them they could now very easily exterminate one another to the last man. They know this. Hence arises a great part of their current unrest, their dejection, their mood of apprehension. And now it may be expected that the other of the two heavenly forces, eternal Eros, will put forth his strength so as to maintain himself alongside of his equally immortal adversary.[8]

Despite the violent opposition which would arise between Freud and Calvin over their differing estimates of the worth and functioning of religion, we begin to discover them in a curious common defense of certain ideas about human nature and conduct. There is in Freud a strong emphasis on the dual destructive and constructive instincts

7. "Freud and American Psychiatry," presented to the American Psychiatric Association on April 28, 1956.

8. *Civilization and Its Discontents*, pp. 143–44.

in man.[9] He points out the importance of the sense of guilt (conscious and unconscious) in human behavior.[10] The psychoanalyst indicates in various ways the multimotivated nature of man and exhibits an acute sensitivity to the complexity and depth of the personality.[11] The category of conflict (within man and between men) and the concept of aggressive impulses are given fundamental positions in his interpretation of human nature.[12] In addition, he holds to a thoroughgoing determinism in the psychic life.[13] His appreciation of the complexity and polyvalence of human life seems to guide him to a perspective which can be neither simply a pessimism nor simply an optimism.

Calvin (1509–64) was a literary humanist, biblical scholar, and theologian. He represents the outlook of the sixteenth century, while Freud represents that of the twentieth century; the former speaks in a theological vocabulary and the latter in an unusual scientific one. Allowances must be made for these differences with all they entail. As we compare Calvin and Freud, our attention must therefore be directed to insights and ideas, not simply to words.

It was not superfluous to have spoken first of the biblical myths. Calvin and the other Reformers can be understood as renewing in their day the appeal to biblical themes as the soundest source of information about man and God. For example, alongside of his distinctly theological pursuits, Calvin carried forward throughout his life an outstanding work in the study of biblical texts. It resulted in his writing commentaries on every biblical book but one. The intent was to replace

9. Ibid., p. 103: "The meaning of the evolution of culture is no longer a riddle to us. It must present to us the struggle between Eros and Death, between the instincts of life and the instincts of death, as it works itself out in the human species. This struggle is what all life essentially consists of. . . ." Also pp. 97, 99–100.

10. "Some Character-Types Met with in Psychoanalytic Work," *General Selections from the Works of Sigmund Freud*, ed. John Rickman (New York: Doubleday, 1957), p. 103: "[In some cases] the sense of guilt was present prior to the transgression . . . it did not arise from [the transgression], but the transgression from the sense of guilt." Cf. also *Civilization and Its Discontents*, p. 123; and *New Introductory Lectures*, pp. 148–50.

11. Contrary to this judgment is the evaluation of Philip Rieff, "The Meaning of History and Religion in Freud's Thought," *Journal of Religion* 31, no. 2 (1951), p. 116: "The Freudian reductionism to 'psychic needs' is perhaps an even more grandiose profanation of human multiformity than the Marxist."

12. *Civilization and Its Discontents*, pp. 85, 105; p. 102: "I take up the standpoint that the tendency to aggression is an innate, independent, instinctual disposition in man. . . ."

13. "The Origin and Development of Psychoanalysis," *General Selections*, p. 22: "The psychoanalyst is distinguished by an especially strong belief in the determination of the psychic life. For him there is in the expressions of the psyche nothing trifling, nothing lawless and arbitrary. . . ."

the authority of the church and the councils with that of the Bible. It is not surprising therefore, to discover Calvin reasserting certain biblical themes and myths in his doctrine of man. As a matter of fact, we find Freud and Calvin standing on the same holy ground—the trouble was that Freud did not see the burning bush.

Two salient and correlative features of the Calvinistic theology are the emphases on the all-encompassing sovereignty and consuming glory of God and on the finitude, misery, and corruption of man. With the latter is associated the horrendous term, "the depravity of man." To be sure, man was created in the image of God—he is the "most noble and remarkable specimen of the Divine justice, wisdom, and goodness . . . a clear mirror of the works of God."[14] Before the fall, life was unstained by sin, distress, broken friendships, envy, rape, robbery, or warfare. Afterwards, all these evils burst forth in human life by a kind of necessity.[15] At the fall, by a responsible and free act, man rebelled against the directing divine power operative in his life.[16] Recalling the words of the serpent in the story of the fall ("Your eyes will be opened, and you will be like gods."), we may suggest, as a psychological comment on the side, that Adam's partaking of the forbidden fruit is a rebellion against "father" (God) and that subsequently he labors under a sense of guilt for this attempt at parricide.[17] By his act of rebellion, man in effect committed spiritual suicide.[18] At this point Freud would assert that Eros found itself contested by Thanatos, the death instinct. The pristine image of the Creator was now mutilated and corrupted. Adam's ambivalent and confused state is

14. John Calvin, *Institutes of the Christian Religion*, 7th Am. ed. (Philadelphia: Presbyterian Board of Christian Education, 1936), 1.15.1 and 1.5.3. Also 1.15.3–4, 8. This source is hereafter cited as *Inst.*

15. *Civilization and Its Discontents*, p. 85: "Men are not gentle, friendly creatures wishing for love, who simply defend themselves if they are attacked, but . . . a powerful measure of desire for aggression has to be reckoned as a part of their instinctual endowment. The result is that their neighbour is to them not only a possible helper or sexual object, but also a temptation to them to gratify their aggressiveness on him. . . ."

16. *Inst.* 1.15.8. Also John Calvin, "The Eternal Predestination of God," *Calvin's Calvinism* (London: Wertheim and Macintosh, 1856–57), p. 112.

17. In *Totem and Taboo*, Freud suggests that the sense of guilt which pervades the human situation and has found expression in myths, institutions, rituals, et cetera, is derived from the murder of his father in the primal horde by his sons in the attempt to displace him and to usurp his authority.

18. John Calvin, *Commentaries on Ephesians*, ch. 2, vv. 1–2. Calvin's commentaries on the books of the Bible were published in Edinburgh by the Calvin Translation Society in 1844–56. They have recently been reprinted in the U.S.A. by Baker Book House (Grand Rapids, 1981). Citations from Calvin's commentaries will hereafter be given in abbreviated form; e.g., *Comm. on Eph.* 2:1–2.

transmitted to his descendants. Calvin and Freud both point to the ways in which the past determines the present and the future. After the fall, man finds himself the battlefield for two dynamic powers, one signified by the category of the image and the other designated by the category of the fall or of sin.[19]

For Calvin the term *depravity* seems to mean, not that every thought and feeling is detestable from every point of view, but that each and every faculty or part of the person is damaged by the fall. In other words, every aspect of personality exhibits the tension and conflict between the instincts to life and the instincts to death. This is the sense which attaches to Calvin's saying that man is in bondage to sin, that no herculean efforts of his own will rescue him from this horrible dominion.[20] "Our nature is . . . fertile in all evils."[21] Man's abysmal condition may fairly be described as pathetic. He is not a tragic figure, for the tragic action requires a certain heroism, a certain passion for righteousness or honor, a free and courageous battle against over-whelming odds. But the fallen man is vicious and miserable; he is in bondage to sin and Satan. He is an instrument of demonic powers, an embodiment of aggressive and deadly instincts.

The human condition just described is that prior to the occurrence of faith and in the presence of God. There are dual movements within the person. We do not have the space to describe the place which the sense of guilt plays in man—the guilt attached to parricidal and fratricidal impulses. Nor have we the opportunity to elaborate on the determinism implied in Calvin's views, though it is suggested in the phrase, "in bondage to sin and Satan." In his fallen condition before the advent of faith, man is controlled by two impulses, one constructive and preservative and the other destructive and awry. The latter is, however, dominant; for, left to his own devices, man's inescapable lot is misery and anxiety, confusion and disorder.

What happens when faith appears? To say it in a few words and therefore too simply, faith is enlightenment and the impartation of a new power. With what results? The result is that a transfer of sover-

19. *Civilization and Its Discontents,* p. 97: "Besides the instinct preserving the organic substance and binding it into even larger units, there must exist another in antithesis to this, which would seek to dissolve these units and reinstate their antecedent inorganic state; that is to say, a death instinct as well as Eros; the phenomena of life would then be explicable from the interplay of the two and their counteracting effects on each other." Page 98: "The two kinds of instincts seldom—perhaps never—appear in isolation, but always mingle with each other in different, very varying proportions and so make themselves unrecognizable to us."

20. *Inst.* 2.3.5; *Comm. on Acts* 15:9; Paul Wernle, *Der evangelische Glaube* (Tuebingen: J. C. B. Mohr, 1919), 3, 211.

21. *Inst.* 2.1.8.

eignty is achieved from the destructive instincts to the constructive ones. Eros, Freud would say, is now in the ascendancy. Note well, however, that the ambivalence of human nature is not thereby overcome. Both life instincts and death instincts are still operative, but now the former dominate. The theologian expresses this by saying that, even after the gift of faith and after the impartation of justification, the saved man remains a sinner and stands constantly in need of repentance. Repentance, which is the work directed to the restoration of the divine image, is never finished, at least in this life (nor can any man be completely psychoanalyzed and therefore be rendered completely free from conflict).

After the reversal, then, the tensions of life remain, but a different logic characterizes them. The power infused by faith is not uncontested. The opposition to sin and Satan continues, except now man enters the fray better armed. (After psychoanalytic therapy is there not a battle yet to be fought? Does not the patient go into the contest better armed?) According to Calvin, the Christian life in faith exhibits certain tensions which are symptomatic of this inner warfare. The assurance which comes with faith is attended by doubt.[22] "The pious heart perceives a division in itself."[23] In Calvin's writings, there is a curious set of antithetical statements about assurance in faith. It is free from doubt, yet it is not free from doubt. It does not hesitate, yet it does hesitate. Security is to be found in it, but nevertheless it is beset by anxiety. The faithful have a firm assurance, but they also waver and tremble. We cannot here discuss how Calvin resolves these apparent paradoxes.[24] For our present purposes the point of interest is that the tension between assurance and doubt is clearly exhibited, according to the Reformer, by the person to whom the gift of faith has been imparted. There is a similar treatment between trust and fear.[25] The faithful also display a tension between misery and hope.[26] They go forward "constantly groaning, partly from a consciousness of their weakness, partly from an eager longing for the future life [which they envisage in hope]."[27] A more careful examination of the writings of Calvin would show, we are sure, evidences of other tensions and con-

22. *Comm. on Heb.* 11:11; *Inst.* 3.2.17.

23. *Inst.* 3.2.18.

24. Some of the texts which deal with this problem are *Inst.* 3.2.15, 17–19; *Comm. on I Pet.* 1:5; *Comm. on Rom.* 5:2; 8:35.

25. *Comm. on Gen.* 32:6; *Comm. on I John* 2:3; *Inst.* 1.2.2; 3.2.12, 17, 23.

26. *Comm. on Rom.* 5:3, 5; 8:25; *Comm. on II Thess.* 1:4; *Comm. on I Pet.* 1:3; *Comm. on Ps.* 19:8; 48:2; *Inst.* 3.8.1; also see Leon Wencelius, "l'Idée de joie dans la pensée de Calvin," *Revue d'Histoire et de Philosophie religieuses* 15:70–109.

27. *Comm. on I Cor.* 15:9.

flicts which the theologian sensed in the precarious lives of both the saved and the unsaved. These remarks should be sufficient, however, to indicate that, while faith brings a reversal in the direction of the development of the personality, both the prefaith state and the post-faith state exhibit the dualism celebrated under the biblical myths; expressed in different categories, it is Freud's dualism between Eros and Thanatos. Both the Reformer and the psychoanalyst have, in addition, a common appreciation of the complexity of human nature and of the inescapable and powerful factors of strife, self-love, and self-destruction in the person. We should add that, after the reversal which comes in faith, man is in "bondage to God" as regards the operations performed in him by the divine spirit. Thus Calvin defends a determinism in both the postfaith state and in the prefaith state. This can be correlated with the theologian's doctrines of the persever-ance of the saints and of predestination. If space permitted, one could also describe how Calvin interpreted the crucifixion-resurrection theme in terms of the movements of the psyche. There is a sense in which the man of faith is crucified with Christ and is resurrected with Christ— and the one does not occur without the other.

Our remarks may indicate in some measure that a strong practical motive lay behind Calvin's theological thought. It is shown by his acute sense of the misery and tragedy of the terrestrial life and of the urgent need for a remedy for its illnesses. The technical theological problems he discusses are connected to a living context. Some of the central questions with which he deals are these: "How can a man and how should a man live in this miserable, broken world?" "How can a man enjoy felicity in spite of misery?" "How can there be peace in the midst of distress and destruction?" Both Calvin and Freud were deeply concerned with these issues. Calvin handles them within a theo-logical framework, while Freud deals with them within a naturalistic framework which includes a commitment that the pleasure principle regulates the psychic processes.[28] The early Bertrand Russell expressed a similar sensitivity to the deadly aspect of life and nature, though he came to it from another, quite different perspective:

> The beauty of Tragedy does not make visible a quality which in more or less obvious shapes, is present always and everywhere in life. In the spectacle of Death, in the endurance of intolerable pain, and in the irrevo-cableness of a vanished past, there is a sacredness, an overpowering awe, a feeling of the vastness, the depth, the inexhaustible mystery of existence, in which by some strange marriage of pain, the sufferer is

28. "Beyond the Pleasure-Principle," *General Selections*, p. 141 *et passim*; "The Ego and the Id," *General Selections*, p. 234 *et passim*.

bound to the world by the bonds of sorrow. . . . The life of Man is a long march through the night, surrounded by invisible foes, tortured by weariness and pain. . . .[29]

Freud and Calvin would contend that the larger number of those "invisible foes" are internal to the person. This does not, however, lessen in any respect the deadliness of that threatening aspect of the world. Nor does it moderate in any way the urgency of the search for salvation. We may interpret the psychoanalyst and the Reformer as consenting in the verdict of Gabriel Marcel that

> despair is possible in any form, at any moment and to any degree, and the betrayal may seem to be counselled, if not forced upon us, by the very structure of the world in which we live. The deadly aspect of this world may, from a given standpoint, be regarded as a ceaseless incitement to denial and to suicide. It could even be said in this sense that the fact that suicide is always possible is the essential starting point of any genuine metaphysical thought.[30]

However uncomfortable they make us feel, the Calvinistic and Freudian themes of the "depravity" of man, of the ambivalence of human nature, and of determinism give a realistic, though difficult, foundation for constructing a proper understanding of man's life and of its context, natural and supernatural. It is with issues such as these that every theologian and philosopher should be required to begin his thinking. No apology should be made for the difficulties these insights present to system makers among the philosophers and theologians; for things should be made as difficult as possible for those engaged in momentous activities.

The image of man entertained by Calvin is, as we have seen, similar in many respects to that held by Freud. In summary, some of the points of agreement we discover are these:

1. An appreciation of the depth and complexity of the psyche.
2. A recognition of the dualistic nature of man.
3. A defense of the doctrine of determinism in the psyche life.
4. An awareness of the continual conflict in man between creative impulses (God—Eros) and destructive impulses (Satan, sin—Thanatos).

29. Bertrand Russell, "A Free Man's Worship," *Mysticism and Logic and Other Essays* (London: George Allen and Unwin, 1951), pp. 54, 56.

30. Gabriel Marcel, "On the Ontological Mystery," *The Philosophy of Existence* (London: Harvill Press, 1954), p. 14.

5. The idea that a hidden or unconscious work in man is determinative of his overt behavior.
6. The contention that the investment of psychic energy in others,
   which we term unselfishness, is essential to the preservation of
   life and the achievement of maturity.
7. A sense of the precariousness of life and of the urgency of salvation due to the presence of powers or instincts in man which
   are deadly.
8. An expression of confidence in the possibility that the creative
   impulses (Eros) can triumph over the destructive ones (Thanatos)—that is, a faith and hope in salvation.
9. The urgent insistence that knowledge of one's self is a necessary
   condition for felicity or salvation.
10. A recognition of the significant role of guilt in the psychic life
    and in behavior.

We have deliberately overlooked the many important points of difference between Calvin and Freud, for this topic has often been treated
by investigators. Less frequently, however, are the similarities between
the Freudian image of man and the Calvinistic one discussed. Some
merit may then attach to this paper, if it has succeeded in indicating
a measure of harmony between Freud and Calvin and in suggesting
more generally that the psychoanalytic and theological perspectives
on human nature and conduct have some things in common.

The psychology of religion has, since its inception, been caught between the positivistic-reductionistic strivings of modern scientific aspirations and the humanistic and holistic visions of theology. At the heart of this ambivalence exist different conceptions of the nature of man. Current shifts from behavioristic, adjustmental, and mental health models to humanistic and actionistic formulations provide the opportunity for a rapprochement of theological and psychological principles. The integration of these ideas in a "Theological-Psychology of Religion" is viewed as offering new theoretical foundations for the development of a rigorously based empirical religious psychology—one with solid footing in objective research, but which is not detached from explicit theological values.

Images of Man and Dimensions of Personal Religion

Values for an Empirical Psychology of Religion

Bernard Spilka

Historically, man per se was the province of religion. The growth of biological science and medicine seemed to reduce human life to the level of a complex machine, while the advent of psychology tended to abstract man from his worldly and possible other-worldly contexts and turned him in upon himself. Thus it was that Freud (1957) theorized that religion was a normal product of psychic development to be cast aside with the coming of maturity. William James (1908:299–300) put faith in the pragmatic mold by stating: "if the hypothesis of God works satisfactorily . . . it is true." As one wag put it, psychology first lost "its soul, then its mind, and then consciousness; but strangely enough it still behaves" (Baker, 1963:1).

The foregoing remarks suggest an historical process by means of

Reprinted from *Review of Religious Research* 11, no. 3 (1970):171–82. Used by permission.

which man became dehumanized, as science usurped him from religion. In the framework of current psychology, this decline has resulted in the study of logical constructs and/or intervening variables, not of man himself. Hence, some troubled psychologists have asked in puzzlement, "Where is the perceiver in perception, and the learner in learning?" The shift from absolutist to relativistic physics further reduced the significance of man from at least a fairly well circumscribed object of study to one in a contingent universe.

The process of trivializing man has not occurred without resistance. Hume (Becker, 1968:22) countered the Newtonian world view by asserting that "the science of man is the only solid foundation for the other sciences." In a similar vein, Diderot (Becker, 1968:3) claimed that "it is the presence of man that renders natural existence interesting. . . . Man is the unique end from which we must begin and to which everything must return." Indeed this is the problem—to formulate a systematic view which without qualification acknowledges the human component in the social and behavioral sciences.

Valuations in the Psychology of Religion

Admiration of the empirical method by psychologists of religion has been mixed. The view that religious phenomena go far beyond what may be scientifically revealed is natural to most workers in this field, since their roots are originally within the religious domain itself. Data thus tend to take a back seat to extensive discussions which invariably do two things: (1) these efforts usually remain quite detached from research findings; and (2) there is reluctance to grapple with factors which underlie this obvious ambivalence toward the objectification of religion. Moberg (1967) has raised somewhat overlapping considerations relative to the sociology of religion, suggesting limits to social scientific research which demand serious reflection.

In essence, we may be observing the operation of apparently conflicting assumptions underlying social science and theology about the nature of man. Only recently has attention been focused on this problem (Chein, 1962; Doniger, 1962; McLaughlin, 1965; Pattison, 1965; Platt, 1965; Thomas, 1962). Unfortunately most of these attempts have not been directed at producing the kind of rapprochement which would result in a viable theoretical foundation for a research- or empirically oriented psychology of religion. It is therefore felt that psychology and theology must be openly coordinated and integrated, or the prevailing confusion in the psychology of religion is likely to continue.

To accomplish this goal, the development of a "Theological-Psychology of Religion"[1] may be necessary. As will be evident, this overlaps considerably with the notion of a humanistic psychology of religion (Royce, 1967; Strunk, 1970), and Pruyser's (1968) call for a restructured "Dynamic Psychology of Religion" to deal with both individual psychology and public theology and religious activity. The above reference to a "theological psychology" may, however, cause many social scientists to shudder, for theology is stereotyped as transcendental in concern. Novak (1968) counters this view and succinctly describes the position taken here when he asserts that

> the astute reader of theological discourse will soon discover that every sentence in such discourse, however obliquely, refers to human actions, or dispositions, or programs. . . . The "Kingdom of God" . . . has an other worldly, apocalyptic concomitant; yet, in its own right, it is a concrete this-worldly ideal. Theology studies ultimate visions of communal relationships and personal identity, insofar as these affect actual human experience (p. 52).

The task is therefore clear—to explicate images of man's nature from psychology and theology, to reveal a growing commonality of outlook, and finally to demonstrate the ramifications this has for a systematic empirical and scientific psychology of religion—a theological one in essence.

Psychological Images of Man

Models of human nature in psychology are by no means simple, even though the mainstream of psychological thought stresses a reductionistic mechanism. The sources for activating this mechanism are primarily of environmental origin as befits the powerful position of behaviorism. It is therefore not surprising that psychology is denoted, in many quarters, "behavioral" science. Sperry (1965:76) describes the "general stance of modern behavioral science" as "objective, mechanistic, materialistic, behavioristic, fatalistic, reductionistic," while Bertalanffy (1968:189) speaks of this approach as "the robot model of human behavior." Chein (1962:8) summarizes these views as resting "on the false assumption that . . . every determinant of behavior is *either* a body-fact *or* an environment-fact."

When acceptance of a biological-vegetative framework is paramount, behavioral explanations become couched in terms of mech-

---

1. The choice of an appropriate term for this effort is a difficult one. We need both a theology of psychology and a psychological theology. The phrase "Theological-Psychology" is an approximation. Any more useful and compatible language would be acceptable to the writer.

anistic contiguity, tension reduction, and homeostasis. Tension is aroused first by tissue needs and physiological drives. If this is reduced in the presence of social elements, interpersonal values and skills are mechanically conditioned. It is also assumed that the energized person will remain active until the sources of his tension are sated. The goals of behavior are not growth but equilibrium, "certain favorable steady states" (Stagner, 1961:19).

This is the stuff learning theories are made of, and as McClelland (1955) poignantly observes, learning is synonymous with adjustment. One learns to adjust to the conditions that exist, not to change them. The content of what is learned is irrelevant, for we are process oriented—learning, thinking, perceiving, which takes place *within* a vegetatively conceived being, whether rat or man. The "adjustment" model of life further implies the rightness of the circumstances in which one exists. The task is to fit in, conform, adjust to the prevailing environmental order. Man is primarily a passive being to be molded by his environment, it is hoped a benign one, a la Skinner (1948). The position is succinctly treated by the founder of behaviorism, John B. Watson (1924:11), who affirmed that "Behaviorism . . . takes the whole field of human adjustments as its own," but

> psychology has little to do with setting of social standards of action, and nothing to do with moral standards. It does lie within her province to tell whether the individual man can act in accordance with such standards, and *how we may control him* or lead him *to act in harmony with them*" (Watson, 1919:2) [Italics added].

The adjustment model, in verifying the correctness of the order of things (physical, social, political, and moral), strengthens the hand of clinical professionals in whom society has invested some power over persons defined as deviant. Here, adjustment models combine with those of medical-biological origin to connote maladjustment as "mental illness." The notion of illness supportively implies that the disturbed person is the relatively passive victim of circumstances—of an internal disease process. As an unwilling and unfortunate pawn of nature, the "patient" is put in the hands of the expert (psychiatrist, physician, or psychologist) for "treatment." Subvocally, the problem is an internal one, possibly somatogenic in origin, permitting the affected individual to be abstracted from the world for appropriate handling until he returns to an adjusted state of "mental health." Implied again is the correctness of the objective conditions that exist and compliance is the virtue to be sought and honored. Conformity and mental health are thus synonymous.

Recent years have witnessed the development of counterthemes which deny these radical determinisms of either self or environment. Thus one hears of "humanistic" psychology (Bugental, 1967; Severin, 1965), "existential" psychology (May, 1961), and "action" psychology (Pratt and Tooley, 1967). The referent of normal gives way to ideal, and man the adjuster and reactor is supplanted by man the actor. The search is for an understanding of man in context: not in *interaction* where he is conceptualized as distinct and separate from all else, but in *transaction* where he is always part of something larger (Chein, 1962; Ittleson and Cantril, 1954). Passivity now yields to activity and control to freedom. The goals of this are evident in Pratt and Tooley's (1967:156) admonition that "*both* scientific and social progress are suspended when man's first agency, action, is idle."

Adopting this view, Ittelson and Kilpatrick (1966) and Bruner and Postman (1948, 1949) have repeatedly demonstrated that one's purposes, needs, and expectations influence what is perceived. Even in the radically behavioristic domain of learning, action views of how people learn have been peripherally present since the early days of research in this area (Hilgard and Bower, 1966). In recent years, Mowrer's (1960a, 1960b) willingness to utilize such language as "hope" and "joy" in his formulations illustrates how learning functions are increasingly being seen in the large and more realistic perspective of the total person.

Motivation theorists have also challenged mechanistic tension-reduction models of human behavior. Goldstein (1939), Rogers (1963), and Maslow (1962) speak of a force for positive growth, a tendency to "self-actualize" oneself, to utilize one's capacities to their fullest. Goldstein (1963:147) sees the inevitable development of self-actualization in an "urge to perfection."

A somewhat related view of human motivation has been proposed by Robert White (1959, 1960) and adopted by Bruner (1966). Emphasizing the motive to be competent, this position counters traditional conceptions of "mental health" and "adjustment." Effectiveness is the goal of activity, and this may imply some degree of adapting to circumstances plus efforts to change existing conditions. Each situation will therefore include behavior that, in the transactional view, is based on the creation of maximal opportunity for future self-determination and potential development. In like manner, Coleman (1960:32) asks "whether man is in fact an active and responsible agent with 'free will' or a puppet whose behavior is determined by forces beyond his control."

Images of Man in Religion and Theology

The distinction made in the title for this section is necessitated by the rather frequent and large discrepancies one observes between (1)

the practice of established religion and (2) the body of doctrine justi-
fying the existence of a church and individual faith. The transformation
of the latter to the former is a cyclical tale of inspiration and institutionalization in which spirit is repeatedly submerged by pressure from
vested power and the dehumanization of dogma and practice. In turn,
there is the fractionation of formal religious bodies by a resurgence of
creative and humanizing forces demanding spiritual relevance (Glock,
1964; O'Dea, 1961). Theologically man is the subject of religion, but
institutionally he has often become its object.

In the course of religious formalization, churches tend more to mirror social forces than to mold them. As Marty (1964:180) states,
"Religious groups in our current society ordinarily serve as the *reac-
tors*. They may hitchhike on secular elements of change." Moberg
(1962:63), in discussing "the new American piety," observes that "secularism . . . as a central theme prevails; 'the American Way' is the
main creed." The same position is affirmed by Herberg (1960), among
many others (Gilkey, 1967; Johnson, 1952; Winter, 1962). Formal religion and the church thus act as agencies for social conformity and the
suppression of deviance, but this need not be oppressively enforced.
Identification with the church has a positive appeal of its own so that
the faithful acquiesce willingly in reducing their freedom by valuing
conforming modes of thought and action. Shades of *Walden Two* (Skinner, 1948:218) in which Frazier explains, "We can achieve a sort of
control under which the controlled, though they are following a code
much more scrupulously than was ever the case under the old system,
nevertheless *feel free* . . . in that case the question of freedom never
arises."

Institutional religion and psychology frequently share a common
view of man, the machine model. The former may do so reluctantly,
but all too often in practice it values the status quo and resists change.
Just as Skinner (1953:447–48) maintains that "the hypothesis that
man is not free is essential to the application of scientific method to
the study of human behavior," so many devout churchmen validate
the inference that freedom may counter the "application of the religious method to man." Southard (1965) poignantly discusses the
realization of these ideas in the methodology of "programming" as it
may be applied in religious education. He points out that the philosophical assumptions and implications of such procedures are usually
forgotten in the enthusiasm generated by the development of these
rather exciting instructional methods.

At this juncture, it should be apparent that generalizations are being
offered; by their very nature, such are inherently false. The foregoing
positions are by no means exhaustively valid, any more so than those

that follow. Nevertheless, they do describe in broadly accurate terms a reality that has been repeatedly confirmed.

Just as institutional religion implies an adjustment perspective, the theologies of the great religions have, at their core, maintained images of man that stress growth, freedom, capability, and action. The doctrine of free will embodies the idea of action in its fullest sense. Free will in Judaism "sees man creating a destiny that impinges on the infinite" (Baeck, 1948:123). Aquinas (1952: Vol. 1:436) stresses the essential association between reason and freedom: "In that man is rational, it is necessary that he have free choice." Niebuhr (1942:17) maintains "the essence of man is his freedom."

Both psychologists and modern theologians are quite loath to accept the notion of a total unfettered freedom of human action that the doctrine of free will might imply. This view is well expressed by scholars whose feet are firmly planted within both psychology and theology. Thus, Van Kaam (1962:5) declares that "the human will is neither the absolute ruler imagined by the will-power Christian nor the product of libidinal and cultural determinism expounded by psychoanalysis and behaviorism." Elsewhere he observes, "It is true that my behavior is conditioned, but I can influence the kind of conditioning by the meaning I freely impose on my tendencies and my environment" (Van Kaam, 1968:125). Nuttin (1962:159) similarly avers that "a free act ... is not the resultant pure and simple of a process governed by influences of environment and physiological factors, but there is also another principle behind it—the self-determination of a person."

In opposition to the conformist orientation of institutional religion, the tenet of free will is consonant with the position of action and humanistic psychology. Both strongly support the possibility of man shaping his situation and circumstances to elevate that which is *good* over that which is socially *right*.

The Transactional Perspective

We have seen an increasing awareness by psychologists of the role of an active organism rather than a reactive one throughout the realm of behavioral science. This viewpoint has long been established in traditional theology. A true appreciation of action must include the nature of the reality in which behavior is embedded; to accomplish this the term *transaction* has been introduced. Ittelson and Cantril (1954:3) define it as carrying

> the double implication (1) that all parts of the situation enter it (the total life situation) as active participants, and (2) that they owe their

very existence as encountered in the situation to this fact of active participation and do not appear as already existing entities merely interacting with each other without affecting their own identity.

Pratt and Tooley (1964) emphasize the action aspect of the transactional field when they claim that "man . . . can never be considered as more *nor* less than the creature *and* creator of his transactional world" (p. 52). Heschel (1965) and Van Kaam (1968) are fine expositors of a similar outlook in theology. Of the greatest significance is that these principles offer an heuristic framework for a "Theological-Psychology of Religion."

Directions for a "Theological-Psychology of Religion"

Contemporary discussions of personality and mental disorder seem to stress three major aspects of the person-world transaction: (1) the relation of the individual to himself as illustrated by Organismic and Self-Concept theories and research (Combs and Snygg, 1959; Goldstein, 1939; Kelly, 1955; Wylie, 1961); (2) the relation of the person to the social world as found in Mirror-image, Social-Interpersonal, Biosocial, and Social Learning views (Goffman, 1959; Kluckhohn, Murray, and Schneider, 1953; Rotter, 1954; Sullivan, 1953); and (3) the relation of the individual to an integrative ideal such as the search for meaning, realization, or some ultimate (Bertocci and Millard, 1963; Frankl, 1963, 1967; Ungersma, 1961). These approaches overlap, and most students of personality employ more than one in their formulations. Ideally, the effective personality demonstrates a realistically based high degree of self-regard, a positive pattern of social relationships involving appreciation of and respect for the individuality of others, and a clear sense of identity which is associated with a progressive and constructive philosophy of life. The characteristics of Maslow's (1954) self-actualizing person may be conceptualized in this manner with surprisingly little effort.

The foregoing general dimensions of an adequate or better actualized personality have their counterparts within Judaeo-Christian theologies. Some explication of these referents from both the psychological and theological domains will now be undertaken to demonstrate their complementarity.

Self-significance

In discussing "the purpose of creation," Maimonides (1956:277) identified self-knowledge with accurate comprehension of "the true nature of everything." His discussion of those "who constantly strive to choose that which is noble" (p. 261) is one facet of a positive evaluation of self through awareness of its likeness to that of the creator. Baeck (1948:189) also extols "the faith of man in himself," for through it, he asserts, "life acquires the strength to possess and choose itself; and that is its eternal-significance, its moral freedom." Free will and effectiveness are thus premised on a positive and constructive self-understanding.

In Catholicism, Aquinas (1952: Vol. 2: Part 2; Questions 3, 25–27, 44) speaking of the virtues refers to an obligation to oneself in the sense of maintaining health, proper care of the body, and apparently mental well-being. Though this is the lowest of these positive obligations, it is still of basic importance in Thomistic philosophy.

Various Protestant theologians embrace similar elements. Beginning with Scripture, Brunner (1936) includes, under the concept of love, love of self and neighbor. Niebuhr (1942:259) speaks of the "self in contemplation" and the "self in action." Like many psychologists whom he criticizes, Niebuhr carries out a rather detailed analysis of self-insight and adequacy.

Many of the analyses of self-love, self-regard, self-obligation, and valuation found in religious literature bear a remarkable likeness to views held by members of the psychological-psychiatric community. Noteworthy here is the discussion offered by Kurt Goldstein in *Health as Value* (1959:179). This centers about "the essential significance of the phenomenon of health for man's self-realization." The centrality of self-oriented theories in contemporary psychology is well represented by the summary of twelve such positions in a currently popular text (Hall and Lindzey, 1957). The basic assumption underlying these views is that all behavior implies a concept of the self, and that to the extent this valuation is consistent, integrated, and positive, the individual responds in a mature and constructive manner. It is, of course, not fortuitous that scholars who espouse such views stress holistic-cognitive images of man and explicitly deny behavioristic conceptions. These treatments reveal the coincidence of theological and psychological outlooks, hence the ease with which they can be united in the construction of an empirical psychology of religion.

Operationally, the above identification recommends the assessment of individual religion with personality-type items and scales usually considered beyond the realm of religious measurement. Dittes (1969) strongly supports this approach; however, work relating faith to self and ego functions has been dubiously productive. It is fair to add that such efforts have not been well formulated. The answer may lie in simply using indices of self-adequacy as one set of religious criteria without regard to their association with other variables assessing spiritual orientation.

Social Significance

From the golden rule and the social gospel to the death of God and situation-ethics debates of today, man was and is primarily viewed as an ethical and social being. The scriptural admonition to "love thy neighbor as thyself" joins the high prescription for self-regard with a similar valuation of others. Rabbi Akiba termed this the highest ethical commandment (Cohen, 1968:7). Aquinas (1952) similarly places the obligation to others above that to the self. The moral core of faith is nowhere better clarified than in Einstein's (1967:71) assertion, "There is no higher religion than human service. To work for the common good is the greatest creed."

Social scientists increasingly regard man as first and foremost a social being. Mowrer (1961:126) claims that "the supreme anguish comes (for man) . . . from the rupturing of his sociality." He cites Karl Menninger to the effect that "mental illness must be a reaction to some kind of feeling of rupture with the social environment" (Mowrer, 1961:126). Adler (1929:264) summarized his theory in the view that "social interest and social cooperation are . . . the salvation of the individual." Two of the main criteria offered by Maslow and Mittelmann (1951:15) for mental well-being are the "ability to satisfy the requirements of the group" and "adequate emancipation from the group or culture."

The likelihood of agreement between theologians and psychologists on the importance of one's social outlook and actions would not appear to be a source of difference, but rather of unity. Paul Johnson's position of Dynamic Interpersonalism (1966:759) demonstrates such congruence when he notes that "interpersonal psychology meets a theology of relationship." The psychological goal of social effectiveness and the religious aim of "following a moral life" therefore combine easily to provide additional footing for a "Theological-Psychology of Religion."

There is a massive amount of research examining the social perspectives of apparently religious individuals. Though the majority of churchgoers and those who assent to the dogma of faith appear to negate humanitarian motives (Kirkpatrick, 1949) and associate themselves with prejudices and discrimination (Allport, 1954, 1966; Dittes, 1970; Spilka and Reynolds, 1965), there is reason to believe that their religious outlook is a consensual one (Allen and Spilka, 1967). Great difficulty has been encountered trying to distinguish this form of personal religion from a committed faith. Dittes (1969), however, may again be correct when he recommends consideration of measures of social outlook and behavior as criteria of personal religion. The work of Allport and Ross (1967) and Allen and Spilka (1967) supports these as relevant additions to current criteria in the psychology of religion.

Ultimate Significance

It was noted earlier that a third referent also provides for a similar combining of psychology and theology. This relates to active man's searching for some direction to make his life relevant and meaningful. Theologians have always perceived the aim of human existence as a search for ultimate significance, which is usually phrased in terms of God or the divine. One need not mention the wide variety of definitions and outlooks on what these concepts have come to mean; the central point is that whatever the referent, it is perceived as a fundamental striving for integration, direction, security, personal effectiveness, and above all, relation in absolute sense. Aquinas (1952:401) thus tells us that "the proper end of faith is the joining of the human mind with divine faith." Within the Thomistic system, one's obligation or positive commandment to love God takes precedence above all else. It is as if comprehension of the purpose of life will always subsume proper appreciation of charity and self-regard. Classical Judaism also stresses that duty to God is primary to self- and other-love (Cohen, 1949); but according to Baeck (1948:35), the problem is "not so much of what God is in himself, but what he means to man."

Among modern Protestant theologians, Cox (1965) distinguishes the meaning- versus the naming-process relative to the concept of God. The former he feels to be a function of history and the social order. In a parallel vein, Cogley (1968) returns us to the position of Frankl (1963): namely, "the search for relevance will have to be a major mark of religion, the theological enterprise *par excellence*" (Cogley, 1968:142).

As psychology discovers higher dimensions of motivation, some behavioral scientists see the identity of their concerns with those of religionists. Szasz (1960:118) claims that "life for most people is a continuous struggle, not for biological survival, but for a 'place in the sun', 'peace of mind' or some other human value." Rollo May (1940:13) also suggests that "people suffer personality breakdowns because they do not have meaning in their lives," and Victor Frankl (1963) takes this "search for meaning" as the root of all human motivation. Jung (1962:229) saw such a lack of meaning as basically a problem "of finding a religious outlook on life."

Among recent developments, Elkind (1970) has constructed a cognitive theoretical approach which argues that religion is a natural product of normal mental growth. Somewhat similar is Blake's (1962) view that there exists a basic "spiritual" need within the human personality equivalent in significance to biological, personal, and social motivational categories.

Turning to the operational sphere, there are a number of referents for "this search for meaning." It is still quite valid to look for such a direction in adherence to established religious institutions. Strommen (1963) found this with respect to Lutheran youth. To the extent they are knowledgeable with regard to their faith and demonstrate behavioral commitment, their social and personal outlooks tend to be positive and progressive (Strommen, 1967). Spilka and his associates have obtained similar evidence (Allen and Spilka, 1967; Spilka and Reynolds, 1965). Dean and Reeves (1962) also show how identification with a religious system may counter personal alienation. Moberg (1967) cautions against the view that these operational approaches exhaust all there is to religion. If his position is valid, we should recognize that the discrepancy between the correlations we obtain and that ideal of 1.00 with regard to the significance of faith may, in part, be a function of a "spiritual" component that constitutes the essence of religiosity.

One cannot disregard the meaningfulness to individuals of ideologies other than those found in the Judaeo-Christian tradition. The likelihood that these are not as independent of the latter as many might like to believe does merit exploration. It is more important to realize that the search for meaning and relevance may take a wide variety of forms, and the quest itself is both psychologically and theologically significant.

A Perspective for Research

It is obviously true, as Dittes (1969) notes, that psychologists of religion will have to broaden their perspectives greatly in order to understand what they should be studying. Utilizing traditional criteria as an entree into the "religious search for meaning," it has been possible to demonstrate the multidimensional nature of personal religion (Spilka, Read, Allen, and Dailey, 1968).

Delineation of various religious forms provides a framework for understanding their correlates in a contemporary and historical sense. In this way the self-, other-, and meaning-aspects of each type of personal religion can be operationally denoted. The outcome would be a picture of different kinds of religionists, and criteria of faith would necessarily include a wide variety of personality, attitude, and value measures not usually associated with the psychology of religion. This necessarily requires extensive theory development, something psychologists of religion have only weakly undertaken.

It should be evident that there are strong trends within psychology to resurrect man *in toto* from a misplaced emphasis on him as a compound of variables and fractionated processes. Current humanistic-psychological versions of man *qua* man are basically similar to the views of man held in Western theology. A natural step would be explicitly to combine common elements from theology and psychology. Hiltner's desire to treat "psychology as a theological discipline internal to theology itself" (1961; p. 251) then would be a step closer to realization. The barriers between religion and psychology would be removed in the construction of a "Theological-Psychology of Religion" pertinent to both disciplines. This should elicit the kind of information and perspective that must form the groundwork for a true understanding of man; he is objective, yes, but not detached.

References

Adler, A. 1929. *The science of living.* Garden City, N.Y.: Doubleday.

Allen, R. O., and Spilka, B. 1967. Committed and consensual religion: a specification of religion-prejudice relationships. *Journal for the Scientific Study of Religion* 6:191–208.

Allport, G. W. 1954. *The nature of prejudice.* Reading, Mass.: Addison-Wesley.

————. 1966. The religious context of prejudice. *Journal for the Scientific Study of Religion* 5:447–57.

Allport, G. W., and Ross, J. M. 1967. Personal religious orientation and prejudice. *Journal of Personality and Social Psychology* 5:432–43.

Aquinas, T. 1952. *Summa theologica.* 2 vols. Great Books of the Western World. Chicago: Encyclopedia Britannica.

Baeck, L. 1948. *The essence of Judaism.* Rev. ed. New York: Schocken.

Baker, R. A. 1963. *Psychology in the wry.* New York: Van Nostrand.

Becker, E. 1968. *The structure of evil.* New York: George Braziller.

Bertalanffy, L. V. 1968. *General system theory.* New York: George Braziller.

Bertocci, P. A., and Millard, R. M. 1963. *Personality and the good.* New York: David McKay.

Blake, J. A. 1962. Faith as a basic personality need. *Pastoral Psychology* 13:43–47.

Bruner, J. 1966. *Toward a theory of instruction.* Cambridge, Mass.: Harvard University.

Bruner, J. S., and Postman, L. 1948. Symbolic value as an organizing factor in perception. *Journal of Social Psychology* 27:203–8.

————. 1949. On the perception of incongruity: A paradigm. *Journal of Personality* 18:206–23.

Brunner, E. 1936. *The divine imperative.* Philadelphia: Westminster.

Bugental, J. F. T., ed. 1967. *Challenges of humanistic psychology*. New York: McGraw-Hill.

Chein, I. 1962. The image of man. *Journal of Social Issues* 18:1–35.

Cogley, J. 1968. *Religion in a secular age*. New York: Praeger.

Cohen, A. 1949. *Everyman's Talmud*. New York: Dutton.

Cohen, H. 1968. *Justice, justice*. New York: Union of American Hebrew Congregations.

Coleman, J. C. 1960. *Personality dynamics and effective behavior*. Chicago: Scott, Foresman.

Combs, A. W., and Syngg, D. 1959. *Individual behavior*. Rev. ed. New York: Harper.

Cox, H. 1965. *The secular city*. New York: Macmillan.

Dean, D. G., and Reeves, J. A. 1962. Anomie: A comparison of a Catholic and a Protestant sample. *Sociometry* 25:209–12.

Dittes, J. E. 1969. Secular religion: Dilemma of churches and researchers. *Review of Religious Research* 10:65–81.

————. 1970. Research of variables in religion. In *The handbook of social psychology*, edited by E. Aronson and G. Lindzey, vol. 5, 602–59. Reading, Mass.: Addison-Wesley.

Doniger, S. 1962. *The nature of man in theological and psychological perspective*. New York: Harper.

Einstein, A. 1967. Quotation. *New York Times Magazine*, 19 November, 71.

Elkind, D. 1970. The origins of religion in the child. *Review of Religious Research* 12, no. 1, 35–42.

Frankl, V. E. 1963. *Man's search for meaning*. New York: Washington Square.

————. 1967. *The doctor and the soul*. New York: Bantam.

Freud, S. 1957. *The future of an illusion*. Garden City, N.Y.: Doubleday.

Gilkey, L. 1967. Social and intellectual sources of contemporary Protestant theology in North America. *Daedalus* 96, no. 1.

Glock, C. Y. 1964. The role of deprivation in the origin and evolution of religious groups. In *Religion and social conflict*, edited by R. Lee and M. E. Marty, 24–36. New York: Oxford University.

Goffman, E. 1959. *The presentation of self in everyday life*. Rev. ed. Garden City, N.Y.: Doubleday.

Goldstein, K. 1939. *The organism*. New York: American.

————. 1959. Health as value. In *New Knowledge in Human Values*. Edited by A. H. Maslow, 178–88. New York: Harper and Row.

————. 1963. *Human nature in the light of psychopathology*. New York: Schocken.

Hall, C. S., and Lindzey, G. 1957. *Theories of personality*. New York: Wiley.

Herberg, W. 1960. *Protestant, Catholic, Jew*. Rev. ed. Garden City, N.Y.: Doubleday.

Heschel, A. J. 1965. *Who is man?* Palo Alto, Cal.: Stanford University.

Hilgard, E. R., and Bower, G. H. 1966. *Theories of learning*. 3d ed. New York: Appleton-Century-Crofts.

Hiltner, S. 1961. Conclusion: The dialogue on man's nature. In *The nature of man*, edited by S. Doniger, 237–61. New York: Harper.

Ittelson, W. H., and Cantril, H. 1954. *Perception: A transactional approach*. Garden City, N.Y.: Doubleday.

Ittelson, W. H., and Kilpatrick, F. L. 1966. Experiments in perception. In *Frontiers of psychological research*, edited by S. Coopersmith. San Francisco: W. H. Freeman.

James, W. 1908. *Pragmatism*. New York: Longmans, Green.

Johnson, P. E. 1952. Do churches exert significant influence on public morality? *The Annals of the American Academy of Political and Social Science* 280:125–32.

————. 1966. The trend toward dynamic interpersonalism. *Religion in Life* 25:751–59.

Jung, C. G. 1962. *Modern man in search of a soul*. New York: Harcourt, Brace and World.

Kelly, G. A. 1955. *Psychology of Personal Constructs*, vol. 1. New York: Norton.

Kirkpatrick, G. 1949. Religion and humanitarianism: A study of institutional implications. *Psychological Monographs* 63, no. 9.

Kluckhohn, C., Murray, H. A., and Schneider, D. M. 1953. *Personality in Nature, Society, and Culture*. 2d ed. New York: Knopf.

McClelland, D. C. 1955. The psychology of mental content reconsidered. *Psychological Review* 62:297–302.

McLaughlin, B. 1965. Values in behavioral science. *Journal of Religion and Health* 4:258–79.

Maimonides, M. 1956. *The guide for the perplexed*. New York: Dover.

Marty, M. E. 1964. Epilogue: The nature and consequences of social conflict for religious groups. In *Religion and social conflict*, edited by R. Lee and M. E. Marty, 173–93. New York: Oxford University.

Maslow, A. H. 1954. *Motivation and personality*. New York: Harper.

————. 1962. *Toward a psychology of being*. New York: Van Nostrand.

Maslow, A. H., and Mittelmann, B. 1951. *Principles of abnormal psychology*. Rev. ed. New York: Harper.

May, R. 1940. *The springs of creative living*. New York: Abingdon-Cokesbury.

May, R., ed. 1961. *Existential psychology*. New York: Random House.

Moberg, D. O. 1962. *The church as a social institution*. Englewood Cliffs, N.J.: Prentice-Hall.

————. 1967. The encounter of scientific and religious values pertinent to man's spiritual nature. *Sociological Analysis* 28:22–33.

Mowrer, O. H. 1960a. *Learning theory and behavior*. New York: Wiley.

————. 1960b. *Learning theory and the symbolic processes*. New York: Wiley.

————. 1961. *The crisis in psychiatry and religion*. Princeton, N.J.: Princeton University.

Niebuhr, R. 1942. *The nature and destiny of man: A Christian perspective*. New York: Charles Scribner's Sons.

Novak, M. 1968. Secular saints. *The Center Magazine* 1, no. 4, 51–59.

Nuttin, J. 1962. *Psychoanalysis and personality*. New York: New American Library.

O'Dea, T. F. 1961. Five dilemmas in the institutionalization of religion. *Journal for the Scientific Study of Religion* 1:30–39.

Pattison, E. M. 1965. Contemporary views of man in psychology. *Journal of Religion and Health* 4:354–66.

Platt, J. R., ed. 1965. *New views of the nature of man*. Chicago: University of Chicago.

Pratt, S., and Tooley, J. 1964. Contract psychology and the actualizing transactional-field. Special edition, *International Journal of Social Psychiatry* 1:51–69.

————. 1967. Action psychology. *Journal of Psychological Studies* 15:137–231.

Pruyser, P. W. 1968. *A dynamic psychology of religion.* New York: Harper and Row.

Rogers, C. R. 1963. The actualizing tendency in relation to "motives" and to consciousness. In *Nebraska symposium on motivation,* edited by M. R. Jones, 1–24. Lincoln, Neb.: University of Nebraska.

Rotter, J. B. 1954. *Social learning and clinical psychology.* Englewood Cliffs, N.J.: Prentice-Hall.

Royce, J. R. 1967. Metaphoric knowledge and humanistic psychology. In *Challenge of humanistic psychology,* edited by J. F. T. Bugental, 21–28. New York: McGraw-Hill.

Severin, F. T. 1965. *Humanistic viewpoints in psychology.* New York: McGraw-Hill.

Skinner, B. F. 1948. *Walden two.* New York: Macmillan.

————. 1953. *Science and human behavior.* New York: Macmillan.

Southard, S. 1965. The Christian individual in a "programmed" world. *Religious Education* 60:209–14, 243.

Sperry, R. W. 1965. Mind, brain, and humanist values. In *New views of human nature,* edited by J. R. Platt, 71–92. Chicago: University of Chicago.

Spilka, B., and Reynolds, J. F. 1965. Religion and prejudice: a factor-analytic study. *Review of Religious Research* 6:163–68.

Spilka, B., Read, S. J., Allen, R. O., and Dailey, K. A. 1968. Specificity vs. generality: The criterion problem in religious measurement. Paper presented at the 1968 convention of the American Association for the Advancement of Science, Dallas, Texas, December 30.

Stagner, R. 1961. *Psychology of personality.* 3d ed. New York: McGraw-Hill.

Strommen, M. P. 1963. *Profiles of church youth.* St. Louis: Concordia.

————. 1967. Religious education and the problem of prejudice. *Religious Education* 62:52–58.

Strunk, O., Jr. 1970. Humanistic religious psychology: A new chapter in the psychology of religion. *Journal of Pastoral Care* 1970(24):90–97.

Sullivan, H. S. 1953. *The interpersonal theory of psychiatry.* New York: Norton.

Szasz, T. S. 1960. The myth of mental illness. *American Psychologist* 15:113–18.

Thomas, O. C. 1962. Psychology and theology on the nature of man. *Pastoral Psychology* 13, no. 121, 41–46.

Ungersma, A. J. 1961. *The search for meaning.* Philadelphia: Westminster.

Van Kaam, A. 1962. Religion and the existential will. Insight 1, no. 1, 2–9.

————. 1968. *Religion and personality.* Garden City, N.Y.: Doubleday.

Watson, J. B. 1919. *Psychology from the standpoint of a behaviorist.* Philadelphia: Lippincott.

————. 1924. *Behaviorism.* New York: Norton.

White, R. W. 1959. Motivation reconsidered: The concept of competence. *Psychological Review* 66:297–333.

————. 1960. Competence and the psychosexual stages of development. In *Nebraska symposium on motivation,* edited by M. R. Jones, 97–141. Lincoln, Neb.: University of Nebraska.

Winter, G. 1962. *The suburban captivity of the churches.* New York: Macmillan.

Wylie, R. C. 1961. *The self concept.* Lincoln, Neb.: University of Nebraska.

Summary

This section of readings considered several understandings of human nature from the viewpoints of Christian theology and Western psychology.

Shinn limits himself to the implications of God's acts in history and in Jesus for the image of man/woman. He emphasizes the gift of freedom given to persons by God in salvation and notes its effects on self and other understanding.

Whitlock analyzes the Hebraic viewpoint and emphasizes the *unity* of the person from this perspective. In wholeness humans acknowledge their relationship to God and their revolt against Him. Selfhood, according to Whitlock, results from the courage to admit that true personhood comes from God.

Stuermann and Geocaris's comparison of Calvin and Freud concludes that they are more alike than different in their assertions that there are destructive and evil tendencies in human nature. Both Calvin and Freud emphasize the importance of a sense of guilt and the need to take responsibility. They differ radically in their analysis of remediation. For Calvin salvation comes through faith. For Freud freedom comes through analysis.

Spilka, while noting the similarities of humanistic psychology to certain theological motifs, places his emphasis more on the creative potential (cf. *imago Dei*) in humans than he does on the limitations (cf. sin). He notes the implications of such an emphasis for social service and the psychological study of religion—including counseling that is informed by faith.

Questions for Dialogue

1. How do the writers of these essays differ from each other and how are they similar?
2. Are there significant points of view or shades of opinion regarding human nature which are not considered by these writers?
3. In what ways do views of human nature influence the manner in which persons interact or relate to each other?
4. Are views of human nature crucial for the practice of counseling? Why, or why not?

Additional Readings

Books

Baker, O. H. *Human nature under God.* New York: Association, 1958.

Gorsuch, R., and Malony, H. N. *The nature of man: A social-psychological perspective.* Springfield, Ill.: Charles C. Thomas, 1974.

Hampden-Turner, C. *Maps of the mind.* New York: Macmillan, 1977.

Meehl, P., Klann, R., Schmieding, A., Breimeier, K., and Schroeder-Slomann, S. *What, then, is man? A symposium of theology, psychology and psychiatry.* St. Louis: Concordia, 1958.

Stern, E. M., and Marino, B. G. *Psychotheology: The discovery of the sacredness in humanity.* New York: Paulist, 1970.

Stevenson, L., ed. *The study of human nature.* New York: Oxford University, 1981.

Articles

Balswick, J., and Ward, D. The nature of man and the scientific models of society. *Journal of the American Scientific Affiliation* 28, no. 4 (1976):181–84.

Dole, A. A., and Rockey, P. B. Toward rigorous but ert models of man. *Journal of Religion and Health* 16, no. 2 (1977):87–91.

Fichter, J. H. The concept of man in social science: Freedom, values and second nature. *Journal for the Scientific Study of Religion* 11, no. 2 (1972):109–21.

Pattison, E. M. Contemporary views of man in psychology. *Journal of Religion and Health* 3, no. 4 (1965):354–66.

Roth, N. The dichotomy of man: Religion versus science. *Journal of Religion and Health* 15, no. 3 (1976):151–58.

The Experience
of Living

In contrast to the foregoing section, this section deals with everyday living. Human nature is one thing; human experience is another. Most persons do not think about their lives in general from moment to moment. They are engrossed in responding to present events. The essays in this section discuss these reactions as they are experienced in human emotions and as they are understood in contemporary psychology and by Christian faith.

Rogers's essay, titled "The Phenomenology of Helplessness: A Psychological and Theological Problem," deals with feelings of futility that accompany the experience of losing power over one's life. He notes, "The problem for many today is a total loss of confidence in any stable or caring ontological reality which might give support, meaning or moral structure to life." He suggests that "there may be other ways in which the experience of helplessness is realistic and constructive."

Finch continues this theme of finding hope through despair in his essay, "The Message of Anxiety." He suggests that anxiety is to be affirmed, not avoided. As he states, "My first proposition, then, is that all anxiety is both normal and inevitable." As a clarification of this bold assertion, he concludes, ". . . anxiety is a creative directive to be oneself in truth, relentlessly."

This same thought is discussed by Morosco in his article, "Theological Implications of Fear: The Grasshopper Complex," in which he states, "Fear in itself is neither sin nor piety; other factors make this determination." Morosco relies heavily on the Biblical mention of fear and concludes that "In contrast to unreal and illegitimate fear-objects, the results of living in tension with the truly All-powerful and Impendent One are said by Scripture to be wholly positive. The Psalmist declares that wisdom begins with the fear of the Lord. . . ."

Finally, Narramore's essay, "Guilt: Where Theology and Psychology Meet," includes a discussion of the Ideal, the Disciplinary, and the Punitive Selves. He suggests that "while confession . . . may help resolve anxiety over the fear of punishment or rejection coming from violation of specific moral standards, it will do nothing to resolve a deep-seated feeling of self-devaluation over one's felt weakness and inadequacy. . . . The fear of punishment and the lack of self-esteem require very different treatments both theologically and psychologically."

While the reader cannot expect to glean a perspective on every human emotion from reading these articles, she/he can expect to better understand experience in general and how to ascertain a psychological or theological perspective on any emotion with which she/he may come in contact.

Despair based on a feeling of helplessness is the most profound of human experiences. Desperate efforts to cope with and overcome these feelings are considered. Both the experience and the attempts to deal with it are normal even if they are often neurotic and ineffectual. Even some religious solutions lack substance. Courage, based on a leap of faith, is suggested as the optimal approach to this problem.

The Phenomenology of Helplessness

A *Psychological and Theological Problem*

William R. Rogers

> *But it is just in that cold, abominable half-despair, half-belief, in that conscious burying oneself alive for grief in the underground for forty years, in that acutely recognized and yet partly doubtful hopelessness of one's position, in that hell of unsatisfied desires turned inward, in that fever of oscillations, of resolutions determined forever and repented of again a minute later—that the savor of that strange enjoyment of which I have spoken lies.*
>
> *I will explain: the enjoyment was just from the too intense consciousness of your own degradation; it was that you yourself felt that you had reached the last barrier; that it was horrible, but it could not be otherwise; that there was no escape for you; that you never could become a different man;* that *even if time and faith were still left you to change into something different, you would most likely not wish to change; or if you did wish to, even then you would do nothing; because perhaps in reality there was nothing for you to change into.*
>
> — *Fyodor Dostoevsky*, Notes from the Underground

Utter helplessness, compounded by the painful awareness of the inner ambiguities generating that helplessness, is a paralyzing and perplexing experience. It seems to devastate the possibilities of hope, of action, of confidence, of faith. And yet in the midst of it there may

Reprinted from *Soundings* 52, No. 3 (1969): 334–49. Used by permission.

be a subtle enjoyment of those very perceptions that illuminate the destructive forces collapsing the spirit into its frightening trap. The intrigue of such insights, however, just tightens the knot of one's feeling of helplessness.

The phenomenological power of such an experience of helplessness is illustrated in the following notes written by a young woman in psychotherapy:

> I feel emotionally very bare—not barren but exposed—so that everything that comes by can toss a little dent into me. Sometimes I want terribly just to be protected and kept safe and hidden from everything so that I don't have to feel anymore. But nothing and no one in the world will take me at my least for only that—they only take me for what I can do or will be doing, and they expect me to keep doing things and if I don't, they leave. I can't do anything and I want to stop faking, but instead I have to keep fighting with myself and to keep up with everyone else. It's impossible ever to rest, or relax because to do that means to lose everyone—like being in a hospital where suddenly no one cares about you really at all; they just lock you up and tell you to get well. No one wants me for what I am really at my worst—only for what I might be, in what I might grow into, but I don't know whether I can ever grow into any potentialities unless someone cares about my inabilities and emptiness. I know my parents would take me back no matter what happened to me, but I cry when I say it. Maybe one thing I need to do now is just to stop crying—sometimes I feel so much on the edge of losing myself. Sometimes it's pretty frightening riding so close to the edge.
>
> I tried to chop my wrist up last night, not because I was violently trying to commit suicide but because I didn't care anymore. It wouldn't have bothered me at all if I'd really done it—it doesn't make any difference what I do. God, I tried to be better and get well, but I'm not and I can't stand it anymore.
>
> I was thinking today of a poem you might know from Stephen Crane's *The Black Riders:*
>
>> In the desert
>> I saw a creature, naked, bestial,
>> Who, squatting upon the ground,
>> Held his heart in his hands,
>> And ate of it.
>> I said, "Is it good, friend?"
>> "It is bitter—bitter," he answered,
>> "But I like it,
>> Because it is bitter,
>> And because it is my heart."

It is hard to admit how much attractive pull this kind of image has for me—how necessary it seems sometimes to escape from society and feed on the kind of confusion and suffering which seem more vital and central to me than anything else. Sometimes the agony of facing myself alone seems the only sustenance for and proof of any wholeness in my life at all.

Even the possibilities of caring and support from another person seem to exaggerate the sense of helplessness.

> I hate people who love me and are good to me because they make me feel constantly guilty. I can't love them or do anything good for them. There's nothing good about me and I keep proving it because I have to or I'm only stupid and guilty. I'd rather be evil and unbalanced—at least it's being something. But really I'm not evil in regards to having no moral standards and I'm probably in many ways as balanced as anyone else. I simply have no will power and someday I'm going to have to pay like hell for it. There are many things I'd like to be. I want to be strong enough to really love and care about someone, maybe about many people. I'd like to be some kind of full self and not a cold, staring moron. But I wouldn't really because it's impossible to be always worthwhile and good and I can't stand failure.

The feeling of internal trappedness and the suffering that results from it occur at various points in individual lives. It is probably one of the most typical experiences encountered in psychotherapy. The awareness of internal conflict between self and others may paralyze an individual to the point that he feels an utter loss of control in his own life. Helplessness can be defined as this experience of the loss of self-determinism coupled with a feeling of utter futility in regaining intrinsic control or initiating action. Clinicians who have worked with people during periods of psychotic breakdown will recognize this experience of the loss of control or the loss of self-determination as the most frightening to a patient. Recognition of personal helplessness may be central not only to the clinician's recommendation for institutionalization but also to the patient's desire for a protected environment in which therapeutic and institutional controls can safeguard him during the implosion of his internal controls and fragmentation of personal identity. Probably nothing is as terrifying to an individual as the sense that everything that is happening in his own mind is overpowering him with its own irrational and chaotic force before which he stands utterly helpless.

This experience of intense inner conflict and helplessness is even further exaggerated for many people today by their experience of the overwhelmingly complex economic and political structures of society. Children face an educational system in which the academic demands and system of evaluation are external to their own control. Young men face a compulsory military system which confronts them with moral dilemmas, frequently insoluble, and certainly determinative in their lives for a period of many years. Adults face a complex credit economy with an endless system of debts locking them into vocational and social conventions in ways that frequently choke criticism and conscience within the system. Meanwhile we are all bombarded with convincing evidence of genetic coding from the biologists, of behavioral determinants and learning reinforcement schedules from the psychologists, of social class conformism data from the sociologists, and of political machine control from the political scientists. One wonders what sustains those fleeting glimpses of freedom and the hope of self-determinism amid such evidence of these exterior determinative processes and the felt weight of their dehumanizing demands. These historical and cultural dimensions of the experience of helplessness receive vivid comment from a writer like Paul Goodman:

> People believe that the great background conditions of modern life are beyond our power to influence. The proliferation of technology is autonomous and cannot be checked. The galloping urbanization is going to gallop on. Our overcentralized administration, both of things and men, is impossibly cumbersome and costly, but we cannot cut it down to size. More dramatic inevitabilities are the explosions, the scientific explosion and the population explosion. And there are more literal explosions, the dynamite accumulating in the slums of a thousand cities and the accumulating stockpiles of nuclear bombs in nations great and small. Our psychology, in brief, is that history is out of control.
>
> Furthermore, the way of coping with complexities, when we do cope, only complicates them further, thus if there are too many cars, we build new highways; if administration is too cumbersome, we build in new levels of administration; if there is a nuclear threat, we develop anti-missile missiles; if there is urban crowding and anomie, we step up urban renewal and social work; if there are ecological disasters because of imprudent use of technology, we subsidize research and development by the same scientific corporations working for the same ecologically irrelevant motives; if there is youth alienation, we extend and intensify processing in the schools.[1]

In the religious sphere there is an additional dimension of helplessness which even further complicates the cultural and psychological stranglehold. Though the helplessness dominant in the experience of Luther in his inability to be loving and obedient before God is not very typical today, there are contemporary forms of spiritual helplessness which may be even more shattering. Though depressed about his own response, Luther never questioned the existence and continuity of God's

---

1. Paul Goodman, *Like a Conquered Province: The Moral Ambiguity of America* (New York, 1966), pp. 101–2.

presence. But the problem for many today is a total loss of confidence in any stable or caring ontological reality which might give support, meaning, or moral structure to life. To one who is aware of the defensiveness, wish-fulfillment, and illusion in much of religion, the magical thinking of some theology, the Kantian critique of the limits of reason, the Kierkegaardian despair at the abyss and uncertainty of all proximate stabilities, the manipulative socioeconomic utility of much of the institutional church à la Marx, and the frequently misread "Death of God" theology, the possibilities for any kind of security in his quest for meaning and a viable faith become very dim. Many of the intellectual forces of our time drive hard toward nihilism and a conviction about absurdity in both human life and reality itself. We can do little but plod along, bored in our technological Eden, numbed by the injustices of human degradation but caught in the absurd counterplay of forces far beyond our control, allowed only the grotesque alternatives of laughter or utter despair. To our cry, "Where is God?" comes only the distress signal, "God is dead."

Though undeniably bleak, the experience of helplessness certainly invites careful psychological and theological analysis. From a psychological point of view, we note Freud's observation that under conditions of stress regression frequently occurs, returning an individual to a psychological state typical of the strange mixture of security and impotence of a child in the face of authority figures who have massive control over him. This was also pertinent to Freud's discussion of man's need for God, for not only does one have an overrated and unrealistic image of a good father undoubtedly frustrated in its fulfillment in childhood, but also a real but denied need for protection. Man feels but cannot admit his need to be safe, to be protected, and in his state picks up memories of the dependency relationship of childhood which may then be displaced upon a figure more powerful than man which might save him from his helplessness. Of course such a fantasied wish for a power in the universe which "watches over man and brings all his concerns to a happy ending"[2] can have no object in reality, and therefore for Freud there is no God. The narrowness and "genetic fallacy" of such a conception of God have been amply commented upon; but the pervasiveness of man's desire for dependence and protection is undeniable. And this desire, particularly under conditions of stress, helps explain in part why one's experience of helplessness may take on neurotic proportions reminiscent of the loss of power or control experienced in childhood.

Karen Horney's discussion in *Neurosis and Human Growth* gives a

---

2. Sigmund Freud, *New Introductory Lectures on Psycho-Analysis* (1933), p. 228.

similar notion of the essence of the neurotic process, developed around the concept of "basic anxiety." Basic anxiety is the experience of being "isolated and helpless in a world conceived as potentially hostile" and is rooted essentially in the childhood experience of rejection and sub-servience to the control of cold or erratic parental figures. It is out of such experiences, Horney believes, that one attempts to develop an idealized image of himself as competent to overcome such helpless-ness, though of course the recognition of the degree of self-deception contained in such an idealized image may even further intensify a later experience of neurotic helplessness.

A further pertinent psychological comment about helplessness is suggested in the analysis of why individuals develop a compulsion to repeat childhood situations of loss and impotence. One could also ask why dreams, supposedly functioning as forms of wish-fulfillment, fre-quently contain scenes of personal paralysis utterly antithetical to an experience of control. Such phenomena, Freud suggests, are attempts to gain mastery, through repetition, over those events which are experienced as controlling. However, such mastery, though perhaps rehearsed in the mind, can scarcely be called satisfactory or effective in overcoming the real social and interpsychic helplessness of the individual. The continuing impotence of such repetition, even when helplessness is analyzed and understood, is well documented both by Dostoevsky's Underground Man and by the case material cited earlier. Misery rather than mastery seems too often the result—the misery of further despair and neurotic self-pity.

Such self-pity also points to the potential narcissistic character of the experience of helplessness. To become increasingly trapped in the analysis of one's own predicament, indeed, even to enjoy that trap-pedness, suggests a kind of self-indulgence. Despair, doubt, and perplexity over seemingly irresoluble ambiguities in one's life, while appearing externally in the form of self-abnegation and depression, may, underneath this, be a form of self-aggrandizement in which a person cherishes his view of life and the world as most profound, sophisticated, and perceptive, and demands in addition that others give support to him in the form of concern, reassurance, or repeated proofs of personal significance. In therapy such narcissistic control may be evidenced in the client's strategies which at times drive the therapist into a corner of helplessness. The last paragraph of the case material cited earlier shows one way in which the helping activity of the therapist can be immobilized, accentuating the awareness of help-lessness on the part of both client and therapist. "No despair is entirely without defiance," observed Kierkegaard. Despair, depression, and the overwhelming experience of helplessness, defiant in its hostile separation of the self from others, is narcissistic in both its concentrated focus on the self and its demands for increasing amounts of love and assurance from others.

Such a criticism of the neurotic possibilities of the feeling of helplessness points to another psychological-theological problem. Not only is there the deceit of the neurotic attempt to control, concealed by its opposite—the appearance of powerlessness and impotence—but also there is in this the essence of hubris, the implicit pride that one's development rests in his own efforts about which he despairs so thoroughly in his helplessness. There is also the pride represented by hidden demands for others to proffer reassurance of personal worth, a demand which at the theological level comes dreadfully close to the idolatry of demanding that God demonstrate Himself as redemptive and prove the worth of His creation.

It would be folly, of course, to offer this sort of theological or psychological observation to an individual experiencing feelings of helplessness as a tactic for initiating change. Understanding of the narcissistic, prideful, or neurotic function of the experience of helplessness may be useful, but it should not be assumed that these are the only dimensions which felt helplessness may take existentially. Furthermore, there are many tactics that individuals themselves initiate as ways of attempting to move beyond the experience of helplessness, some of which may deepen the self-deceptive processes but others of which may be productive.

One way of attempting to deal with helplessness is *delusion*, the pretense that there are no real problems that one cannot overcome. Although trapped by inner struggles, the individual may pacify himself with endless distractions that trivialize life, or at best he may feel a spurious sense of power in the articulateness with which he can describe his dilemma. Dostoevsky illustrates this well: only rarely does the Underground Man recognize that he is lying to himself. Such delusion undoubtedly reaches its most intense proportions in the paranoid reactions which may accompany withdrawal and social impotence, in which a person feels that he is indeed the controlling figure, dominating men and ideas, his grandiosity suspect not to himself but in the presumed persecutory intimidations of others (this betraying an even deeper helplessness, of course).

Some have pointed out that such delusional or magic thinking with its credibility gap between what we say and what is real also functions on the level of our national experience of helplessness. We claim to be concerned about morality, but we look at hippies in the park and delude ourselves about the businessmen's morality, hidden in hotels across the street. We claim to be concerned about the lack of law and order in demonstrations and picket lines, but delude ourselves about the powerful though less accessible crime syndicates and political boss organizations. We claim to be concerned about pollution of the water and the air, but conceal our inactivity and failure to allocate money for programs to check this. We claim to be concerned about Appalachia but forget that we only squeaked out minimal help through an old highway bill. Most especially, we claim to desire peace in Vietnam, but we send in more troops, bombers, and battleships. We say we will meet anywhere for peace talks but then turn down the first seven offers for such talks. Such delusions, which conceal our helplessness in coping with major national problems, are obviously very dangerous.

A second mode of escaping helplessness may be through a *flight into sensuality*. For some, an antidote to social and psychological helplessness may be sought in an assertion of sexual potency. Over and over again, however, clinicians discover that such solutions frequently lead to boredom, disillusion, and eventually an increased sense of helplessness as this kind of sex becomes empty and one is all the more desperate about shallowness of relationships. One could also point to the abuses of psychedelic drugs. Despair over impotence in one's personal relationships or passive curiosity may lead a person to turn to the undulating brilliance and reflective ecstasy (or perhaps despair and horror) of a drug-induced experience outside any of the controls of a therapeutic setting. While perhaps expansive for some, the tragic component of such uncontrolled experiences is that they often lead to a sense of increased isolation and a desperate clinging to fewer and fewer relationships or internal realities to keep from plunging irrevocably into the nonproductive world of those who have "freaked out." The difficulties of personal recovery, plus the awareness that friends made on the drug scene will not understand or be sympathetic to any attempt at reentering a world of constructive participation, suggest a continuation of one's helpless position even if he wishes change. (One should, of course, distinguish this privatistic abuse of psychedelic drugs from the therapeutic use of these powerful agents under appropriate clinical conditions.)

Escape from helplessness may also be sought through *obsessions and mechanistic calculations*. Individuals may become obsessed with controlling small things in life that are manageable in order to evade the major complexities which seem overwhelming. One may escape into a series of relatively meaningless calculations which are readily accessible through pseudoscientific research, budget preparations, astrological maneuvers, or baseball percentages. The most grossly dehumanizing extension of this form of escape is probably in the box scores given every day for deaths in Vietnam. Such death scores also carry the phony implication that if we maintain a kill ratio in which we have a lower number of absolute losses of human lives, somehow the enemy will give up. The logic of this thinking is disastrously erroneous. The greatest danger in calculating such scores, of course, is that we overlook the basic moral irony of the fighting itself, where freedom and democracy are supposedly defended by measures that are neither democratic nor free.

A fourth mode of escaping helplessness is through *resignation*. As Horney put it, "If you don't care about anything, nothing can hurt you." Resignation can take the form of apathetic adjustment to an automated, technological society, in which protection of the smooth-running machine becomes itself a virtue, obliterating anxiety about individual helplessness in the face of the complexity of that machine. With young people, resignation in the form of dropping out may be tempting at the point that one experiences initial success but then gradual disillusionment in his efforts to change political or social systems. For middle-class adults, a focus on privatism marks a similar resignation: a retreat into the safety of one's own family and a focus on consumer goods, in relation to which one may experience at least limited power and choice. Yet as Goodman and others point out, this is "privacy purchased at a terrible price of anxiety, exclusion, and pettiness, the need to delete anything different from oneself and to protect things that are not worth protecting."[3] Such privatism may lie behind our current concern with law and order, a concern which frequently reflects the dominance of property values over human values. There seems to be almost an obsessional mass neurosis with protection of property, accentuated undoubtedly by the affluence of a culture in which we insulate ourselves against moral attacks on the means of attainment and distribution of property. Anxiety about property values and production rates may also have far more to do with the race problem than traditional social prejudice. In any case, resignation to the status quo may numb one from a crushing experience of personal helplessness, at least for a time.

Still another defense typically employed as protection against the experience of helplessness is the process of *identification with symbols of power*. It is perhaps commonplace to note that in psychotherapy the client frequently identifies with the therapist in ways that represent more than simply a displacement of affect in the transference neurosis. There is frequently identification with the psychological power of the therapist, his empathetic and analytic capacity, and frequently his values. This identification, taken with the concomitant dependence on

3. Goodman, *Like a Conquered Province*, p. 107.

the therapist, may help explain the heightened feelings of helplessness that many clients experience as they near termination of the therapeutic relationship. In their social relationships, suppressed persons identify with power symbols like magic, gods, superstitious rites, bull fighters, or big automobiles. Perhaps attention to guns and the furious protest over gun control acts may represent a similar desire of men in otherwise frustrating circumstances to identify with a symbol of power. Ironically, one might also add that the peace emblem has itself become a symbol of power for many young people, representing a militant defiance of established structures and a radical hope for change, in spite of continuing experiences of helplessness.

This suggests still another mode of coping with helplessness: the *anticipation of some explosive, apocalyptic event* that will suddenly change the shape of the world and free the individual from his confines. The prisoner anticipating liberation or escape; the neurotic anticipating some massive insight that will realign his internal tumult; the youth anticipating a radical freedom in adulthood; and the revolutionary anticipating a new regime: all demonstrate this flight from helplessness. Some anticipation of apocalypse may lead to patience and waiting, and hence offer temporary solace in enduring one's condition. For others there may be the wish and the energy to hasten radical change through explosive rage and violent destruction of the repressive system or its symbols. Such frustration and rage may be just as fearsome in the exsoldiers or small property owners who have both good arms and training in violence as in the radicals whom they seek to put down. It is fearsome as well in the proposals for using nuclear military tactics as the apocalyptic solution to an experience of helplessness in a military-diplomatic conflict which drags on with little evidence of resolution.

All these modes of spurious escape from the experience of helplessness have their corollaries in religious temptations. Men have deluded themselves about helplessness through fantasies of an eternal reality completely disassociated from this present life, and have sought pious repose from the agonies of the spiritual quest. Jesus Himself struggled with the temptation to "change stones into bread" and thus vitiate the reality of His struggle in the wilderness. Religious men have turned to obsessions with religious ritual and form, as Freud so well pointed out, and have retreated to mechanical calculations of church membership, contributions, building programs, and ecumenical policy. Religious men have resigned themselves to blasé and passive accommodation to the routines of the church and the abuses of the world. Religious men have identified with the symbols of power in ecclesiastical institutions and, idolatrously, even with the divine Being itself.

And religious men have become so absorbed in apocalyptic visions anticipating eschatological cataclysm that they have ignored the dimensions of reality and responsibility in those levels of redemption already at hand.

All such attempts at escaping the experience of helplessness in either the psychological, the social, or the religious realm are at best palliative and temporary, at worst deceitful, dehumanizing, deluded, and demonic. None of them points toward any genuine establishment of hope, deliverance, or new life either in terms of individual growth or in the restoration of a meaningful relationship with ultimate sources of power and healing. Yet where else may one turn?

While it is clear that both the experience of helplessness and attempts to escape this experience may be fraught with neurotic implications, there may be other ways in which the experience of helplessness is realistic and constructive. The humanistic psychologists, as well as many theologians, are helpful at this point in the ways they deal with ontological anxiety and ontological guilt. There is clearly a sense in which every man must face the termination of his own being, confront death realistically, and accept his own finitude. Man is indeed helpless in the face of this reality. And yet the anxiety generated by this ontological awareness may be one of the most constructive features in enabling man to face the realistic possibilities and limitations of his life and to ask what is possible and what it means.

Rollo May and Ronald Laing have dealt with man's experience of ontological guilt as a recognition of our final helplessness in attempts to experience another person in the full authenticity of his own inner reality, or in attempts to fulfill our own potentialities for growth and depth of experience. We are guilty of continual incompleteness in our own growth toward wholeness, and we are guilty of inevitably mis-understanding the intentionality and genuineness of another man's internal experience. Yet the acceptance of helplessness in our ultimate failure in both these respects may function positively in allowing us to dispel the desperate and prideful strategies that we too easily employ to defend our limited understandings. We may be enabled to accept humbly our genuine ontological posture and to be receptive to those modes of personal revelation and divine revelation which emerge only after frantic attempts at control have been abandoned.

This is close to the theological recognition that man is ultimately finite, and dependent upon a transcendent source of creativity, healing, and meaning. One of the most systematic theological statements of this recognition, built around man's awareness of his finite helplessness, is given by Schleiermacher in *The Christian Faith*. For Schleiermacher the essence of the religious experience, as well as the source for theological reflection, was focused in the consciousness of being absolutely dependent. This feeling of dependence was not only related to but identified with man's relationship to God. Some may argue that the feeling of absolute dependence was more of a rational, theoretical category in Schleiermacher's dialectic of knowing, doing, and feeling than it was a genuine existential phenomenon. Yet Schleiermacher goes to considerable lengths to identify the feeling as "immediate," and to differentiate it from an objective consciousness or a representation obtained only by self-contemplation. The feeling of absolute dependence carries the double conviction that while one is helpless in his own power to know and to do, he is completed or made whole through his relation with those ontological processes upon which his life depends. Feeling, and especially the feeling of absolute dependence, marks a particular life-moment in which there is a miraculous blending of unity and diversity—a blending in which diffusion and centrality come into a dynamic cohesiveness, thus marking the ultimate but fleeting optimal condition of man's ontological possibility. Hence the feeling of absolute dependence, with its realistic indictment of man's attempt to control his ultimate destiny by himself, takes on a form which recognizes the constructive extension of the experience of helplessness insofar as it is receptive to a recognition of this ultimate relationship.

Other theologians also recognize that the realistic dimensions of helplessness may be central in the establishment of genuine faith. Kierkegaard and Tillich have written about this quite explicitly. Not only may one experience helplessness over specific failures and weakness in his own life, and specific political and social problems in public life, but also one may come to the point of feeling helpless over helplessness itself or of reaching despair over despair itself. "Despair over something is not yet properly despair," wrote Kierkegaard in *Sickness Unto Death;* and it may be that this condition is necessary for some as a transition toward the possibility of belief and action. Dostoevsky's Underground Man comes close to this profound despair. But as long as one experiences the enjoyment or pseudosophistication of his experience, he can hardly move beyond the trappedness of his own narcissism. When one allows the full intensity and awesome fear of his experience of helplessness to emerge, however, particularly in a therapeutic or religious context, there may come with this experience a profound awareness of being sustained, of being given life, of being held or received, in spite of cynicism about the possibility of any such restoration. The young woman cited in the case material described this latter feeling with a fantasy of being at the bottom of a dark well for days and days, thrashing about, but finally hitting what she knew was the bottom of the well and finding that her insulated, mummylike wrappings were at last unwound so that she could emerge into the light again: free, vulnerable, but a new person.

The content of what is discovered at such a point of transition is not always clear. One senses healing and deliverance, coupled with a profound sense of inner discovery and a significant recognition of a supportive relationship; but why or how one is sustained, or the exact parameters of this experience of renewal, are usually less clear. The forcefulness, but in some sense contentlessness, of this experience is what led Tillich to use the term "radical faith." One has radical faith because it is faith profoundly validated by the experience in spite of lack of final resolve or stable clarity about the best way to define the source and power of the experience. This is close to what Kierkegaard meant also when he wrote about the leap of faith—a leap that enables one to transcend the inevitable ambiguities of his helpless self-consciousness. This too is radical, not so much in its possible transcending of intellectual paradox but in its recognition and reception of a new depth of life and experience which is too forcible in man's personal life and too ubiquitous in his cultural life to be denied or simply rationalized as a defensive escape. We retain Freud's caution that religion *may* be man's response to his feeling of helplessness, but it may also be a more profound and realistic response to a genuine experience of being redeemed from utter helplessness and given new possibility of life. The real test of possible neurotic dimensions in this experience would undoubtedly come in the sort of life processes to which such experience leads. If it were simply to silence doubt and enervate one into delusional security, obsessive acts, moral resignation, or apocalyptic irresponsibility, then it might indeed be suspect; but if it leads one to risk himself further in attempts at deeper understanding and more profound exposure and encounter with other men, moral action, and an open and expectant posture in anticipation of new truth, then I believe one must trust its authenticity.

What emerges in this open renewal is not so much a set of specific answers or intellectual resolutions as a general sense of hope, deliverance, joy, and expectation. That such hope can emerge out of an experience of overwhelming helplessness recalls other analyses such as those of Marcel, Pruyser, and Pluegge, all of whom have studied the process of hope emerging under conditions of helplessness, particularly in relation to tragedy and death. Hoping, they suggest, is a response to tragedy, and can really only occur when one is visited by calamity or the threat of calamity, as in the recognition of one's own death. Pruyser cites Pluegge's clinical account of persons dealing with terminal illness, noting the progression of stages moving from a "waiting" period involving denial, delusion, and self-deceit, similar to the delusion discussed earlier; through a period of "pining" characterized by anxiety, rebellion, and despair; and culminating in a "hope" characterized by patience, tolerance, and humility in the face of reality. As Marcel said, "There is an aspect of chastity in hope," as one stands in all modesty before reality as it is, but finds that even in the midst of what he was afraid he could not endure, he does endure, and is sustained with a sense of power far beyond all expectation.[4]

This also suggests a view of mental illness espoused by men like Anton Boisen and Ronald Laing, who have demonstrated that out of the personality disintegration and felt helplessness of mental illness, an individual may in fact be opened up to new levels of personal and interpersonal experience formerly excluded by neurotic defenses. From the chaos there may emerge a more realistic, profound, and viable view of oneself and his world. "Madness," says Laing, "need not be all break-down. It may also be break-through. It is potentially liberation and renewal."[5]

Probably nothing less forceful than the symbols of death and resurrection, or the emergence of a new creation, can signify the emergence of new life experienced out of the death of paralyzing helplessness. "Resurrection means the victory of the new state of things, the New Being born out of the death of the Old."[6] Though there are myriad ways of attempting to escape the terror and impotence of the old helplessness, these can be, as we have seen, only temporary, delusional, defensive, and at many points dangerous. Here we see in addition that they may prohibit the profoundly redemptive and recreative experience that is possible only when one has the courage to face the realistic helplessness of his own limited control, limited understanding, and finite being. Because of the narcissism in peculiar enjoyment of helplessness, or the fear of its overwhelming immobilization, or the various forms of self-deceit and apathy by which we try to convince ourselves that the helplessness is not real, we may indefinitely evade the troublesome but potentially releasing acknowledgment of genuine helplessness. Yet only with this acknowledgment may we be freed from neurotic defenses against fear and finitude which drive one into the terrors of helplessness, and in its idolatry. Only with this acknowledgment, furthermore, will we be freed to accept our ontological reality as paradoxically dependent but completed (made whole) in that expe-

---

4. Paul Pruyser, "Phenomenology and Dynamics of Hoping," *Journal for the Scientific Study of Religion* 3 (1963): 86–96.

5. R. D. Laing, *Politics of Experience* (London, 1968), p. 92.

6. Paul Tillich, *The New Being* (New York, 1955), p. 24.

rience of new life, an experience which because of our helplessness seems to bring actualization through the power of Being itself. We know our wholeness in juxtaposition to our despair. Surely resurrection happens now—and again and again.

Plato, Paul, Pierre Teilhard de Chardin, Henri Bergson, and Sören Kierkegaard are similar in that they all affirm the power of "anxiety" in motivating persons to seek ultimate rather than temporary answers to life's dilemmas. Anxiety is affirmed as normal, inevitable, and growth producing. Conscience is the voice of anxiety and should be listened to because it propels one into authentic existence. "Spirit" in humans is that part of them that will not allow them to live less than their potentials call them to live.

The Message of Anxiety

John G. Finch

Always anxiety . . . and the psychiatrists usually are afraid of anxiety. They don't know what anxiety is. Anxiety is the excitement, the élan vital which we carry with us, and which becomes stagnated if we are unsure about the role we have to play. If we don't know if we will get applause or tomatoes, we hesitate, so the heart begins to race and all the excitement can flow into activity and we have stage fright. So the formula of anxiety is very simple. Anxiety is the gap between the now and the then. If you are in the now, you can't be anxious, because the excitement flows immediately into ongoing spontaneous activity. If you are in the now, you are creative, you are inventive. If you have your senses ready, if you have your eyes and ears open like every small child, you find a solution (Perls, 1969, pp. 2–3).

In discussing my subject, The Message of Anxiety, I would like to trace very briefly, through the history of thought, some suggestions that will enable us to draw together both the importance and the magnitude of our study. It is my feeling that what anxiety has gained in power to terrorize, by virtue of being misunderstood, it has lost in meaningfulness. By approaching anxiety from a historical point of view it is my hope that we can see it constructively and use it creatively. My method will be to liken it to and in fact identify it with observations of a phenomenon that has made its appearance at various

Reprinted from *A Christian Existential Psychology: The Contributions of John G. Finch*, edited by H. Newton Malony (Washington, D.C.: University Press of America, 1980), pp. 153–74. Used by permission.

points in the writings of philosophers, physicists, theologians, and psychologists under diverse names, but whose meaning can be better comprehended in the phrase "the creative directive." This seems to be true on a universal scale, as expressed vividly by St. Paul in the phrase, "The whole creation has been groaning in travail together until now" (Rom. 8:22). What Paul has described on a universal scale and then applies to individuals in the words—"And not only the creation, but we ourselves, who have the first fruits of the Spirit, groan inwardly as we wait for adoption as sons, the redemption of our bodies" (Rom. 8:23)—gives me the cue to suggest that this creative directive is anxiety nudging and pushing us to be ourselves in truth, relentlessly, until perhaps we are the full expression of God's creation.

At this point, let us turn to Plato, from whom St. Paul undoubtedly learned a great deal. Plato suggests, having borrowed this from an unidentified teacher,

The good is that at which all things aim; the good for man is happiness, and happiness is the realization of man's essential nature. The virtue, or excellence, of a thing is the full development of the potentialities of its essential nature.

The Nicomachean Ethics is part of a vast scientific and philosophical system to which a teleological view of the universe is basic: all things are to be understood in terms of their purposes, the ends toward which they tend, ends inherent in their forms and integral to their nature (Magill, 1961, p. 157).

Could this not be put more simply by suggesting that there is a built-in creative directive to be oneself, in truth, relentlessly? And I am suggesting that we see this creative directive as anxiety, since this, too, is an ontological fact, empirically and phenomenologically observed.

Let us turn next to a more contemporary witness—the late Pierre Teilhard de Chardin. In his works, he portrays this built-in urge or directive as the "within" or "consciousness" or "interiority." It too is no less a creative directive that urges toward some form of higher achievement. Thus in the process of evolution, this "within" or "consciousness" creatively materializes itself in creation. So he says:

The material of the world has a propensity driving it from the simple to the complex. It has an inherent preference, a natural tendency toward the complex.

[It is] this cosmic phenomenon [that] must be explained . . . [in] one sufficient, logical explanation. He calls it the "within" of things. . . . In man, who stands at the summit of creation, the evidence of a "within" or "consciousness" is immediately obvious and undisputed (Kopp, 1964, pp. 28–29).

Thus, to borrow his imagery, if we can see man at birth as being at point Alpha, propelled by what Teilhard de Chardin calls "interiority" or the "within" or "consciousness" or what I have termed the creative directive to be oneself in truth, then the directive would be to move from point Alpha to point Omega. Thus to attempt to resist moving in the direction of Omega would create an upheaval or tension which I term anxiety, because that would be a violation of its natural, built-in goal. Nor could we, I believe, term this anxiety neurotic, for we have to distinguish between the neurotic's refusal to be himself (the neurotic handling of anxiety) and the basic wholesomeness of the creative directive or nudge of one to fulfill his potential. To put it the other way, it is to confuse the cause with the effect, i.e., anxiety with neurosis. So, to quote this Jesuit priest-philosopher-theologian-scientist:

According to this, to follow Christ is not a flight from the world, but submission to the world. Worship does not mean putting God before all things, but seeking God in and through all things, giving oneself with heart and soul to the act of creation which is taking place all the time, associating oneself with it and thus, through work and research which, rightly viewed, is worship, to bring the world to final perfection in Point Omega (Kopp, 1964, p. 58).

If we pause for a moment to examine this notion with reference to the work of Henri Bergson, the idea of the creative directive seems to be expressed in the *élan vital*. According to him, there is "a vital impetus, an imminent teleology within the life force itself" (Runes, 1962, p. 37). It does not seem too difficult to see this forward creative thrust being thwarted by circumstances, by a reluctance to be oneself in truth and thereby creating some indefinable feelings which we have come to call anxiety.

Bergson describes this force as

an interesting force that shows itself in living things, an *élan vital* that has endured through the ages, accounting for the creative evolution of life and of instinct and intelligence in living things (Magill, 1961, p. 767).

But Bergson goes further in suggesting—like Teilhard de Chardin and, indeed, like St. Paul—that *élan vital* is necessary if we are ever going to be able to comprehend the complexities of life as a whole. It is not the individual alone, nor the individual parts alone, but *all* of creation that "groans" for fulfillment.

Bergson's thought has been very well summarized in an article in *Masterpieces of World Philosophy in Summary Form* (Magill, 1961), where the notion of the creative directive is so clearly perceived:

> The production of instinct and intelligence is an experiment in which the *élan* has been articulating divergent but complementary tendencies that have lain dormant in it from the beginning. Through the resultant clarification it is readying itself to combine the desirable features of each in a new capacity that will transcend both. Intuition manifests itself in situations in which men are not dominated by disintegrated thoughts— in the crises of life where problems press in and drastic action is required, and in moments of intense joy, sadness, or commiseration. In such cases and for a brief time we know our own inner being and that of others in a much more intimate fashion than we do when we sit in our studies and describe ourselves. Life then becomes aware of itself, of duration, and of the world, not through the distorting mediation of concepts, but directly and immediately. Man in his present state cannot maintain such insight for long, but if the *élan* is successful it will develop beings who can. What the nature of that intuition will be, and whether the *élan* will attain its goal of complete self-consciousness and complete dominance over matter, we cannot tell.

> The self is not a continuously creative, pure-burning center of energy, for it can lapse into periods of lethargy during which it approaches the status of a physical thing.

> Matter is tired life. If the *élan* is a flowing current, then matter is a congealing of it. If the *élan* is a cosmic tension, then extension is the interruption or disappearance of that tension (p. 767).

Allow me to juxtapose my formulation: Anxiety is the creative directive to be oneself in truth, relentlessly.

Let us turn next to Freud. Here we have a curious double legacy, which both contaminates and at the same time acts as a corrective to his findings. The strong rationalistic scientific bent in Freud is a reflection of his times. Logical positivism was the prevailing mood, and science, with its methodology, was the temper of the Enlightenment. It was with this bias that Freud quite deliberately cast his lot. His impatience with such doctrines as "vitalism" and "entelechy" forced him to coerce his data onto the proverbial procrustean bed. While dedicated to science, he yet had no little trouble with such phenomena as kept emerging in his research with patients. Consequently, his "nineteenth-century biological presuppositions prevented him from seeing the psychological context of such problems. ([Karen] Horney refers to 'biological' in the sense of chemical-physical mechanism)" (May, 1950, p. 139). Is this the problem we encounter in Freud's concept of libido? Is it possible that because of his strong scientific bias he misconstrued the evidence in suggesting that the libido was (1) sexual craving, or (2) any erotic desire or pleasure? Also, Freud's usage of the term was far from consistent, and he "continually changed his usage as well as the concepts for which Libido was proposed; and . . . his followers have not in general been more consistent" (English and English, 1958, p. 294). May this be further reason to emphasize his dilemma?

Then, if we add to this observation the statement from English and English that "common to all uses is the idea of some sort of psychic dynamics or energy, an irrational and instinctual determiner of both conscious and unconscious processes" (1958, p. 294), I feel we are skirting on the very edge of what I have described as the creative directive to be oneself in truth, relentlessly. As a matter of fact, I feel, if I may presume to say so, not only that my nonmechanistic description seems to fit the situation better than the words *dynamics* or *energy*, but that anxiety as I have delineated it will make Freud even more intelligible wherever he discusses libido.

Now, of course, I am well aware that we run counter to the notions of science and the logical positivism on which it is based. But then, I'm not so sure that men of science want the monopoly of being the sole purveyors of truth. Objectivity and the elimination of variables are sufficient preoccupations for science. Nor need it be a contest between science and philosophy, between the existential and the logical approaches. The question is not: Are these nonscientific means of acquiring knowledge viable and valid? Rather, after all our scientific conditioning, how flexible can we be to entertain the truth conveyed in poetry, in myth, in paradigm and parable, in story and paradox, in illustration, in simile and description? For these are indeed the vehicles of truth and wisdom no less than those of other methodologies.

I shall try not to labor the point, so let me suggest very briefly that in attempting to understand anxiety biologically and to interpret its causes biologically, we have misconstrued its meaning and become somewhat afraid of it. I reiterate: Anxiety is good, and in essence constructive. It is also my contention that there is no such thing as neurotic anxiety. There are only neurotic ways of handling anxiety.

I am indebted to the tremendous amount of constructive scientific research that has dedicated itself to tracing anxiety reactions in the human organism, but let us not thereby assume that we now know what anxiety is. For instance, Isidore Portnoy says,

The pattern of organismic response in acute stress appears to involve the hypothalamic-thalamic-cortical connections in its upward discharge, and the hypothalamic-sympathetic-adrenal medullary system in its downward discharge, with the familiar peripheral effects of sympathetic excitation—raised blood pressure and pulse rate, inhibited peristalsis, palmar sweating, dryness in the mouth, etc. At the same time, involvement of the parasympathetic branch of the autonomic system, expressed peripherally in increased frequency of urination, emptying of the rectum, slowing of the heart rate, and lowered blood pressure, etc., are frequent aspects of the anxiety picture, particularly when stress is prolonged. These parasympathetic expressions may dominate the anxiety picture, as may also expressions of the participation of the somatic nervous system in the downward discharge. While the synergistic action of the sympathetic-adrenalin and vago-insulin mechanisms appears to be a physiological necessity for the organism's capacity to fight or flee in the face of danger, the precise factors which account for the dominance of sympathetic or parasympathetic response in anxiety remain rooted in deeper aspects of personality functioning, the dynamics being as yet unclear (1959, p. 313).

The above is a most lucid result of a great deal of dedicated scientific research. It leaves open one idea with which Portnoy seems to agree: "Anxiety remain[s] rooted in deeper aspects of personality functioning, *the dynamics being as yet unclear*" (my italics). I am most grateful to be able to recognize anxiety through the various physiologic changes that take place. It is gratifying to discover preventive treatment of physical maladies by recognizing their psychogenic nature. All too frequently what I have called the message of anxiety goes unheeded.

It is this message to which I wish to speak more expressly. I have written thus far about anxiety in general. I have attempted to give it a more than scientific base. I believe I have indicated that vitalism, hormic psychology, entelechy, Bergson's *élan vital*, Teilhard de Chardin's "within" or "consciousness," and even Freud's theory of libido are really not so drastically different, but indeed may very well be saying the same thing. I have gone further in suggesting that anxiety is the creative directive to be oneself in truth, relentlessly. It remains now for me to proceed to elaborate this observation.

My first proposition then is that all anxiety is both normal and inevitable. It is intrinsically human to be anxious. I agree with Portnoy that

normal anxiety is an inevitable accompaniment of healthy growth and change in the direction of greater freedom, autonomy, and creativity as we move toward increasing fulfillment of our innate constructive potentialities (1959, p. 310).

I go beyond Portnoy when he construes this as "normal," as opposed to neurotic, anxiety (see above). For, as I have pointed out, it is not anxiety that is normal or neurotic but our response to and lack of understanding for the meaning of the message of anxiety.

In his book *Psychology and the Human Dilemma* (1966), Rollo May attempts to make the same distinction between neurotic and normal anxiety. Cause and effect seem to be confused in this treatment. For if "the anxiety that comes from conforming, to escape this loneliness, is the neurotic transformation of the original normal anxiety," or if "dogma leads to neurotic anxiety" (p. 80), then, as I have suggested, it is not the anxiety that is neurotic but our utilization of anxiety. I feel this distinction is necessary so as to enable us to distinguish the message and *constructive* power of anxiety. When May suggests that "neurotic anxiety . . . is a reaction . . . and is managed by various kinds of blocking . . ." (p. 80), then I can see an important distinction, viz., that the patient is choosing to mismanage a normal, good experience by essentially refusing to heed the message of anxiety. Thus the neurosis becomes more acute while the wholesome power of anxiety, the creative directive, pushes ever harder to make the patient reckon with the message.

I feel sure there is no serious difference in our points of view except that I emphasize that all anxiety is normal, and in keeping this emphasis I feel we are better able to separate the person from his neurotic behavior. In this way the patient's perspective is clarified, that if anxiety can be used neurotically, the patient can recognize anxiety and become aware of its beneficence as an ally, rather than take refuge from it.

I am inspired by Sören Kierkegaard to believe that

> if we observe children, we find this dread (or anxiety) more definitely indicated as seeking after adventure, a thirst for the prodigious, the mysterious. . . . This dread (anxiety) belongs to the child so essentially that it cannot do without it; even though it alarms him it captivates him nevertheless by its sweet feeling of apprehension. In all nations in which the childish character is preserved as the dreaming of the spirit this dread (anxiety) is found, and the deeper it is, the more profound is the nation. . . . Dread has here the same significance melancholy has at a far later point where freedom, after having passed through imperfect forms of its history, has to come to itself in a deeper sense (1946, pp. 38–39).

My second proposition is that since anxiety is an authentic human condition, authentic to man's ontology, then as long as one is increasing his authenticity, anxiety both facilitates and directs his response. That is to say that when one is being true to his own nature, a creative level of anxiety is maintained. But when there is a violation of the nature of one's being, anxiety is backed up like a dammed river and the intensity of anxiety increases. This increase is described and defined well in the earlier quotation from Portnoy. This distress signal informs the person that he is not behaving authentically. This is when one may heed the message and choose to live in harmony with himself or disregard the message and become increasingly sick. This is where neuroses and psychoses become inauthentic ways of responding to the message of anxiety. So, it must also be pointed out that inasmuch as inauthentic responses detract from authenticity and create neurotic compromises with inner reality, these compromises can result only in the intensification of anxiety, for the directive of anxiety is to be oneself in truth, relentlessly.

My third proposition is somewhat speculative in this attempt at a theoretical structure, but here it is: It is my feeling that the conscience is at the heart of anxiety. Since anxiety is a nebulous power that activates and drives the being to fulfillment, the focal point of anxiety might be termed "conscience."

If we traced historically the notion of conscience, we would discover it has always been. All religions—Eastern and Western, all cultures, even all psychologies have run up against this same bedrock and indeed, in greater or lesser measure, have posited themselves on it. Religions have tried to provide forgiveness for its violation; cultures have had to use it for their survival; psychology has attempted to explain it away, but it has stood firm and immovable—and now I have chosen to introduce this concept for our consideration.

Conscience as a fundamental datum, residing, as it were, at the heart of anxiety, is that aspect of man's being that is not created by the milieu or the superego influences, but is seized on and trained by them. I do not believe it is sufficient to say a threat to life and security constitutes the point of contact with the milieu, for there are numerous notable examples of people who, in spite of anxiety welling up to tidal wave proportions, have gone forward to achieve their true selves or to express their true selves as conscientiously perceived by them. This is a phenomenological fact known to everyone.

I am suggesting that conscience is as authentic as anxiety itself. It is as much a part of the human situation as guilt. As Martin Buber sees it, conscience is that aspect "of the human world whose foundations [man] knows and recognizes as those of his own existence and of all common human existence." The point of conscience in its most basic quality then would be a "doing unto others as we would have them do unto us" (Arieti, 1959, p. 1824). Or, to apply it in terms of authenticity: When we are not realizing our authentic selves, our anxiety focuses in guilt feelings which in turn are expressed in pangs of conscience. Now, it would go far beyond the bounds of this paper to discuss authentic and inauthentic guilt—apart from associating authentic guilt with the violation of the true self and that of others, while inauthentic guilt would be the opposite. It follows, too, that in the approximation of authenticity, one's sensitivity to the authentic skirts along the margin of increased anxiety described as the creative directive to be oneself in truth, relentlessly.

In Rollo May's treatment of conscience I perceive the same creative directive that I have suggested is true of anxiety. He says,

> Conscience, rather, is one's capacity to tap one's own deeper levels of insight, ethical sensitivity and awareness, in which tradition and immediate experience are not opposed to each other but [interrelated. . . . It is] a level on which the individual participates in the tradition, and on that level tradition aids man in finding his own most meaningful experience (1953, p. 215).

Conscience seems to be the voice of anxiety saying, "This is the way, walk in it" (Isa. 30:21). It seems to be the eye of anxiety leading it through the fog of confused expectation, the discriminating guide to filter in and filter out the burdens of the superego and the pressures of the id, if you will, in one's constructive attempt to find oneself in truth.

Let me here add a brief quotation from Medard Boss that suggests a parallel understanding:

> How else could it be possible that man is reminded of this task by his conscience, whenever he does not fulfill it. This call of conscience, these feelings of guilt, will not give him any peace until he has borne out all the possibilities in caring for the things and fellow men of his world (1963, p. 48).

Having discussed anxiety as a creative directive, the following question is appropriate: Why, in view of this healthy, constructive force propelling it in the direction of authenticity, is there a backing-up of anxiety, as it were? Perhaps the most obvious answer lies in the confusion and demands made by the milieu into which the neonate finds itself born. Since we are aware of this aspect of the situation, this question and the answer could be considered superfluous. But I am not so sure we have understood the nature of anxiety if we dismiss it that lightly. Here, I return to Kierkegaard for a more meaningful answer.

Kierkegaard takes the story of Adam and Eve in the Garden of Eden as his starting point. His insight, imagination, description, and penetration into the human situation reach new heights. He sees the condition of innocence in an idyllic setting suddenly stirred by the awareness of freedom. So, to quote him,

> In this state [of innocence] there is peace and repose; but at the same time there is something different, which is not dissension and strife, for there is nothing to strive with. What is it then? Nothing. But what effect does nothing produce? It begets dread [anxiety]. This is the profound secret of innocence, that at the same time it is dread. Dreamingly the spirit projects its own reality, but this reality is nothing, but this nothing constantly sees innocence outside of it. . . . Dread is a sympathetic antipathy and an antipathetic sympathy (1946, p. 38).

Now, of course, this does not seem to be very lucid unless one recognizes it as another description of ambivalence, and if you are struck by its ambiguity, Kierkegaard agrees, as he says, "there is nothing in the world more ambiguous" (1946, p. 39).

However, what he is wrestling with expressing is the quality and nature of anxiety as it posits freedom. Some of our questions will be anticipated shortly. He then moves from the state of repose in innocence to a description of anxiety. Thus he says,

> So when it is related in Genesis that God said to Adam, "Only of the tree of the knowledge of good and evil thou shalt not eat," it is a matter of course that Adam did not understand this word. For how could he have understood the difference between good and evil, seeing that this distinction was in fact consequent upon the enjoyment of the fruit? . . . One assumes that the prohibition awakens the desire (1946, p. 40).

Or, as he says in another place:

> In making the prohibition a conditioning cause one assumes that the *prohibition awakens a concupiscentia* [a predisposition] (1946, p. 37).

To do this,

> One posits a knowledge instead of ignorance; for Adam would have had to have a knowledge of freedom, since his desire was to use it. The explanation therefore *anticipates* what was *subsequent*. The prohibition awakens in him the possibility of freedom . . . the alarming possibility of *being able*. *What* it is he is able to do, of that he has no conception. . . . There is only the possibility of being able, as a heightened expression of dread, because this in a more profound sense is and is not, because in a more profound sense he loves it and flees from it. . . . There is nothing to prevent his having a notion of the terrible. . . . The infinite possibility of being able draws closer for the fact that this possibility indicates a possibility as its consequence (1946, pp. 40–41).

Attempting to paraphrase what is, admittedly, a difficult concept couched in difficult language, I think Kierkegaard is saying that anxiety is that quality intrinsic to the human, and the limitation of human *foreknowledge of consequences* both intensifies anxiety and directs man to choose. Not to choose is to intensify anxiety. To choose is to participate in anxiety. To choose not to choose is to intensify anxiety. For to choose not to choose is to choose inauthenticity neurotically. To choose authentically is to ride on the tide of anxiety in the direction of choosing oneself.

Allow me then to take you into two profound and extremely difficult quotations which lead us to Kierkegaard's concept of man or his ontology:

> Man is a synthesis of the soulish and the bodily. But a synthesis is unthinkable if the two are not united in a third factor. This third factor is the spirit. In the state of innocence man is not merely an animal, for if at any time of his life he was merely an animal, he never would become a man. So then the spirit is present, but in a state of immediacy, a dreaming state. Forasmuch as it is present, it is in one way a hostile power, for it constantly disturbs the relation between soul and body, a relation which endures, and yet does not endure, inasmuch as it has endurance only by means of the spirit. On the other hand, it is a friendly power which has precisely the function of constituting the relationship. What then is man's relation to this ambiguous power? How is spirit related to itself and to its situation? It is related as dread. It cannot do away with itself, so long as itself is outside of itself. Neither can man sink down into the vegetative life, for he is determined as spirit. He cannot flee from dread, for he loves it; really he does not love it, for he flees from it. Innocence has now reached its apex. It is ignorance, but not an animal brutality, but an ignorance which is qualified by spirit, but which precisely is dread, because its ignorance is about nothing (1946, pp. 39–40).

The other passage, in which Kierkegaard discusses the heart of his message, is to be found in *The Sickness Unto Death* (1955):

> Man is spirit. But what is spirit? Spirit is the self. But what is the self? The self is a relation which relates itself to its own self, or it is that in the relation [which accounts for it] that the relation relates itself to its own self; the self is not the relation but [consists in the fact] that the relation relates itself to its own self. Man is a synthesis of the infinite and the finite, of the temporal and the eternal, of freedom and necessity, in short is a synthesis. A synthesis is a relation between two factors. So regarded, man is not yet a self.

> In the relation between two, the relation is the third term as a negative unity, and the two relate themselves to the relation, and in the relation to the relation; such a relation is that between soul and body, when man

is regarded as soul. If on the contrary the relation relates itself to its own self, the relation is then the positive third term, and this is the self.

Such a relation which relates itself to its own self [that is to say, a self] must either have constituted itself or have been constituted by another. . . . Such a derived, constituted, relation is the human self, a relation which relates itself to its own self, and in relating itself to its own self relates itself to another. . . . By relating itself to its own self and by willing to be itself the self is grounded transparently in the Power which posited it (pp. 146–47).

In these two celebrated passages Kierkegaard outlines his ontology. Man, he suggests, has three aspects: body, soul (mind), and spirit. Body and mind are to be brought into harmony with the demands and intentions of the spirit.

"Spirit [is] the absolute of all that a man can be" (Kierkegaard, 1955, p. 176). The objective or goal for which the creative directive exists is to be spirit. Anxiety is the creative directive to bring the body and mind into harmony in the spirit. It is worthy of note that in Kierkegaard's existential psychology, man's chief dilemma is to become a self or spirit. Therefore his basic experience is anxiety, whose twin purpose is to intensify awareness of disharmony with the spirit, while at the same time constituting the relation.

Kierkegaard assigns the power of synthesizing to the spirit. The "spirit," he says, "(is the) third factor. . . . So then the spirit is present . . . it is in one way a hostile power, for it constantly disturbs the relation between soul and body. . ." (1946, p. 39), i.e., the body and the mind. In other words, when the body attempts an inauthentic alliance with the mind, or when alliance results from rationalization, anxiety develops. Or, at this point, the spirit intercepts and disturbs the inauthenticity, causing anxiety. If the mind becomes more astute and creates more ingenious subterfuges in further inauthenticity, once again the function of the spirit is to break up the defenses against inauthenticity. This is what Kierkegaard means by saying, "[the spirit] is in one way a hostile power. . . . [But then] it is a friendly power which has precisely the function of constituting the relationship" (1946, p. 39). In other words, any compromise between body and mind that is not conducive to the objective of spirit—"the absolute of all that a man can be" (Kierkegaard, 1955, p. 176)—or of being a self in truth, relentlessly, is immediately informed by the creative directive of anxiety. For as Kierkegaard says, in such a situation "the spirit relate[s] to itself and to its situation . . . as dread [or anxiety]" (1946, pp. 39–40). It can do no other. Thus it is created. Hence when we speak of mental illness or psychogenic illness, it must be seen as the message of anxiety. Either physically or mentally, anxiety takes its toll if the creative directive to be oneself in truth is not heeded. Allow me, then, to tender an obvious suggestion: When the patient is ill, the most important preoccupation of the therapist must needs be a concern to discover in what way and for what reason the patient is avoiding authenticity.

Kierkegaard makes one further important point. He is radically misinterpreted if his ontology is coerced into phenomenology. When he speaks of spirit, he sees it phenomenologically, but he never construes it as separate from ontology. Spirit does not exist of and by itself in any self-creating sense, but rather is determined by that Power which constituted it.

> This then is the formula which describes the condition of the self when despair is completely eradicated: by relating itself to its own self and by willing to be itself the self is grounded transparently in the Power which posited it (Kierkegaard, 1955, p. 147).

It ought to be pointed out then that when we reduce ontology to phenomenology, we are guilty of the same kind of reductionism of which we accuse science. Certainly, we are spoken to by phenomena, e.g., anxiety. Certainly, phenomena may lead us to larger deductions, but for Kierkegaard phenomena can only be interpreted as meaningfully as they relate to the Spirit that posited them. This is to imply a built-in teleology which I have pointed to as being oneself in truth, relentlessly. *Being oneself in truth* refers to that Other that posited the self. It is very lucidly and insightfully expressed in the statement of Augustine: "Thou madest us for Thyself and our heart is restless until it repose in Thee" (Augustine, 1909, p. 5).

In contrast to this, one notices the total frustration of a detached nihilistic existential psychology symbolized in Sartre's *No Exit* (1949).

Anxiety in the Context of the Developmental Process

Having portrayed anxiety as the creative directive to be oneself in truth, relentlessly; having in my own mind and for our purposes identified it with Teilhard de Chardin's "within" or "consciousness," or Bergson's *élan vital*, or even perhaps Freud's concept of the libido; let me proceed further by using Theodore Lidz's phrase, "an inborn directedness for further growth" (1968, p. 4). Now of course Lidz refers to the organism, though I feel sure he does not limit his statement to that. I am suggesting that the neonate is thrust into life on the tide of anxiety—a terrifying experience described well by Otto Rank in his *The Trauma of Birth* (1952). The helplessness and complete innocence of the neonate make its emergence even more terrifying. But the die is cast, and only the tender, loving care of family and surroundings might be counted on to mitigate the transition from warmth, comfort, security. There is a certain relentlessness about this experience of birth. There is only one way to go, but this is a never-to-be-forgotten experience to long for. And here begins the long, arduous task of moving from the stage of total *dependence* to other stages of growth yet unknown. If any *one* thing is clear to the neonate, it is that it is being carried on the tide of anxiety further and further from the protective womb, into ever new and bewildering experiences. Here rises the conflict of egress and return. The past looks inviting, but impossible. The future looks exciting, but foreboding. And, carried forward on the tide of anxiety, the self attempts every form of self-contortion and reality distortion to escape, only to find that the tide keeps moving it away from the safety of the stage of dependence.

It is then perhaps that the most dramatic bid for dependence is made in what I call the second stage of development—*independence*. This is a stage when the growing child is tremendously aware of his potential, excited about it, but terrified by it. This is what Kierkegaard might term a "sympathetic antipathy or an antipathetic sympathy." Or again, "He cannot flee from dread, for he loves it; really he does not love it, for he flees from it" (1946, p. 40). This is a stage when one wants the privileges of freedom but does not want the responsibility. In this stage the most extraordinary feats of self-distortion take place to remain dependent while making the pretense of self-dependence. That is why I term independence a "pseudo state." An illustration of this state would be a fetus waving its fists defiantly from the womb and shouting, "I am the master of my fate; I am the captain of my soul" (Henley, 1955, p. 985). Anxiety drives one forward, while the unknown future in its unspecificity overcomes one with alarm. Now if it seems I am repeating myself in describing the states of dependence and independence, let me point out that in fact this is true of all stages, since (1) conditions throughout life can be and frequently are used to test return possibilities—indeed whole societies have founded themselves on cradle-to-the-grave security perhaps only because someone has perceived this as a phenomenological fact and capitalized on it— and (2) independence in its thrust is a way of spreading anxiety in such a manner that the milieu will often become anxious enough to cater to the return. Thus it might be said, figuratively speaking, that in independence, anxiety is passing through the narrow gorge of reality in its attempt to test the limits of reality. Hence, too, it will be noted that many of the symptoms are those found in youth.

It is when reality holds firm—like the banks of a cresting river—

that the stage of *self-dependence* is possible. After the most intense struggle, akin only to the trauma of birth; after the painful discovery that one's attempts to transform reality to fit one's own dependency needs is causing more intense anxiety; after the awareness that physical and emotional disturbances are symptoms of this impossibility; one begins to orient one's life in terms of the message of anxiety to be oneself in truth. At this stage one's whole life is reoriented in the direction of self-dependence. It may begin in some meaningful religious experience; it may begin in therapy; it may begin in experiences as varied and unique as human nature is capable of. But at this stage, one might say, we have the birth of the self in self-dependence.

Only now does one begin to feel the meaningfulness of the fourth stage—*interdependence*. It means, not to use and coerce other selves into one's egocentric needs, but to relate with other selves in a real give-and-take, in a mutuality and sharing that assumes full responsibility for oneself but no less responsibility for the other. In the thought of Buber, this would facilitate the development of an I-Thou relation. In this stage we might suggest that anxiety exhibits itself in concern, its intensity being increased by the frustrations of life, while instead of lapsing into compulsivity, anxiety carries one into new and ingenious ways of removing the blocks, with respect of persons as a primary guideline. The source of motivation at this point is a quiet inner serenity rather than a diabolic self-divinization that resembles the dependent child throwing a tantrum.

Of course, a detailed exposition of these stages in the developmental process is not compatible with the limits of this chapter. Moreover, these stages overlap and are not mutually exclusive. But I believe enough has been said to delineate anxiety as the creative directive to be oneself in truth, relentlessly.

In conclusion, allow me to draw attention to some of the main points in this chapter. I have started with an empirically deduced assumption that anxiety is the creative directive to be oneself in truth, relentlessly. I have endeavored to suggest that it is possible to identify anxiety with other expressions of an inner forward thrust such as "entelechy" in Plato, the "within" or "consciousness" of Teilhard de Chardin, the *élan vital* of Bergson, and even the "libido" in Freud. I have further suggested a most important difference from other views, that anxiety is always a healthy experience, propelling one in the direction of selfhood. Anxiety is no more neurotic than any other crisis or near crisis caused by some instrument out of control. The way anxiety is managed can be neurotic, but anxiety itself is a creative directive to be oneself in truth, relentlessly. I have tried also to uncover conscience as an ontological phenomenon at the heart and core of anxiety. Finally, I have tried to point out that anxiety intensifies to block regression to the womb of innocence, dependence, and irresponsibility, while the challenge of the unknown and unspecified directive to be a person in truth is likewise experienced as anxiety. Neurosis results from attempting to remain dependent while anxiety increases because one is bucking the tide of anxiety instead of riding it to one's real destination in selfhood. Let me say one final word. I am suggesting that in psychosis, a deadly compromise has been effected in which the psychotic has "succeeded" in the return to the womb where the security of total dependence eliminates all responsibility. Here, anxiety has been driven underground or sedated from where it may make only an episodic appearance, as in the death throes of a victimized creature, until in the death of anxiety, the creature dies.

In the pages of Scripture the conception of human fear is both sternly prohibited and warmly encouraged. Fear in itself is neither sin nor piety; other factors make this determination. Because of the great importance of fear in the human psyche (both theologically and psychologically), this paper seeks to discover what gives fear its negative or positive quality. Through an analysis of fear in its component elements and stages of development, an attempt is made to derive the theological significance of fear—for discernment in biblical study and in personal-ecclesiastical applications.

Theological Implications of Fear

The Grasshopper Complex

Robert E. Morosco

Theological paradoxes, such as giving with the result of receiving (Luke 6:38) and dying with the outcome of receiving life (Matt. 10:39), are not infrequently uncovered in Scripture. Also under the heading of "paradox" might be included biblical directions regarding the concept commonly labeled "fear." It is well recognized that throughout both testaments prescriptions are issued to "fear not!" and to "stop fearing!" (Gen. 15:1; 21:17; 26:24; Exod. 14:13; Deut. 1:21; Matt. 10:31; Acts 27:24). Just as frequent, however, are exhortations to the contrary. The law, for instance, requires a child to fear his father and mother (Exod. 20:12; Lev. 19:3, *yahrah*, translated "honor" and "revere" respectively in the Revised Standard Version). Scores of texts urge men to fear God (Lev. 19:14; Luke 23:40), the Lord (Josh. 24:14; Prov. 3:7), and even His name (Deut. 28:58). Paul, too, exhorts men to fear the Lord (II Cor. 5:11; 7:1) and Christ (Eph. 5:21, *phobos*, translated "reverence" in the RSV). In Romans 11:20 Paul warns the grafted wild olive branches (Gentiles joined to the Jewish patriarchal roots,

Reprinted from *Journal of Psychology and Theology* 1, no. 2 (1973), 43–50. Used by permission.

i.e., in the church) to fear (*phobeo*, translated "stand in awe" in the RSV), while in Romans 13:7 Paul urges fear to be rendered to whomever it is due ("respect" for, *phobos* in the RSV). Peter tells "the exiles of the Dispersion" to "conduct yourselves with fear throughout the time of your exile" (I Peter 1:17), and the author of Hebrews begins his exhortation not to fail to reach God's promised rest with "Therefore . . . let us fear" (4:1).

Because of the negative connotations generally associated with the English word *fear*, it is not unusual for sensitive pastors, Bible teachers, and Christian psychologists to ignore the positive theological stress upon fear in the Bible, while emphasizing those texts with exhortations to desist from fear. Some translations of the Bible lessen this tension by employing "revere" or "respect" for positive imperatives, while maintaining "fear" in the negative commands. There are, however, texts which suggest that such a simple dichotomy misses the significance of the concept of fear. For instance, Isaiah 8:12–13 uses *yahrah* ("to fear") in parallel negative and positive imperatives. Isaiah is urged by Yahweh not to fear the Assyrian armies, yet, he is to fear Yahweh of hosts. In one line *yahrah* is viewed as an affront to God, in the next it is depicted as a virtue. To assign here two meanings to *yahrah* in corresponding imperatives of the same passages is awkward and suspect, to say the least.

Though the Scriptures sometimes speak of "fear" in the affective sense, the most significant texts are concerned with volitionally controlled or theological fear. There is, however, a relationship between the two. To adequately comprehend the biblical concept of fear, distinction must be made between the *fear-object*, the *fear-conflict*, and the *fear* itself. From the many recorded prescriptions and commandments to initiate, cease, or continue fear, it is evident that fear in the theological sense is not the unpleasant affect or feeling that is often associated with psychological fear (else, authoritative commands would conveniently replace therapeutic analysis). Also, not directly in the view of the biblical authors are the physical contingents linked to fear (e.g., disturbed breathing, increased heart activity, vasomotor changes, perspiration, and musculoskeletal reactions like trembling). Fear, from a theological perspective, is something over which men have control; they have little or no control over these physioemotional reflexes. Unpleasant emotional and bodily aspects of fear seem rather to be accompaniments to unresolved fear-conflicts.

A fear-conflict is the result of the awareness (real or imaginary) of someone or something so impending upon one's secure sphere of existence as to significantly affect it. It is in the defense of one's being—in an attempt to preserve one's self-conceived omnipotence—that the fearer's system is provided temporary super-power with the injection of the hormone adrenalin through the adrenal glands. Whether or not the perceived intrusion is probable is not significant, for the fear-subject believes it to be. And whether or not the fear-object, though impending (and even potent), can actually tamper with the fear-subject's existence does not affect the fear-conflict, for the fear-subject thinks this to be the case. Thus a fear-conflict brings with it a mental attitude of helplessness before an entity which both whelms and looms: this conflict generates the unpleasantness (emotional and physical) which remains with the fear-subject until the conflict with the fear-object is finally resolved.

This means that a fear-object, to exist, must have two legs: (*a*) *almightiness*, which ranges from supreme power in a single area of one's life at a single moment to the complete authority to destroy the existence of the fearer; and (*b*) *impendency* of actually entering the secure domain of the fear-subject. In other words, the fear-object is an entity that threatens to consume the fearer's subjective omnipotence in some area. If either the almightiness or impendency is removed from the fearer's mind, so is the fear-object, and thus the fear-conflict is ended. Once the fear-subject becomes convinced that either his potential fear-object *is not able* to affect his existence or that this entity, though able, *is not going to* affect his existence, the fear-object is dissipated, and the fear-conflict alleviated.

If, for example, while watering one's rose garden, a large, hairy bumblebee (an entity with a certain power) should encroach into the sphere of activity, the result is a fear-conflict with the bee. A grasshopper, however, seldom does more than startle the experienced gardener (barring one who might see this insect as a significant threat to his existence, e.g., a gardener who is unfamiliar with the grasshopper or a wheat farmer who might conceive of a grasshopper blight). Yet even a legitimate fear-object, like a bumblebee, if it is disjoined from the vulnerable sphere of one's activity (e.g., by distance or by the protective wall of a glass jar), becomes a mere object of interest, the now innocuous fear-object arousing curiosity to the same degree that it would evoke a fear-conflict if impendency became a reality (e.g., the popularity of snake pits and lions' dens at the zoo); and the conflict is ended.

Fear-objects begin to be learned early with the assimilation of values from significant people in a person's life, especially his mother and father; although assimilated fear-objects may also be rejected (e.g., those parents who lived close to the Depression era and so fear economic depression may have children who fail to perceive either the potency or impendency of this fear-object). This early learning often fails to reflect reality and so has to be unlearned (through therapy if necessary). Other fear-objects are learned later as one interacts with his environment. It is hoped that a Christian will accept the values contained in Scripture and so will assimilate fear-objects from this source. Fear-objects range, therefore, from inanimate and abstract conceptions (e.g., abandonment, one's own feelings of hostility, lack of financial security, etc.) to personal beings (e.g., mother, father, boss, God, etc.). Some are legitimate fear-objects because they objectively possess the two fear supports the fearer thinks they do, while others are unrealistic and irrational. To the fearer it makes no difference. Thus, it is entirely possible for a fear-subject to drive himself into a state of extreme anxiety, with very little objective reason. And contrariwise, it is possible for one in great objective danger not to experience any threat at all to his being. Fear-objects depend absolutely upon the thinking of their fear-subjects.

Often, a fear-object can be unlearned or dissipated by the fear-subject's gaining an objective familiarity with it, thus becoming persuaded that one or both of its supportive legs does not really exist. Yet, if the fear-object is long standing, the final persuasion of the unreality of its legs may be long in coming (e.g., the unlearning of a long-term hydrophobia or an untheological and fearful opinion regarding God which was learned as a child).

If the fear-object cannot be dissipated through the removal of one of its two legs, there are several subjective ways of existing with an intact fear-object. It can be struggled against, retreated from, or surrendered to. Since by definition an unimpaired fear-object is believed to be all-powerful and impending upon one's life, to resist or struggle against the fear-object subjectively, one must defend against one of these two supports (e.g., by contriving plausible explanations for doing away with either of them—rationalization; by coalescing with another person or a group to whom one or both of the legs of the fear-object is not a threat—identification; or by refusing to acknowledge the reality of the legs—denial, etc.). Ego defenses are also employed to make a psychic retreat from an intact fear-object. Through fantasy, one can escape internally from the domain of the fear-object; by repression a fear-object is removed from one's sphere of existence; by regression one can leave the fear-object with a retreat to an earlier developmental level, etc. Both psychic struggle and psychic retreat temporarily relieve the symptoms of the fear-conflict; but since the conflict itself continues, when the defenses weaken, the symptoms will again rush to consciousness with the not infrequent result that the fear-conflict itself will now be difficult to identify.

A third alternative for dealing with an unimpaired fear-object involves surrender to or acceptance of the realm of authority possessed by the fear-object, genuinely acknowledging the loss of one's personal omnipotence and adequacy in this area. With this particular mode of existence, one is forced into living in a kind of tension of submission to something or someone which has power or authority over his existence. This acceptance of and acquiescence to the fear-object is fear in the theological sense. It is this acceptance of the overwhelming that Jesus demands when He asks man to "fear him who can destroy both soul and body in hell" (Matt. 10:28). This acquiescence to the fear-object allows one to exist with an all-powerful and impending entity by acknowledging that this being legitimately warrants the respect and regard it demands. No negative feelings or unpleasant physical contingents need result, for one is merely nodding to reality. The unpleasantness associated with fear is actually the effect of an unresolved fear-conflict, not the effect of fear itself. Therefore God can be comfortably acknowledged and accepted as the ultimate in fear-objects because He is objectively and unchangeably omnipotent and imminent. A nondivine and less terminal fear-object, like one's employer, can also be acknowledged as supreme in his more limited realm. A still lesser fear-object, such as a snake coiled in one's path, is skirted about in acceptance of his realm; by doing this, the unpleasant feelings and painful bodily reactions of an unresolved fear-conflict are reduced. When the Bible speaks of fear, it is the acquiescence to the fear-object that is meant, hence the biblical translation "revere" or "respect" or "regard" is actually close to what the writers of Scripture had in mind in both their negative and positive statements. Biblical fear is regard, respect, and honor of the fear-object (hence, the septuagintal translation *timao*, "to honor, revere," for *yahrah*. Exod. 20:12; Matt. 15:4; 19:19). Theological fear is not primarily dread of or repulsion for the fear-object, but surrender to its authority.

This brings us to the significance attached to fear in Holy Script. Why is such a private matter like whom or what one fears in life so important theologically? Why does the Bible deal with man's relationship to fear-objects in the imperative tense? The theological significance of fear resides in the fact that through one's fear (i.e., his acquiescence to another's authority) a person's values are revealed (i.e., fear echoes the most esteemed elements in one's value system). A person's fear-objects are accorded his attention, respect, and even servitude. For example, unlike the harmless grasshopper, the bumblebee is not shooed away with a swish of the gardener's wrist. Rather, his path of flight is observed gingerly, and he is given free course wherever he decides to go. Again, when the company's general manager enters the garrulous office party, he usually has the effect of causing a momentary hush so that none will seem to be competing with him for the attention due him. The fear-object is king of his domain; when his domain overlaps with that of the fear-subject, the latter's realm is annexed to the former's, thus making the fear-object king over both regions. Exceptions to this are only the result of an impending greater fear-object; that is, even a mild and passive mother strikes out fearlessly at the bumblebee which approaches the carriage of her helpless infant. Why? Because she places greater positive value on her child than on the state of nonpain she might exchange to protect her infant. The employee seeking to impress the president of his company might risk offending the general manager by continuing to dominate the conversation even when the latter joins in. Why? Again, the reason rests in the higher regard that is placed on the president than on the general manager in the employee's mind.

One's ultimate fear-object is that which he reveres above all else in life. It is that entity to which the fearer has surrendered the final power and authority of his existence. This is the position which legitimately belongs only to the creature's Creator, though this is often not the case. One's supreme fear-object warrants total regard and esteem. The person who fears loneliness or reveres nonloneliness above all things might even give up the most advantageous position of employment that he is capable of attaining in order to move "home" where his friends and family live (and so to relieve his fear-conflict). An individual who reveres financial security most of all might, on the other hand, leave his wife and children on the chance of striking it rich on the other side of the world. One who regards God above all things desires His will above all things in life.

The theological significance attached to fear can be seen in Numbers 13, where the account is given of the twelve Hebrew spies who are sent into the land of Canaan to make reconnaissance in preparation for taking the land. The majority report from the spies, however, is one that reflects great fear or reverence for the land's inhabitants— "We are not able to go up against the people; for they are stronger than we" (v. 31). In other words, Canaan is the domain of its present inhabitants, who are all-powerful as far as we are concerned; therefore, to enter their realm would initiate a fear-conflict, since this would add the element of impendency to the fear-object. The unpleasant physical and emotional reactions of dread would have resulted had the people entered the land and so established a fear-conflict. However, by acquiescing to the authority of the Canaanites, i.e., by fearing them in the theological sense, the people avoided a fear-conflict and so protected themselves. The chapter closes with a disclosure of the people's supreme reverence for the Canaanites: "And we were in our own sight as grasshoppers, and so we were in their sight" (13:33, Amplified Version).

The recorded response of God to the fear of the people is quite severe, even considering the dispossession from this people of the land they refused to enter, in order to give it to Moses and his seed (Num. 14:11–12). From a purely psychological perspective, it seems almost unfair that God should so react to the fear of man. After all, were not the circumstances such that anyone with any sense would have been afraid to enter the territory of the powerful Canaanites? This kind of thinking, though dominated with concern, fails to grasp fully the theological implications of fear.

The great failure in the fear displayed by the Exodus generation—i.e., in making themselves grasshoppers before the Canaanites—inheres in the fact that their concession to the Canaanites (i.e., their fear) declared where this people placed their highest regard and esteem. Their fear reflected who was the potentate of their existence. The people are explicitly told, "Do not fear the people of the land" (Num. 14:9; Deut. 1:21, "Do not fear or be dismayed"), while the positive command regarding the fear of the people is always the same—"You shall walk after the LORD your God and fear him" (Deut. 13:4), and "Fear the LORD your God" (Deut. 6:2), etc. In other words, the highest regard, respect, and esteem of the people was to be put upon their Creator and God, Jehovah. God Himself always desires to be acknowledged as the Supreme One in man's existence. Perhaps it is in response to this failure so to fear God that the prophet Isaiah declares that the inhabitants of the entire earth are in God's eyes grasshoppers (Isa. 40:22), and, therefore, are obliged to revere the Lord! But through this earlier incident with the Exodus generation, the God who redeemed Israel from the slavery of Egypt is revealed to have been relegated to an inferior position in the thinking of the people, while the wicked Canaanites are given a kind of corporate kingship or godship in the people's minds. Thus Joshua and Caleb, who alone of the spies fought the majority decision, identify this reverence for the Canaanites as rebellion against God: "Do not rebel against the LORD; . . . do not fear the people of the land" (Num. 14:9). The people esteemed man over God, and so usurped God's throne. Compare Proverbs 29:25: "The fear of man lays a snare, but he who trusts in the LORD is safe." From the parallelism of this passage it is also evident that a person's fear-object is equivalent to his faith-object. The tension of living is complete dependence (trust or faith) upon another being and is equivalent to acknowledging that this being is the overwhelming force in one's existence (fear). Therefore the spies and the people were trusting in the ability of the Canaanites over and above that of the living God, and this was their tragic sin (Matt. 10:28).

Fear, in and of itself, is not morally evil or wrong; fear is neutral. It is merely respectfully acknowledging the power or authority of an entity. Fear becomes a failing in the personality (not necessarily a sin) when it does not reflect reality, i.e., when the true power-authority of an entity is stressed beyond verity (e.g., the almightiness of money, success, etc.), or when an entity's impendency is pushed to an unreal extreme (e.g., the possibility of total personal rejection, of being destroyed in an earthquake, etc.). No sane person would fail to fear a hungry tiger blocking his way. Why? Because a hungry tiger in one's path objectively possesses the power-authority to destroy a human being and will probably do so if one proceeds to approach him. To be afraid to leave home in Los Angeles for fear that a hungry tiger might devour one (i.e., to avoid a fear-conflict) displays a personality problem, however, since the odds of coming across a hungry tiger in this urban area put the fear-object in the unreal or near-unreal category.

When does fear verge upon sin? It is a dangerous thing to attempt to pass moral judgment upon the fears of others, but there seems to be some criteria for each to analyze his own fears theologically. Since God Himself, in accordance with the reality of His nature, demands to be the highest fear-object in the thinking of His creatures, the possibility of moral error is present whenever someone or something is selected to be revered above Him. When the Exodus generation exhibited their fear of the Canaanites by accepting their will over Jehovah's, they, in essence, had elevated the power and impendency of the Canaanites over the omnipotence and imminence of God, who was with Israel. The Exodus generation had chosen an unreal fear-object that contradicted the reality of God—in His person and His word. This means that fear (acquiescence to a fear-object to resolve a fear-conflict) enters the sphere of sin when it involves raising something or someone above what God says or is. Therefore fear, in the biblical sense, is an act of volition. By surrendering to the Canaanites, the Jews resolved their possible fear-conflict with them; but by doing this they set up hostilities with God and so initiated a fear-conflict with Him, since they were no longer surrendered to the living God as a fear-object. To set up an unresolved fear-conflict with God is sin.

Whenever the principal fear-object in one's life is nondivine, the result, theologically, is sacrilege, because a fear-object is a motivating factor of one's existence. Thus, the Exodus generation refused to enter Canaan, in accordance with the will of the Canaanites and contrary to the will of God (Deut. 5:29; Prov. 3:7; 8:13; 16:6; see also Sirach 2:15—"Those who fear the Lord will not disobey his words"). In Galatians 2 Paul is said to have directly opposed his fellow apostle, Peter, because the latter stood condemned. Peter's problem consisted in his forsaking the habit of eating and having fellowship with the Gentiles, as God had directed him in Acts 10, when James and certain Jews came to Antioch from Jerusalem. With the arrival of the Jews, Peter drew back and separated himself from the Gentiles. Paul explicitly identifies Peter's motivation as "fearing the circumcision party" (Gal. 2:12). In effect, Peter displayed greater regard and reverence for the circumcised ones than for his God (i.e., he acquiesced to his Jewish fear-objects in the face of what he knew to be God's will, and so resolved his conflict with the Jews, but established a fear-conflict with God [see, e.g., John 7:13]). The effect, then, is a kind of idolatry, defined as placing something higher in one's thinking than the living God, i.e., disturbing the legitimate creature-Creator relationship. The correlation between fear and worship can be seen in the kind of things openly worshiped in some heathen lands—snakes, lions, deadly lagoons, etc.— all primitive fear-objects. In addition, Scripture equates fear with worship (Pss. 19:9; 34:11; 96:9; Jer. 2:19; Heb. 12:28; see also the concept of the "God-fearers," i.e., Gentiles who worship Jehovah in the synagogue, Acts 10:2). The Preacher concludes that the whole duty of man is to fear God (Eccles. 12:13), while Jeremiah makes the fear of Jehovah the heart of the new covenant (Jer. 32:39–40). In fact, so closely and so naturally are fear and Jehovah associated that the term "fear" (*yirah*) is actually found in the Bible as a synonym for Jehovah (Gen. 31:42, 53).

In the operation of the church, the temptation is sometimes present to instill in a congregation a higher and "more tangible" fear-object than God, e.g., the acceptance of a church leader or the approbation of onlookers, in order to get the church's work accomplished. The theological term for this is "legalism." The legalistic syndrome is more than following a set of regulations: even the New Testament sets forth prescriptions for believers to follow. Legalism is complying with the norms or standards of someone or some group out of the motivation of fear of being rejected or held in low esteem by that group or person, or out of reverence that this rejection not occur. Included under the heading of legalism is serving for approbation, i.e., serving out of the motivation of fear of not attaining the approval one desires. From this perspective it can be seen how critical it is for the church to adequately understand its complete and unqualified acceptance by God in Christ. The church does not serve Christ out of the fear that its acceptance before God depends on its labor. Rather, the church serves out of the motivation of love it has because God loved it first, gave Himself for it, and has accepted it by reason of the work of His Son.

The psychological mechanics used to replace the fear of the Lord with an illegitimate fear-object are merely applications of the two above-mentioned ways of alleviating fear. If a false fear-object, e.g., the Canaanites or a deacon, is elevated in one's mind above the true and living God, then God loses His sovereign power; thus, in the subject's mind, God no longer has the almightiness necessary to be the fear-object par excellence, and the new false fear-object is given His place. Or, if in one's thinking God can be removed or allowed to drift to a distant place in the far heaven, i.e., if one can think away God's imminence, he no longer impends upon one's life as a fear-object must. The result is a wholly transcendent God who becomes the curiosity object of religion rather than the fear-object of life. This can be seen, for instance, in the Jewish apocalyptical literature written between the testaments: in a frenzy to maintain the transcendence of the Most High, the imminence of God is ignored, and correlatively, the Jewish people are seen to cling to the system of severe legalism which could not accept the grace of God in Christ when He came. The technique of resisting a fear-object by pushing it afar can also be seen in Acts 24:25, where, in response to Paul's presentation of the gospel, "Felix feared and said, Go away for the present; when I have opportunity I will summon you," thus preventing the potential fear-object from impending upon his presence.

In contrast to unreal and illegitimate fear-objects, the results of living in tension with the truly All-powerful and Impendent One are said in Scripture to be wholly positive. The psalmist declares that wisdom begins with the fear of the Lord (Ps. 111:10; Prov. 1:7; 9:10), which suggests that only by fearing Jehovah is reality ultimately viewed as it truly is. In order to replace God with another supreme fear-object, reality has to be distorted (i.e., the character of the living God must be altered). Other positive effects resulting from the fear of Jehovah are said to include happiness (Prov. 28:14; Sirach 1:12), displeasure with evil (Prov. 8:13), prolonged life (Prov. 10:27), and righteousness (Prov. 16:6; Neh. 1:5; Gen. 22:12). In addition, the Bible teaches that only the fear of the Lord can alleviate one's slavery to old fears (Rom. 8:15), such as the fear of death, which the devil is said to use to keep man in slavery (Heb. 2:15), but which for the believer has become innocuous because death has lost its omnipotence or sting (I Cor. 15:55). John says that only a "perfect love," i.e., only the love which exists in relationship with the Divine, is able to "cast out fear" (the fear of death and judgment, I John 4:17–18).

The study of guilt is central to any effective integration of psychology and theology. Guilt, and its related concept, sin, is certainly a central issue of theology. Likewise the phenomenon of guilt is one of the most crucial issues facing psychotherapists. After a brief discussion of the many forms guilt takes, this article traces in outline form the development of the guilt emotion through the process of internalization. Following that an analysis is made of the constituent elements of the guilt emotion.

Guilt

Where Theology and Psychology Meet

S. Bruce Narramore

Over fifteen years ago Meehl (1958) suggested that an analysis of the complex phenomenon of guilt was essential to any adequate rapprochement between psychology and theology. Yet in the intervening years only one major treatise of high quality (Tournier, 1962) has come from authors representing an evangelical viewpoint. Ministers of conservative orientation hold essentially the same view of guilt they did fifteen years ago, and Christian therapists have largely failed to develop any distinctive approaches or new theoretical formulations integrating both biblical and psychological conceptualizations of the experience of guilt.

Because of the crucial role guilt plays in both the psychotherapeutic process and the Christian experience I would like to examine its impact upon personality functioning and draw integrative implications for both the practicing therapist and the minister. I will attempt a survey (from a psychodynamic viewpoint) of the following areas: (a) the manifestations of guilt in daily experience; (b) the origin and development of guilt; (c) the cognitive and affective content of the guilt emotion; (d) the defensive processes designed to avoid the anxiety of guilt; (e)

Reprinted from *Journal of Psychology and Theology* 2, no. 1 (1974): 18–25. Used by permission.

a theological analysis of guilt and its implications for both Christian motivation and therapeutic guilt reduction; and (f) some therapeutic principles for coping with guilt-ridden personalities.

While it will be impossible to go into depth in all of these area, I will attempt to survey the major areas where a psychological perspective can contribute to our theological view of guilt and where our theological conceptions can shed light on important elements of the therapy of guilt. This article will deal with the broad outlines of the psychological development of guilt. It will also present an analysis of the content of the guilt emotion.

The Manifestations of Guilt

Guilt's presence is most clearly experienced by depressed and obsessive-compulsive individuals. In these so-called "guilt neuroses" the ravages of a guilty conscious reach their peak. The acute sense of worthlessness of the depressive and the obsessive doubting or compulsive working of the obsessive-compulsive clearly portray the inner workings of a sadistic conscience. But the influence of guilt is not limited to these more classical expressions. All people occasionally experience pangs of guilt.

The critical person always searching for an object for his accusations, the compulsive housewife, the driven businessman, the overly sensitive or withdrawn person, the responder to a challenge for spiritual commitment, and even the so-called "psychopath" are all suffering from an inability to cope with guilt emotions.

For the present we will simply state that guilt is in some way involved in *all* types of psychogenic pathologies. In some the role of guilt is central, while in others it plays a less vital role. But in all cases it is there in some degree and therapy will be ineffective unless the guilt is properly resolved.

The Development of Conscience

Lying in his crib, the newborn infant has no sense of right and wrong. Although he may be considered "sinful" in a theological sense, he has no awareness of any moral standards. He is consciously amoral.

The Ideal Self

Gradually things begin to change. It isn't long until the infant's parents decide it's time he starts to "learn." When he does something they don't approve they let him know it. When he responds the way they like he is rewarded. During the first few years of life the parents hold out a wide variety of goals, standards, and expectations. Due to the child's idealizing of his (seemingly) omnipotent parents and to their power to punish disapproved behavior the child gradually incorporates their expectations into his developing personality (Schafer, 1968). He knows that when he acts in approved ways he is rewarded and that when he misbehaves he is punished. He also hopes that by conforming to his parents' standards he will some day come to share their power and position. These motives, (a) the receipt of rewards, (b) the avoidance of punishment, and (c) the sharing of his parents' powers, give each child a strong desire to live up to his parents' expectations.

Based largely on these motives parental ideals are gradually incorporated into the young child's life. Along with the expectations of peers and other significant people, he begins to form an image of what he thinks he should become. By adolescence these ideals are firmly embedded in his personality in the form of an ideal self. This ideal self (or ego ideal, as it is sometimes called) is the portion of the personality that contains all of our uniquely human values, standards, and aspirations. This ideal self serves as a goal to motivate our actions and also as a standard by which we judge the acceptability of our behavior. In short, it forms the nucleus of conscience.

The Corrective Self

At the same time children are internalizing a system of ideals, they are also taking in their parents' attitudes toward their misbehavior and their parents' methods of punishment or correction. Just as children develop an ideal concept of what they think they *should* become, they also develop a set of corrective attitudes and actions and gradually take them as their own. The young child spanking his own hands or in a way strangely imitative of his parents saying "No! No!" to himself is evidencing this process of internalization. He is inflicting upon himself the same type of punishment he received from his parents. This type of reaction is one of the first evidences that a child is evaluating his behavior and correcting himself when he is wrong. It is also the forerunner of later guilt emotions.

To elaborate on this process let's look at what happens when a child fails to live up to the expectations of his parents. Briefly, a parent may (a) punish the child, (b) subtly reject the child by being angry at him, (c) shame the child for his failure, (d) ignore the failure, or let the child profit from the consequences of his actions, (e) lovingly accept the child and reason with him about his behavior, or (f) lovingly discipline the child and show him how he can do better. Each of these reactions is taken into the child's personality and has an important bearing on the development of his moral system. We will begin with the first three parental options since they are the source of later guilt emotions and central to the formation of all neurotic problems.

Probably the most common result of misbehavior is some sort of punishment. When a child disobeys he learns to expect retribution. He is told, "Since you did that you must be punished." Gradually the experience of parental punishment begins to instill a deep expectation of retribution. After this happens a few times the child feels anxious even when his parents are not present. He has developed a kind of internalized parent that speaks to him much like his actual parent.

A second type of parental response to misbehavior is a veiled threat of personal rejection. The mother of an adopted child told me of great difficulty controlling her new daughter. She had tried everything and finally found a way that worked. "I tell her," she said proudly, "God doesn't love you when you're naughty."

Unfortunately, it isn't just these obvious expressions of parental anger and rejection that instill a fear of losing love. All human love is in some degree conditional. Most parents actually do love their children more when they are fulfilling their ideals. This very subtle fact helps lay the basis for the child's later fear that if he doesn't live up to someone's expectations he won't be loved.

A third parental response to misbehavior is to try to shame the child into more acceptable activities. Parents often compare one child to another or focus repeatedly on a child's failures. They may also say things like "Shame on you. You know better than that!" or "Naughty, naughty," or "Look what you've done now!" Needless to say, the repeated use of this type of comment can instill deep feelings of guilt and self-abasement in an impressionable child.

Over a period of years these three corrective parental responses are incorporated into the young child's personality. What originally came as an external threat of punishment, rejection, or disesteem is gradually changed into an internal corrective force. Taken together, these three attitudes comprise what I call the *punitive self.* They are the internal equivalents of the punishments the child received from his environment. I designate this set of corrective attitudes punitive because they all involve a hostile, threatening, or rejecting attitude toward the self.

All forms of discipline are not, of course, as potentially negative as the fears of punishment, rejection, and lowered self-esteem. With a minimum amount of anger and frustration parents can also (*a*) ignore a child's failures and let him profit from the consequences of his own behavior, (b) unconditionally love the child and reason with him about the effects of his actions, or (c) lovingly and patiently discipline him and help him see how he can do better. When these parental patterns are imitated and incorporated into a growing child's personality they form another set of corrective attitudes I call the *disciplinary self.* This set of attitudes is very different from the punitive self. It is loving rather than angry. It is patient rather than impulsive. And it is reasonable rather than demanding. This disciplinary self is the forerunner of adult feelings of genuine regret or constructive remorse in contrast to the neurotic guilt coming from the punitive self.

Projection and Omnipotence in the Development of Guilt

It would be easy to conclude from this that the adult emotion of guilt is an exact replica (or nearly so) of the corrective responses one received when he was a child. This, however, is not true. While parental responses are crucial to the development of guilt, they are not the sole determining factors. The child's state of weakness and inadequacy coupled with his perception of his parents' power also helps shape his experience of guilt.

Every child feels small, inferior, and inadequate. At the same time, children also perceive their parents as all-powerful and all-knowing. Most of us have heard reflections of this in children's comments like, "My dad can do anything!" This coupling of a child's feeling of weakness and his perception of his parents' power produces an important dynamic.

When a child becomes angry with his parents he assumes they know how mad he is (since they are thought to be omniscient) and fears they will retaliate with all their (seemingly) awesome power. In short, he projects his own intense anger onto his parents, attaches the great strength he has attributed to his parents to the anger he has projected onto them, and then recoils in fear from the fantasized retribution. In this way the child's conscience actually becomes more punitive than his parents were in reality. Whatever angry punishment the parent actually meted out is compounded by the child's perception of his parent as omnipotent and the child's projection of his own hostility onto the parent.

This dynamic helps explain the severe harshness conscience can take. Even a child with basically well adjusted parents who do not rely on fear motivation can develop a harsh conscience because of the anger within himself. Children with harsh parents are, of course, much more prone to developing punitive consciences, but the sole cause of this development does not lie in the parent.

A Diagrammatic View of Conscience

Based largely on the internalization of the ideals and disciplinary attitudes just discussed we all enter adulthood with a rather well developed moral system. While the content and nature of this moral system varies greatly from person to person, the psychological mechanics involved are essentially the same in every person. This moral system can be conceptualized as follows:

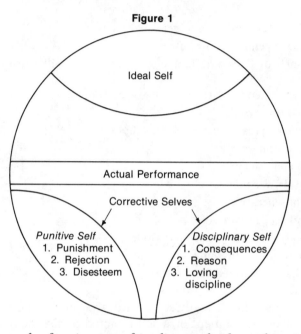

Figure 1

Within each of us is a set of goals, standards, and aspirations, the ideal self. When our performance falls short of these ideals a corrective response is triggered. This corrective response comes either from our threatening, punitive self or from our rational, loving, disciplinary self.

To the extent that the punitive self is in operation we experience feelings of self-condemnation, self-inflicted punishment, and isolation. This type of emotion has been variously labeled false guilt (Hyder, 1971), neurotic guilt (Horney, 1937), or pseudo guilt (Narramore, 1966). To the degree the disciplinary self is in operation we experience a positive self-corrective attitude. While recognizing our faults, we continue to respect ourselves and maturely plan ways of improving our behavior. This type of emotion has been called true guilt, constructive guilt, or existential guilt. For reasons we will see shortly, I prefer not to label the emotions coming from this loving, disciplinary self guilt at all. They are such entirely different feelings based on entirely different parental introjects that I prefer the term "constructive sorrow."

Ingredients of Guilt

Some time ago I asked an audience to write out how they felt when they felt guilty. Here are some of their replies:

Scared, uneasy.

Tense, like maybe I'm going to get caught.

A feeling of impending punishment.

Like if somebody finds out I'll be punished and they will scream what I've done to everyone.

My mind has a tendency to kick itself several times.

Disgusted with myself.

Like a raunchy person or a complete failure.

Stupid, low, remorseful.

Miserable and ashamed.

Rotten inside, worthless.

A feeling of separation.

Lonely and very frustrated.

I feel nobody loves me—especially God.

I find it hard to like myself.

Depressed and separated from others.

These responses fall into three general groupings. The first group reflects a fear of punishment or a self-inflicted punishment. The next shows a loss of self-esteem. And the last indicates a feeling of loneliness, rejection, or isolation. As can be easily seen, these three categories correspond exactly to the three negative attitudes of the punitive self just discussed. These three types of anxiety make up the broader emotion of guilt.

It may surprise some to see that I consider self-esteem one subexperience of the wider emotion of guilt. We are more likely to see self-esteem as the broad issue of one's total identity or overall adjustment, while guilt is viewed as only one of several internal psychic processes that occasionally attack our larger self-image system. I do not believe this is an accurate understanding of the relationship of guilt and self-esteem and in this section would like to demonstrate why by examining the relationship of guilt and self-esteem from three different perspectives. The first is a structural view of conscience. The second is the feeling content of guilt and lowered self-esteem. And the third is the etiology of these two emotions.

To begin, let us take another look at the structural view of conscience presented earlier. We said then that the total moral system is made up of (*a*) a set of ideals or goals (the ideal self or ego ideal), (*b*) a punitive set of corrective attitudes that is the source of neurotic guilt feelings, and (*c*) a disciplinary self that contains the constructive, loving corrective attitudes. Now we can take this diagram one step further. The attitudes of the ideal self can be divided into two groups. One group of ideals contains the positive desires, expectations, and images. This includes the desires for talent, power, intelligence, beauty, and respect. These ideals are formed largely by comparing oneself to others. All children occasionally feel weak and inferior in relation to more powerful adults or siblings. To overcome this feeling of inferiority they strive to reach the place they can feel as big, powerful, and intelligent as their parents. These goals of mastery, power, and intelligence form the core of the positive side of the ideal self.

The other portion of the ideal self is the negative, prohibitive side. It contains all our prohibitions and restrictions, especially those with moral connotations. In contrast to the "thou shalts" of the first set of ideals, this group is made up of the "thou shalt nots." The first group says "become like this and you can feel strong, respected, intelligent,

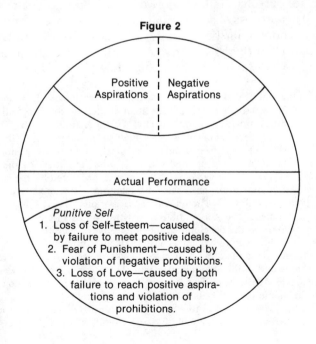

Figure 2

and adequate." The second group says, "If you don't avoid these activities you will be in danger of punishment and must feel bad."

When a child fails to measure up to the positive goals of his ideal self he feels inadequate and inferior. In short, he feels small and insignificant—a failure to be adult or mature. This evaluation leads to the feeling of inferiority, which is experienced as a loss of self-esteem. By contrast, when a child disobeys the negative side of his ideal self he experiences a slightly different emotion. He feels like a wrongdoer (evil) rather than a failure (weak). He fears punishment and retribution over moral disobedience rather than inadequacy and loss of self-esteem. In contrast to the loss of self-esteem or feeling of inferiority, moral transgressions involve more than the fear of being caught and punished. Whereas in low self-esteem the self is *compared* (unfavorably) with another person, in moral violations the self is in danger of *punishment* from the other person.[1] This distinction helps clarify the exact nature of guilt. Some guilt consists largely of anxiety over one's self—our inadequacies and failure—while some guilt is made up of anxiety over anticipated punishment. All guilt (regardless of which aspects of the ideal self has been violated) involves anxiety over losing love.

This explains why we can consider self-esteem to be a subpart of guilt. To the degree that we feel we are living up to the achievement standards of our conscience we esteem ourselves adequate. But to the degree we see ourselves falling short of these expectations we devalue ourselves. This process of self-evaluation forms the basis for our entire self-concept and cannot be logically separated from a study of guilt and conscience. Both the anxiety over punishment and the anxiety over inferiority are laid down in the first few years of life. Both result

---

1. Based on these and related distinctions some authors (particularly those of psychoanalytic orientation) distinguish between shame (what we are here calling loss of self-esteem) and guilt proper. Piers and Singer (1970) for example, write: "The following seem to me properties of shame which clearly differentiate it from guilt: 1) Shame arises out of a tension between the ego and the ego ideal, not between ego and superego as in guilt. 2) Whereas guilt is generated whenever a boundary (set by the superego) is touched or transgressed, shame occurs when a goal (presented by the ego ideal) is not being reached. It thus indicates a real 'shortcoming.' Guilt anxiety accompanies transgression; shame, failure. 3) The unconscious, irrational threat implied in shame anxiety is abandonment, and not mutilation (castration) as in guilt. 4) The Law of Talion does not obtain in the development of shame, as it generally does in guilt."

From a slightly different viewpoint Lewis (1971) also differentiates between guilt and shame. She describes the different ways in which the self experiences the stimuli that trigger shame and guilt. She indicates that shame is triggered by a disappointment or defeat while guilt is set in motion only by a moral transgression. She also suggests that in shame the self feels inadequate or deficient whereas in guilt the self feels adequate but rebellious. And in shame the failure is felt to be involuntary and unpreventable whereas in guilt the violation was willful.

from the failure to measure up to the internalized ideals of parents and significant others. And both are always experienced in combination.

The involvement of low self-esteem in guilt feelings has some crucial implications for both the pastoral and psychological treatment of guilt emotions. Since one component of guilt (low self-esteem) is actually a feeling of inadequacy and weakness, confession of misdeeds will not help alleviate it. While confession (or catharsis) may help resolve anxiety over the fear of punishment or rejection coming from violation of specific moral standards, it will do nothing to resolve a deep-seated feeling of self-devaluation over one's felt weakness and inadequacy. In fact, confessing one's failures can serve to reinforce neurotic self-debasement and actually perpetuate the experience of guilt. Because of this danger, the fear of punishment and the lack of self-esteem require very different treatments both theologically and psychologically.

References

Horney, K. 1937. *The neurotic personality of our time*. New York: W. W. Norton.

Hyder, Q. 1971. *The Christian's handbook of psychiatry*. Old Tappan, N.J.: Fleming H. Revell.

Lewis, H. 1971. *Shame and guilt in neurosis*. New York: International Universities.

Meehl, P.; Klann, R.; Schmieding, K.; Breimeier, K.; and Schroeder-Slomann, S. 1958. *What then is man?* St. Louis: Concordia.

Narramore, C. M. 1966. *Encyclopedia of psychological problems*. Grand Rapids: Zondervan.

Piers, G., and Singer, M. 1971. *Shame and guilt*. New York: W. W. Norton.

Schafer, R. 1968. *Aspects of internalization*. New York: International Universities.

Tournier, P. 1962. *Guilt and grace*. New York: Harper and Row.

Summary

This section considered several commonly experienced human emotions from both theological and psychological points of view. While not exhaustive of all feelings, these discussions are considered representative of the way in which human reactions to life events can be approached.

Rogers depicts "helplessness" as probably the most common problem clients present in therapy. He notes that regression and hyperdependency often occur. Facing helplessness with courage, faith, and hope are recommended by Rogers as constructive means of handling one's despair.

Finch correctly notes that many counselors attempt to do away with anxiety in their clients. He sees this as destructive of human growth and proposes, instead, a model in which anxiety becomes a creative force. He discusses the contributions of Sören Kierkegaard and Rollo May to these ideas and suggests the critical ingredient in personhood is "spirit" through which anxiety can become courage.

Morosco notes that the Bible admonishes persons to "fear the LORD" (Ps. 111:10) as well as to "be not afraid" (Matt. 10:31). He suggests that *both* are true and, in his article, proceeds to detail how this can be so. He concludes that many sin by adopting the "grasshopper complex" as did the Israelites when they discounted their ability to overcome the Caananites. Instead, he notes the biblical call for humility before and trust in the love of God.

Narramore's article is one of several he wrote on guilt. His book on

138

the same theme (coauthored with Counts) is noted below. He correctly notes that guilt is a very familiar concern in counseling and offers a thorough analysis of the phenomenon. He provides a useful developmental model which includes both ideal and cultural dimensions. Although he does not provide a solution in this essay, he concludes that certain forms of guilt require different types of amelioration in counseling.

Questions for Dialogue

1. Identify differences, as well as similarities, in the discussion of human emotions discussed in these articles.
2. On the basis of these essays, construct a model depicting how human responses to life experiences can be both psychologically understandable but religiously inadequate.
3. Identify other human emotions which could be considered within the framework provided by one or more of these authors.
4. Is faith an antidote to helplessness, anxiety, fear, and guilt? If so, how?

Additional Readings

Books

Becker, E. *The denial of death.* New York: Free, 1973.

Ellison, C. W. *Loneliness: The search for intimacy.* Chappaqua, N.Y.: Christian Herald, 1980.

Hart, A. H. *Feeling free.* Waco, Tex.: Word, 1981.

May, R. *The meaning of anxiety.* New York: Ronald, 1950.

Narramore, S. B., and Counts, W. *Guilt and freedom.* Santa Ana, Cal.: Vision House, 1974.

Articles

Boisen, A. T. Religious experience and psychological conflict. *Journal of Pastoral Care* 13 (1959): 160–63.

Grounds, V. C. Therapist and theologian look at love. *Christianity Today* 15, no. 22 (1971): 1000–1002.

Jackson, G. E. The problem of hostility, psychologically and theologically considered. *Journal of Religion and Health* 11, no. 1 (1972): 73–93.

Mauger, P. Psychology, theology and sin. *Pastoral Psychology* 23, no. 227 (1972): 5–11.

Meissner, W. W. Toward a theology of human aggression. *Journal of Religion and Health* 10, no. 4 (1971): 324–32.

Schmitt, R. F., Jr. Suffering and wisdom. *Journal of Religion and Health* 20, no. 2 (1981): 108–23.

Walters, O. S. Christian answers to immaturity. *Christianity Today* 37, no. 3 (1968): 417–28.

The Meaning
of Health

This section includes articles which are the central focus of this volume, namely, the meaning of health. Health is a state of mind and a state of body. Physical, mental, and spiritual health while similar are not one and the same. Ideally all three exist together, but each can exist without the others. As stated in the prologue, wholeness and holiness are two distinct realities. The essays included here discuss many of these issues.

"Sin or Sickness" is a narrative account of three types of mental illness which masquerade, in part, as moral aberrations. Samuel Southard, the author, notes that "the three persons whom we have considered present certain characteristics which will help us to distinguish between sinful behavior that is symptomatic of sickness." These are: unusual and unpredictable behavior, unrealistic attitudes, inner compulsions, and a resistance to reason.

Duke's article, "Religion and Mental Health: A Theological Point of View," defines sin as the human illusion that one can solve all problems alone. In contrast, he suggests that ". . . there has been a growing consensus that man's (sic) health as a creative human being demands that he be understood holistically, and that his growth, not unashamedly, be understood as a process of acceptance, forgiveness, as well as firmness." His essay considers these options.

"Salvation's Message About Health" is Seward Hiltner's attempt to explain the meaning of health from the viewpoint of the Christian faith. He explicates "sin" and redefines "wholeness." As he states, "It is also continually important for the Christian, who must accept what

141

the modern world means by 'health,' to recognize that there is another way, the biblical way, of approaching the context in which health is to be understood. This concept is for the eyes of faith, for as many as are called to have this vision of health in the person as derivative from the creation of God."

Richard Kahoe's essay, titled "A Search for Mental Health," reviews several current understandings of health from the psychological perspective and concludes, "What is noteworthy is the convergence of several disparate lines of research and threads of thought from psychology and from the teachings of Jesus—a convergence around self-centeredness as central to mental illness and the giving of oneself to a higher task as central to mental health."

The last article in this section, "Maturity: Psychological and Biblical," compares Jahoda's criteria for "positive" mental health with the prescriptions of Scripture. Although the content differs, Carter concludes that there is a significant degree of overlap in the two perspectives and that ". . . a mature person in either a psychological or biblical sense is integrated, has a purposeful or goal directed quality about his life, and is open to himself and others; the immature person is disorganized, having either conflicting goals or no goal, and is unaware and unaccepting of various aspects of himself and others."

The reader should expect to have his/her consciousness raised as to the various current conceptions about health and wholeness. The reader should also have increased awareness of the way in which the biblical perspective is both harmonious with or critical of these understandings.

Sin and sickness, evilness and illness, immorality and emotional disturbance—are often confused and mistaken for each other. The tendency is to categorize behavior as sinful, evil, and immoral when, in truth, persons are suffering from mental illness. Manic-depressive psychosis, senile dementia, and involutional melancolia are each illustrated in case studies wherein their true natures were identified by pastors who had enlightened points of view.

Sin or Sickness?

Samuel Southard

Every pastor is called upon to judge between sin and sickness in the lives of his people. We may be unprepared to make such decisions, but community opinion concerning a parishioner may be determined by our opinion. This does not mean that the pastor can take the place of a medical doctor or psychiatrist and diagnose the type of sickness. Nor does it mean that he can take the place of God and pronounce specific judgment upon a sinner. Instead, we must determine the moral accountability of a man for his actions. Was he acting in a voluntary, responsible manner, or did he act out of compulsion, not knowing what he did or said?

These questions can be answered only in relation to specific people because the community asks them in relation to specific individuals. In this article we will present the story of three people whose illness raised moral questions. They are chosen because they represent types of illnesses in which these questions are raised either by the community, the family, or the person himself. The three illnesses are manic-depressive psychosis, simple senile dementia, and involutional melancolia.

The first person we will discuss found himself in difficulty with his community because of his actions. Before marriage, he was known as a "wild, but likable, fellow." After marriage, people said that his wife "settled him down." He and his wife attend church regularly. About

Reprinted from *Pastoral Psychology* 11 (1960): 31–34. Used by permission.

a year ago their pastor noticed that John, the husband, would become restless during church and would often leave his seat and walk outside. When seen later on in the day he seemed calm. Following several weeks of this type of behavior, he would sit in church with his eyes downcast. During these days he would refuse to pray in public, although he had freely done so on previous occasions. When the pastor mentioned this to John, the latter replied, "I feel so sick inside, I can't do it. I am afraid my heart is bad." The pastor asked if he had seen a doctor. "I'm not afraid to die," said John. The pastor was puzzled.

A few days later the wife called to say that John had left the house the night before without saying where he was going. A friend told her that he had decided to take a trip to Florida. "Has he ever done this before?" asked the pastor. "Well," she said, "on several occasions he gets real excited and takes off for some city. I tell you, pastor, it worries me because I don't think he knows what he's doing. He's a good husband, but when he gets in these moods, he'll drink—and—well, he's had some trouble with women, too."

John was picked up by the state police and returned home to jail. The pastor and his wife sought the advice of the family doctor, who asked that a psychiatrist in a nearby town examine him. John was transferred to a private hospital and given shock treatments. The psychiatrist explained to the pastor that John was a "manic depressive." He pointed out that the parishioner would alternate between moods of depression, in which he could not pray and felt guilty, and moods of elation in which he would become restless and reckless. For years these mood swings had been gradually increasing in height and depth, until now they were noticeable to all.

The pastor visited John in the hospital upon his return home. The man needed much support, for he was generally rejected in the community because of his recent escapades. His lodge excluded him because he had been seen with women of low character on his drinking sprees. The pastor, on the other hand, pointed out to his deacons that John did this only during one of these periods of elation, and that he was ordinarily a sober and continent gentleman. Although there was some dissension in the church, this speech prepared the way for John. As a result of this acceptance, John drew closer to the church. He began to pray at home, which he had never done before. In the following two years he has had no severe mood swings and has been promoted in his job.

In this case, the pastor's acceptance of his parishioner into the community was as vital a ministry as the shock treatment. Both were based upon the diagnosis of sickness rather than sin, and both were instrumental in his recovery.

Another type of illness that leads to "immoral" behavior is caused by organic degeneration of the brain in older people. This is in contrast to our previous example, for no one has found any physical cause for manic-depressive psychosis. The "simple senile dementia" which we will now discuss may have many causes, but an organic basis can often be demonstrated. At the present time this particular field of psychiatry is under intensive study as the longevity span of Americans increases.

Families are often so distressed by the "moral" degeneration of a grandmother or grandfather that it may be months before a doctor can see the patient and establish the fact that sickness rather than sin is the cause. Consider, for example, Mr. Ambrose, who was for years a respected layman in his church and president of a neighborhood bank. At the age of seventy he began to make obscene remarks to his wife. He could not remember where he would lay down his glasses, but could vividly recall events of years gone by. At times he would storm about the house, cursing. He had always been considered a mild-tempered gentleman. Finally, he began to walk about the street, giving coins to all the children he saw and telling strangers that they were his own children. The consternation caused by this action can be illustrated in a remark of his daughter: "It was bad enough for him to say those things about white children, but he's claiming black children too!"

Several months after he first became irritable with his wife, Mr. Ambrose went into several stores and wrote out checks to pay for the bills of indigent customers. When his family was faced with the necessity of paying out several hundred dollars to meet these bills, they finally agreed to consult their family doctor. The latter advised hospitalization, but the family resisted this and kept Mr. Ambrose at home until he became untidy. After repeated assurances from the doctor and the pastor that Mr. Ambrose was sick and needed treatment, they took him to a state mental hospital.

In this instance, the pride of the family caused them to brush aside medical advice. The sons and daughters, thirty to fifty years of age, told the pastor how horrified they were at the conduct of their father and had agreed to keep him at home "under guard" if necessary. The pastor was most successful in interpreting the action of the old man as a sickness to the teenage grandchildren, who were less concerned about property settlements, guardianships, etc., than their parents. The "righteous indignation" of the family toward the father was soon

forgotten as they plunged into the business of dividing up his estate.
The sins of the children followed the sickness of the father.

In neither of these two examples have the persons talked about their
own sinfulness, although John, the manic-depressive, regretted the
actions that were a part of his illness. Our third example, however,
concerns one who was absolutely convinced that he was a lost man,
judged and condemned for his sins. Now this would not be considered
sickness in some men—rather we would praise God for these signs of
repentance. But the man of whom we are now speaking was a fifty-
year-old minister, honored by his church and the community. Pastor
Johnson had served one church for fifteen years. He had the normal
anxieties of the pastorate and of his home life. However, at the age of
forty-nine his mother died in a mental hospital. He said little about
it at the time, but his friends noticed his "moodiness." Several months
later his income tax was returned by an investigator who wished to
ask about some convention expenses which he had listed. Although
the investigator was satisfied, and his tax was accepted as in order,
Pastor Johnson began to be anxious. He told his wife and close friends
that he had been dishonest. He went to the local Bureau of Internal
Revenue and asked that his income tax returns for the past few years
be checked. He was assured that all was in order. His wife then began
to notice his suspiciousness of strangers. He confided in a friend that
"the FBI is after me." A few days later he was quite depressed. He
wept to himself, and declared that he was unworthy to be a minister.
His speech and motions slowed down until he seemed to walk in a
dream. He asked his assistant to take over all the duties of the church
for him.

By this time the church was worried. The elders approached his
wife and asked if he had been seen by a doctor. She replied that he
thought it was useless, but that she had urged him to make an appointment. The chairman of the board of elders then told the pastor that
the church would be glad to finance any medical treatment that would
be necessary. Pastor Johnson shook his head and said, "I know I am
to die for my sins." He said little else until visited by a psychiatrist
who happened to be an elder in a neighboring church. He dreaded
hospitalization and could not tell why. However, he did accept a few
weeks in a private hospital where he received shock treatments and
psychotherapy. During that time he admitted his deep fear that he
would die in a mental hospital as his mother had done. He also confessed to a great deal of physical weakness in the last year, which he
attributed to worry and anxiety. He felt quite guilty about this, for he
believed that a minister should always be "up and about for the Lord."

After his release from the hospital, Pastor Johnson continued to have weekly counseling sessions with his hospital psychiatrist. During that time he would talk over some of his deeper anxieties and fears about his future as a husband, father, and pastor. For many years he had successfully combated these fears, but now he felt that they were overwhelming him. The psychiatrist told him that he was to be commended for his steadfast courage. But now he was fighting additional odds because of the involutional changes which were taking place in his body. These chemical changes alone could cause depression.

Through talking out his anxieties and receiving a great deal of support from his church, Pastor Johnson was able to return to his pulpit after an absence of one year. During that time the church had paid all his hospital bills and his salary. The pastor reduced his work load and spent more time with his family and in recreation. Several years later he accepted a small village church which made less strenuous demands upon him.

In this case the pastor was fortunate to serve a church which identified with him and supported him in his illness. The membership attributed his anxieties about income tax and "sinfulness" to sickness. There were no evil rumors for him to overcome when he returned to his work. By this thoughtful and understanding distinction between sin and sickness, a congregation restored their minister to health and the maximum of service which he could accept.

The three persons whom we have considered present certain characteristics which will help us to distinguish between sinful behavior and behavior that is symptomatic of sickness. Their actions were unusual and unpredictable. (John, for example, would jump up and leave the church.) Their behavior was not in keeping with their usual mode of conduct. (Mr. Ambrose's wife was shocked when he cursed her, for she had never heard him curse before.) Their attitudes were not consistent with reality. (Pastor Johnson was anxious even when reassured about his income tax.) They were not amenable to "reason." None of them would accept logical arguments, even about going to a hospital. Some inner compulsion which they could not express seemed to guide them. When Pastor Johnson talked about dying, he was serious. He admitted to his psychiatrist that he contemplated suicide before he was hospitalized. A sick man can damage himself or others unless we see his sickness and accept responsibility for interpreting this to him and his family.

It may not be possible or even profitable for psychotherapists and theologians to engage in protracted debate about the existence of God as the source of human love, but it is certainly worthwhile to realize that in both disciplines there has been a tearing down of false gods masquerading as judges or authoritarian father figures, determined to support and defend society's mores as the revelation of divine truth.

Religion and Mental Health

A Theological Point of View

Robert W. Duke

It is not unusual for a seminary student on probation to confess that he is experiencing scholastic difficulties because of personal problems which vitiate the quality of his work and, in fact, impede his conscious effort to improve. Indeed, long experience justifies the observation that personal matters such as identity, vocational goals, marital problems, the great expectations of others, as well as feelings of guilt concerning solemn vows once made in the sight of man, all play their part in the process by which and in which a man thinks and acts. The pastor who thinks, as he prepares his sermon, that he is confronting only a congregation of rational men and women need but examine his own internal life to realize how limited an understanding of man that is!

This commonplace is simply a phenomenological point of contact between the psychologically oriented disciplines and the biblical description of man. Each in its own way speaks of man as a body-spirit continuum, so cunningly fashioned that no one part of that organism may function except that its influence is felt in the entire human being. Both points of view, as they focus on man, magnify this symbol. The Cartesian dualism of thought and extension, that is, of man the thinking animal, who in serene detachment imposes order upon the eruptive flux of experience, shaping it according to the order-

Reprinted from *Pastoral Psychology* 21, no. 204 (1970): 14–18. Used by permission.

ing principles of his mind, is no longer an acceptable image of the way
in which man thinks and acts.

There is a fund of experiential data, the contributions from a variety
of disciplines, suggesting that man's affective, bodily, feeling-concerns
play a prominent role in his image of himself. Indeed, it is commonly
accepted that a vast world of unconscious or subconscious needs and
desires lie latent at the threshold of conscious behavior, largely unrec-
ognized, but immensely important in shaping a man's style of life, his
social behavior, and the goals he deems to be eminently important for
him. Indeed, it appears that man's inveterate process of rationalization, a technique of self-deception he employs to mask the truth from
himself under the guise of reason, enables him to deny these facts of
his own psychic life. T. S. Eliot grasps this process in the following
images:

> We only ask to be reassured
> About the noises in the cellar
> And the window that should not have been open:
> Why do we all behave as if the door might suddenly open, the curtains
>   be drawn.
> The cellar make some dreadful disclosure, the roof disappear,
> And we should cease to be sure of what is real or unreal?
> Hold tight, hold tight, we must insist that the world is what we have
>   always taken it to be.[1]

There is, furthermore, a common ground shared by psychotherapy
and religion with respect to their understanding of man's relation to
other men. The Old Testament understanding of man, aptly pictured
in H. Wheeler Robinson's famous image of "corporate personality,"
finds its analogues in contemporary sociological and psychological
descriptions of man's intrinsic relations to the primary groups from
which he springs. The New Testament witness to man's essential participation in the society from which he comes is confessed in many
places; one of particular note is I John 4:19, "We love, because he first
loved us." In this personal relationship, the Christian is born out of
the womb of the church through the sacrament of baptism. He is given
a name, and a way of life is fashioned for him in which he grows.
Whoever he will become as a person, the experiences of love, security,
faith, and trust will have been, as it were, implanted through those
initial relations.

Man does not make himself out of himself in isolation, and no
understanding of how man acts and why he thinks the way he does

---

1. *The Family Reunion*, Part I, Scene 1, p. 39 (Harcourt, Brace).

may ignore his origins. To be sure, the interpretation given to the sources of these relations and their meanings vary, but from a phenomenological point of view, one can hardly ignore their striking similarity. Indeed, it is not uncommon for students of man's social nature to refer to John Donne's famous phrase, "No man is an island entire of itself; every man is a piece of the continent . . . ," when seeking to describe mankind's interdependence. It is not without significance that few trouble to note that the original source of that striking thought is a meditation on the church in which Donne says, "The Church is catholic, universal, so are all her actions; all that she does belongs to all. When she baptizes a child that action concerns me, for that child is thereby connected to that Head which is my Head too, and engrafted into that body whereof I am a member. And when she buries a man, that action concerns me: all mankind is of one Author and is one volume."[2]

These intricate relations between man and society and within himself direct our attention to another place of meeting between psychotherapy and religion in terms of a common reexamination of what is meant by sin, and how a man receives forgiveness, and learns to accept himself. For a long time, Protestant theology, dominated by a Pelagian view of man in terms of his free will, taught that by conscious effort man could work out his own salvation. The so-called doctrine of works is characteristic of a large segment of American Protestantism, which subverted its biblical allegiance and sold itself to rationalism. Now certainly, words like "sin," "forgiveness," and "guilt" mean different things when psychotherapists and theologians first begin to talk together, and yet both might well find themselves agreeing with Luther when he speaks of "free will."

> I wish that word "free will" had never been invented. It is not in the Scriptures, and it were better to call it "self-will" which profiteth not. Or, if anyone wishes to retain it, he ought to apply it to the new-created man, so as to understand by it the man who is without sin. He is assuredly free, as was Adam in Paradise, and it is of him that Scriptures speak when they touch upon our freedom; but they who lie in sins are unfree and prisoners of the devil; yet because they can become free through grace, you can call them men of free will, just as you might call a man rich, although he is a beggar, because he can become rich. But it is neither right nor good thus to juggle with words in matters of such seriousness.[3]

2. "Meditation XVII." *The Complete Poetry and Selected Prose of John Donne* (Modern Library).

3. Kerr, Hugh T., Jr., ed. *A Compendium of Luther's Theology*, p. 91 (Westminster Press).

Both the psychologist and the pastoral counselor would share, I believe, the common opinion that the student suffering from scholastic deficiencies, referred to initially in this article, is not going to overcome his academic difficulties by sheer will power, through attention to the demands of his intellect together with a rigorous exclusion from his conscious mind of all other concerns. Indeed, it might be possible to go further and observe that the academic problems may not be the real issue at all, but that his questions about vocation, his relations with the opposite sex, or lack of them, and his feelings of guilt about his own failure direct attention to deeper issues which must be confronted. One might well ask how he interprets his own situation. Does he falsely conceive of himself as a sinner? Does he convict himself, actually superficially, mistaking a neurosis for something far deeper, having to do with a total view of himself and his relation to the one whom he calls God? There is indeed a wretchedness of which the apostle Paul speaks, the deep-rooted and ultimately creative conviction that a man cannot work out his own salvation, that he is in bondage to and captive of "the law of sin which dwells in my members." But that insight into the genuine sources of help is the gracious fruition of the endless self-analysis of a mature conscience, revealing a person of great personal strength who is able to admit his need for help, his dependence upon another, as well as his dissatisfaction with his life.

Rightly understood, the Christian doctrine of sin is the most hope-giving relation a man can accept as an interpretation of his own nature. Sin, in this view, is not a series of discreet moral lapses like smoking, drinking, swearing, as well as signs of virtue by which a prideful man may appear humble and a sinful man good, but is rather a basic disposition of man to create the illusion that he can solve his own problems because the basis of his salvation lies within himself. Indeed, one might penetrate more deeply and observe that, as in Paul's situation, a man's knowledge of himself is not actually a product of his own private self-examination, but is a knowledge communicated to him. Paul's self-understanding developed in relation to his meditation upon the God who revealed Himself in Jesus Christ. He knew who he was because he had come to know who Christ was to him and for him. The "I" conferring identity on him was the product of a relationship with God in Christ. It was this kind of knowledge which supported Paul, encouraged him, and was the enabling power which held him together, directing his total energies in endless acts of self-giving, a process, incidentally, which paradoxically only served to strengthen rather than weaken his psychic energy.

It would be possible to describe some dimensions of Paul's dilemma psychologically without suffering from the mistake of psychologism, by observing that Saul, the law-abiding Pharisee, suffered from a bad conscience, a punitive and deceptive notion of the law, and consequently from an egocentricity which did nothing to increase his self-respect. It seems to me that, once again, there is a point of encounter between psychotherapy and religion in their agreement that there is a world of difference between self-love and egocentricity, and that man's genuine understanding of himself is both a revelation and a discovery found in relationships. The therapist serves a most creative function when through the process of counseling he enables the patient to see for himself that there is a distinction between what Paul Tournier calls " 'functional guilt,' which results from social suggestion, fears of taboos or losing the love of others," and " 'value guilt,' that genuine consciousness of having betrayed an authentic standard." This "is a free judgment of the self by the self."[4]

I have sought so far to stress certain key terms such as the self and others, community, and relationship; words whose symbolic connotations are meaningful in both theological and psychological disciplines. I would like now to advance the argument a step further by examining a certain quality of those relations which is productive of psychological and religious health. It has always struck me as a point of overwhelming significance, particularly in view of the one-sided interpretations easily made of him, that Karl Barth's lengthy and exhaustive description of man's sinful nature is subsumed in his *Church Dogmatics* under the "Doctrine of Reconciliation." That is, the judgment upon man's propensity for self-annihilation made by religion is pronounced within the framework of a profound and unyielding acceptance of man for what he is, as he is, without excuse; accepted because he is man, because he is God's own creature. There is, it seems to me at least, a sound basis for health in this relationship, because it is a penetrating yet compassionate look beyond the disguises, beneath the masks, below the surfaces of cordial deception, to the sick turmoil writhing within, inverted in its overt form into gestures of serenity and obedience.

I refer you now to a passage from Barth's lecture, "The Humanity of God":

We have to regard each human being, even the oddest, most infamous or wretched, from the point of view that on the basis of the eternal decision of God, Jesus Christ is also his Brother, God Himself is also his

4. *Guilt and Grace*, p. 64 (Harper & Row).

Father. On that assumption we have to associate with him. If that is already known to him, we have to strengthen him in it. If he does not yet know it or knows it no longer, it is our job to impart that knowledge to him. When the humanity of God is perceived, no other attitude is possible to any fellow man. It is identical with the practical recognition of his human rights and his human dignity. If we refuse it to him, we should, on our side, be renouncing Jesus Christ as our Brother and God as our Father.[5]

It seems to me that this understanding of the way in which man is viewed moves beneath the superficial levels of judgment to a determined, suffering acceptance which is self-authenticating, making possible a new kind of person.

Counseling relationships within the church, based on law, tend to substitute new laws for a new person. The rigid person comes to the pastor hoping to be chastised, anxious to be pronounced guilty, desiring to be penalized, hoping for the word of authority which will solve his dilemma. Nothing of the deep-rooted reasons for behavior is satisfactorily explored, the person's self-hate is increased, much to his satisfaction and shame. Strangely enough, if the person were to slip and fall from grace again, there is always the assurance that the combination of guilt, condemnation, and good works will somehow solve the problem, until the next time. My point is that there is no new creation, there is no new being, and there is no relationship which makes this transformation possible. The New Testament talks about new persons, new in the sense that their entire life is reoriented through an admittedly painful but permissive relationship in which other persons, serving as priests to one another, enable the individual gropingly, haltingly, but with increasing confidence to achieve some new and healthy understanding not only of his own life—its genuine goals and needs—but of the demands and promises of religion.

It may not be possible or even profitable for psychotherapists and theologians to engage in protracted debate about the existence of God as the source of human love, but it is certainly worthwhile to realize that in both disciplines there has been a tearing down of false gods masquerading as judges or authoritarian father figures, determined to support and defend society's mores as the revelation of divine truth. Furthermore, there has been a growing consensus that man's health as a creative human being demands that he be understood holistically, and that his growth, not unashamedly spoken of in terms of sanctification, be understood as a process of acceptance, forgiveness, as well as firmness.

5. *The Humanity of God*, p. 43 (John Knox Press).

That portion of Protestant worship, often conducted in such a matter-of-fact fashion, which deals with our corporate confession and absolution, ritualistically embraces a fundamental religious attitude. In religious terms it symbolizes the heart of the counseling process. One confesses because he knows that he is accepted. One tells all, because he knows he is known. One admits all, because he knows that this searching honesty is an essential ingredient in the process of his own spiritual growth. Whether or not this relationship is an experience of the depths of human love as a process of personal transformation, or whether it is actually an empirical manifestation of the love of God controlling us, is of course an act of faith. It does seem to me, though, that the pastor's own faith, his own understanding of who he is, and the nature of his calling are fundamental to the meaning of the relationship developed. I find these words from a sermon by Karl Barth most illuminating at this point, and shall close with them:

> We should get the simple truth straight, dear friends. We are in the world not to comfort ourselves, but to comfort others. Yet the one and only genuine comfort we may offer to our fellowmen is this reflection of heaven, of Jesus Christ, of God himself, as it appears on a radiant face. Why don't we do it? Why do we withhold from them the one comfort of mutual benefit? Why are the faces we show each other at best superior looking, serious, questioning, sorrowful and reproachful faces, at worst even grimaces or lifeless masks, real Carnival masks? Why don't our faces shine?[6]

---

6. "Look Up to Him!" in *Deliverance to the Captives*, p. 48 (Harper & Row).

Salvation has a "from," a "to," a "by," and a "feeling" dimension. It is a direction, not a condition based on the fact that to be human is to be spirit—not have a spirit. Sin is bondage and salvation is freedom. The meaning of health in the New Testament is different from health as currently conceived. While modern views of health attempt to get body and mind together, the biblical view never perceives them as separate and views health as uniting humans to God.

Salvation's Message about Health

Seward Hiltner

Salvation in the New Testament

1. *Salvation has a 'from' dimension.* The person or group who knows and experiences salvation is thereby rescued from some kind of bondage or undesirable previous condition. This is variously interpreted as salvation from bondage to the law, or from libertarianism, or from 'flesh' (*sarx*), in Paul's use of that term to refer to what we now call inordinate and compulsive preoccupations. We are saved from the power of sin, and from death as an enemy. Whether as person or group, we are saved not from every preexisting condition but from everything that means bondage in actual fact.

It is important to note that no fundamental distinction is made between the kinds of bondage which, while we were enslaved by them, we recognized as bondage—and those other types of bondage that are seen in their true light only after we have been saved. A man who has a disease knows he is in bondage then. A man following Paul's 'lusts of the flesh' may not at that time know he is in bondage, but may become aware of the true situation only after his rescue. Therefore, the one accurate way of appraising what is bondage is retrospective.

2. *Salvation has a 'to' dimension.* The person or group is saved to live in and enjoy Paul's 'fruits of the spirit', such as love, joy, and

Reprinted from *International Review of Missions* 57, no. 2 (1968): 157–74. Used by permission.

peace. In modern language, the 'to' represents in each instance the opposite of any particular bondage. Generally speaking, the 'to' is thought of in terms of freedom, of release, of an exultant relaxation of the previous tension. It is like awakening to find that one has just crossed an abyss, of which one was perhaps unaware while the crossing was taking place.

In the reflection of the person or group, the 'from' and the 'to' dimensions are inextricably interrelated. If one has been under bondage to the law, then the new reality rises above the law although it does not negate the law's intent. If one was under bondage to impulses, then the new reality brings discipline through discipleship. If the bondage was disease and thus limitation of function, then salvation from it means relative ease and flexibility of function. It is impossible to define salvation, and its meaning for any person or group, without concomitant reference to the 'from' and 'to' dimensions, and the relationship between them.

3. *Salvation has a positive feeling dimension.* Taken in and of itself, an exultant positive feeling might of course be deceptive, as Paul had to remind the Corinthians. But when seen in proper context, and along with the other points we are noting, then it is impossible to think of salvation as grim lack of emotion and feeling.

This point is more important than appears at first glance. A consistency is called for between the actual situation and one's feelings. The positive feeling, however, even though its initial elation will have to give way to a quieter joy, just as a honeymoon fades into a happy marriage, can never become business as usual, or be taken for granted. But this means that a complete forgetting of the bondage from which one has been released would be an enemy to the proper feeling tone here and hereafter. No longer is there compulsive preoccupation with the bondage of the past, but neither is it forgotten.

4. *Salvation has a 'by' dimension.* This is of course by God in Jesus Christ. It is, however, referred to in various ways in order to demonstrate and clarify different but equally important aspects of the central truth. When we say that it is by grace, we emphasize God's love and goodness and His call for an active response of true gratitude. This grace, seen through our faith, highlights what God has done to change our perspective in acknowledging the person and work of Jesus Christ as effective agent of our salvation, and induces our continuing belief and trust in Him. There are of course other aspects than those we have named. In Hebrews, for instance, we find the declaration of the consistency of God's saving acts now in Jesus Christ, and previously in His dealings with the Jewish people as His agents for the salvation of mankind.

When the 'by' is fully spelled out, there is always a 'not by' set against it. It is by faith not works, by grace not merit, by truly hearing God and not yelling at Him, by seeing Jesus on the Cross and not solely as risen. Even when the 'not by' is not articulated, it can always be supplied if the 'by' is given.

5. *Salvation is in every dimension of time.* The *kairos* has come, and thus salvation is real only if it is, most obviously, now. It is time fulfilled. We are to put behind us the things that are past, in the sense that they are no longer to be our ruling preoccupations. But we are not to forget them, nor fail to remember that in our past as in our present God was striving mightily to save us. And looking ahead to the things that are before, we are to be neither complacent nor anxiously apprehensive. If salvation is a fact now, then it is equally a fact of past and future, even if we cannot spell out details of the future or blot out details of the past. Salvation is contemporaneous. And it is the realism of this contemporaneity which enables us to deal with both past and future appropriately, looking to the past with sorrow but without guilt, and to the future with prudent confidence but without apprehensive anxiety.

6. *Salvation is a direction, not a status or condition.* Even when salvation has caught us up, and all of life past, present, and future is approached in a different way, we are not automatically wrapped in something which eliminates sin and removes either the prospective fact or fear of death, or which gives us infallible guidance on our decisions by some heavenly radar. Especially Protestantism, in interpreters such as Luther and Reinhold Niebuhr, have correctly sensed that this means the necessity of some uneasiness in Christian persons or groups. Even saved, we are constantly moving in realms of ambiguity. What we do have is a kind of direction-finder, but not a detailed map.

If salvation is thought of as a status or condition, rather than as a direction, then it may result in the worst forms of arrogance on the one side or irresponsibility on the other. It may be linguistically awkward to ask, "Are you in process of being saved?" But it is more accurate than, "Are you saved?"

7. *The object of God's saving is man as spirit.* Man does not *have* spirit. He *is* spirit. His spiritual nature is his whole nature, and it carries two equally important corollaries: first, that spirit means man in his true unity and integrity; and second, that his wholeness and integrity are derivative from God as Spirit. Man's soma and his psyche are parts of him, indispensable aspects. But they cannot be regarded as forming a coordinate series with spirit. Spirit answers a different kind of question.

Salvation is directed to man as spirit, that is, to man in his true integrity being made derivatively in the image of God, and with the image restored through the person and work of Jesus Christ. If a man is in this process of being saved, in the larger sense of his genuine unity, what happens to his psyche and his soma? The New Testament writers were tempted, at this point, to beat the drums and to allege that true salvation of man as spirit automatically means cure of body and mind. Happily, the temptation was resisted. To be sure, the new faith will have a positive effect upon body and mind. But some conditions in psyche or soma or both may have become relatively irreversible. And, on the other side, if salvation healed all diseases automatically, then the search for salvation would become calculating prudence. As we have seen in the story of the man born blind, and healed by Jesus, calculation must be completely set aside. Accept Jesus as Lord in order to get over your virus infection? This is an unthinkable sequence of events in the New Testament.

This list of seven mutually reinforcing and equally indispensable aspects of salvation could of course be added to for purposes of clarification. We could note that the focus is on the ever-present relation of person and group, the one never becoming a mere derivative of the other. We could see the fellowship as plainly nurturing the person into the salvatory process, and then the person as naturally moving into the fellowship to aid its purposes.

We could also elaborate upon the church, the kingdom of God, the resurrection of the body, and many other points that follow from the basic understanding of the salvation, by God through Jesus Christ, of man and mankind. There would also be the work of the Holy Spirit, the meaning of divine providence and of sanctification, of the means of grace, of the nature of forgiveness, and much else. For Christian thought hangs together and is all of a piece. Yet I think it may be argued that the indispensable dimensions of salvation have been given in the seven schematic points, and that these others are implications of them, if we begin our inquiry at the point of salvation.

Since, however, the principle opposite of salvation is sin, we do need to complete this compendious account of salvation by a brief analysis of sin. This too may be done schematically but in shorter form.

1. *Sin is that part of man's bondage for which he is responsible.* From the perspective of salvation, sin is the word for man's central predicament. It is not necessarily related to tornados, earthquakes, or microbes.

2. *Sin is both actual and original.* That is, sin is both individual or voluntary, and collective or of social inheritance. There can be neither

condemnation by assigning blame, nor white-washing by pleas of being victimized. Both factors are always involved.

3. *The meaning of sin can be grasped only through metaphors.* The principal ones which have been used are rebellion, alienation, and missing the mark, with the last predominating in the New Testament. Each metaphor seems suited to a particular age, but each adds dimensions of meaning which no era can afford to discard. The metaphor of alienation, along with that of the net or web, seems best communicative for our own day.

4. *The news of sin is good news.* The person or group who grasps and accepts the enormity of sin could not possibly do so unless prevenient grace were at work; so that even the bare beginnings of repentance, or sad acknowledgment of sinfulness, are indications of constructive change in direction, and therefore, good news.

5. *Salvation breaks the power of sin but does not make man sinless.* A fundamentally new direction has been taken, so although there is no map to be followed among life's ambiguities, slips cannot be what they were before, provided there is persistent turning again to the source of salvation, Jesus Christ, for forgiveness and redirection. But any perfectionism that alleges sinlessness mistakes salvation to be a condition rather than a direction, a possession rather than a gift.

6. *While in the salvatory process, we are to 'sin bravely'.* The focus of our attention, as Luther saw so clearly, is to be on putting on Christ to our neighbor humbly but energetically. It is not to be on a finicky avoidance of any sin, for that may result in the worst sin of all: smug pride and obsessive self-concern.

7. *From the perspective of salvation, sin is the decisive enemy.* But in this actual world in which God has given some freedom to all creatures and all events, many lesser enemies stand in the way of various aspects of man's values: his life, his physical and mental health, his social organization, etc. Although salvation is to be sought first, it implies a consequent pursuit of the supportive values, and a continual struggle against other enemies.

Health in the New Testament

In modern thought, four assumptions are made about that to which the term *health* refers. Later on, we shall examine these assumptions, and the implications that have been drawn from them in modern reflection concerning health. What we cannot do is to include these assumptions in the meaning we assign to the term *health* when we ask what the Bible says about it. For these assumptions are not found in the New Testament. That does not mean the New Testament is against them. It simply means that it makes different kinds of assumptions about what is being referred to by the notion of 'health'.

The first modern assumption is that *health is a condition of the individual person*. To be sure, we have public health and many measures to ensure that all members of a community will have their health protected or restored. But the primary reference is to the individual. The second and related assumption is that *we use 'health' as referring only analogously to conditions at the social or cosmic levels*. We do not deny the validity of partial analogies. But all analogies are projected from the individual person, and none in the other direction. The third modern assumption about what health refers to is that *we begin with soma and pride ourselves on growing attention to psyche*. In too many instances, psyche is still barely noticed. But in no quarter is there repentance for the kind of thought that produced the categorical division. The fourth assumption is that *health is something everybody wants as well as needs*. That is, health is a secular value transcending all lines of division, belief, religion, philosophy, or politics. Thus, health is defined as something to be seen in its own context.

When we turn to the New Testament, however, we find none of these assumptions at work.

1. *Whatever health may be, it is a condition of the individual person only derivatively from cosmic 'wholeness'*. One does not begin from individual toothaches and viruses and then make social or cosmic analogies. The method is the other way round. Individual illness is relative lack of wholeness, and is actually to be understood as a symptom of the disrupted and broken relationships in the whole creation. This is of course no denial of the reality of illness and disease, nor is it a theory of causation in the scientific sense. It is simply a quite different way of looking at these phenomena. It is radically different from the modern way.

2. *Although relatively free functioning (or restoration of functioning) of either soma or psyche or both are seen as positive values, they are not viewed as ends in themselves, as if that context were sufficient*. Health and healing are good at every level, but the higher (integrating more complexities) levels supply the total context. The Good Samaritan got the injured man to the inn and did not preach him a sermon; but the central message of the story is about his higher commitment which enabled him to transcend provincial enmity. When the Gadarene was restored and 'in his right mind', he was forbidden simply to tag along behind Jesus, and was sent back to the very place where he had first become mentally ill. Acts of healing can and should be done at every needed level. But both the motivation toward them and the appraisal

of their significance are to be seen in a context transcending the acts themselves.

3. *Whatever health of psyche or soma may mean, they are regarded as equally necessary aspects of the same reality.* The reason for this is that they are seen as derivative aspects of cosmic wholeness, so far as it exists and is not negated by the cosmic disruption. There is no special disposition, as in the modern world, to think of soma as clearly real, and then of psyche as maybe real and perhaps related. Health of psyche-soma, however, although a positive value, is not to be equated with general 'wholeness'.

4. *The Bible does not recommend any instrumentalities, even faith, for the purpose of maintaining health or effecting healing.* This is partly because the biblical concern was not scientific or technical, partly because of the status of medicine in biblical days, and partly because the biblical focus simply was elsewhere. But with its realism based in the Jewish tradition, this was no denial of the need for appropriate instrumentalities. It simply was not the job of the biblical writers to consider them, except in avoiding the calculation which might lead to a pursuit of the more restricted value of health or healing by the wrong use of salvation as instrumentality.

5. *The highest value is cosmic wholeness (or its restoration), in which the salvatory process enables us to participate both now and hereafter. That highest value is not 'health' in any more limited sense.* We must not be misled by the common terms and derivations into overlooking the whole context of the New Testament treatment. There is no biblical warrant for taking 'health' in an individualistic, focally somatic sense which has no context beyond relatively free functioning, and escalating it to the top of the scale of values.

In attempting to set forth the New Testament understanding of 'health' in a somewhat more restricted sense than that of salvation or wholeness, it is no part of our intention to suggest that nothing else in the Bible bears upon the modern understanding of health. But unless we keep clearly before us the differences between current concerns and those of the New Testament, we shall fail to do justice to either.

Modern Views of Health

We already suggested four modern assumptions about what is referred to today as 'health'. These view the locus of health as the individual person, the meaning of health as only an analogy if extended to the group or cosmos, the psyche and soma as things we must try to bring together, and the value of health as applying to every person.

On the basis of these assumptions, several theories of health can be set forth, some of them more articulately and others more epiphenomenally, to give the following conceptions of disease and illness. These views are not mutually exclusive; yet, finally, some choices must be made among them.

1. *Health is simply the absence of impairment of function.* If the person is able to carry out the functions which are statistically necessary (such as eating, walking, sleeping, and working), without undue pain or stress, then in this epiphenomenal kind of definition, he is healthy even if he has some structural defect. He might have poor eyesight corrected by spectacles, only one kidney compensated for by the other, or but one arm compensated for functionally by the other arm, the feet, and the mouth. This kind of conception can also be carried over into the psychic realm, where the relative absence of stress, anxiety, and guilt would be similar to the relative absence of pain and stricture of movement. The model lying behind this conception of health tends to be mechanical. There is health when the parts work both separately and together.

2. *Health is the positive capacity to engage in and enjoy functions.* This conception differs from the first in its attempt to make a more positive statement. It presupposes the absence of impairment of function, and then adds that performance of function should bring subjective feelings of satisfaction or enjoyment. The model behind this theory is still basically mechanical, but it is 'mechanics with a heart', somewhat like the older vitalism in biology.

3. *Health is the capacity of the whole human organism to adapt itself to a constantly changing external and internal environment.* This is the homeostatic theory of health. It emphasizes the capacity of the organism, seen somatically or psychically or both, to return after stress situations to integrated stability. It also stresses health as 'successful communication' between parts and whole. The model behind it is cybernetic in nature.

4. *Health is viewed as the condition which results from a combination of appropriate human relatedness and appropriate energy investment.* Freud's conception of health as proper 'love and work' is a good illustration of this view. Here the focus of health is on the overall relationship between the person and his environment, rather than on the capacity to restore temporarily impeded function. The model behind this theory seems to be like the quantum theory in physics, or perhaps even like a lifestyle.

5. *Health is seen as the top of the hierarchy of all human values.* This theory begins by making no distinction between health and wholeness in every sense of the latter term. It then proceeds by regarding the

integration of complexities as an unlimited good. On this basis, when any good integrative thing or process is found, it is subsumed under health as wholeness. Thus all values which focus on the person are taken to be real or authentic health. The model here is somewhat like a ladder. Every time one climbs a higher rung, he finds that health was there before him. It is also like an expanding series of concentric circles, with health as the widest and most far-flung.

6. *Health is the organism's contributing optimally to the community or collectivity.* We do not know to what extent this conception of health prevails in totalitarian countries. It is of course rare in Western countries. If set forth in extreme form, it would make health much like a beehive. However, a subtle version of it is found in Jung, where the theory becomes a dialectic between individuation and relation to collectivity.

7. *Health is the organismic 'enabling' or base value needed in some degree for all other values to rest upon.* This view can accept the intent of conceptions 1 through 4, but must reject views 5 and 6. Unlike views 1 through 4, however, it guards against both health as an epiphenomenon or result, and health as a possible value seen only for its own sake. It insists that the human meaning of health is a combination of its indispensability and its functions as a base or as an 'enabler'. Health neither competes with love, justice, wisdom, peace, and creativity, nor does it guarantee them. It is no substitute for them; but they are impossible without some degree of health. The model lying behind this conception shows health as the base of a pyramid. Without it the walls of the pyramid, other values, could not be erected. But the base is just that, and not a substitute for the top, nor any assurance that the walls will be correctly built.

Christian Critique of Modern Health Conceptions

It is my contention that the modern theory of health best supported by the New Testament understanding of both salvation and health is the seventh, which regards health as an enabling value. The biblical account cannot be against any of the first four views of health, provided they are in some way set into a larger and more appropriate context. But since none of these views supplies such a context, then the vote goes to the enablement theory, which may of course draw content from any or all of the first four views.

The New Testament must stand clearly against the fifth view, which sees health as escalating so as to absorb all other values. It is this view of health which becomes a direct competitor to the Christian understanding of salvation in Western countries. In certain nations, it may be the sixth, or collectivist, view of health that the New Testament must oppose. In principle, the views of health which with Christianity cannot be reconciled are those which, either by secularization or imperialism, render the need for salvation irrelevant. In the Christian view, health is the base even for salvation. But health in any modern sense is not to be equated with salvation; it does not substitute for salvation; and it does not guarantee salvation. On the other hand, there can be no degree of salvation, for person or group, without some degree of health. Any improvement in health always offers a potentiality for progress in the salvatory process.

This conclusion may be further supported by returning to the seven indispensable dimensions of salvation as delineated in the first section.

The person whose health is enhanced or restored *from* a previous condition of some degree of illness or disease has added a great positive value. This is equally valuable if, before, he had pain and distress, or if he had a cancer of which he was unaware and which had so far produced no pain. But the release, restoration, and enhancement that come with effective treatment are not what his life is for. They simply enable him to get on with those values.

By the same token, the *to* which he reaches when there is healing or enhancement of health provides a positive freedom in which new values may be pursued more diligently or joyfully. But it is not sufficient to define the new joy and peace in terms of subjective feelings which carry no action consequences.

On the other hand, if the person released from illness finds no enhancement of *positive feeling* in the process, then it is dubious whether the new condition has embraced the psychic area.

The fourth dimension of salvation noted was *by* God's action in Jesus Christ. If a man has enough health, or enough is restored to him, to enable him to pursue other values, then he knows that ultimately this base is a gift. To be sure, it is a gift for which he exercises some stewardship through diet and exercise and untangling mental conflicts; but it comes finally from grace, and his proper response is gratitude. If, on the other hand, he begins to think of health itself as the highest value, the attitude moves subtly from gratitude to achievement. And the *by* is then likely to be forgotten.

The fifth dimension of salvation was concerned with *time*. The man with health enhanced or restored rejoices in a relatively free-functioning present as he could not in the past, and does not quail before a prospective future as he had previously done. With no value but this health he could very easily feel guilty about his past and apprehensive about his future. If, however, health is to enable, then past and future, along with the present, fall into place.

The sixth dimension saw salvation as *direction*, not condition. The man with health restored or enhanced (if health is an enabler) is not preoccupied with his new and better condition, but turns at once to ask himself what he is going to do with it, what values he intends now to pursue. If, instead, he wonders, "Now that I have more health, how can I get even more than this?" he becomes narcissistically turned in upon himself and, in the obsession of his cultivation, may lose the health he has.

The seventh dimension of salvation asserted that the *object of God's saving action is man as spirit.* Under the enabling theory of health in the modern sense, the provision of a more or less sound health base which can support various values shows health to be a necessary aid to spirit. If there were no health at all, there would be no man and no spirit. Health and spirit do not operate in watertight compartments; but at the same time, health exists to serve spirit, not the other way round. More spirit does not necessarily mean more health, provided the health base was relatively adequate to start from. In contrast, if health is seen as the highest value, or the summa of values, then it is likely to be so viewed that man ceases to grasp his unity and integrity as spirit. He no longer even wants to become what he truly is.

All seven of the dimensions of salvation, therefore, reinforce the understanding of health (in the modern sense) as an enablement, and not as topmost value. A similar set of arguments could be set forth against the view of health in the purely collectivist sense. As we shall see, the Western temptation to focus exclusively upon individualism in relation to health requires correction. But this cannot be done by assigning no value to the person, including the health base that enables him to be a person in community.

Having examined the advantages of the enablement theory of health in light of the several dimensions of salvation, we may now return to the four basic assumptions of the modern world concerning what is meant when the word *health* is used. We have already noted that the New Testament does not make these assumptions about what health is. We have also pointed out that the discrepancy is not necessarily because the Bible is against these assumptions, when in proper context, but because its concern and focus lie elsewhere. Let us look at these assumptions once again, in the light of the biblical understanding of salvation.

The first modern assumption is that *health is a condition of the individual person.* We saw that the Bible comes at it the other way round. But the Bible is, derivatively from cosmic health, also clearly interested in the health of the person and therefore has, inferentially, no objection to calling 'health' something which is primarily related to individual welfare—so long only as, in the larger context, it is recalled that any health of the person is corollary to the cosmic health created by God, and so long as salvation is not thought of as a kind of summation of all the individual healths. After all, the crux of the modern assumption is necessary attention to individuality, which is a proper working out of the biblical intent.

We noted the second modern assumption as using *'health' only analogously in relation to conditions at social or cosmic levels.* This is really the other side of the first assumption. In view of the very different technologies developed for fostering health in the individual person— whether through clinical and public health measures or those needed to foster 'health' in a group, between races or nations—it is the part of wisdom to apply different terms to the foci of these respective tasks. The biblical criticism would appear only if 'health,' when formally associated with the person, were escalated as if nothing had to be done to races or nations except 'heal' their 'illness,' by some amateur extrapolation of medicine to disrupted bureaucrats everywhere.

We noted the third modern assumption about health as trying to *get soma and psyche back together.* The New Testament can have no quarrel with this aim, since it never saw the two as separate. What it does say is: go ahead and bring them together, without losing any of the modern differentiated knowledge; but watch your attitude in the process; do not be proud of your achievement; be repentant about why it took so long to get round to it. Psyche and soma are not entities, but valid and essential perspectives upon the total functioning human organism.

The fourth modern assumption about health is as *something everybody both wants and needs.* In revealing some of the psychic complexities which also affect soma, medicine and psychiatry have shown that health is not clearly something that everyone wants unambiguously; and sociology and anthropology show similar ambiguity for groups. On the other side, it is true that the desire for health, at least in the formal sense, has been advancing very rapidly. After politics, every new nation looks first at its food production and its medical facilities. In a general sense, health has been secularized even amongst us. Granted the world situation, we should deem it a proper inference from the Bible to welcome this fact—but again, only so long as health is an enabling value and not at the top of the value hierarchy.

But salvation too, as the New Testament understands it, is for all men individually and collectively. The Christian can be for health as a secular, i.e., as a fully ecumenical value, so long as he sees it as a base upon which salvation may be built. He cannot separate salvation from health, as if salvation were independent of health. But neither can he become so occupied with health in the modern sense that he regards salvation as equivalent to health or as absorbed by it.

It is also continuingly important for the Christian, who must accept what the modern world means by 'health,' to recognize that there is another way, the biblical way, of approaching the context in which health is to be understood. This concept is for the eyes of faith, for as many as are called to have this vision of health in the person as derivative from the creation of God. But this vision of the Christian can in no way be used to bar him from accepting the modern understanding of health, if the enablement theory is applied.

We are not justified by health alone. But we cannot be justified by grace through faith alone unless we have some health.

The Christian Concern for Health in the Modern World

I shall consider first the kind and degree of attention to health that seems appropriate in the light of the foregoing discussion. I shall then turn to the proper concern of the Christian and the church for the restoration of health, and for the maintenance and enhancement of health.

Attention to Health. It seems crystal clear that, with health as an enabling value, very serious attention to health is called for, both that of ourselves and of all other men. Since the Bible is no respecter of special methods, all demonstrably effective methods are to be approved. Thus there can be no quarrel with any science and technology that demonstrate what is and is not effective, unless morally or otherwise they should use methods that subvert values beyond health itself. The time has come when we should, without qualification, apply this same criterion to the basic health of the psyche, also understood as an enabling value. The provincial prejudices against psychiatry for calling a spade a spade about sex, hostility, inner turmoil, and the like, receive no warrant from Christian thought as I conceive it. I am of course against all faddisms, because they are not engaged in serious and discriminating inquiry about their relative effectiveness.

When health is seriously threatened, it is very human to be wholly preoccupied with it until restoration is brought about. Although I believe that such preoccupation ought not to be the normal condition of Christians, I see nothing in the compassion of Christian understanding that would regard such preoccupation, under threat, as reprehensible. It is high time that we got over the repressive moralism under which the better attitude when confronted with serious illness is to smile and to try to please God by professing calm and joy, when the actual interior is churning with negative feelings of all kinds. God made us men and not angels. What is needed is honest acknowledgment and sharing of such feelings, not their repressive denial. God understands them. We should also.

It is true, however, that the tendency to escalate health in the modern sense has gone so far that many persons, in confronting serious illness, have added needless anxiety because they have no other real value but health. Our main help here, I think, can be in a realistic lifting up of this whole matter in our congregations, our hospitals, and elsewhere. We are almost the sole critical interpreters of 'justification by health alone'. We need to do more of it, at the same time that we are helping those threatened to acknowledge and let God receive their true, although temporary, negative feelings.

Yet despite the health cult, there is in nearly every land a group of people—usually men—who identify virility and masculinity and autonomy with paying as little attention as possible to health. They may never see a physician unless an accident occurs. They should be helped to see that attentiveness to health is part of our humanity and not, as they often think, of weakness or femininity.

What is the Christian view towards attention to various practices of physical and mental hygiene? The principal answer is reasonable attentiveness to reasonably demonstrated procedures, all the way from brushing the teeth and counting calories to having a friend to whom unresolved hostilities may be expressed. I think we must be very alert to the cultural provincialism of many of our individually most cherished health-supporting practices. The use of alcoholic beverages, for instance, is caught in such provincialisms, in both directions. I rather doubt that Jesus is necessarily for suntan, or for icy dips before breakfast.

On the question of how much attention to health, except at the points where we are of necessity preoccupied under threat, the general answer is that health best performs its enabling function when reasonable rules are observed and when it is otherwise not given much thought. As our Western societies proceed towards more affluence, it seems very likely that we shall have more persons at least tempted to pamper their health. Let us suppose that a person in early adult years resolved to protect his health above all things: proper diet, never a psychic strain or worry, no risk or involvement, just the right amount of exercise, a weekly medical examination, no shovelling of snow, and never an exotic dish! These days, he might live to be a hundred. But would not his attentiveness to his own health be, in fact, idolatry? If health is an enablement, then he has spent his whole life, to change the metaphor, in sharpening tools that have never been used. I believe that the temptations in this direction will increase so rapidly that we must at once begin to expose this kind of idolatry of health.

Although I hold no special brief for the few saints of masochistic disposition who used poor health as a kind of badge demonstrating their Christian devotion, I find myself very much more suspicious of those moderns unwilling to risk even the slightest aspect of their health for Christ's sake. Among more sophisticated persons, this reluctance takes increasingly the form of no deep emotional involvement, because such commitment might produce strain and blood pressure. Do we not need to interpret these matters as excluding equally foolhardy carelessness and narcissistic self-protection, no matter how sophisticated the form?

The Restoration of Health. The process of restoring health is healing. It is bringing back something which has been impaired as to either direction or schedule. When our reference is to health in the modern sense, then the healing process demands to be carried out under overall medical direction. There is every warrant from Christian thought in general medical oversight and management.

This point is very different, however, from alleging the health omnipotence or omnicompetence of physicians. If other professional and subprofessional persons are not on the health team captained by the physician, then the resources being used to foster the healing process are out of date. Further, the same is true if these persons are not given opportunity to share, albeit under the physician's chairmanship, in the decisions about both diagnosis and treatment. The day has passed in which the physician could interpret his captaincy of the health team as dictatorship.

Among the members of the health team captained by the physician is the priest or ordained minister. Even though his larger concern, both as Christian and as professional representative, is with the salvation of the sufferer, as a member of the health team he must work under the chairmanship of the physician or else his 'lone wolf' efforts, no matter how well intentioned, may contribute negatively to the health base without which there can be no salvation. To work as such a team member requires some real shifts in the psychological attitude of many clergymen. But it becomes more essential with every year that passes, especially with the increase in medical knowledge and skill. This does not mean that the pastor must take orders from the doctor. There may indeed be situations in which the pastor, having shared and listened, must conscientiously do something which his team and its captain do not favor. What he can never do is refuse to consult and to listen.

This kind of active cooperation needs to be fostered in mission hospitals and clinics wherever they exist. The two-kingdom theory of the management of mission medical enterprises, under which the physician took care of 'health' and the evangelist dealt with the 'spirit,' is no longer tenable. If pastors do not know how to work on a healing team, then they must be taught. And if physicians do not know how to include intelligent pastoral work in their team operation, then they too must learn.

Such cooperation is, however, of equal importance in hospitals, clinics, and community health centers that are conducted under secular auspices. From the point of view of the secular health institution, the chaplain is present for sociological reasons, i.e., because he represents something available in the normal community, and because the best healing takes place when as much as possible of normal community life is represented. In the church, we have of course additional reasons for wanting to be present. But the presence of an atheist as captain of a medical team provides no excuse for the clergyman to resort to being a lone wolf and consulting nobody.

It seems to me that there are two general courses of action clearly blocked out for the medical missionary enterprise, lest our healing institutions eventually become anachronisms. The first is to deploy medical and health personnel, in any area, focusing on the type of care not yet supplied by national medicine. This means, for instance, more pediatricians and psychiatrists in a situation where surgery and ophthalmology and internal medicine are increasingly well performed by national medicine. Simply clinging to the conception of medicine as led by surgery and internal medicine, regardless of other resources available, makes little sense. But the proper movement may demand severe shifts in attitude.

The other essential is educating national pastors in how to work with medical teams, whether Christian or national. I do not see how this is possible except through the leadership of the medical mission movement itself, and that means administrative leadership and fund deployment by physicians, even though the primary supervision of such education must be by pastors who have themselves had special education. We now have ample precedent in the extensive movement of clinical pastoral education in the United States, and this movement has now been extended to several other countries including Holland, Canada, Australia, New Zealand, and, in a limited way, to the Scandinavian countries.

Maintenance and Enhancement of Health. Support by the church of all valid types of preventive medicine and public health is of course called for. Inoculations against such diseases as smallpox and poliomyelitis; prenatal and well-baby clinics; mental health clinics; and all facilities of similar function can do much to protect health before serious illness can take hold.

Except in pioneer or emergency situations, I see no particular reason why the church should be more interested in such services when it manages them and finances them than when they are under other kinds of competent administration. But for many years to come, the situation in regard to preventive medicine as well as medical care will still be acute in many parts of the world. So long as this fact is true, we shall need to use all the resources we have in the church to try to meet the massive pain and suffering. But with modern economic productive capacity, and except for pockets, this situation will happily not last forever. We should not allow ourselves to become attitudinally attached to it as a permanent condition.

The 'health' people must, I think, very rapidly establish more and better working relationships with the 'social action' people. For, especially with modern productivity, and modern medical skill, the issue of how long it will take to get basic health care and preventive medicine to various parts of the world may depend more on good social action than on good usage of church medical resources.

As to what can be done preventively by congregations, I find myself at this stage a little alarmed at the apparent romanticism in viewing the congregation as a 'community of healing.' It is and must be a 'community involved in salvation,' concerned with its own mutual relationships and with the need of all men everywhere. Since health as a base is in some degree a prerequisite for potential engagement in the salvatory process, of course every congregation must be concerned about health care all over the world. But this seems to me quite different from trying to cash in on the popularity of health in the modern sense, and then subtly shifting the definition over to the different method of the Bible. Health and salvation are by no means categorically separated; but if we live in the modern world, they are by no means the same thing either.

Reviews several sets of psychological concepts that reflect the general position that mental health and mental illness are separate dimensions—not just the opposite or absence of one another. The impact of these concepts is that mental illness involves a defensive ego orientation, and mental health involves a growth-related task orientation. The position is related to concepts of conventional morality and some explicit teachings of Christ regarding self-denial and giving one's life for a greater cause. In the review of psychological concepts, S. E. Asch's "task-orientation" is juxtaposed with a "self-orientation" implicit in C. R. Roger's theory. F. Herzberg's job factor theory, the concepts of coping and defending, and G. W. Allport's intrinsic and extrinsic religious orientations also depict similar dichotomies of mental health and mental illness. Relationships between theology and psychology in general are discussed.

A Search for Mental Health

Richard D. Kahoe

For most of its history psychology has been preoccupied with mental illness and has accepted the assumption that mental health is adequately defined as the absence of mental illness. Increasingly this assumption has been questioned, and the present article relates my own search, and that of others, for a concept of mental health independent of the concept of mental illness. In fact, in recent years this search has been shared by so many psychologists (e.g., Jahoda, 1958) and the distinction between mental health and mental illness has become so familiar that the distinction may seem passé. Therefore, I can claim no basic originality in this paper. What is noteworthy is the convergence of several disparate lines of research and threads of thought from psychology and from the teachings of Jesus Christ—a convergence around self-centeredness as central to mental illness and the giving of oneself to a higher task as central to mental health.

Reprinted from *Journal of Psychology and Theology* 3, no. 4 (1975): 235–42. Used by permission.

Self-Centeredness

I can take my departure from the venerable psychological construct of the self. One of my most vivid undergraduate psychology memories is the enthusiasm of a professor over Carl Rogers' (1951) recently propounded self theory. That well-systematized theory included these four basic propositions:

1. Every individual exists in a continually changing world of experience of which he is the center.
4. The organism has one basic tendency and striving—to actualize, maintain, and enhance the experiencing organism.
5. Behavior is basically the goal-directed attempt of the organism to satisfy its needs as experienced in the field as perceived.
8. A portion of the total perceptual field gradually becomes differentiated as the self (pp. 483–97).

To a psychological community already looking for viable alternatives to psychoanalysis and behaviorism, Rogers's theory had a great deal of appeal. His orderly propositions were soon challenged, though— by the social psychologist Solomon Asch (1952). In an implicit confrontation of Rogers's concepts (he never mentioned Rogers or his writings by name), Asch audaciously asked, "Is the ego the center of the world?" (p. 289). Then he proceeded to examine a point of view that sounds unmistakably Rogerian—the "doctrine that asserts that the individual is the center of reference for all that he does and experiences" (pp. 289–90). This doctrine, he said,

> proposes that action begins with the needs of the organism and directs itself to the surroundings to gratify these needs. . . . It asserts as a general principle that the needs to which an individual is responsive are always needs referring to itself and that the environment is a heap of materials and means for their fulfillment (p. 290).

Asch concluded that in the context of self and ego theories "the axiom about organism-centered action becomes a doctrine of self-interest at the human level" (p. 290).

Task-Centeredness

Having set up a Rogerian view of self, Asch proceeded to present empirical evidence suggesting that persons are not inherently ego- or self-centered. It is true that since we come to know the world only through physical senses, our experiences are necessarily seen as "mine," but most of those experiences refer, not to "me," but to things "out there." A pain, for example, has clear ego reference, and we can relate objects to our right or left, in front or behind, but many other experiences are independent of the self. As Asch said, "We compare the size of two objects without comparing either to our own height; a statement about the sum of two numbers is a fact about numbers, not about ourselves" (p. 293).

The behavior of children provides rich observations for sources of motivation. Some of their behaviors obviously relate to their biological needs, but when the obvious physical needs are satisfied, a child may be even more active. They explore their object world, "moving, lifting, dropping, and turning" (p. 298). They show motivations for making, constructing, and mastering tasks and objects. The child of two or three, in that "first stage of independence," insists on climbing steps, dressing, and opening doors without assistance; the emphasis is on doing, not on merely attaining the goal of the activity. The orientation of such a child is what Asch called "task-centered."

Traditional psychology acknowledged only "ego-centered" motivation. Thus a person who was strongly motivated was characterized as being "ego-involved," and the apathetic person was not "ego-involved." Asch suggested that there may be two fundamentally different kinds of motivational orientation. Task-orientation finds its motivating force in the task itself, and may better characterize the kind of behavior traditionally attributed to "ego-involvement." An ego-orientation, on the other hand, is primarily motivated by the needs of the self and shows qualitative differences from a task-orientation. Apropos children's behavior again,

> There are obvious differences between a child who is absorbed in play
> and a child who, while playing, notes whether he is observed and praised
> and whose activity lags in the absence of an onlooker (p. 303).

To abridge Asch's evidence and conclusions considerably, I might conclude with his implication that the "task-orientation frees one for seeing and understanding situations in their own terms [whereas] focusing on the self may interfere with giving oneself freely to the task" (p. 311).

Before temporarily leaving the subject of task-centeredness, I should comment on some more recent denotations of the term. In the social psychology of leadership and small-group work "task-centered" has been contrasted with "person-centered." In these contexts "task-centered" has usually had a pejorative connotation insofar as a leader focuses on the "job to be done" to the detriment of the personal needs of those under one's leadership. In the sense Asch and I have used the term, such a connotation is inappropriate in that a leader's "task," whether in a small group, industrial setting, or volunteer organization, would typically involve both social needs of the group and the job they have assumed.

Motivation-Hygiene Theory

Another line of thinking relates more closely to my own interests and research for the last dozen years. In the mid-1950s a group of industrial psychologists at Western Reserve University were studying job satisfaction—what things made people happy and unhappy with their jobs. In the book *The Motivation to Work* (Herzberg, Mausner, and Snyderman, 1959) they reported a study in which two hundred accountants and engineers were asked to recollect incidents in which they were especially well satisfied with their jobs and those in which their jobs gave special dissatisfaction. The findings, in short, were that in relating positive job situations workers most often mentioned variables intrinsic to their work—amount of responsibility, enjoyment of the work, feeling of achievement, and professional achievement. These variables (called "motivators" in motivation-hygiene theory) were seldom factors in unhappy job situations. Rather, dissatisfaction was related to such "hygiene" factors as fairness of company policies, relationships with one's supervisors and peers, and working conditions—factors extrinsic to the work itself. The extrinsic factors or "hygienes" were seldom mentioned positively as related to job satisfaction.

Thus it would seem that one set of factors has the potential for job satisfaction and a largely independent set of variables relates to unhappiness on the job. The chief investigator in this study, Frederick Herzberg, concluded that no amount of hygiene or extrinsic factors—working conditions, security, company policies—can lead to genuine positive job satisfaction. Positive feelings come only from such motivators as achievement and growth, the intrinsic job factors. A number of subsequent studies in industrial psychology have challenged the generality of Herzberg's conclusions for job satisfaction and dissatisfaction, but the following implications do not depend crucially on the facts of applied industrial psychology.

In collaboration with a clinical psychologist, Herzberg (Herzberg and Hamlin, 1961; 1963) extrapolated his findings into a general theory of mental health. Herzberg had observed that, in contradiction to the trend of the job motivation study, there were a few workers who manifested no job motivations other than those extrinsic to the work itself. It thus appeared that they were oriented toward those factors which operate only to remove dissatisfaction or avoid unpleasantness and which have no capacity for positive growth experience. Only an orientation toward intrinsic job factors can provide meaningful achievement or self-actualizing experience. As Herzberg said in a way reminiscent of Asch, "Growth is dependent on some achievements, but achievement requires a task" (1966, p. 78).

Consequently Herzberg proposed two separate dimensions for mental health and mental illness. People who are oriented toward motivator or intrinsic incentives (related to a job or other life experiences) will be truly mentally healthy if their intrinsic and extrinsic needs are satisfied. Even if neither set of needs is met, though, they will not be mentally ill—only unhappy and unfulfilled. However, those who are oriented toward the extrinsic, avoidance needs can never be mentally healthy. If their extrinsic needs are not met they may become mentally ill, but even if those needs are met, they will still be maladjusted (1966, pp. 81–91).

Some confirmation of Herzberg's interpretation of the intrinsic and extrinsic job factors was produced in research with one of my students at a Baptist college.[1] We administered a job motivation inventory to identify students who were at the high and low extremes on the intrinsic and extrinsic job orientation dimensions. Then we analyzed their responses to a personality inventory to see what personality traits characterized the two dimensions. The intrinsic orientation was based on endorsement of such job-related incentives as "doing the kind of work I feel is really important," "to be placed in charge of a job and see that it is done right," and "acquire further knowledge and skills." Students high on that dimension responded positively to personality test items like "I enjoy planning and deciding what each person should do" and "I am known as a hard and steady worker"—the kinds of things you might expect.

Somewhat more surprising, though consistent with Herzberg's theory, was the extent of maladjustment manifest by the high extrinsic students. On the job inventory they had rated as important such commonplace needs as "To get along well with my boss," "Physical safety," "Good salary," "Having plenty of time to get a job done," and "Being kept informed about company policies." The related personality items were predominately defensive, avoidance, and anxiety-ridden, like, "Every now and then I get into a bad mood and no one can do anything to please me," "The thought of being in an automobile accident is very

1. Kahoe, R. D., and Polk, J. D., Jr., "Personality scales assessing intrinsic and extrinsic motivational variables," Southwest Baptist College *Faculty Studies Bulletin* 2 (1971): 38–42.

frightening to me," "Sometimes I feel I am about to go to pieces," and "When I am cornered I tell that portion of the truth which is not likely to hurt me."

A substantial amount of other research tending to support Herzberg's basic notions about the implications of intrinsic and extrinsic motivations has been done but defies summary in this paper. The most extensive summary is in a paper by Haywood (1971), and an example of personality and attitude correlates can be found in an article by Kahoe (1974b).

Coping and Defending

Another set of concepts comes from the neo-Freudians or ego psychologists. Whereas psychoanalysts have long emphasized the "ego-defense mechanisms," it has been relatively recently that the "coping" mechanisms have been given due emphasis. Norma Hahn, who has done considerable research on the mechanisms, makes the following distinction between the two methods of handling conflict:

> Coping behavior is distinguished from defensive behavior since the latter by definition is rigid, compelled, reality distorting, and undifferentiated, whereas the former is flexible, purposive, reality oriented, and differentiated (1965, p. 374).

In trying to measure coping and defending tendencies as personality characteristics, Hahn found that in general the two orientations were independent, not related either positively or negatively. She suggested that "the absence of pathology does not necessarily insure the presence of competence" (p. 378) or vice versa. That is, one may avoid the reality-distorting defense mechanisms but also be unable to cope with their conflicts; or one may manifest tendencies to use both defense and coping mechanisms.

The Harvard University educational psychologist Jerome Bruner (1966) has related coping and defending tendencies to an educational setting. Bruner was working with children referred to a guidance clinic for "learning blocks," in an effort to investigate learning effectiveness and find procedures to quantitatively differentiate normal children and ineffective learners. After some months of study it became apparent that the crucial differences were not quantitative but qualitative. "The learning activities of our disturbed children had certain distinctive features that had very little directly to do with the nature of effectiveness. . . . Their efforts [were] to defend themselves from the activity of learning and its consequences" (p. 131). The school work set off conflicts, anxiety, and panic which called for self-defense and utterly blocked coping efforts. Bruner concluded that the coping-defending distinction is

> one of the differences between psychological health and illness. . . . Coping respects the requirements of problems we encounter while still respecting our integrity. Defending is a strategy whose objective is avoiding or escaping from problems for which there is no solution that does not violate our integrity of functioning (p. 129).

In some tentative, unpublished research I did several years ago I attempted to relate Hahn's measures of coping and defending to the intrinsic and extrinsic orientations derived from motivation-hygiene theory. Empirically they seemed not to be related in any straightforward way, but the conceptual definitions suggest some kind of kinship or parallel between the two sets of constructs. Certainly both construe mental health and mental illness as dichotomous variables.

Intrinsic and Extrinsic Religious Orientations

A final line of evidence for the distinction between mental health and illness comes from the thinking and research of the late Gordon Allport. In extensive investigations of both prejudice and religion, Allport (1968) faced the paradox that in numerous studies churchgoers, religiously oriented people, showed more prejudice on the average than did nonchurchgoers. In attempting to resolve this problem Allport discerned two dimensions of religiosity, an extrinsic and an intrinsic religious orientation. People with the extrinsic orientation use their religion to serve other needs—"security and solace, sociability and distraction, status and self-justification" (p. 243). As Allport further said, "In theological terms the extrinsic type turns to God, but without turning away from self" (p. 243).

Persons with intrinsic religious orientations live their religion, making it the master motive of their lives. Other needs are brought into harmony with the religious beliefs, and the person endeavors to embrace and fully follow their creed. Allport found that it was apparently the extrinsically oriented churchgoers (the great majority) whose prejudice made religious populations appear to be more biased. Intrinsically religious persons are not only less prejudiced than the extrinsically oriented ones, but Allport found that in some studies they were also less prejudiced than nonchurchgoers (1968).

Whereas Allport generally construed intrinsic and extrinsic religious orientations as bipolar opposites, Feagin (1964) established that they are independent dimensions, just as are intrinsic and extrinsic job motivations and coping and defending tendencies. Feagin also found that the extrinsic religious orientation was positively correlated with racial prejudice and that the intrinsic religious orientation was unrelated to prejudice. I found a similar pattern of relationships for dogmatism (Kahoe, 1974a) and for authoritarianism (Kahoe, 1975) and other relationships that support a parallel between mental health and illness and intrinsic and extrinsic religious orientations respectively. I also found that intrinsic religion had a strong correlation with intrinsic motivation and that extrinsic religion had a weaker but statistically significant relationship with extrinsic job motivation (Kahoe, 1974a). Dittes (1969) reviewed research regarding the intrinsic and extrinsic religious orientations in the *Handbook of Social Psychology*, and Hunt and King (1971) performed a similar service more recently in an article in the *Journal for the Scientific Study of Religion*. (The latter journal had four other articles on the concepts in the same issue.)

Integration with the New Testament Message

I have drawn from recent psychological research and theory several converging pairs of concepts which reiterate the theme: Mental health is not just the absence of mental illness or its opposite. The two are different processes and function relatively independently of one another. I might adopt a general model from biology, identifying the respective dimensions with the processes of growth and homeostasis. The task-oriented, coping, intrinsic dimensions all connote achievement and growth. Ego-orientation, defensive, and extrinsic orientations pose as avoiders, preservers of the status quo but actually as degenerating factors, for where no growth occurs, atrophy seems inevitable.

To return to a major concept of Carl Rogers—self-actualization—it can be seen as a paradox that self-actualization does not come from direct concern with the self. Rather, one must be involved with a task outside oneself in order to be self-actualized. As Asch said, "The ego needs to have interests wider than itself, not to be always looking at itself, not to be always watching its own feelings and looking out for its own interests" (1952, p. 320). True self-interest is not self-seeking nor self-defensive but finds growth from the challenges offered by the environment. In many ways this is not a new insight. It is suggested by the adage, "A person all wrapped up in oneself makes an awfully small package." More salient, the renunciation of self-service is implicit or explicit in the world's major religions. I find both the warning against self-interest and the prescription of a task-orientation in Christ's declaration:

If anyone wishes to be a follower of mine, he must leave self behind; day after day he must take up his cross, and come with me. Whoever cares for his own safety is lost; but if a man will let himself be lost for my sake, that man is safe (Luke 9:23–24, *New English Bible*).

As we examine the teachings of Christ further concerning these concepts we recognize that mental health and mental illness are not usual New Testament or theological categories. Nonetheless we might assume that the New Testament prescription for the optimum life with God through Jesus Christ would at least incorporate what we would call mental health and exclude mental illness. Apropos our theme, the relationship to one's "self" figures prominently in Christ's teachings and in the gospel records. The above Scripture about denying self and taking up one's cross is only one of about seven specific iterations of these principles (see also Matt. 10:38–39; 16:24–26; Mark 8:34–36; Luke 14:27; 17:33; and John 12:25–26), and Jesus' response to the rich young ruler reflects essentially the same ideas in an individual context (Matt. 19:21–22; Luke 18:22–23). Excessive concern about money was also the villain in the parable of the laborers in the vineyard (Matt. 20:1–16). Most modern readers could probably empathize with the complaining workers more readily than with the apparently stingy employer (with whom Christ might be identified). Yet Herzberg's theory tends to confirm Christ's position that the workers' concern with extrinsic material rewards was misplaced. We infer from the parable, then, that labor in Christ's vineyard is intrinsically rewarding and extrinsic reward should not be expected beyond some minimum level.

Jesus proclaimed the principle of self-denial in the Sermon on the Mount with instruction not to worry about food, drink, and clothing (Matt. 6:25–34; Luke 12:22–29). In the psychological theories self-denial is not seen as an end in itself, of course, but only because self-actualization is better attained through a task-orientation. So also in Jesus' teachings self-denial is always a means to the spiritual fulfillment of the individual. To continue with Luke's account of the Sermon:

Set your mind upon his kingdom, and all the rest will come to you as well ... your Father has chosen to give you the Kingdom. ... Provide for yourselves purses that do not wear out, and never-failing wealth in heaven (Luke 12:31–33, *New English Bible*).

Similarly we find Christ repeatedly citing the Old Testament commandment "Love your neighbor as yourself" (Lev. 19:18; Matt. 19:19; 22:39; Mark 12:31) with the implication that self-love is normal and by no means condemned in the godly person. There is no inconsistency here, for as we have seen, self-denial (in the sense of refusing to be self-centered) is consistent with self-actualization, self-acceptance, or self-love. There may even be a degree to which people cannot engage in the kind of self-denial I am talking about until they truly accept themselves.

Conclusion

Probably at this point the psychological and biblical parallels I have drawn demand some kind of general examination. On the one hand, a too ready acceptance of identity between the psychological and theological concepts would leave me open to a charge of syncretism which Pruyser (1968) has identified as the fault of combining disparate ideas within a formula that is "to trite to be false and too meaningless to be correct" (p. 95).

On the other hand, the psychological constructs might be charged with contamination from moral or religious preconceptions. Braginsky and Braginsky (1974) have accused contemporary psychology of being "culture-bound," subservient to moral and religious as well as political and economic interests of society. They would not be surprised to find psychology espousing concepts congruent with traditional morality, but they would hardly approve of it. Surely we would agree that the thinking of psychologists as well as other scientists is influenced and even limited by their world views. In the case of some of our theorists there are quite obvious influences. Herzberg (1966) has related his motivation and hygiene orientations to two Old Testament views of man. The hygiene or extrinsic orientation was related to the model of Adam, the natural man whose basic motivation was the avoidance of pain. Intrinsic motivation denotes a second side of man's nature, epitomized by Abraham, in whom God recognized "that man is capable, that he had been given innate potential" (p. 16). Allport's familiarity with theology undoubtedly influenced his recognition (or invention?) of the intrinsic and extrinsic religious orientations. The impress of traditional moral views may have been made in more subtle forms on other theories I have reviewed.

While I recognize that the realms of theology and psychology are largely separate, giving different views of a multifaceted universe, it is equally obvious that they have areas of overlap. The nature of man is the most notable of these, and the present article has been specifically directed at a part of that study. Therefore both theology and psychology bear on the nature of mental health and mental illness—fully functioning man and malfunctioning man. Theology or religion, having had historical precedence, was naturally in a position to reach certain insights long before psychology was. If we assume that there is an innate nature of man (and not just fabrications of the different disciplines), then it should be no surprise that the realities would lead psychology to at least some of the same conclusions that theology had reached. As a representative of a still different discipline, physiology, Hans Selye came to a conclusion similar to the one advocated in this article; noting that all living organisms share a quality of self-centeredness, he observed that "it may well be the original sin that the Bible talks about" (Gordon, 1974, p. 70).

The disciplines of theology and psychology have basically different methodologies. Psychology stresses empiricism, but it is becoming increasingly obvious that we can be empirical only in testing our hypotheses. The source of our hypotheses is more subjective. It does not bother me that my psychological constructs or yours may have been partially determined by religious or moral presuppositions, either consciously or unconsciously. Quite probably, insights of other disciplines such as theology can and should stimulate psychology, producing a hybrid vigor that keeps us from forgetting man and becoming preoccupied with minutiae. Regardless of the source of ideas, constructs, or hypotheses, if empirical data are objectively collected, analyzed, and interpreted, I should consider the psychology viable. The psychological constructs reviewed above and the view presented of mental health and mental illness may represent such a cross-fertilization of psychology and theology.

References

Allport, G. W. 1968. *The person in psychology.* Boston: Beacon.

Asch, S. E. 1952. *Social psychology.* Englewood Cliffs, N.J.: Prentice-Hall.

Braginsky, B. M., and Braginsky, D. D. 1974. *Mainstream psychology: A critique.* New York: Holt, Rinehart, and Winston.

Bruner, J. S. 1966. *Toward a theory of instruction.* Cambridge, Mass.: Belknap.

Dittes, J. E. 1969. Psychology of religion. In *The handbook of social psychology,* edited by G. Lindzey and E. Aronson, vol. 5. 2d ed. Reading, Mass.: Addison-Wesley.

Feagin, J. R. 1964. Prejudice and religious types: A focussed study of southern fundamentalists. *Journal for the Scientific Study of Religion* 4:3–13.

Gordon, A. 1974. Four words to live by. *Reader's Digest,* February, 69–72.

Hahn, N. 1965. Coping and defense mechanisms related to personality inventories. *Journal of Consulting Psychology* 29:373–78.

Haywood, H. C. 1971. Individual differences in motivational orientation: A trait approach. In *Intrinsic motivation: A new direction in education,* edited by H. I. Day, D. E. Berlyne, and D. E. Hunt. Toronto: Holt, Rinehart, and Winston.

Herzberg, F. 1966. *Work and the nature of man.* Cleveland: World.

Herzberg, F., and Hamlin, R. M. 1961. A motivation-hygiene concept of mental health. *Mental Hygiene* 45:394–401.

————.1963. The motivation-hygiene concept and psychotherapy. *Mental Hygiene* 47:384–97.

Herzberg, F.; Mausner, B.; and Snyderman, B. 1959. *The motivation to work.* 2d ed. New York: Wiley.

Hunt, R. A., and King, M. 1971. The intrinsic-extrinsic concept: A review and evaluation. *Journal for the Scientific Study of Religion* 10:370–74.

Jahoda, M. 1958. *Current concepts of positive mental health.* New York: Basic Books.

Kahoe, R. D. 1974a. Personality and achievement correlates of intrinsic and extrinsic religious orientations. *Journal of Personality and Social Psychology* 29:812–18.

————.1974b. The psychology and theology of sexism. *Journal of Psychology and Theology* 2:284–90.

————.1975. Authoritarianism and religion: Relationships of *F* scale items to intrinsic and extrinsic religious orientations. *JSAS Catalog of Selected Documents in Psychology* 5:284–85. (Ms. no. 1020)

Pruyser, P. 1968. *A dynamic psychology of religion.* New York: Harper and Row.

Rogers, C. R. 1951. *Client-centered therapy.* Boston: Houghton Mifflin.

Five dimensions of maturity are outlined and described: having a realistic view of oneself and others, accepting oneself and others, living in the present but having long-range goals, having values, and developing one's abilities and coping with daily living. A parallel description of biblical maturity is also made on these dimensions, but differences in content are noted. Psychological maturity is grounded in the image of God in man as created but fallen for both the Christian and the non-Christian, but the additional aspects of biblical maturity are grounded in the renewed image.

Maturity

Psychological and Biblical

John D. Carter

Though their terminology may vary when psychologists describe maturity, they focus on five basic dimensions: (*a*) having a realistic view of oneself and others; (*b*) accepting oneself and others; (*c*) living in the present but having long-range goals; (*d*) having values; and (*e*) developing one's abilities and interests and coping with the task of living. While the list could be extended or elaborated upon in more detail, these dimensions cover the basic aspects of maturity.

In her review of maturity and conceptions of positive mental health, Jahoda (1958) organized the material into six dimensions which overlap those described above.

Psychologists are not the only ones to speak of maturity. The New Testament repeatedly uses the concept to describe the character of Christian experience. The biblical word for maturity is *telios*, which is translated "perfect" in the King James Version and "maturity" in most recent versions. Its basic meaning is mature, complete, or fully developed, and refers to the potential of the person or thing to grow, develop, or become complete. First, the psychological dimensions of

Reprinted from *Journal of Psychology and Theology* 2, no. 2 (1974): 89–96. Used by permission.

maturity will be examined and then their beautiful parallels in the Scripture will be elaborated upon.

The Psychological Perspective

A realistic view of oneself and others involves an accurate objective evaluation of oneself and others. Maslow (1970) lists this dimension first in describing self-actualizing people. Allport (1961) calls it self-objectification: the ability to know and understand oneself, to recognize how one's present behavior and reactions were influenced by similar experiences in the past. This dimension also represents the whole development of the ego in Freudian thinking (Freud, 1960).

A realistic view of the self often may be obtained by asking oneself several questions, such as, "What kind of things can I do best?"; "What are my strengths and weaknesses?" At the same time it is necessary to ask, "Would others agree and have I had some success in my area of strength?" It is important to realize that people often have more than one real talent and a host of lesser abilities. In addition, one's talents and abilities are often related to one's interests (Allport, 1961). Often a person finds that he is good at doing the things he likes to do or can learn to do them more quickly than someone who does not share those interests. The variety of interests an individual has is related to the variety of his abilities. Consequently, in gaining a realistic view of the self, an examination of one's interests may be very helpful in discovering one's abilities and potential.

The immature person often makes one of two errors in gaining a realistic view of himself. The first is to assume he is very capable or talented in one or more areas when he is not. Coupled with this error is the assumption that others have little or no real ability, having achieved their office, job, or position of responsibility by coincidence. This first error is often observed in children and particularly in adolescents who seem convinced that they can do things much better than just about anyone. This is also the error of the "armchair" or "Monday-morning quarterback" who is certain he could have done a much better job than the real player. The second error, which is characteristic of the individual with an immature or unrealistic view of the self, is the reverse of the first. This person says he is untalented and really can't do anything very well. In fact, he says most anyone can do almost anything better than he can. A person with realistic self-perception avoids both errors. He knows his strengths and his weaknesses and does not over- or underestimate either. He can also laugh at himself (Allport, 1961). Just as there was a correlation between one's view of himself and others in both errors of immaturity, so there is a close relationship in a realistic view of self and a realistic view of others. When a person can perceive his own strengths, abilities, and talents as well as his lack of ability in certain areas, then he can also perceive the talents of others accurately.

One may see that his friends and neighbors have similar strengths or weaknesses or quite different ones. (Since an accurate view of self and others is related, one can begin to grow by starting with either. However, since everyone spends more time with himself and has more information about oneself, it is often easier to begin with oneself.)

The second aspect or dimension of maturity—accepting oneself and others—is closely related to the first. Rogers (1961) so stresses the importance of this dimension of maturity that he divides it into its components and discusses each separately. Adler (Ansbacher and Ansbacher, 1956) repeatedly stresses the acceptance of others, calling it social interests and social feeling—a feeling of brotherliness toward one's fellows. For Sullivan (1953), relating to others in a healthy way and mutually meeting each other's needs is the very nature of personality.

Accepting means allowing, believing, or recognizing something as true or real in one's inner experience. It does not imply that whatever needs to be accepted is good, valuable, or right, but only that it really exists. For example, everyone has a variety of hopes, fears, desires, and aspirations. They are not all good or desirable but they are all real. Their reality must be accepted if one is to be mature. The reality of these worthwhile desires and fears must be accepted as existing now in order for change or improvement to occur. Suppose a child gets in trouble with the neighbors by walking on their grass and picking their flowers, but his parents say to the neighbors he is a good boy and wouldn't do such a thing. The longer the parents fail to accept the reality of the child's bad behavior (and thus their relationship to it), the more likely is the child to continue and the more the relationship with the neighbors will degenerate.

In addition, acceptance means that the self or other selves are approved as persons or personalities apart from however many imperfections exist. The immature individual often confuses some specific habit, attitude, or action with the total person and rejects the person rather than accepting the total person as worthwhile and more important than the undesirable aspect.

The third dimension of maturity is living in the present but having long-range goals. For Adler (Ansbacher & Ansbacher, 1956), maturity involves living in the world of others and finding meaningful work. The productive orientation described by Fromm (1947), which touches on several dimensions, includes meaningful work for the person and for the common good. Rogers (1961) calls the multitude of feelings that are related to the network of interaction patterns involved in living "being complexity"—i.e. as one is involved in many interpersonal relationships both in the home and occupationally with both positive and negative feelings. A person is all of these feelings, i.e., he is a complex being in the present.

Living in the present means facing and coping with one's present circumstances and situations. This involves dealing with and acknowledging the importance of oneself, job, church, friends, family, etc. Each of and all these situations could be described as "where I am." Each of these situations or circumstances has some positive and negative qualities; that is, it meets some needs but not others. The mature person is aware of these qualities and his needs. He is able to see what is good and bad as well as what can be changed and what cannot in each situation. In each the mature person has some goals that he would like to see accomplished and is aware of the present state of progress toward these goals. The immature person tends to live with the "if only" or the "when" attitude; that is, "if only it were as good as it used to be" or "won't it be grand when." For either case, there is little or no acceptance of the present situation and the person's responsibility in it and for it or for changing it.

In addition, the mature person is aware that the present is not all that it could be or all that he would like it to be. Consequently he develops goals toward which he directs the course of his activity and life. Maslow (1970) refers to this quality in terms of a mature people being characterized by a high degree of autonomy, i.e., the ability to set their own goals. White (1959) describes a related aspect of goal setting as competence, the learned ability to cope with life tasks and to establish one's own goals in the situation. These goals usually are spread over several areas of life, such as familial, vocational, economic, and personal. The goals vary as to their clarity, permanence, and desirability. As he moves toward them the mature person assesses his progress and directs or redirects his effort as needed. He may even change his goals; i.e., he remains master of his goals, and they remain flexible. The immature person tends to be mastered by his goals, becoming rigid and rejecting others or himself for not obtaining or making satisfactory progress toward his goals.

Having values at first may not appear to be a very psychological concept, but most psychologists recognize implicitly, if not explicitly, the existence of values for the mature or healthy person. Frankl (1963) describes having values in terms of the will to meaning which organizes all of one's life. Allport (1961) speaks in a similar way of mature people having a unifying philosophy of life, while Maslow (1970) says the mature have a strong ethical sense and are able to resist the cultural pressure to conform. Rollo May (1967) speaks of values in terms of choice and the courage to decide how one is going to live. Values for the psychologist, therefore, must be self-chosen. They are not values the individual accepts because he is coerced by a society or a religion. Rather they are chosen by the mature person and integrated in the person's self-concept and behavior. They are thus not external but internalized values. Internalization and integration of values in the person implies harmony within the personality and purposefulness of his plans and actions. The immature person operates without values, e.g., a psychopath or a child, or with a rigid threatening set of moral values, e.g., an obsessive-compulsive individual or a preadolescent (White, 1964). Some immature persons alternate in various ways between these polarities. In the one case there are few values and in the other case they are coercive-threatening-external rules. The mature person is free of coercion because his values are self-chosen and he acts accordingly. His values may be that of society or religion but they have become his own by choice and internalization. Having values is clearly related to the long-range goals described above.

The developing of one's abilities and interests and coping with the problems of living is the final characteristic of maturity. The first characteristic focuses more on self-perception while this last one focuses on developing one's potentials and skills and then utilizing them to create, make, and do things both from necessity and for fun. This last quality has certain global and integrative quality which Freud would call reality orientation. In general, Rogers and Maslow would call it self-actualization. More specifically Maslow (1970) would refer to mature people as problem-centered while Schactel (1959) refers to this ability to be involved in life as allocentricity, the ability to concentrate intensely on problems outside of oneself. Mature people are interested in their job, home, family, community, church, themselves, etc. Of course their degree of interest may vary from area to area, but they have interests. They are not only capable of purposeful, creative action but they like to do things. They have a high degree of ability to concentrate on the task at hand but also to leave it when necessary. The immature person seems to have more dislikes than likes and has not developed his creative abilities nor the ability or interest in coping with life's daily tasks.

Coleman (1970) summarizes a great deal of the psychological discussion of this final aspect of maturity as a task-oriented approach to life versus a defensive orientation. The immature person is trying to protect or defend himself from life, the world, others, and himself as well, while the mature person is involved in the tasks of life. He is able to modify his approach and try an alternate approach and able to accept a substitute goal and make compromises when necessary.

The Biblical Perspective

Turning from the psychological perspective to the biblical one, the parallel becomes evident. The Bible asks man to have a realistic or objective view of himself and others. The basic requirement is to perceive the self, others, and the world from the divine perspective. God views each and every man as fallen and in need of a Savior (Rom. 3:23). Once man recognizes his need for a Savior and responds he becomes a new creature, with a new relationship to God, other men, and the world (II Cor. 5:17). Another aspect of a realistic biblical view of self and others is the recognition of natural traits and abilities, as well as one's spiritual gifts (Matt. 25:25–26; I Cor. 12:14–25) and place in the body repeatedly articulated (I Cor. 12:14; Eph. 4:4). A realistic perception of the needs of others, both believers (Gal. 6:2) and unbelievers (Matt. 25:34–40), is the biblical expectation as well as a divine view of the social order (Rom. 13:1–3).

A second aspect of biblical maturity involves the accepting of oneself and others. Perhaps the clearest statement of this principle is given by Jesus, "Love your neighbor as yourself" (Matt. 22:39). It is important to note the love of neighbor is dependent in quality and amount on love of self—love of self in the sense of acceptance as described above. Acceptance means allowing the biblical view of sinfulness and fallenness to be true or real in my inner experience both before and after I become a Christian. Sinfulness and fallenness are not eliminated by being saved. Righteousness always belongs to Christ and is legally attributed to the person by God. It does not become a personal quality so the person can brag (Phil. 3:9; Eph. 5:9) either before God or others. A corresponding view of others is also characteristic of the spiritually mature. A second aspect of acceptance of the self and others is recognizing that both self and others are more than sinful and fallen. Each person is created in God's image (Gen. 1:27) and is also fallen (Rom. 5:12) and is redeemed or in need of redemption. God loves everyone whom He created, which means everyone is worthwhile as a person. Hence everyone should be accepted as a person. Acceptance as a person does not imply approval of all of the person's behavior or motives. However, the Bible calls the mature believer to a very high level of love for other believers (I John 3:16), to a deep sensitivity to their weakness (Heb. 12:12) and to the whole body as brothers in Christ (I Cor. 12:25–26). The biblical words *agapeo, philo,* and *koinonia* call for a greater depth of warmth and mature relationship than perhaps any psychologist emphasizes other than Carl Rogers, who came from a Christian home (Rogers, 1961).

Third, living in the present with long-term goals is basic in the Scriptures. Now is the day of salvation, for both the believer and the unbeliever. Salvation has an eternally present aspect. While the Bible describes the future life with God, there is a very heavy emphasis in present actions and attitudes. The believer is to manifest the fruit of the Spirit in his life. Christ makes an observable difference in the believer's ongoing action. It is the carnal or immature who does not show a currently observable change. In fact, believers are warned not to long to leave the world but to live in it now (I Cor. 5:9–10). The words "abide" and "grow up in Christ" are repeatedly used to emphasize the current ongoing focus of the Christian. However, the Christian life is also described as a race with a prize (Phil. 3:14). Most clearly Paul makes the third aspect of maturity the model of the mature Christian life, "As many as would be perfect [mature—*telios*] be thus minded" (Phil. 3:15). He describes his previous life in Judaism (Phil. 3:4–6) which he then gives up for Christ (Phil. 3:8), but the process does not end at that point. In verse 10 Paul goes on describing the model, "That I may know him, the power of his resurrection, the fellowship of his suffering being made comformable to his death." This last verb is a present participle and is the strongest possible way of stressing ongoing action—the focus is on the present. However, Paul further elaborates the model of maturity by saying it is not as though I am already perfect (mature) but . . . I press to that which is before . . . , I press toward the mark of the high (upward) calling of God (see Phil. 3:14). Thus the model of the Christian has a present focus with long-range future goals.

A fourth characteristic of Christian maturity is having values which are self-chosen. Joshua in the process of conquering and possessing the land appeals to the Israelites, "Choose this day whom you will serve . . ." (Josh. 24:15). Values are a "package plan" because they involve an integrated set of motives and actions, not just something one says he thinks is right. The value-packages are clearly indicated in the descriptions of the works of the flesh and the works of the Spirit. Paul in Philippians 3:8 describes a complete values reorganization in which a total set of values and accompanying actions are reinterpreted and reversed. However, the value reassessment is an ongoing process, "Not as though I had already attained or were already perfect but this one thing I do, forgetting those things which are past, I press toward the mark" (Phil. 3:12–14). Thus the process of reassessing is an ongoing process which merges with the realistic evaluation of the self and the focus on the present, but it is pulled forward and clarified by the long-

range goal of "high calling of God." It is the commitment of the self
to a set of values that reorganizes the person and gives him an identity.
For the Christian this is union with Christ which is so characteristically described by Paul with the phrase "in Christ."

The final characteristic of the mature Christian is developing one's
abilities and interest in everyday living. The development and use of
one's talents and gifts (Eph. 4:7) is a necessary part of Christian
maturity since they are given to the church for the work of the ministry
(Eph. 4:12). Timothy is encouraged to rekindle the gift of God within
him (II Tim. 1:6). The encouragement of growth toward Christian
maturity seems to be the purpose of the gifts and the goal of the
ministry (Eph. 4:15–16). Interest in everyday living involves working
to support oneself (II Thess. 3:10) as well as for one's family (I Tim.
5:8). Interest in the daily tasks is not to be neglected or done grudg-
ingly (Eph. 6:6; Col. 3:22). Thus the developing of one's abilities, talents,
and gifts begins to merge with Christian values and a biblically appropriate perception of oneself and others. This merger produces
congruence in the mature Christian of all that he says and does (James
2:26; I John 3:18). Perhaps this is best illustrated in the epistle of
I John where the apostle describes three criteria of mature Christian
faith: believing the truth (Jesus is the Christ), loving the brotherhood,
and practicing righteousness. These three criteria are repeated three
times in the epistle. These criteria tend to focus on three different
aspects of the human person. Believing the truth has a strong cognitive
component, while practicing righteousness has a strong behavioral
focus, and loving the brothers involves the emotional-motivational
aspects. These joint criteria thus emphasize the unified or integrated
aspect of Christian maturity in the personality. The mature Christian's
behavior, beliefs, and emotions are thus organized in a consistent,
congruent, and unified pattern. He is interested in his daily life because
this is where God has placed him (Phil. 4:11; Heb. 13:5; I Cor. 7:21)
and he acts as unto the Lord (Eph. 6:8). Every task or sphere of activities is infused with spiritual meaning and interest. He recognizes that
every good thing in life is from God (James 1:17) and that there is
much that is worthy of his attention and enjoyment in this life (Phil.
4:8). Furthermore, the mature believer is aware that the mandate to
subdue the earth (Gen. 1:28) has never been revoked. On the other
hand, the immature Christian is torn by conflict because he is pulled
in two directions (James 1:8; 4:8) and because he is unclear about his
identity, that is, he has not reckoned himself dead to sin and alive to
God (Rom. 6:11). He has not embraced his identity as a new man or
self but rather tries to operate as the old man which he is not.

Conclusions

By way of summary, the five aspects or dimensions of maturity have been outlined: a realistic view of self and others, accepting oneself and others, living in the present but having long-range goals, having values, and the ability and interest in coping with the tasks of living. The parallel between the psychological and biblical implications has been developed and illustrated. However, when all five aspects of maturity are taken together a new dimension emerges: self-actualization. In discussing the five aspects a certain degree of overlap was evident. The overlap occurs because a mature person in either a psychological or biblical sense is integrated, has a purposeful or goal-directed quality about his life, is open to himself and others, while the immature person is disorganized, having either conflicting goals or no goal, and is unaware and unaccepting of various aspects of himself and others.

As each of the aspects of maturity have a psychic and biblical parallel, so the whole process of self-actualization has a parallel. Psychologically, actualization means developing one's body, mind, and emotions into a fully functioning person. Biblically it is the same; that is, the process is parallel but the content is different. The non-Christian may actualize his full potential as a person made in God's image but fallen. The fall limits the potential and direction of self-actualization. It does not prevent the person from becoming a good, healthy, kind, and developed person, since the image is more fundamental than the fall. The fall marred the image of God in man (Berkhof, 1941). Some Christians seem almost to reverse the pattern, emphasizing the fall so much that it appears that fallen man is only tainted by the image. Counts (1973) calls this latter view "worm theology."

Many non-Christians show varying degrees of behavior and attitudes similar to the fruit of the Spirit. An individual may develop his humanity (the God-given divine image) by utilizing the principles of psychology and mental health with and/or without the aid of a therapist into a more mature, healthy, self-actualized person. The fact is simply that most non-Christians are neither "Hitlers," rapists, nor addicts, because everyone can live at a higher level than this. However, the most fully functioning non-Christian will not be characterized by a relationship to Christ or the body of believers, nor will he be motivated by agape love, and his self perception and perception of the cosmos will not be Christianlike in character.

The Christian, on the other hand, actualizes his potential as created, fallen, and redeemed. In the Christian the image is being renewed (Eph. 4:24; Col. 3:10). Christ becomes the model or ideal for the Christian and the Scripture his guidelines. Since the Christian is related to the God of the universe he becomes more in harmony (if he is growing and maturing) with the divine purpose and pattern in both himself and the world. This is the meaning of the renewing of the image, but note that it is a process—the removal of the effects of the fall on the image.

Christian self-actualization moves toward perfection after Christ (Phil. 3:10–14). The non-Christian can become *complete* as a created and fallen man while the Christian becomes *complete* or rather *perfected* as created, fallen, and renewed.

References

Allport, G. W. 1961. *The pattern and growth of personality*. New York: Holt, Rinehart, and Winston.

Ansbacher, H. L., and Ansbacher, R. R. 1956. *The individual psychology of Alfred Adler*. New York: Basic Books.

Berkhof, L. 1941. *Systematic theology*. Grand Rapids: Eerdmans.

Coleman, J. C. 1960. *Personality dynamics and effective behavior*. Glenview, Ill.: Scott, Foresman.

Counts, W. M. 1973. The nature of man and the Christian's self-esteem. *Journal of Psychology and Theology*. 1:38–44.

Frankl, V. 1963. *Man's search for meaning*. New York: Washington Square.

Freud, S. 1960. *The ego and the id*. New York: W. W. Norton.

Jahoda, M. 1958. *Current concepts of positive mental health*. New York: Basic Books.

Maslow, A. H. 1970. *Motivation and personality*. New York: Harper and Row.

Rogers, C. 1961. *On becoming a person*. Boston: Houghton Mifflin.

Schactel, E. 1959. *Metamorphosis*. New York: Basic Books.

Sullivan, H. S. 1953. *The interpersonal theory of psychiatry*. New York: W. W. Norton.

White, R. W. 1964. *The abnormal personality*. New York: Ronald.

—————.1959. Motivation reconsidered: The concept of competence. *Psychological Review*. 297–333.

Summary

This section discussed health from several points of view. Although physical health was not considered in as much detail as mental and spiritual health, the wholeness of persons was emphasized and many of the ideas expressed here would be applicable to health in general.

The import of Southard's article is its concern that the emotional and physical condition of persons be evaluated before they are labeled as morally or spiritually guilty of sinful behavior. Much that is termed willfully bad is, in fact, a result of mental disturbance which calls for treatment—not censure. Making these distinctions is a complex but necessary task.

The theological dimensions of mental health noted by Duke include references to the emotions, to interpersonal relationships, to the freedom of the will, and to egocentrism. He emphasizes the power of the Christian gospel to enlighten persons and the ability of the Christian church to transform them into new and healthy beings.

"Salvation" is understood by Hiltner to mean the understanding of life grounded in the revelation of God in Christ. He notes that the Christian faith saves persons "from" sin and "for" service. His critique of conventional views of health serves as both an affirmation and corrective of implicit assumptions inherent in these positions.

Kahoe writes as a Christian psychologist. He correctly notes that contemporary behavioral science has no option other than to conceive mental health in terms of persons' abilities to take care of themselves and to master the tasks they undertake. In addition, they fulfill their inner desires for self-actualization. While psychology has difficulty in making sense of self-sacrifice, the Christian faith perceives such acts to be at the center of self-fulfillment. Kahoe concludes that faith may serve as a corrective for science in this regard.

Maturity may be a synonym for positive mental health, according to Carter. It emphasizes a developmental perspective in which an *optimal* state of being is achieved. He finds many similarities in the biblical and psychological points of view. However, Christian faith emphasizes the model of Jesus and "perfection" (i.e., maturity) is defined as becoming more like Christ. Psychology has no such ideal figure at the center of its model.

Questions for Dialogue

1. What difficulties can you think of which might make the distinction between sickness and sin a problem? Taking the opposite concern, what differences between health and salvation might be difficult to perceive?
2. What similarities can you see among the several authors in this section in regard to their understanding of the Christian critique of "health"?
3. Are "health," "wholeness," "maturity," and "holiness" one and the same? Utilize the prologue essay as well as the readings in this section in answering this question.
4. What types of critiques might social/behavioral sciences use in evaluating religious understandings of "health"?

Additional Readings

Books

Ellens, J. H. *God's grace and human health*. Nashville: Abingdon, 1982.

Goldbrunner, J. *Holiness is wholeness*. New York: Pantheon Books, 1955.

Homans, P. *Theology after Freud: An interpretative inquiry*. New York: Bobbs-Merrill, 1970.

Jahoda, M. *Current concepts of positive mental health*. New York: Basic Books, 1958.

Articles

Cox, J. L. Health and salvation in the ethical ideal. *Journal of Religion and Health* 20, no. 4 (1981): 307–16.

Ludwig, D. J., and Weber, T. Development of religious perception: Integration of life. *Journal of Psychology and Theology* 2, no. 2 (1974): 140–48.

Miller, S. H. Religion: Healthy and unhealthy. *Journal of Religion and Health* 4 (1965): 295–301.

Sfero, M. H. Sin as neurosis—neurosis as sin: Further implications of a Hadachic metapsychology. *Journal of Religion and Health* 17, no. 4 (1978): 274–87.

Smith, D. E. The next decade of dialogue: Religion and health. *Journal of Religion and Health* 13, no. 3 (1974): 161–79.

Stark, M. J., and Washburn, M. C. Beyond the norm: A speculative model of self realization. *Journal of Religion and Health* 16, no. 1 (1977): 58–68.

The Process
of Healing

The psychological and theological implications of psychotherapy are considered in this section. As distinct from the next section, Methods of Therapy, the readings in this section explore the theories undergirding the therapeutic endeavor. The basic issue underlying all of the essays is "How shall the endeavor of counseling by one person with another be understood theologically?"

Oden considers the thinking of one theologian, Dietrich Bonhoeffer. Although Bonhoeffer's idea of a "religionless Christianity" had great impact on religious thinkers, it had not been related to secular therapeutic efforts such as counseling. Oden states emphatically, ". . . if the therapeutic process is able to nurture authentic human existence even without the church's proclamation being heard, this does not mean that Jesus Christ is not at the center of things (here as always), but that He is taking shape in the world without that Word being consciously heard and understood, and that there is no reason for the church to be embarrassed by the presence of the Holy Spirit apart from the church, or for the theologian to rush to the therapist and tell him he cannot accomplish this healing without Christ!"

The late Paul Tillich, in his essay, "Theology and Counseling," makes a somewhat different, but related, point in his effort to dignify the counseling task. He poignantly notes that the church is both the object as well as the subject in counseling. He helpfully distinguishes pastoral counseling from psychotherapy. He states, counseling ". . . deals with special forms of psychological disturbances and human relationships in which these disturbances occur and pastoral counseling deals with them in relation to an *ultimate* concern and not in relation to preliminary concerns, as for instance social and psychological and bodily health."

In "Counseling and Evangelical Theology," Peters proposes yet another point of view. He concludes, quite correctly, that psychology has shown much recent interest in the place of values in counseling. In counterbalancing theology and psychology he notes that they both deal with human experience and he asserts, "It becomes the charge of the evangelical pastor to continue in his loyalty to the authority of the Word. In the conviction that the basic needs of the troubled personality are anticipated in the teachings of the Bible, he can speak of a theological basis for the principles of counseling. On the other hand, since the Bible is not a guide to methodology, the insights of psychology have their rightful place in the ministry of the evangelical pastor."

The philosopher, H. L. Parsons, notes the distressing manner in which faith and reason have typified the distinction between religious and secular counseling. He calls for a combination of the two and argues, "Theology and therapy *can* be integrated because they deal with a common problem: what must I do to achieve health? But they *will* be integrated only if, however different, they succeed in giving a common answer to that problem. This means they must employ a common method. And it turns out that the only method which is susceptible of commonality, of community, as John Dewey has pointed out, is the general method of empirical inquiry and creative communication—the method of science." This is a novel approach when compared to the foregoing essays.

The reader of this section should expect to have his/her consciousness raised regarding the several approaches that can be taken to understand better the underlying presumptions of the healing task. Although she/he will not find unanimity in these viewpoints, she/he will find a common concern that healing be intentional and self-conscious.

"Worldly theology," Bonhoeffer's term for religion in a world come of age, has much promise for the understanding of psychotherapy. "Two sphere" (grace/nature) thinking has permeated modern Christian thought, much to its own detriment. Christ and the world cannot be separated. Wherever therapy is, theology is present. Helping which nurtures selfhood is Christian, regardless of whether or not the name of Jesus is mentioned. Client-centered therapy is discussed as representative of this "unconscious Christianity."

Theology and Therapy

A New Look at Bonhoeffer

Thomas C. Oden

Although Dietrich Bonhoeffer's thought on religionless Christianity continues to have an explosive impact upon secularizing Protestantism, little effort has been made to relate it to actual secular academic disciplines. Ironically Bonhoeffer has been read and appreciated chiefly by religious people, however much his theology protests against *homo religiosus*. The unfinished task in Bonhoeffer studies is now to engage him in conversation with those for whom religion is mostly a thing of the past.

We shall limit our discussion to the promise of worldly theology for one specific major life-option of our time: psychotherapy, an area in which Bonhoeffer's contribution may have as much relevance as it has had for social ethics, ecclesiology, or the renewal of the laity.

Although most students of his biography know that Dietrich Bonhoeffer was the son of a well-known authority on psychotherapy and neurology, a professor of psychiatry at the University of Berlin, and that Dietrich's childhood was spent in a setting thoroughly familiar with Freudian psychoanalysis and the psychotherapies of the 1920s, little or no attempt has been made to ask about the martyred theologian's own view of the healing process or the possible relevance of his theological method for psychotherapy. It is curious that in *Die Mündige Welt*,[1] the four volumes of essays assessing Bonhoeffer's work,

Reprinted from *Dialog* 5, no. 2 (1966): 98–111. Used by permission.
1. (Munich: Chr. Kaiser Verlag, 1956).

with such distinguished contributors as Barth, Ebeling, Ernst Wolf, and Regin Prenter, none of his interpreters so much as mentions his relevance for pastoral care or secular psychotherapy.[2]

Yet for many of us the issues between Protestant theology and psychotherapy remain mostly muddled and unresolved. We still await an honest, congruent conversation between a theology of revelation and a psychotherapy of self-understanding, or between a theology of God's self-disclosure and a therapy of human self-disclosure. Most of the attempts at a rapprochement (Thurneysen, Tillich, Hiltner)[3] have been abortive, either by diluting revelation or by misunderstanding therapy. Frankly, as I have listened to various contemporary theologians hopefully for some fresh word on this conversation, it has been a bit disappointing, until the insight suddenly dawned recently that virtually everything Bonhoeffer was saying about the "matured world," the concreteness of Christ's formation in the world and worldly Christianity, offers a penetrating new clue for pursuing this somewhat stagnated dialogue which has been trying to break through for thirty or forty years now.

Although admittedly Bonhoeffer has said very little directly about the therapeutic process as such, his whole style of theologizing, his basic *modus vivendi* as theologian, may give us the possibility of grappling with the issue in an amazingly original way. So our purpose will be to listen attentively to the maturing Bonhoeffer, especially the hunted and imprisoned Bonhoeffer of the war years[4] (which was his

2. Likewise in the briefer American assessment of *The Place of Bonhoeffer*, ed. Martin Marty (New York: Association, 1956), in which Bonhoeffer's work is reviewed with respect to its implications for biblical studies, theology, liturgy, ethics, sociology, etc., it is also telling that no such reference was made to any significance of Bonhoeffer's thought for psychology or counseling.

3. Cf. a critique of these efforts, Thomas C. Oden, "Revelation in Psychotherapy," *Continuum* (Summer, 1964).

4. Returning from America to Germany in 1939 to continue his leadership of the makeshift, illegal, Gestapo-hunted seminary at Koslin, Bonhoeffer began to work on a new approach to ethics which he viewed as a long-term project. Written in hiding during the years 1940–43 and deposited in such varied places as a Bavarian Benedictine monastery and a summer estate in Pomerania, posthumously edited under the title *Ethics*, this group of essays provides many indications of how Bonhoeffer's thought first began to take shape on the question of the worldliness of the Word of God, which we shall argue has profound significance for the dialogue with psychotherapy. On April 5, 1943, Bonhoeffer was arrested for conspiring against the Hitler regime. From Tegel prison, however, he continued to develop these new lines of thinking, which are now collected in his *Letters and Papers from Prison* (London: SCM, 1953). In 1944, after the failure of the plot to kill Hitler, he was moved to a tighter-security Gestapo prison in Prinz Albrecht Strasse in Berlin, later taken to Buchenwald as a special prisoner, and subsequently, after a brief court-martial, hanged in the concentration camp in Flossenburg, April 9, 1945, only a few days before that area was liberated by the American army.

most creative period, though it never should be separated from his previous churchly and discipleship-oriented period) with the view in mind of asking how he might provide us a new *Fragestellung* for the continuing theology-therapy dialogue.

Thinking in Terms of Two Spheres

Virtually all attempts to engage Protestant theology in conversation with psychotherapy have been infected by a disease which Bonhoeffer has called "thinking in terms of two spheres."[5] From better to worse discussions of theology and therapy—from Eduard Thurneysen to Erich Fromm, from Paul Tillich to Fulton Sheen, from Seward Hiltner to Norman Vincent Peale, none seems to have escaped this mind set of thinking in terms of two spheres.[6]

To think in terms of two spheres means to divide reality up in two antithetical categories: sacred/secular, divine/worldly, revelation/reason, grace/nature. The pernicious danger Bonhoeffer sees in this is that the Word of God is reduced to a partial matter, a part of reality amid other realities, instead of participating in reality as a whole. All "two sphere" thinking imagines that there are realities which lie outside the reality that is in Christ.

Thinking in terms of two spheres would suppose, for example, that the psychotherapeutic process is something that might be perceived as lying outside the reality of grace. The trouble with such thinking is that it creates

the possibility of existing in a single one of these spheres, a spiritual existence which has no part in secular existence, and a secular existence which can claim autonomy for itself.[7]

The prototypes of such bifurcated thinking are (a) the monastic movement which separates the sacred from the secular; and (b) the secularism of the nineteenth century which tries to choose the secular against the sacred. To both of these Bonhoeffer protests:

So long as Christ and the world are conceived as two opposing and mutually repellent spheres, man will be left in the following dilemma:

5. Dietrich Bonhoeffer, *Ethics* (London: SCM, 195ɔ), pp. 62ff.
6. Even the most perceptive and mature discussion of this subject yet produced by Protestant theology, Albert C. Oulter's *Psychotherapy and the Christian Message* (New York: Harper and Brothers, 1954), expresses this bifurcation of thought in certain passages.
7. Bonhoeffer, *Ethics*, p. 63.

he abandons reality as a whole, and places himself in one or the other of the two spheres.[8]

Consequently, the problem in our dialogue with therapy is to break the spell of "thinking in terms of two spheres," a habit as chronic among secularists as it is among religionists. For according to the Christian confession,

> There are not two realities, but only one reality, and that is the reality of God, which has become manifest in Christ in the reality of the world.[9]

To deal with reality is to deal with that reality which has been dealt with by God in Jesus Christ. To perceive it as anything less than reconciled is to perceive it inadequately.[10]

> The reality of God discloses itself only by setting me entirely in the reality of the world and when I encounter the reality of the world it is always already sustained, accepted, and reconciled in the reality of God.[11]

Therefore one can never experience "the reality of God without the reality of the world or the reality of the world without the reality of God."[12]

As we deal with psychotherapy and the kerygma, we do not confront two spheres standing side by side, competing with one another, attacking each other's frontiers ("If that were so, this frontier dispute would always be the decisive problem of history").[13] No, we cannot pursue the dialogue on any other assumption than that "the world, the natural, the profane and reason are now all taken up into God from the outset."[14]

But if such worldly realities as psychotherapy are already circum-

---

8. *Ibid.* Bonhoeffer is here assuming a concept of *reality* which must be grasped if we are to proceed meaningfully. Reality means: that which God perceives, knows, judges, creates, and redeems. All concepts of reality which do not take into account God's own dealing with the world in the Christ event are, in Bonhoeffer's view, abstractions. "The place where the answer is given, both to the question concerning the reality of God and to the question concerning the reality of the world, is designated solely and alone by the name Jesus Christ. . . . In Him all things consist" (Col. 1:17). Ibid., p. 61.

9. *Ibid.*, pp. 63ff.

10. This Barthian concept of reality, which Karl Barth draws from Colossians, Ephesians, Augustine, Calvin, and others (cf. *Church Dogmatics*, III/1), is pursued by Bonhoeffer with more relentless worldly-directed consistency than by Barth himself.

11. Bonhoeffer, *Ethics*, p. 61.

12. *Ibid.*, pp. 61–62.

13. *Ibid.*, p. 64.

14. *Ibid.*

scribed by grace, what becomes of the church and its pastoral care?
Does the church have any territory to call its own in the world?

> The space of the church is not there in order to try to deprive the world
> of a piece of its territory, but precisely in order to prove to the world
> that it is still the world, the world which is loved by God and reconciled
> with Him. The Church has neither the wish nor the obligation to extend
> her space to cover the space of the world. She asks for no more space
> than she needs for the purpose of serving the world by bearing witness
> to Jesus Christ and to the reconciliation of the world with God through
> Him.[15]

Applying this to the therapeutic process, one might say that the
church is not trying to take over the therapist's secular function or
extend her space over the therapeutic process. The church does have
a legitimate space within the world, but only that which is necessary
for her unique service and witness.[16]

The central theme of Bonhoeffer's *Ethics* is: "Whoever sees Jesus
Christ does indeed see God and the world in one. He can henceforth
no longer see God without the world or the world without God.[17]
Consequently, Bonhoeffer proposes,

> It is now essential to the real concept of the secular that it shall always
> be seen in the movement of being accepted and becoming accepted by
> God in Christ.[18]

True secularity is thus defended and affirmed by authentic Christian
proclamation, if it is the case that

> there is no real possibility of being a Christian outside the reality of the
> world and that there is no real worldly existence outside the reality of
> Jesus Christ.[19]

15. *Ibid.*, p. 68.

16. Bonhoeffer's thinking on the worldliness of the Word of God during the war
years is not an altogether new reflection. For as early as 1928, while serving a curacy
in Spain with a German-speaking congregation, he was already expressing such
thoughts: "Here one meets men as they are, far from the masquerade of the Christian
world; people with passions, criminal types, small people with small aims, small urges
and small misdeeds—all in all, people who feel themselves homeless in both senses
of the word, who thaw out when you speak to them in a friendly way—real men; I
can only say I have the impression that these of all people stand much more under
grace than under wrath, but the Christian world in particular stands much more
under wrath than under grace." *Gesamelte Schriften I*, ed. E. Bethge, quoted by G.
Ebeling in *Word and Faith* (London: SCM, 1963), pp. 283–84.

17. Bonhoeffer, *Ethics*, p. 8

18. *Ibid.*, p. 65.

19. *Ibid.*, p. 66.

So now we ask the strange question: How does psychotherapy as a humanistic process participate in the reality of Jesus Christ, and how does Christ take form in and through that special relationship of so-called secular healing?

The Embarrassing Jurisdictional Dispute Between Therapy and Theology

Why do we choose psychotherapy as a special test case for the validity of Bonhoeffer's worldly theology? Because therapy continues to be one of the more dramatic examples of how our secular society, through ostensibly worldly and humanistic means, helps troubled persons to overcome many forms of guilt, interpersonal brokenness, and suffering which once were thought to have only a religious solution. There depression is being undercut by human self-understanding, neurotic guilt is being transformed into self-acceptance, the demons are being overthrown! In that sense psychotherapy represents something of a problem, even an embarrassment, to a theology of revelation. For if it is possible for humanistic, agnostic therapists to do all this, what are we religionists left to do? To whom do we appeal in jurisdictional disputes over who cures what ailments?

Bultmann, in his conflict with Heidegger, draws the boundary in an interesting way. Admittedly, he says, Heidegger can speak of the possibility of authenticity and healthy human existence, in a formal (ontological) sense, but he cannot make this an actual, or realizable (ontic) possibility for a particular person. He can only *describe* in a formal or general sense what authenticity means, as being open to the future, taking the past upon oneself, etc., but to *conceptualize* health is quite different from *actualizing* it, or making it *choosable* as an *existenziel* ontic possibility.[20]

If we accept this distinction,[21] it is clear that Bultmann's boundary with Heidegger does not apply to psychotherapy, however legitimate this jurisdictional settlement may be with respect to existential philosophy. The boundary dispute becomes much more delicate when we deal with someone like Carl Rogers, who not merely *talks* about the formal ontological possibilities of authentic human existence,[22] but more so goes about the process of *realizing* authenticity in persons to

20. Cf. Thomas C. Oden, "The Alleged Structural Inconsistency in Bultmann," *The Journal of Religion*, July 1964, pp. 194ff.

21. It is defended by this writer in *Radical Obedience: The Ethics of Rudolph Bultmann* (Philadelphia: Westminster, 1964), chs. 2 and 3.

22. Cf. his essay, "A Therapist's View of Personal Goals" (Wallingford, Pa.: Pendle Hill, 1959).

a recognizable degree, not merely describing but *mediating* to the troubled person a relationship in which he can grow toward congruence and health, self-acceptance, and reconciliation with himself and the world.[23]

Bonhoeffer's thought on worldly Christianity helps us to reframe the issue precisely at the point where Bultmann's boundary is inadequate for distinguishing between theology and therapy. For if indeed God and the world are one in Christ, and that really to know the world is to know its participation in Jesus Christ, and to know Jesus Christ is to know His taking form in the world, then the whole boundary dispute must be reconceived. The clues to Bonhoeffer's transformation of the question may be found in the following concepts: (1) "unconscious Christianity," (2) the emancipation of worldly processes, (3) the natural, (4) formation, and (5) relative autonomy.

In his letter from prison of July 27, 1944, he speaks of *"unconscious Christianity"* as "a subject with which I am more and more concerned."[24] He draws upon a distinction made in the Lutheran doctrine of infant baptism, in which there is a kind of unconscious faith (*fides directa*) which makes the sacrament efficacious. It is not a deliberate, reflective, conscious faith (*fides reflexa*) but a faith *for* the child, a representative faith mediated through the *sanctorum communio*. So he proposes an interesting analogy between faith in infant baptism, and the presence of a sort of "unconscious faith" among natural men which might be present, for example, in the therapeutic process, with grace fully present in any case. However absent may be the *fides reflexa* (the conscious response of man to the Word of God in Christ) in the therapeutic process, one may nevertheless be open to Christ's taking form in him to move him toward authenticity.

What Bonhoeffer wants for secular processes is that they be *"emancipated for true worldliness,"* i.e., "for the state to be a state," or in our case, for psychotherapy to *be* psychotherapy. "The primary implication for secular institutions of the dominion of Christ ... is not, therefore, the conversion of the statesman or the economist,"[25] or the therapist, in an individual sense, but instead the maintaining and enhancing of their genuine worldliness. The goal is not to "Christianize" the state, economy, or the healing process, but instead to help them function toward their proper ends of justice, production of health.

23. Thus Rogers is much more an embarrassment to a theology of revelation than Heidegger, for to whatever degree authenticity may take ontic shape in the therapeutic process, it challenges the church's claim to uniqueness.

24. Bonhoeffer, *Prisoner for God* (New York: Macmillan, 1957), p. 172.

25. Bonhoeffer, *Ethics*, p. 293.

The purpose and aim of the dominion of Christ is not to make the worldly order godly or to subordinate it to the Church, but to set it free for true worldliness.[26]

In a truly perceptive conclusion to his essay on " 'Personal' and 'Real' Ethos,"[27] Bonhoeffer says,

When the Church perceives that a worldly order is on some few occasions possible without the preaching being heard (but still never without the existence of Jesus Christ), this will not impel her to disregard Christ, but it will elicit from her the full proclamation of the grace of the dominion of Christ. The unknown God will now be preached as the God who is known because He is revealed.[28]

Thus if the therapeutic process is able to nurture authentic human existence even *without* the church's proclamation being heard, this does not mean that Jesus Christ is not at the center of things (here as always), but that he is taking shape in the world without that Word being consciously heard and understood, and that there is no reason for the church to be embarrassed by the presence of the Holy Spirit apart from the church, or for the theologian to rush to the therapist and tell him he cannot accomplish this healing without Christ! Instead such processes will elicit from the church grateful acknowledgment of the grace of Christ in the midst of worldly relationships, and wherever her preaching is able to be heard she will say that the God who is hidden in the world has made himself known in Jesus Christ.[29]

Bonhoeffer was distressed that Protestant thought had almost

26. *Ibid.*, p. 294. Bonhoeffer is quick to avoid a serious misunderstanding on this point, however: "The emancipation of the worldly order under the dominion of Christ takes concrete form not through the conversion of Christian statemen, etc., but through the *concrete encounter* of the secular institutions with the Church of Jesus Christ, her proclamation, her life." The fuller emancipation of such worldly processes as psychotherapy takes form through the concrete encounter of the practicing therapeutic community with the living Christian community and its living Word, proclaimed and celebrated in Word and sacrament. Psychotherapy will not be truly free for worldly functioning until it sees its own process reflected in the light of the kerygma.

27. Bonhoeffer's criticisms of Otto Dilschneider's *Die evangelische Tat* (Bertelsmann, 1940).

28. Bonhoeffer, *Ethics*, p. 296.

29. Bonhoeffer, *Prisoner for God*, p. 166. In his letter from prison of July 18, 1944, Bonhoeffer argues that the aim of Christian proclamation from the beginning is to call forth authentic human existence: "To be a Christian does not mean to be religious in a particular way, to cultivate some particular form of asceticism (as a sinner, a penitent, or a saint), but to be a man. . . . The religious act is always something partial, faith is always something whole, an act involving the whole life. Jesus does not call men to a new religion, but to life." What is therapy searching for other than wholeness, health, authenticity, to be a real man? So far as therapy achieves this, the church can only rejoice.

entirely abandoned the concept of *"the natural"* to Catholic ethics. He felt that this was a substantial loss which cut Protestant thinking off from intellectual tools for dealing with questions of worldly existence. For if grace should be so misunderstood as to make nature unimportant, a dangerous blind spot results in Protestant fideism. Bonhoeffer wanted to recover the concept of the natural, but on the new basis of this Christological interpretation of reality. So with uncommon originality, he defined *the natural* as "the form of life preserved by God for the fallen world and directed towards justification, redemption, and renewal through Christ."[30]

Mark carefully the distinction between unnatural (neurotic) and natural (moving toward health and full-functioning):

> The natural is that which, after the Fall, is directed toward the coming of Christ. The unnatural is that which, after the Fall, closes its doors against the coming of Christ. There is indeed only a relative difference between that which is directed towards Christ and that which closes its doors to Christ.[31]

If so, then both natural and unnatural, sickness and wholeness, are defined relative to Christ. If Christ is the presence of the healing reality in the midst of the world, neurosis is closedness to this reality, and health is openness.[32]

Having only recently read Abraham Maslow's *Toward a Psychology of Being*,[33] in which he powerfully argues that there are within human nature reliable resources for self-fulfillment, I was surprised to find astonishing agreement in Bonhoeffer, who says,

> It is in the last analysis life itself that tends towards the natural and keeps turning against the unnatural and bringing about its downfall. This, in the last analysis, is what underlies the maintenance and recovery of physical and mental health. Life is its own physician, whether it be the life of an individual or the life of a community; it wards off the unnatural because the unnatural is a destroyer of life; only when life itself is no longer able to offer the necessary resistance do the destructive forces of the unnatural carry off the victory.[34]

---

30. Bonhoeffer, *Ethics*, p. 103. Following a strongly Lutheran distinction between *creatura* and *natura*, between the creaturely and the natural, he says, "Through the fall the 'creature' becomes 'nature.' The direct dependence of the creature on God is replaced by the relative freedom of natural life" (p. 102).

31. *Ibid.* p. 102.

32. *Ibid.*, p. 103. Reason remains the organ of knowledge of the natural, although the natural is fully knowable only under the illumination of Christ. "Certainly reason does not now cease to be reason, but is now fallen reason, perceiving only the datum of the fallen world."

33. (New York: Van Nostrand, 1962).

34. Bonhoeffer, *Ethics*, p. 105.

In this connection Bonhoeffer notes with appreciation the viewpoint of psychotherapist Fritz Künkel, for whom "life" is always the "final corrective of what is psychically unnatural and diseased."[35] Neurotic conflicts are unnatural in that the natural processes have not learned to fend off their self-destructive features. But along with Maslow, Erikson, Boisen, and Rogers, Bonhoeffer would agree that the natural processes direct one constantly toward authenticity.

In a theology of revelation so consistent as Bonhoeffer's, one is amazed to hear a good word spoken for genuinely naturalistic optimism:

> In this context there is a solid basis for that optimistic view of human history which confines itself within the limits of the fallen world. . . . We are referring here to an entirely immanent optimism, one which is entirely rooted in the natural.[36]

Anyone who has seriously considered Roger's therapy, which continually relies upon the natural resources of the self for self-affirmation and self-fulfillment, is struck by a very persistent, stubborn, almost incredible faith in the strength of human nature to fight against neurosis and move the self toward authenticity, and a radical optimism directed toward the resources within itself for appropriate self-direction, provided one is given a safe context for self-exploration. Of all places to find corroboration of this, one would hardly expect it in this thoroughly christological orientation of Bonhoeffer.

Another concept which Bonhoeffer's thought brings to the rethinking of this jurisdictional dispute is that of concrete *formation*.[37] Authentic existence is existence which is being concretely formed into the likeness of true man, Jesus Christ, characterized by freedom from guilt, freedom for the neighbor, and openness to the future. If such concrete formation takes place in psychotherapy, however unconsciously Christian, it is a cause for rejoicing. The formation of which Bonhoeffer speaks is not our forming of ourselves or formulating plans, programs, or policies to shape our world, but instead God's taking form in us, as that form is preeminently known in Jesus Christ. Paul tells the Galatians that his task is unfulfilled "till Christ is formed in you" (Gal. 4:19). In effective psychotherapy we can see, perceive, and experience authentic human existence taking form in us, and therefore, however unconsciously, our "being found in him" (cf. Phil. 3:9; Rom. 8:29).

35. *Ibid.*
36. *Ibid.*, p. 106.
37. *Ibid.*, pp. 17–25.

The concept of formation bears on therapy in that in the therapeutic process, where authenticity is being at least partially achieved, the Christian can perceive something much more than human interaction. He can see there true humanity, i.e., Jesus Christ, taking concrete form, and that even amid human brokenness men are responding to the accepting reality (mediated through the therapist) which is made known once for all in Christ, and under whose initiative all healing takes place.[38]

"Relative Autonomy." To speak of the lordship of Christ over secular processes such as psychotherapy does not mean that such processes are made subject to an alien rule, for "He came unto his own,"[39] and "by him all things consist."[40] It is under the lordship of Christ that these secular processes "attain to their own true character and become subject to their own innate law."[41] This does not mean that they are governed by what Bonhoeffer calls "the arbitrary rule of a so-called 'autonomy' which is fundamentally nothing but lawlessness, *anomia.* . . ."[42] Therapy must be allowed to function in terms of its own innate processes, but it is not in the last sense interpretable from within its own limited framework.[43]

Thus we find Bonhoeffer supporting a *"relative autonomy"* for secular processes:

> There is good reason for laying stress on the autonomy of, for example, the state in opposition to the heteronomy of an ecclesiastical theocracy; yet before God there is no autonomy, but the law of the God who is revealed in Jesus Christ is the law of all earthly institutions.[44]

There is a sense in which the therapeutic process is autonomous (it has its own law innate within itself), but viewed from the kerygmatic perspective all so-called autonomous processes "consist in Him."[45]

38. But does Christ take form in the world apart from the church? The extent to which His form is present in secular processes is unclear in Bonhoeffer's thought, but it seems that much that Bonhoeffer says about "the natural" and religionless Christianity implies precisely that.

39. John 1:11.

40. Col. 1:17.

41. Bonhoeffer, *Ethics*, p. 293.

42. *Ibid.*, p. 203.

43. Psychotherapy is not autonomous in a spurious, lawless sense. For authentic autonomy means that a process is subject to laws innate within itself.

44. Bonhoeffer, *Ethics*, p. 325.

45. *Ibid.*, pp. 70–71. Bonhoeffer speaks of an inauthentic "love for the world which is enmity toward God (James 4:4) because it springs from the nature of the world as such and not from the love of God for the world. The world 'as such' is the world as it understands itself, the world which resists the reality of the love of God. . . ."

When reality is bifurcated, however, and the world is viewed as if it owned its existence apart from God, the result is the "love of the world," against which the New Testament speaks. It simply fails to love the world as God loves it. "Life which posits itself as an absolute, as an end in itself, as its own destroyer."[46]

The great limitation of a spuriously autonomous psychotherapy is not that it fails to elicit any healing or authenticity, but that it would define authenticity only from within the narrow range of the client's own self-understanding, instead of his being understood by God.

Can we therefore say that the fully functioning person experiencing effective therapy is indeed, however unconsciously, a man of faith—freed to be open to the future, accept himself in the past, etc.? If so, there is one addition that must be made. The Christian community believes that this kind of ambiguous, fragmented, "unconscious Christianity," or natural authenticity, has a right to experience a deeper understanding of its own inner reality, viz., the incarnation, the word that God takes shape in us. Christ's coming is that point in history where we have been freed to know fully that we are indeed accepted by God himself, not merely by our therapist or ourselves, and that the future is guaranteed by the God who has made himself known as trustworthy in Jesus Christ.

Client-Centered Therapy: A Promising Analogy to the Worldliness of the Word

Although Bonhoeffer knew nothing of the approach to therapy developed by Carl Rogers, there are many aspects of his view of God's participation in the broken world which are surprisingly analogous to the client-centered therapist's participation in the frame of reference of the troubled person.

It is astonishing how similar is Bonhoeffer's discussion of "the responsible man" to Roger's view of *"the fully functioning person."* In his essay, "A Process Conception of Psychotherapy," Rogers describes the last state of the therapeutic process in these terms:

> Experiencing has lost almost completely its structure-bound aspects and becomes process experiencing—that is, the situation is experienced and interpreted in its newness, not as the past.[47]

46. *Ibid.*, p. 106.
47. Carl Rogers, *On Becoming a Person* (New York: Houghton Mifflin, 1961), pp. 152–53.

Again in his essay, "The Fully Functioning Person," Rogers says:

> For the person who was fully open to his new experience, completely without defensiveness, each moment would be new. . . . Consequently such a person would realize that "What I will be in the next moment, and what I will do, grows out of that moment and cannot be predicted in advance either by me or by others."[48]

Similarly Bonhoeffer says of the responsible man that

> his conduct is not established in advance, once and for all, that is to say, as a matter of principle, but it arises with the given situation. He has no principle at his disposal which possesses absolute validity . . . but he sees in the given situation what is necessary and what is "right" for him to grasp and to do.[49]

. Note also how Bonhoeffer's language about God the healer corresponds with the nondiagnostic, empathetic function of the helper in client-centered therapy:

> While we are distinguishing the pious from the ungodly, the good from the wicked, the noble from the mean, God makes no such distinction at all in His love for the real man.[50]

If in our Protestant pastoral office we have been overly busy distinguishing sheep and goats, the effective therapist has been making no such distinction at all in his emphatic positive concern for the man as he is. Even as Rogers does not allow diagnosis to invade the psychotherapeutic relationship, Bonhoeffer also agrees that God does not permit us to

> classify men and the world according to our own standards and to set ourselves up as judges over them. He leads us *ad absurdum* by Himself becoming a real man and a companion of sinners. . . . God sides with the real man and with the real world against all their accusers.[51]

Admittedly certain forms of psychotherapy (especially psychoanalysis) have concerned themselves more with diagnosis, so that some therapists have tried to classify the client in terms of their own conceptual framework and diagnostic standards, but such is not the most

48. *Ibid.*, p. 188.
49. Bonhoeffer, *Ethics*, p. 197.
50. *Ibid.*, p. 10.
51. *Ibid.*

helpful aim of the therapeutic relationship, according to Rogers, whose views we are following here. Rather the therapist leads the troubled person in a unique way by following him through his own expressions of inner conflict, sharing his situation as companion, entering his frame of reference, siding with him in the form of understanding, regardless of who may be against him. And it is only in the consciousness that someone is truly unconditionally for him in understanding and positive regard, and with him amid his internal conflicts, that real healing is achieved.[52]

In distinguishing between the ultimate and the penultimate, Bonhoeffer affirms that in Protestant theology the last word is always justification of the sinner by grace alone. The question of the *penultimate*, however, has to do with the "things before this last thing," taking with relative seriousness the human words before this last divine word. Furthermore, he asks whether the last word is always the most appropriate word, in every situation. He uses an example which, for our discussion, is of most interest, inasmuch as Bonhoeffer seldom refers to his own functioning as pastoral counselor:

> When I am with someone who has suffered a bereavement, I often decide to adopt a 'penultimate' attitude, remaining silent as a sign that I share in the bereaved man's helplessness in the face of such a grievous event, and not speaking the biblical words of comfort which are, in fact, known to me and available to me.[53]

Even in this brief statement we can see an attitude toward suffering which fundamentally reflects the basic characteristics of what Carl Rogers would call "the helping relationship." Basically he is sharing in the sense of limitation which the bereaved is experiencing, and the best way he can signify this is not by verbalizing about how the person is helpless, but by demonstrating his sharing in his helplessness through *silence* which itself is a sort of helplessness in the form of language.

Bonhoeffer then asks himself why, in this context, he does not go ahead and witness to the ultimate.

52. *Ibid.*, p. 12. "The despiser of men despises what God has loved." It is so easy to despise that which is caught in inauthenticity, guilt, and anxiety, both in ourselves and others. The therapist regards suffering with unconditional positive regard. Yet for Bonhoeffer, it is only in the light of the incarnation, in which we see ourselves as having been concretely loved, that it is possible in the fuller sense to accept the real man, to achieve empathetic acceptance. "It is only through God's being made man that it is possible to know the real man and not to despise him. . . . The real man can live before God, and we can allow the real man to live before God side by side with ourselves without either despising or deifying him."

53. *Ibid.*, p. 84.

Is it because of some mistrust of the ultimate word? Or is there some good positive reason for such an attitude, namely, that my knowledge of the word, my having it at my fingertips, in other words, my being, so to speak, spiritually master of the situation, bears only the appearance of the ultimate, but is in reality itself something entirely penultimate? Does one not in some cases, by remaining deliberately in the penultimate, perhaps point all the more genuinely to the ultimate, which God will speak in His own time . . . ?[54]

The good client-centered therapist, likewise, refuses to impose upon the troubled person some kind of ultimate interpretation which in effect would falsify his empathetic participation in the limited situation of the other. That would simply demonstrate his own spurious "mastery" of the situation, and more deeply his unwillingness to share seriously in the internal reality of the individual's conflict. Bonhoeffer suggests that such a "penultimate" attitude embraces the whole domain of the Christian life, but "especially the whole range of Christian pastoral activity."

Only five days before the attempt to assassinate Hitler failed, Bonhoeffer proposed this strange formula: The God who is with us is the God who forsakes us.[55] In this connection, he quotes Mark 15:34, Jesus' expression on the cross, "My God, my God, why hast thou forsaken me?" Likewise in therapy, it is the empathetic therapist, the one who is for us, who in a sense *"forsakes"* us, leaves us to ourselves, even amid anger, agony, and anxiety.

God allows himself to be edged out of the world and on to the cross. God is weak and powerless in the world, and that is exactly the way, the only way in which he can be with us and help us. Matthew 8:17 makes it crystal clear that it is not by his omnipotence that Christ helps us, but by his weakness and suffering.[56]

The analogy here between God's action and the therapist's empathy is startling. For Rogers has repeatedly described the helping relationship as one in which the only way one can help the troubled person is to be with him in empathetic acceptance and unconditional positive regard. And so it is perhaps in the effective therapeutic process that God's power is *silently* being made known, not coercively or in traditional language, but as the God who is present in weakness and suf-

54. *Ibid.*, p. 85.
55. Bonhoeffer, *Prisoner for God*, p. 164.
56. *Ibid.*

fering, sharing our human condition, and taking form concretely in the midst of the world.[57]

Religionless Christianity and Religionless Psychotherapy

Thus far most of the writings we have discussed are contained in the 1940–43 essays on *Ethics*. From April 5, 1943, to April 9, 1945, Bonhoeffer was imprisoned. The ideas which emerged during this period have become so very influential in Protestant theology that, in addition to Barth and Bultmann, Dietrich Bonhoeffer has become the leading spokesman of a whole new school of "worldly theology."[58] It was especially during the summer of 1944 that his thinking on religionless Christianity emerged with real force, in which he set forth a constellation of embryonic theological proposals which have piercing relevance for our dialogue with therapy.[59]

If one were to identify the central theological events of the past generation, in addition to Bultmann's publication of "The New Testament and Mythology," and Pope John's call for an ecumenical council, one might also place in that category the letter which Bonhoeffer wrote to Eberhard Bethge on April 30, 1944, from Tegel prison, in which began to develop this whole line of thinking:

> You would be surprised and perhaps disturbed if you knew how my ideas on theology are taking shape. . . . The thing that keeps coming back to me is [that we] are proceeding towards a time of no religion at all: men as they are now simply cannot be religious any more. . . . Our whole nineteen-hundred-year-old Christian preaching and theology rests upon

57. He who would truly behold the process of human healing, *ecce homo!* Behold the man in whom the real world is made known, the world which God has reconciled. Behold "the lived love of God," behold the man, in whom healing is manifested, in whom "God is willing to be guilty of our guilt. In a manner which passes all comprehension God reverses the judgment of justice and piety, declares Himself guilty toward the world, and thereby wipes out the world's guilt. God Himself sets out on the path of humiliation and atonement, and thereby absolves the world." (*Ethics*, p. 9). If you would really understand such secular processes as psychotherapy, Bonhoeffer declares, look at them as they really are, as worldly relationships toward which God's own Yes has been addressed.

58. The institutional manifestations of this movement are the German evangelical academies with their dialogical approach to the world, the ecumenical lay movement and much that goes on under the name of renewal of the church, the ministry of the laity, holy worldliness and the world come of age. Much of this worldly theology emerged with real force only at the very end of Bonhoeffer's career.

59. We will focus the remainder of our discussion on that section of his letters from prison during the summer of 1944, from April 30 until October, 1944.

the "religious premise" of man . . . but . . . the linchpin is removed from the whole structure of our Christianity to date.[60]

He then asks what might result:

If we had finally to put down the Western pattern of Christianity as a mere preliminary stage to doing without religion altogether? . . . How can Christ become the Lord even of those with no religion?[61]

In several letters, Bonhoeffer points to the center of his thinking during the summer of 1944. On June 27, 1944, he wrote,

This world must not be prematurely written off. . . . Christ takes hold of a man in the center of his life. You see how my thoughts are constantly revolving round the same theme.[62]

Three days later he wrote:

Let me briefly summarize what I am concerned about: it is how can we reclaim for Christ a world which has come of age?[63]

The question is:

What is the significance of a Church . . . in a religionless world? How do we speak of God without religion, i.e., without the temporally-influenced presuppositions of metaphysics, inwardness, and so on? How do we speak . . . in a secular fashion of God? In what way are we in a religion-less and secular sense Christians, in what way are we the *Ekklesia*, "those who are called forth," not conceiving of ourselves religiously as specially favoured, but as wholly belonging to the world? Then Christ is no longer an object of religion, but something quite different, indeed and in truth the Lord of the world.[64]

---

60. Bonhoeffer, *Prisoner for God*, p. 122.

61. *Ibid.*, pp. 122–23.

62. *Ibid.*, p. 154.

63. *Ibid.*, p. 157.

64. It is unfortunate that the one who introduced us to the notion of religionless Christianity never had time to give us a clear definition of religion. Although we might properly suppose that he has Barth's definition of religion in mind, he never validates this assumption. Again and again he uses the analogy of religion to circumcision as a condition for justification (*Prisoner for God*, p. 123). Once he suggested that religion means "to speak on the one hand metaphysically, and on the other hand, individu-alistically" (*Ibid.*, p. 125). Elsewhere religion means variously, "individualistic con-cern for personal salvation" (*Ibid.*), "concern for the next world" (*Ibid.*, p. 126), reli-ance upon a *Deus ex machina* (*Letters and Papers from Prison*, p. 114), or using God as a "working hypothesis" (*Ibid.*, p. 163).

His letter of June 8, 1944, dealing with the relation of science to Christian faith, however, can be directly and clearly applied to our discussion with therapy, wherein he most candidly admits,

> It is possible nowadays to find answers to these problems which leave God right out of the picture. It just isn't true to say that Christianity alone has the answers. In fact, the Christian answers are no more conclusive or compelling than any of the others. Once more, God cannot be used as a stopgap. We must not wait until we are at the end of our tether; He must be found at the centre of life.[65]

The same letter discusses the modern man from an historical perspective, arguing that from the thirteenth century on there has been a movement toward autonomy. Man has discovered the laws by which he lives, manages the world, political affairs, and psychology.[66]

> Man has learned to cope with all questions of importance without recourse to God as a working hypothesis. . . . It is becoming evident that everything gets along without God, and just as well as before. As in the scientific field, so in human affairs generally, what we call "God" is being more and more edged out of life, losing more and more ground.[67]

Is not this the setting of the present dialogue? Although Protestant theology has borrowed much from modern psychology, it has nonetheless yearned to cling to some territory which would remain distinctively religious. Yet psychotherapy has become increasingly sure of itself, able to get along quite well without the so-called "God" of religion (to be distinguished from the God known in Christian faith, the God who reveals himself in Jesus Christ). Both Catholics and Protestants, however, continue to view the secularizing development with frenzied alarm as defection from the truth.

A Christian apologetic has emerged, therefore, to try to prove to this world come of age that it needs religion, that it cannot live without it. Admittedly, many of these once sacred questions have been surrendered to the secular world view, but certain issues like guilt and death we continue to reserve for specifically religious answers, although the range of these questions seems to be getting smaller and smaller.[68] But what if, one day, even these "ultimate questions" should be taken over by secular hands and answered without the God of religion?

65. Bonhoeffer, *Prisoner for God*, pp. 142–43.

66. *Ibid.*, p. 145. In our time this process of increasing autonomy has "reached a certain completion."

67. *Ibid.*, pp. 145–46.

68. We religionists "live, to some extent, by these ultimate questions," i.e., we make a living, so to speak, parasitically, on the fact that we still have a little territory in the healing of man which is religious and which secular thinking cannot handle.

How should worldly theology respond to this process of increasing autonomy? Bonhoeffer's answer: utter honesty, repentance, and intellectual sincerity. "We have to live in the world *etsi deus non daretu.*"[69]

This whole historical process, climaxed by Freudian psychoanalysis, by which God is pushed more and more out of space in the world, the process by which the world has come of age, calls for an abandonment of a false religious conception of "God," and a "clearing of the decks" for the authentic proclamation of the kerygma.[70]

It is precisely because the church has been fighting this rear-guard action for self-preservation and trying to keep its place in the modern world as if that were an end in itself, that it has lost its chance to speak to the modern world, so busy has it been with the task of defense. So now we are in a new situation in which

> traditional language must perforce become powerless and remain silent, and our Christianity to-day will be confined to praying for and doing right by our fellow men. Christian thinking, speaking, and organizing must be reborn out of this praying and action.[71].

Bonhoeffer therefore differs fundamentally in his view of pastoral care from Thurneysen who would continue to rely so exclusively upon the traditional language of the church.[72]

If Bonhoeffer's rejection of "religion" on behalf of Christian faith is accepted, its consequence will be the frustration of at least 90% of the attempts by both psychologists and religionists writing on this subject in the last generation. Such writings as those of Allport, Tillich, Jung, Fromm, Mowrer, Guntrip, Biddle, McKenzie,[73] and others attempting

69. Bonhoeffer, *Prisoner for God*, p. 163.

70. *Ibid.*, p. 164.

71. *Ibid.*, p. 140. Meanwhile, it may not be helpful to explain to the troubled in therapy their situation in terms of the traditional language of the church, moving back archaically to the ancient language from modern language. Rather we must learn to translate our traditional categories into this new secularized language, which is the meaning of Bonhoeffer's "nonreligious interpretation of religious concepts."

72. There will come a day when we will again be able to utter the word of God, but it will be in "a new language, which will horrify men, and yet overwhelm them by its power . . . until then the Christian cause will be a silent and hidden affair." *Ibid.*, pp. 140–41.

73. Gordon Allport, *The Individual and His Religion* (New York: Macmillan, 1950); Paul Tillich, *Systematic Theology*, vol. 3 (Chicago: University of Chicago, 1964); Carl Jung, *Modern Man in Search of a Soul* (New York: Harcourt, Brace, and Co., 1933); Erich Fromm, *Psychoanalysis and Religion* (New Haven: Yale University, 1950); Hobart Mowrer, *The Crisis in Psychiatry and Religion* (New York: Van Nostrand, 1961); Henry Guntrip, *Psychotherapy and Religion* (New York: Harper and Brothers, 1957); W. Earl Biddle, *Integration of Religion and Psychiatry* (New York: Collier, 1962); John G. McKenzie, *Nervous Disorders and Religion* (New York: Collier, 1962).

a rapprochement of psychology and religion are based on a concept of religion which any post-Bonhoefferian theology will reject. Although psychotherapy may have much in common with religion in general, this does not mean that it therefore has an ally in Christian proclamation about the God who loves us in spite of all our religious pretensions and grasps us amid our inauthentic attempts to grasp reality apart from His own gracious self-disclosure.

Religion of the sort Bonhoeffer describes and protests must be rejected not only by Christian faith but also by psychotherapy. Of course it is already being rejected by psychotherapy, which needs no *deus ex machina* to bail it out at the crucial time. Let us then pursue the dialogue between therapy and theology on the assumption that we are discussing the relationship between a religionless psychotherapy and a religionless Christianity, and see where this takes us. This at least appears more promising than the more or less innocuous attempts of the religious psychologists such as Allport or Jung, or the psychological religionists such as Tillich or McKenzie.

An Assessment of Theological Resources for the Emerging Dialogue

We conclude our discussion of Bonhoeffer's relevance to secular psychotherapy by reviewing his own assessment of the major voices in Protestant theology, asking how they are more or less adequate in their conversation with therapy.

1. The strong point of *theological liberalism* was that it accepted a lively relationship with the newly matured world and did not try to turn back the clock. In relation to psychotherapy, e.g., it ventured out (against more orthodox protests) to learn (albeit uncritically) all it could about man's sickness and health when viewed autonomously and abstractly apart from revelation. Its Achilles heel was:

> It allowed the world the right to assign Christ his place in the world: in the dispute between Christ and the world it accepted the comparatively clement peace dictated by the world.[74]

Most of the legion of American discussions of psychotherapy have been trapped in this accommodationist process.

2. The gut issue of worldly theology against *Tillich's* view of psychotherapy[75] is his decisive use of the concept of religion.

74. Bonhoeffer, *Letters and Papers*, p. 108.
75. Tillich, *Theology of Culture* (New York: Oxford University, 1959), pp. 112ff.

Tillich set out to interpret the evolution of the world itself—against its will—in a religious sense, to give it its whole shape through religion. That was very courageous of him, but the world unseated him and went on by itself; he too sought to understand the world better than it understood itself, but it felt entirely *mis*understood, and rejected the imputation. (Of course the world does need to be understood better than it understands itself, but not "religiously" as the religious socialists desired.)[76]

For Tillich, with his definition of religion as ultimate concern, psychotherapy becomes an arena in which religious concerns are expressed, just like art or philosophy. But for Bonhoeffer, with his Barthian definition of religion as man's outmoded, inauthentic quest for God, the worst possible category through which to interpret these secular functions is the notion of "religion," which is already negated by God's self-disclosure in Christ.

Tillich's view that the Christian proclamation speaks primarily on "the boundary situation" of man is likewise challenged by Bonhoeffer, who says: "The church stands not where human powers give out, on the borders, but in the center of the village."[77]

Against Tillich's method of correlation and theology of culture Bonhoeffer says:

It is necessary to free oneself from the way of thinking which sets out from human problems and which asks for solutions on this basis.[78]

In typical Barthian fashion, Bonhoeffer rejects a method of correlation (allowing culture's questions to frame the questions for theology), inasmuch as all biblical thinking moves "not from the world to God but from God to the world,"[79] and the divine initiative is as much present in framing the theological question as it is in speaking to its solution.

The same thing that disturbed Bonhoeffer about Tillich's theology also bothered him about much of the psychotherapy he knew.

We have, of course, the secularized offshoots of Christian theology, the existential philosophers and the psychotherapists who demonstrate to secure, contented, happy mankind that it is really unhappy and desperate, and merely unwilling to realize that it is in severe straits it knows nothing at all about, from which only they can rescue it. Wherever there is health, strength, security, simplicity, they spy luscious fruit to gnaw at or to lay their pernicious eggs in. They make it their object first

76. Bonhoeffer, *Letters and Papers*, p. 109.
77. Bonhoeffer, *Prisoner for God*, p. 124.
78. Bonhoeffer, *Ethics*, p. 320.
79. *Ibid.*

of all to drive men to inward despair, and then it is all theirs. That is secularized methodism.[80]

Secularized methodism is a term of utmost contempt for Bonhoeffer, for it signifies what is worst in Protestant pietism being taken over and "used" by the world come of age, viz., a methodology which convinces men they are in the worst possible predicament, only then to propose itself as the only solution. Like much secularized methodism, Tillich's theological method lends itself to

> "priestly" snuffing around in the sins of men in order to catch them out. It is as though a beautiful house could be known only after a cobweb had been found in the furthermost corner of the cellar, or as though a good play could be appreciated only after one had seen how the actors behave off stage.[81]

3. *Barth* was first to perceive of these efforts to try to clear a space for religion in the world as a failure to understand Christ as the center of the world (even when unacknowledged). If attempts such as Tillich's are still "unintentionally sailing in the channel of liberal theology," Barth's decisive contribution to theology, "his greatest service (the second edition of his *Epistle to the Romans*, in spite of all its neo-Kantian shavings),"[82] was his sharp distinction between religion and Christianity. Barth initiated the line of thought which views Christianity (God's quest for man) as opposed to religion (man's quest for God). But Barth did not finish what he started.

Barth's crippling inadequacy is his "positivist doctrine of revelation,"[83] which does not leave room for "nonreligious interpretation of theological concepts," making sense of the kerygma in secularized language. So his program has tended to lapse into conservative restoration of the Calvinist-Augustinian tradition, instead of being truly open to the twentieth century.

4. Only *Bultmann* seemed to Bonhoeffer to be aware of Barth's limitations, and tried to transcend them with his proposal on demythologizing. Bonhoeffer was giving much reflection to the demythology controversy during his prison days. On May 9, 1944, he wrote,

> My view of it today would be not that he went too far, as most people seem to think, but that he did not go far enough. It is not only mytho-

80. Bonhoeffer, *Prisoner for God*, p. 146.
81. Bonhoeffer, *Letters and Papers*, p. 117.
82. *Ibid.*, p. 109.
83. Bonhoeffer, *Prisoner for God*, p. 126. Barth says in effect, "Take it or leave it: Virgin Birth, Trinity or anything else, everything which is an equally significant and necessary part of the whole which later has to be swallowed as a whole or not at all."

logical conceptions, such as the miracles, the ascension and the like (which are not in principle separable from the conceptions of God, faith and so on) that are problematic, but the "religious" conceptions themselves. You cannot, as Bultmann imagines, separate God and miracles, but you do have to be able to interpret and proclaim both of them in a "nonreligious" sense. Bultmann's approach is really at bottom the liberal one (i.e., abridging the Gospel), whereas I seek to think theologically.[84]

In one of his last letters (August 3, 1944), he encloses an outline of a proposed book, which he prefaces with this remark:

The Church must get out of her stagnation. We must move out again into the open air of intellectual discussion with the world, and risk shocking people if we are to cut any ice.[85]

Although he never had an opportunity to pursue it himself, Bonhoeffer would undoubtedly have welcomed a serious discussion between a theology of revelation and a secular psychotherapy which has taken over so many priestly functions, but it would have certainly been a dialogue and not a monologue. It could never be a mere listening to the therapists as if they were to lay down the rules of the game, or to assign a place for Christ in the processes of life.[86]

One might conclude this discussion with a selection from "Thoughts on the Baptism of D. W. R.," written in prison for his godchild on the occasion of his baptism. Among several reflections from his Tegel prison cell, he writes,

Despite everything, however, I can only say I should not have chosen to live in any other age than our own, though it is so regardless of our

84. *Ibid.*, p. 125. Doubtless Bonhoeffer has misunderstood Bultmann, in that Bultmann's view of myth does not have the objectivist character Bonhoeffer attributes to it. Bultmann is not trying to get away from miracle or myth, but to understand them existentially in terms of this-worldly language, which I believe is also the basic intention of Bonhoeffer's "nonreligious interpretation of religious concepts." Bonhoeffer acknowledged only one of the two parts of the demythology task, i.e., he would speak of demythology without also speaking of existential interpretation of the kerygma. When Bonhoeffer explains that what he means by "non-religious interpretation of religious concepts" is to ask "how we may reinterpret in the manner 'of the world' . . . the concepts of repentance, faith, justification, rebirth, sanctification and so on," (*Ibid.*, p. 126) it becomes clear that essentially he is in agreement with Bultmann's framing of the problem, if not entirely with his proposed solution.

85. *Ibid.*, p. 177.

86. Bonhoeffer feared that not many postwar theologians would combine a Barthian Christology with a deeply enmeshed concern for the world, and indeed how few there have been, with perhaps Gollwitzer and Hromadka coming the closest in political affairs. But who has pursued a post-Barthian rapprochement with psychotherapy?

external fortunes. Never have we realized, as we do today, how the world lies under the wrath and grace of God.[87]

In an era of political momentum in which there is a great deal of resentment against the twentieth century itself, and in this waning era of Protestant pietism in which there remains the greatest temptation to withdraw into an introverted religious shell amid the vitalities of the twentieth century, here in the imprisoned Bonhoeffer we find a joyful affirmation of the modern world as precisely the world which is created, judged, reconciled, and known by God in Jesus Christ.

87. Bonhoeffer, *Prisoner for God*, p. 137.

Theology provides the foundation for counseling. The manifest church embodies the New Being in that it represents the entrance into the world of a new reality, i.e., Jesus the Christ. But it does so only partially, therefore, it both offers and stands in need of counseling. True counseling is based on a recognition and courageous acceptance of human finiteness. This is the human predicament which can be overcome only by accepting our acceptance of God. All neurotic anxiety is based in ultimate anxiety about our being accepted.

Theology and Counseling

Paul J. Tillich

Both theology and counseling are functions of the church. Theology, in its doctrine of the church, tries to give the theoretical foundations of both theology itself and of counseling. Counseling receives its theoretical foundation from theology, and sometimes it is not only in the receiving position but also the giving: the theologian needs counseling—personally and for his theological work.

Let me speak first about the theology of the church insofar as it has implications for counseling; then about theology and man's predicament insofar as it has implications for counseling; and finally about the counselor and other helpers.

The Implications of the Church's Theology

The church can be briefly described as the community of the New Being: that community in which the new creature, the new reality, the new aeon, or—most abstractly—the New Being, is actualized. Where there is *New* Being, there must be *Old* Being, and the New Being must *do* something to the *Old* Being—not abolish it but transform it, for the Old Being is the being of estrangement from what we,

Lecture delivered in Marsh Chapel, November 14, 1955, before the Fourth Annual Workshop sponsored by the Boston University School of Theology and the Pastoral Counseling Service.

Reprinted from *Journal of Pastoral Care* 10, no. 4 (1956): 193–200. Used by permission.

and life generally, essentially are. And what has to be done with this Old Being is reconciliation and transformation.

This reality of the church between Old and New Being is expressed in all its functions. All functions of the church have one side according to which they belong to the Old Being, and they have another side according to which they proclaim and actualize the *New* Being. The church belongs to the state of universal estrangement, but the church knows about this state, even its own involvement in it, and the church embodies *New* Being, Reconciled Being, *Re*united Being.

We find this ambiguous situation, which characterizes the church, in all its functions. We find it in preaching, which has in itself the problem of human self-expression and which, at the same time, is supposed to bear in itself the message of the New Being. We have it in the cult, which is a creation of human decision and which, at the same time, is supposed to embody the great expressions of the New Reality in which we can participate. We have it in social and individual ethics, which are dependent on the social and psychological situation of human beings, our insights into them, and our participation in them, and which at the same time are supposed to give answers. We have it in missions—missions at home and missions towards other religions—where we bring our own religious culture, which is in the same estrangement and judgment as the other religious cultures. But at the same time, in this human vessel and in these estranged forms, which are *our own* religious culture, we are supposed to bring something which has *judged and transformed* our own religious culture. This is the ambiguity of religious life; it is the ambiguity of the church and all its functions.

And let's be very honest about it, since most of those who are here this afternoon are leaders of churches: it is not only the fact that the churches are finite—which means that they have shortcomings, errors, and failures—but there is more involved in the ambiguity of the churches: they also are in the predicament of mankind as a whole. And this predicament includes pride, self-elevation, arrogance; it includes will to power, it includes desire for undue self-realization, and it even includes *"unbelief,"* which does not mean lack of belief in some doctrines but rather separation from God, turning away from Him. All this is also true of the two functions of the church about which I am supposed to speak here: theology and pastoral counseling. They also are in finitude and error, in estrangement and lack of spiritual power.

But a second thing must be said. Very often the church is in danger of considering itself the subject, and others the object, of its actions. But all functions of the church are directed not only toward others but also toward the church itself. Not only are the functions of the church directed toward the church itself—its members, its leaders, and its institutions—but also toward the church are directed the spiritual functions of men not living within the community of the church. The church is not only the subject, dealing with man's cultural and spiritual functions, but is also the object of them. The church is always subject and object at the same time. It is preached to and preaches. It *receives* the ethical problems and preliminary solutions. It *receives* political structures. It becomes *object* as much as subject in all these respects. And now again, applying it to our subject: the church also receives theological methods and forms of procedure, and not only does the church counsel but it *is* counseled. It *is* counseled not only in all of its counselors but also in its leadership, in the deciding groups in it, in its totality.

Let me immediately derive from this a very important point for all counseling. Never feel you are just the subject having objects whom you counsel. Whenever this happens, the act of counseling is humiliating for the one counseled. But always act—and not only act: *feel*, in the depths of your own being—as though you participated in an act of communion with those whom you counsel. Tell them sometimes (not always, and not as an external law) that you are in the same predicament as they are. *Confess*, if you want *them* to confess. Don't be one-sided in the subject-object relationship into which counseling can easily fall. If this is true of the church as a whole, if this mutuality is needed with respect to all cultural functions, then it is certainly needed with respect to all individual functions, and especially to the most *personal* function, which we call counseling.

On the other hand, all this reduction of ecclesiastical arrogance of which I spoke earlier does *not* mean that the church cannot claim to have a unique message, a message of something which has happened, namely the manifestation *within history* of that which judges and transforms and may fulfill history.

Now we must live in this tension. And I think it is an extreme temptation for ministers who in all ecclesiastical functions are accustomed to being the leaders, to make themselves into subjects over against the objects of their activities. Actually they are neither, but they are those who express something under which both the subject and the object, the leader and the layman, the counselor and the counseled, stand. And perhaps every minister should counsel himself in this respect and ask himself whether he has fallen into this distortion of his function.

Who is supposed to engage in this act of pastoral counseling? In

principle every Christian, according to the law of the universal priesthood of every Christian, a most precious heritage of the Reformation.

Now this possibility is not always actual, but it is very often so.
And if it is actual, something is fulfilled which is the ultimate solution
of the great problem with which we are dealing, namely, the personal
union of the pastoral counselor and any other helper. But in order to
reach this, we must first, as always, have a clear, well-defined distinction of functions.

In terms of definition, pastoral counseling must be clearly and
sharply distinguished from helping in all other respects. The function
of the minister is different from the function of him who helps the
body, or the social situation, or the psychological disease. This difference must not be blurred by a mixture of the functions. Counseling is
an act which is a part of a larger activity, namely, pastoral care. Pastoral care, in the name of the church, deals with its members
individually. It does so in terms of consolation, of encouragement, of
teaching, of technically good advice.

Counseling is another element in the same reality. It deals with
special forms of psychological disturbances and human relationships
in which these disturbances occur. And pastoral counseling deals with
them in relation to an *ultimate* concern and not in relation to preliminary concerns, as for instance social and psychological and bodily
health. This is the difference between the kinds of functions. Wherever
a minister gives counsel, he should do it in the light of the eternal.
And he never should do it simply as a substitute for a physician or
social worker or psychoanalyst, or whatever other help exists. He should
be aware that *functionally* he represents the church, that he represents
the New Being, *in spite* of its ambiguity, and that this representation
makes him perform a function different from the others. The ideal is
the universal priesthood and therefore the possibility that *every* helper
also helps in the light of the eternal. But this ideal cannot be reached
at all if one tries to reach it by confusion of the functions.

The Theological Implications of Man's Predicament

Now I come to the second step of my consideration, namely, the
theology of man's predicament and the function of counseling in relation to this predicament. I have already said that the church
participates in the ambiguity of the human situation. Man, as created,
is good. Being as being is good. This we must maintain against ancient
and *modern* manichaeism (and the newer manichaeism often appears
in the attire of naturalism and existentialism). But on the other hand,
man's existence is an estranged existence; it is distorted; it is *not* in

its essence—and this we must maintain against idealism, moralism, progressivism, old and new, and especially new.

If this is the human situation, if man has a *predicament* which can be described as estrangement from his essential being, if it can be described as "man against himself" (Menninger) or in terms of "no exit" (Sartre), then the question is, "What has counseling to do in this situation?" Let me bring it together under three terms: judgment, acceptance, and transformation.

Judgment means honestly facing the reality of man's estranged predicament. Acceptance means accepting the other one and oneself in the name of Him who accepts us *both*. Transformation means participating, together with those whom we counsel, in the power of the New Reality, which is the reality of love. These three things are the characteristics of counseling in the name of the New Being.

Man is finite. He comes from nothing and goes to nothing. And the awareness of his finitude is anxiety. He stands under the bewildering power of temporality which forces him every moment to realize that this moment already has vanished and will never return. He is tied to the law of transitoriness, and he is aware of this in the anxiety of having to die, in the horror of being no more.

Now how does this threefold analysis apply? Judgment towards finitude means facing it, not jumping over it, not even with the cheap consolation of endless continuation of life after death. This is a distorted, not even Platonic, and certainly not Christian, consolation of those who have lost the meaning of eternity.

Accepting the situation of being finite; *judging* ourselves as finite; and then bringing people into the situation in which we accept their anxiety about this state and help them to accept it themselves: we can do nothing else. Counseling in which we would say, "Oh, your sickness is not so bad, there is very little danger of your dying"—this or the other consolation of which I spoke does not mean acceptance. Acceptance means the courage to face our real situation. And acceptance of the other one means accepting his anxiety and not trying to minimize it, to deny it, to bully him into beliefs in order to overcome his anxiety—beliefs which in any case would not be able to do this.

The question remains, "In what power can we do this?" We can do it only in the power of that which transcends finitude: in the power of the eternal, which is just the opposite of endless continuation of the finite. And in doing so, we may have the grace that *both* of us, counseled and counselor, might in a great moment be grasped by the presence of the eternal and *both* of us be enabled to accept *courageously* the true judgment that we are finite. And if this happens, then a transformation into the eternal has taken place.

I could apply this to other forms of finitude, such as loneliness, illness, accidents, insecurity, weakness, and error. They all belong to our finitude and must be judged as concomitants of our finitude, which we cannot deny in their reality but which we are able to accept. In every special case you yourselves are educated enough theologically, and humanly, to give the special answer, in the light of the eternal; an answer which is not cheap consolation, nor an admonition to believe something unbelievable, but to accept finitude in the light of the eternal to which we belong.

The human predicament also involves the fact of being guilty, the threat of that despair which is connected with the questions of guilt. Here also the first thing is judgment. And I say this with a special emphasis because counselors and analysts are often accused of being lenient, permissive, letting people do what they want, lacking in the power of judgment. *This is not helpful at all.* The negative must be honestly faced as negative.

But then immediately we come to the second point, namely, acceptance. But all acceptance is an acceptance "in spite of," otherwise it doesn't do justice to the actual feeling of guilt. This is the feeling of an estrangement which is tragic but also responsible, which is unavoidable and universal, but at the same time everyone's responsibility. Perhaps the most profound work of the counselor is to help the other one to accept himself in the situation of guilt. This *cannot* be done by suspending judgment, but it can by no means be done at all by continuing and strengthening moral demands. If you do *this*, you are under the judgment of every good analyst and have forgotten what the Reformers, Augustine, and Paul experienced, namely, that the law condemns and destroys if it is not preceded by forgiveness. There must be acceptance without suspending judgment.

Now this is most difficult in a culture such as ours, especially in Protestant churches such as ours which are thoroughly distorted moralistically, and where the constant danger is that the people who come to you can sin in individual acts about which they have special guilt feelings, and they expect from you a repetition of other laws, or the same laws, which will serve to deepen their guilt feeling. The deepest guilt feeling always comes from the message of grace, *not* from the proclamation of the law. Here analysis and pastoral counseling are in agreement.

This act of acceptance, because it is an act of reunion (or love, which is the reunion of the separated) is at the same time transformation. One can transform *only* through acceptance, *never* through commands!

It is not the counselor as an *individual*, who really accepts—that is what I always tell my psychoanalytic friends: "Who are you to *accept* somebody?" But you can accept somebody if you realize that you both equally are accepted, so that the power of acceptance works through you and through him. And it is not you alone who accepts, you a questionable human being, who perhaps needs counseling and analysis as much as your patient does. You both stand in the need of acceptance-*in-spite-of*!! When this is realized, we have a relationship which in itself has the character of transformation.

A third element of the human predicament is the disturbances, confusions, doubts, and feelings of meaninglessness, of emptiness, of nothingness—"the encounter with nothingness" (Kuhn), as existentialism has been described. Here again the first step is judgment— seeing and facing, as the great existentialists have done, the reality of our nothingness, of our meaninglessness, of the tremendous depths of emptiness, of doubt, of cynicism in our civilization. The Christian counselor should realize that he has great allies in the existentialist literature and art, allies which have had the courage to see and to express this point of negativity, of meaninglessness, accompanying finitude and guilt. Perhaps this last element is the most important in our present situation. The counselor must realize that the religious symbols he uses in his counseling often are up against grave doubt, questioning, and desperate cynicism, such that they are of no avail.

The first thing is to face the situation of this kind of emptiness and the next is to accept the situation. Now this is most difficult, especially for ministers, because for them the traditional symbols are so much beyond doubt, in many cases. This is the situation with those who have become habitual Christians, whereas for the *best* Christians (if the phrase may be used) doubt is an element of their existence; thus they can participate in the doubt of the others. Then they can accept because they themselves, with their doubt and their emptiness, and their anxiety of meaninglessness, are accepting themselves. This is the second step, *acceptance*. Out of this may come a moment in which an ultimate certainty, beyond any doubt—namely, the certainty of ultimate seriousness—unites the counseled and the counselor. This is the seriousness of facing reality, the seriousness of accepting a distorted, empty and meaningless reality. And it *might* happen that in this point of seriousness the counselor and the one he counsels will find themselves.

A Comparison of Functions

Now I come to a comparison of the functions of the Christian counselor, or pastoral counseling, and helping generally. The basic difference is that the pastoral counselor always speaks under the dimension of

the eternal, even if he knows that he himself is judged by this dimension, must be accepted by it, and *might* be transformed—or might not.

The helper, in all other respects, is not necessarily in this relationship. This produces profound problems, both personal and theoretical.
The personal problem cannot be easily solved by the distinction of
functions. Certainly we must clearly and logically distinguish these
two functions. But the question is, "To what extent is that possible?"
The minister as counselor cannot escape some medical judgments, as
he cannot avoid some social judgments, about the situation of the
counselee. Of course he will test them by the physician and by the
analyst. Nevertheless the way in which he has them tested by the
doctor or analyst is in itself a kind of medical judgment. Now here is
an overlapping which cannot be avoided because we *live*, and are not
well-ordered according to the structures of symbolic logic.

The physician, the social worker, the psychiatrist, is a human being,
and that means that he is not without an ultimate concern, however
hidden and suppressed this may be. But an ultimate concern means
an ultimate presupposition in the dimension in which the minister
speaks directly and performs his function. He may be a naturalist, an
existentialist, even an idealist—which is probably the farthest removed
from the Christian attitude—but in any case, he has a hidden ultimate
concern and a hidden presupposition. And although, if he is a good
psychoanalyst or doctor, he will consciously avoid influencing his
patient with his world view, as the minister will avoid influencing his
parishioner with respect to medical or psychoanalytic measures, it is
not possible to avoid this completely. As to the counselee, we can say
that a definitely determined sickness needs medical help in the bodily
as in the psychological respect. General disturbances do not demand
a doctor—we all have general disturbances almost every day—but a
neurotic compulsion, in which we feel that a part of our being has
split off from its totality, needs medical attention exactly as does a
sick limb of our body. But now the question is, "If this is a good logical
distinction, can the two things really be separated? Is it possible, in
the medical respect, bodily as well as psychological, to separate special fixed forms of disease from the total process of life and from the
total process of personality?"

Now to a certain extent it is possible, otherwise the doctors couldn't
exist, and the ministers even less, but this relative distinction never
can be a real separation. And here we are in the same trouble in which
we were before, in respect to the counselor. He who is sick, for example, he who has definite compulsive symptoms, he who has definite
symptoms of bodily organs which do not function in the totality of his

life process, certainly should go to the doctor. But, is he not at the same time a totality and *unity?* And here the problem arises.

Now I can only say what I said of judging and accepting. We must judge that this is the situation and face it. And we must accept our human situation as we have it today, as it *is,* and by courageously accepting, we may transform it. This transformation might mean a partial return to something which once upon a time was a reality, namely, the reality of the unity of all helpers in one person and in one function. This ideal, as all such ideals, could not keep itself alive, for the simple reason that special functions develop in their full possibilities only if they are separated. We never would have had medicine if we remained in the situation of the medicine man, and the same applies to the minister. But isn't there involved, in this idea, a reality which perhaps in *another way* might be fulfilled? I would not say this if I were not convinced that the real *helper* unites *all* elements of help and that a psychoanalyst is the *greater* the more he can at the same time be a priest, and the priest is the greater the more he can at the same time be a healer. The ancient church knew about this ideal and had examples of it, and in Jesus, as a symbol of His actions, they are united.

Now this is the ultimate answer. How far this answer is from reality, we don't know, but we can know that it is not completely away and that the very fact of our cooperation in meetings like this, and in many other forms similar to this, is an indication that we at least have come to the point of judging our situation—and if we do this courageously, then acceptance and transformation might follow.

The differences between counseling and psychotherapy are in degree not kind. Pastoral counseling is different, however, and is a function of the church. Unfortunately, theology is often considered to be dogmatism by mental health professionals at the same time that they have become more aware of the place of values in counseling. The pastoral role of "priest" is a significant one in spite of the fact that there is a "priesthood of all believers" to which even secular counselors are called. The importance of guilt, forgiveness, and love in all counseling is considered and similarities among helpers are noted.

Counseling and Evangelical Theology

Frank C. Peters

Early in my ministry I heard a specialist in pastoral counseling compare ministers of evangelical persuasion with ministers of liberal persuasion. It was the speaker's contention that evangelicals were committed to ideas whereas liberals were interested in people. The lecturer then went on to convince his audience that the meaningful psychological action was in the one camp and the cause of much of the trouble was in the other.

Evangelicals have in the past been somewhat skeptical of the heavy psychological baggage which has characterized many programs designed to train men for the gospel ministry. Today most evangelical training institutions offer courses which utilize the insights gained from psychology. Perhaps the including of lectures on counseling in the W. H. Griffith Thomas Memorial Lectures is further evidence that evangelicals are open to further insights from the behavioral sciences.

Counseling, as we will use the term in these lectures, refers to a relationship in which one person endeavors to help another to understand and to solve his adjustment problems. The term covers a wide area of procedures: advice giving, psychoanalysis, information giving, interpretation of test scores, encouraging the counselee to verbalize

This article is the first in the series of W. H. Griffith Thomas lectures delivered by Peters in November 1968, at Dallas Seminary.

Reprinted from *Bibliotheca Sacra*, January 1969, 3–15. Used by permission.

his difficulties, and working through his emotions. The objectives of counseling have been identified by the Committee on Definition, Division of Counseling Psychology, American Psychological Association, as "to help individuals toward overcoming obstacles to their personal growth, wherever they may be encountered, and toward achieving optimum development of the personal resources."[1]

In lecturing to ministers and theological students it becomes imperative to differentiate between counseling and pastoral care. Pastoral care includes much more than counseling and involves a number of ministers resident in the New Testament church. All of these gifts were given for the "edification of the saints," and are used by the Holy Spirit toward the growth of the individual believer. Counseling, then, becomes one significant aspect of pastoral care.

There is a difference of opinion as to whether counseling and psychotherapy are in all essential respects identical. C. H. Patterson[2] argues that the nature of the relationship which is considered basic in both counseling and psychotherapy is identical and that the methods and techniques are also the same. Tyler, attempting to differentiate counseling from psychotherapy, states that it is not the job of counselors "to remove physical and mental handicaps or to get rid of limitations."[3] This is the work of the therapist, which "is aimed essentially at change in developmental structures rather than at fulfillment."

In these lectures we shall view the difference as one of degree and kind. Where the client is seriously emotionally disturbed, the process is called psychotherapy and is seen as a remedial process designed to restore the normal level of functioning. In counseling we aim to develop the client's full potential or assist him in actualizing his best self. When help is offered in a medical setting, we will use the term *psychotherapy;* if it is a nonmedical setting, we speak of counseling. I am assuming that pastors generally do not attempt to cope with serious emotional disturbances and, of course, their setting is nonmedical. We shall therefore use the term *counseling* for our purposes.

Pastoral counseling, in its present form at least, is perhaps an innovation within the evangelical church. I am sure that many of the older men in the ministry today would readily admit that they heard very little, if anything, about counseling in their seminary days. Today the

1. American Psychological Association, Division of Counseling Psychology, Committee on Definition, "Counseling Psychology as a Specialty," *American Psychologist* 11 (1956): 282–85.

2. C. H. Patterson, Counseling and/or Psychotherapy?" *American Psychologist* 18 (1963): 667–69.

3. Leona Tyler, "Theoretical Principles Underlying the Counseling Process," *Journal of Counseling Psychology* 5 (1958): 3–10.

movement has established its own literature and has become quite popular in the church. Centers for clinical training of theological students are readily available as are also courses in counseling in almost all seminaries. Almost all pastoral conferences feature some topic concerning counseling on their programs.

The experimental groundwork in pastoral counseling has come almost exclusively from psychology and psychiatry. This has made for a shift in emphasis in pastoral care. Whereas the counseling of earlier days was related to theology, today it centers more in psychology. As Hulme correctly suggests: "The impetus for the new movement has come more from the laboratories of the psychological sciences than from the scholarship of theologians. It is a psychologically oriented 'Seelsorge.' "[4]

This, then, means that pastoral counseling as we know it today has developed alongside of rather than within the framework of theology. It would seem to me that the task of the evangelical theologian of today would be to relate the insights which counseling has acquired from the behavioral sciences to the basic premises of an evangelical theology.

Unfortunately, theology in the minds of most psychologists is related to dogmatism and authoritarianism. As such it would stand in direct opposition to the scientific method and free inquiry. To proceed from certain theological presuppositions also smacks of advice-giving, which has become the unpardonable sin in counseling. All of this confronts the evangelical theologian and pastor whose interests and work lead him into the field of counseling with the mammoth task of integrating two disciplines which seem to be unwilling bedfellows.

Thorne shows sympathy for a pastoral counseling which assumes theology and says that "the validity of revealed truth would be tremendously strengthened if science could clarify some of the relationships involved."[5] This, I believe, is an excellent insight for the evangelical pastor. Since the pastor accepts revealed truth as ultimate authority, he often proceeds too easily and too quickly to the "answer" without understanding the dynamics of the distorted relationships or without helping his parishioner toward such an understanding. Counseling becomes a form of proclamation rather than a process of investigation and a means toward achieving insight.

Before we discuss the role of theology in the counseling ministry of the evangelical pastor, it might be advantageous to inquire whether counseling as it relates psychology and medicine has any philosophical

4. William E. Hulme, *Counseling and Theology*, p. 1.
5. Frederick C. Thorne, *Principles of Personality Counseling*, p. 482.

presuppositions. If such presuppositions exist in counseling psychology, surely the pastoral counselor would be allowed the same privilege even though the presuppositions themselves might be different from those of the counseling psychologist.

In recent years psychologists have shown interest in the place of philosophy and values in counseling. Cribbin[6] did an extensive piece of work in reviewing over two hundred texts and journal articles to ascertain the role of philosophy in modern guidance. He found that counselors do have a number of basic presuppositions which they bring to the counseling process.

Whenever a profession develops rapidly to advanced stages it will be noticed that the development of a basic philosophy tends to lag behind. In the early stages of counseling, very little was written on the issue of philosophy and values in counseling and much was written on the techniques of counseling. I believe it would be correct to say that the general emphasis in the counseling field up to 1950 was on methods, techniques, and services. Relatively few contributions pertaining to philosophy and values were found. The situation was not noticeably different by 1960. In the April, 1960, *Review of Educational Research*, the review of the literature on the philosophy of counseling for the preceding three years found this type of article outnumbered thirty to one by articles on methods and procedures.[7]

Professional journals have published numerous articles since 1960 which deal with basic philosophical and ethical issues. C. G. Wrenn[8] states frankly that although relatively few authors pretend to possess a consistent philosophy or systematic psychological view, it is of utmost importance that knowledge of man's behavior be seen in the framework of the meaning of his existence in the universe.

What a counselor believes will inevitably play an important role in his relationships with his clients. The value orientation of the counselor need not be expressed verbally to be effective. His "counseling style" and the subtle reinforcements by gestures and expressions communicate the counselor's pleasure or displeasure with the counselee's position. Perhaps this is the reason why the theorists of various "schools" of thought find that a majority of their clients talk about themselves and their problems in a way which fits into the theoretical

6. J. J. Cribbin, "Critique of the Philosophy of Modern Guidance," *Catholic Educational Review* 53 (1953): 73–91.

7. John F. McGowan and Lyle D. Schmidt, *Counseling: Readings in Theory and Practice*, pp. 96–97.

8. C. G. Wrenn, "Philosophical and Psychological Basis of Personnel Services in Education," in Personnel Services in Education, *Yearbook National Society for Studies in Education*, 1959, Part II, Chap. 3.

framework of the counselor. The counselee finally says what he feels the counselor wants him to say.

I do not believe that it is sound practice for counselors to keep their values hidden from their clients nor do I believe that this is ever truly possible even if it were desirable. The counselor who attempts to conceal his value orientations from the client will usually be perceived by his client as uninvolved in the relationship. Complete objectivity or impersonality, while a necessary ideal in the scientific method, must be viewed in the light of what actually happens in the counseling relationship. However, this does not mean that the counselor would necessarily employ directive means to transfer his beliefs and values to his client. Respect for the client's individual freedom would preclude the use of overt persuasiveness. Statement of the counselor's beliefs and values should be viewed as part of an honesty relationship which encourages the counselee to state honestly his views and feelings concerning himself and his orientation.

I am proceeding, then, on the assumption that the evangelical pastor has accepted counseling as part of his ministry and realizes that the insights of the behavioral sciences must be taken seriously. However, the evangelical pastor is unwilling to minimize the role of theology in counseling. He is aware that the pastoral counseling movement has its origin primarily among those of the liberal theological movements within Protestantism and that there has been a natural resistance toward affording theology a prominent place in pastoral counseling.

Edward Thornton,[9] in speaking of the role of theology in pastoral counseling, makes mention of the apprehensiveness which characterizes the relationship between theologians and counselors. Like newlyweds, says Thornton, they are uncertain of their relationship to each other and therefore exchange sweet words while anxiously remaining on guard lest the relationship expose concealed weaknesses. The time has come, I believe, for evangelical theologians to declare the honeymoon over and to initiate a very frank appraisal of both the conflicts and the possibilities inherent in the relationship of theology and counseling. Pastoral counseling must remain a distinctive Christian discipline rather than a "how to do it" area of study.

Since both theology and psychology are related to human experience, they must be allied in the important discipline of counseling. There is a danger of having a theology which is largely removed from life or a psychology which attempts to speak authoritatively to all of man's needs.

It becomes the charge of the evangelical pastor to continue in his

9. Edward E. Thornton, *Theology and Pastoral Counseling*, p. 15.

loyalty to the authority of the Word. In the conviction that the basic needs of the troubled personality are anticipated in the teachings of the Bible, he can speak of a theological basis for the principles of counseling. On the other hand, since the Bible is not a guide to methodology, the insights of psychology have their rightful place in the ministry of the evangelical pastor.

The evangelical pastor must begin by rejecting the position which would set up a uniquely "evangelical therapy." The clinical evidence is all too clear that a disbelieving therapist can be effective in providing a client with a genuine self-awareness and openness to experience. In many cases it would be better for a parishioner to be treated by a skillful therapist who is not a Christian but who respects the role of faith and values in human experience, than to be further confused by a well-meaning Christian whose therapeutic skills are highly questionable.

I believe that many of the major assumptions of evangelical theology have no direct bearing on counseling as it is presently practiced. I shall therefore choose three areas of theological concern which, I believe, would have direct bearing on the counseling process. These are the areas in which every evangelical pastor must seek to integrate biblical authority and psychological insights.

The Priesthood of All Believers

There is both need and room for a thorough examination of the basis, meaning, and development of the doctrine of the priesthood of all believers. It is time that evangelicals take this doctrine out of the slogan category and set it in its true context as a most essential and determinative element in the theology of the church. The New Testament knows two forms of priesthood—the priesthood of Christ (Heb. 6:20; 7:26–27) and the priesthood of all believers (I Peter 2:9; Rev. 5:10). The people of God in the New Testament stand in an entirely new relationship and emerge as a kingdom of priests—a new and redeemed community.

The doctrine of the priesthood of all believers is the basic doctrine which underlies Luther's teaching on the seven outward "marks" of the true church. He proclaimed it "for certain, and firmly established that the soul can do without everything except the Word of God."[10] Calvin in amplifying the threefold office of Christ quite unashamedly holds the following points of view: There is no priesthood save that of Christ who is the only High Priest. It is the business of every Christian

10. Quoted by Cyril Eastwood in *The Priesthood of All Believers*, p. 2.

to offer spiritual sacrifices because he belongs to a royal priesthood.[11] For Calvin, then, the priesthood of believers is based on the fact that Christ is our mediator and receives us into His fellowship of His service for mankind.

My intentions are not to belabor one of the great doctrines stemming from the Reformation, but rather to investigate its significance for the pastor and counselor. Even a cursory investigation of the implications of this doctrine reveals that the pastor ministers to priests. His counseling and pastoral care should never violate the priestly prerogatives of those to whom he ministers. As Paul Miller puts it, the Christian minister is "a servant of God's servants."[12]

The neurotic counselee or parishioner often sees his pastor or counselor in a role of mediatorship. He feels thwarted in his direct approach to God and therefore seeks a substitute approach—a human mediator. Freedom for a neurotic person is both a goal and a threat, as Erich Fromm has so well illustrated in his book *Escape from Freedom*. Freedom implies responsibility, and responsibility can be dangerous and threatening.

Hulme[13] points out that there is no insurance against a pastor assuming the role of priest simply because he is a Protestant minister. The inclination to assume mediatorial powers for another is as frequently of psychological origin as of theological indoctrination. An immature pastor may not be aware of the need in himself to make people dependent on him. Counseling, good counseling, enables parishioners to help themselves. In order to do this, they, the parishioners, must be encouraged to develop for themselves their own priesthood capacities.

The biblical doctrine of the priesthood of believers places certain necessary limits on pastoral counseling. Counseling which takes evangelical theology seriously may not violate the priestly prerogative of parishioners and, therefore, must never become an end in itself. Counseling must help the parishioner to do his own mediating; it must help him to move beyond the human counselor to the divine counselor and that as quickly as possible. Unless the parishioner becomes increasingly more dependent on God and decreasingly dependent on the counselor, the process has failed the biblical ideal for Christian growth.

Psychologists have been looking for a concept which might guide them in their efforts to maintain a proper relationship with the counselee which fosters growth in the client and decreases the dependence relationship. "Psychological weaning" can become a real problem.

11. *Ibid.*, p. 67.
12. Paul M. Miller, *Servant of God's Servants.*
13. Hulme, *Counseling and Theology*, p. 122.

There are always people who use counseling as a crutch and an escape, always hoping that the counselor will do for them what he knows they must do for themselves. I would submit to you that the evangelical pastor who takes his theology seriously can structure his counseling on the basis of the universal priesthood of believers and will thus experience one of two things. His counselee may mature, accept responsibility, and come to the point where he does not need the counselor. On the other hand, the counselee will realize that he cannot switch his responsibility to the counselor and will terminate the relationship. In either case, the counselor will find himself without a job.

Guilt and Forgiveness

A second doctrine which has implications for counseling is that of guilt and forgiveness. Early in the history of psychotherapy, Freud recognized that guilt played an enormous role in the neurotic syndrome. In his attempt to explain this psychological phenomenon, he advanced the theory that, as a result of a too intense socialization, some individuals develop so great a fear of their sexual and hostile feelings that, eventually, they even deny these feelings access to consciousness. When these impulses clamor for recognition and expression, the ego experiences the characteristic effects of depression, anxiety, and guilt. Mowrer,[14] reviewing Freud's "impulse theory" of neurosis, suggested as early as 1950 that a theory of guilt be acknowledged by psychologists.

For Mowrer, emotionally ill persons are typically guilty persons whose guilt is real rather than illusory.[15] It would seem, then, that pastoral counseling would be strategically relevant since theology deals with the problem of man's guilt and forgiveness. However, since pastoral counseling has been so largely inspired and patterned by secular psychotherapy, it has fallen short of its mission. If one takes the neurotic's guilt seriously and agrees at least in part with Mowrer[16] that neurosis is a medical euphemism for a "state of sin" and social alienation, then the cure must go beyond mere "counseling."

The issue which militates against taking guilt seriously in psychology is the problem of determinism. Determinism is a natural corollary of naturalism in philosophy and has deeply entrenched itself in psychology. Influential schools of psychology have convinced our generation that man, because of various types of determinism, is not

14. O. H. Mowrer, *Learning Theory and Personality Dynamics.*
15. Mowrer, *Crisis in Psychiatry and Religion*, p. 91.
16. *Ibid.*, p. 108.

genuinely responsible for his behavior. If that is true, his guilt is a farce and must be treated not as a cause of his neurosis but as part of it.

Not all psychologists have been happy with a mechanistic and deterministic philosophy. Mowrer writes,

> There is, as we know, a widespread tendency—sometimes called "scientism"—to assume that human beings cannot be "responsible" for *anything*, that we are all just cogs in a vast cause-and-effect complex and are in no way accountable for anything we do or anything that happens to us. Such a doctrine, aside from its lack of genuine scientific justification, is devastating: no society could endure which thoroughly accepted it—and neither can an individual.[17]

Another prominent psychologist who has opposed the reductionist tendency is Gordon W. Allport. He argues thus:

> Strict determinism would have to say that no one ever does anything. The person does not live his life; it is lived for him. He is no freer than a billiard ball responding within a triangle of forces. The two major forces are internal drive and environmental pressures. To these two Freud added a third, namely, man's super-ego. This force, however, is only a derivative of parental and social teaching (environmental forces). The ego, having no energy of its own, is a victim of these tyrants.[18]

Man is genuinely responsible for his behavior, as the biblical doctrine of sin teaches, and pastoral counselors must be on guard not to succumb to pressure to water down human responsibility. The answer is not to minimize sin, but rather to make forgiveness more operational. A therapy which gives the patient a combination of hormones and tranquilizers will not be enough, nor is it sufficient to gain insight into the forces that have molded personality. Unless the client accepts his responsibility, he cannot truly experience the therapeutic release which true forgiveness brings.

The Pelagian denial of determinism is no help to me as a psychologist whose orientation is to evangelical theology. I am all too aware of the determining forces of heredity and environment. It would seem to me that the Augustinian emphasis on responsibility in the face of determining influences reminds the individual that he concurred in the moral decisions which led to his sinful state. This realization of responsibility leads to a repentance with hope rather than a remorse in despair. The sinner accepts his responsibility so that he can be truly

17. *Ibid.*, p. 58.
18. Gordon W. Allport, *Pattern and Growth in Personality*, p. 561.

forgiven by grace. Any discussion of forgiveness is possible only where responsibility is taken seriously and where repentance is evidence of this responsibility. Furthermore, any discussion of forgiveness in psychology must take seriously the difference which exists between psychology and biblical literature on this point.

If guilt is real, forgiveness must be as real as guilt in order that it function in a therapeutic way. As we have seen from earlier references, Mowrer has a clear message concerning the reality of guilt in the life of the sufferer. Interestingly enough, his concept of forgiveness is scarcely adequate to cope with his arguments concerning the demands of such guilt on the sufferer. He considers forgiveness "as something of an anachronism," and chides clergymen for trafficking in a "questionable commodity."[19] Freud, while recognizing the psychological value of forgiveness, was repelled by the audacity of it. In this Freud joins the company of the contemporaries of Jesus who raised objections to forgiveness.

The evangelical counselor sees forgiveness grounded firmly in God's forgiveness of us. Forgiveness is not an inner psychic phenomenon that does not involve an external agent. It is not the absolution of the ego from the superego. Christian forgiveness has deep historical roots in the life, death, and resurrection of Jesus Christ, and any discussion of forgiveness apart from this event will fall short of the biblical message. The Christian psychologist with evangelical convictions will not hesitate to proclaim such a forgiveness when the question of guilt is projected by his client.

The evangelical counselor is completely unapologetic about basing his pronouncements on forgiveness—not on human insight, but on divine revelation. The forgiving love of God comes to man through the self-disclosure of God. The final healing power of life is for us, and in Jesus Christ we are forgiven and accepted. In our prodigality, alienation, estrangement, frustration, guilt, and hostility, we find that we are still loved of God and through Jesus Christ are received into sonship. Such forgiveness is not the product of human experience but rather runs its course within human experience.

Therapeutic Self-assurance

One of the desired effects of forgiveness is self-acceptance, a very important aspect of any therapeutic encounter. Unless the counselee

19. Mowrer, "The Almighty's Unmighty Ministers," *The Christian Century* 79, no. 42 1962): 1254.

is able to stem the ever-increasing tides of self-rejection, there is little
hope of his ever becoming a fully functioning person.

In therapy, just as in divine forgiveness, the individual comes to see
his alienation from himself in a deeper dimension. Since he is willing
to drop the heavy armor of his defenses, he becomes ever more aware
of his predicament and his inability to cope with it. It is the evangelical
conviction that his self-acceptance does not come from finding great
resources in himself, but rather from understanding and experiencing
what it means to be "accepted in the beloved."

Forgiveness means that God accepts us radically. The gospel invites
us to accept our acceptance and that in spite of all self-rejections. Our
acceptance of ourselves is not based on a sudden goodness which has
obliterated all the scars of previous conflict, but rather on the insight
that God has accepted us amid our phoniness.

Oden compares divine forgiveness with the acceptance the counselee experiences with his counselor. When God accepts us in our sins
He does not affirm our pretense and our sham.

> Similarly, the therapist does not affirm neurosis. He does not like sick-
> ness. He affirms the *person* who is wrestling with neurotic compulsions
> *amid* his sickness and *in spite* of his pretenses, distortions, projections,
> and absurdities in order that he might bring more of his experience into
> conscious awareness and acceptance. . . . There is a significant analogy
> between the radical divine acceptance which is the subject of the Christian
> kerygma and the radical therapeutic acceptance which enables the client
> to accept himself.[20]

Evangelical theology reminds the counselor that he is not the source
of acceptance, but that he serves as a communicator of divine acceptance. Such communication comes through word and through the
client's experience with another human being who also accepts him
"for Christ's sake." The effective counselor offers the individual the
possibility for self-acceptance by accepting him as he is. But in doing
this he is not only expressing personal openness to a fellowman in
distress, but rather he is performing what Oden calls a "representative
ministry" whereby he implicitly communicates to the client through
the relationship what acceptance in the midst of guilt actually means
in human experience.

The psychotherapeutic injunction that the basis for acceptance of
others is self-acceptance is quite compatible with evangelical theology.
We love our neighbor as we love ourselves was the message of Jesus.
A rejection of self never leads to a wholesome acceptance of others.

20. Thomas C. Oden, *Kerygma and Counseling*, p. 62.

Forgiven man comes to value himself anew in the light of God's astounding valuation of him. Thus christological humanism is a deeper affirmation of man than the often shallow romantic humanism that undergirds much of psychotherapy today.

Effective psychotherapy in the context of evangelical theology places man in a new relationship to himself. Redeemed man who understands his relationship to God through the message of Scripture is now truly free to become himself. His goal is to become that which in Christ he truly is.

The precondition of loving others is the understanding that one is loved. As the client comes to perceive himself as genuinely valued by God, he finds in this relationship the dynamic to move out toward others in love and ministry. It is expressed by John in a nutshell when he affirms, "In this is love, not that we loved God, but that he loved us. . . . If God so loved us, we ought also to love one another" (I John 4:10–11).

An inaccurate contemporary duality of thinking permits many to perceive therapy as practical and theology as theoretical. They both deal with the same human problem and therefore should be integrated. This is possible, however, only if theology remains supernaturalistic. Theology and therapy can be synthesized through an empirical scientific approach to the study of values. Theologians see ultimate values in human experience and therapists can keep such values in mind even when dealing with practical human problems.

Theology and Therapy

H. L. Parsons

To many people in our society theology and therapy appear poles apart. Theology deals in dry abstractions, remote from the pace and passion of our daily living; therapy is a practical technique for getting people out of jams. Theology sits smugly on the faded, musty shelves of the past; therapy is a modern thing, streamlined, efficient. Theology speculates on supernatural mysteries; therapy is simple and understandable. Theology concerns itself with eternal, celestial things; therapy, with temporal, terrestrial matters.

This divorce between the two—once married and of one flesh—is accepted by many clergymen and, perhaps, by more psychologists. It is accepted because a deep dualism pervades our thinking—the dualism between supernaturalism and naturalism, religion and science, faith and reason, value and fact, God and man—and therefore between theology and therapy.

Men have responded to this dualism in various ways: they have blindly accepted it; they have believed that where this life leaves off the next begins, that the church is *in* the world but not *of* the world, that the work of the minister lies over and beyond the work of the doctor and psychiatrist; they have rejected religion as a tattered banner of a long-lost cause; they have turned their souls away from the natural order, with its godless science, moving into puritan commu-

Reprinted from *Pastoral Care* 12 (1953): 215–23. Used by permission.

nities to keep themselves undefiled. Following similar lines, clergymen and psychologists have variously defined the relation of theology and therapy. For some, the work of the minister is sacred, the work of the psychiatrist is secular, and never the twain shall meet. For others, the two fields meet but do not overlap. For still others, theology is an expendable remnant of antiquity, to which the minister in the pulpit should make a polite and passing concession, but which he must perforce abandon as he goes about his therapeutic work in counseling, calling, and the like in the community. Finally, some—obviously not psychiatrists—believe that psychiatry is the work of the devil.

Note that either the old dualism is maintained or that what has been traditionally known as religion is swallowed up in psychotherapy. This is why most ministers, faced with the alternatives of a dualistic division of labor on the one hand and an absorption into another field on the other hand, choose to cling to the old dualism. Much of the speaking and writing on this subject is tolerant, even condescending—but unyielding. Each side, religion and psychiatry, is ready to remind the other that it has a monopoly over special, unique, and important truths and techniques, and that it is determined not to yield ground to an alien who is less capable; and, having made clear that it will not compromise, it then makes loving protestations of its willingness to "cooperate" with the other fellow.

And so the dualism persists, for there can be no meaningful synthesis or integration until each side approaches the other in the spirit of seeking a higher and richer perspective which includes but transcends both. In spite of the very valuable work of such groups as the Council for Clinical Training over the past twenty-five years, I do not believe that great numbers of ministers have managed to see their fundamental theological work as of a piece with that of psychiatry's. The major reason is that in the main the theology taught in the seminaries is some brand of supernaturalism. God, the ultimate Value who gives health and makes all things anew, is unknown and unknowable, like the wind that bloweth where it listeth. Hence salvation, the process or outcome of achieving health, is essentially an unknown and unknowable process, an activity of "blind" or "absurd" faith which issues in a peace that likewise passes understanding. Such theology, with its theory of salvation, can never be integrated with a therapy which begins with precisely opposite premises: that the value of life is here and now, that it may be studied by rational-empirical methods, and that through such study we may provide conditions for its emergence into human life; and that salvation or health is a natural process which, while not completely "controlled," can be studied and facilitated by the human mind and human techniques.

The Need for Integration

How, then, can theology and therapy be integrated? First, we must ask, *Why* must they be integrated?

Theology and therapy deal with the same problem: What must I do to be saved? How can I achieve the more abundant life? Health, wholeness, wholeheartedness (to use a word used by both Horney and Jesus)—these are the generic aims of those who theorize about the good life and those who try to bring it into realization. Traditionally, theology has tended to emphasize those factors in the saving process which are not in human control, while modern therapists, although acknowledging processes beyond man's conscious control (such as the impulsive factors pointed out by Freud or the creative processes pointed out by Jung, Otto Rank, and Rogers), have tended to emphasize factors which lie within man's control.

One may ask: But do both theology and therapy deal with the problem of God? And the asker might answer: If they do not then we are thrown back into the abyss of dualism, or else "theology" becomes mere "psychology"; if they do, then therapy, which has not been supernaturalistic, must become so. But the first alternative is what we do not desire, and the second, if we did desire it, is now practically impossible. Psychiatry is part and parcel of the revolt against the "medieval synthesis of supernaturalism."

This dilemma is resolvable because it is based on a false premise: that theology must be supernaturalistic. Yet in recent times some theologies have been frankly naturalistic, and on that account no less theological than their predecessors. Theology, of whatever kind, deals with what is of Ultimate Value for human living, regardless of whatever else it may deal with. It aims to discover by one cognitive method or another that Ultimate Value, and, derivatively, the good life. Theologians who prefer to use the generalized rational-empirical method of the sciences will necessarily confine themselves to the realm of nature, since the realm of nature is all that they can observe by means of such a method. They automatically eliminate any "supernatural" realm, since whatever is in nature is what some human mind has had or can have (in principle) some relation to, and since, as Whitehead says, "If anything out of relationship, then complete ignorance as to it."[1] To be actual is to be in relation to something else; we can give no other sensible meaning to actuality. True, there are many events we do not now know (have no conscious relation with) and will never

1. A. N. Whitehead, *Science and the Modern World* (New York: New American Library 1948), p. 26.

know. But we may say of such events *as events* that they have relations to other events, and that *in principle* they are knowable. Otherwise we are talking nonsense.

Now I submit that a desire for consistency, for knowledge that is all of a piece, for integration between religion and science, value and fact, theology and therapy—the desire for wholeness—is one deep in our natures, and one which cries out for fulfillment. In science and philosophy this desire is reflected by the standard of logical coherence; in art, by the principle of "unity in variety"; in personal life, by integrity; in interpersonal relations, by love; in religion, by wholeheartedness, or unity with God.

A glance through the psychiatric literature will make it clear that this drive for integration, for progressive levels of integration, is fundamental to the human organism and is the one resource which the therapist can count on in his attempts to help render the broken individual whole again. This principle of integration as the binding fact of organic life is also receiving widespread recognition in the physical and biological sciences[2] and the social sciences[3] and is being lifted into attention and apotheosis by ethicists and theologians. Many of the old theologians recognized it, but removed it from inquiry by maintaining it could not be understood by man.

Because we live and move and have our being within an experience that is a seamless garment, and because there is this process at work within that experience to weave its parts into mutually supporting and enriching patterns, we shall remain essentially dissatisfied so long as our theologies and our various ideas and techniques of therapy remain at odds with one another. Not all things can be completely or ideally integrated—at least not within the lifetime and the limitations of your or my personality and probably not within the lifetime of our universe. But we do require a minimum, basic integration, if only to enable us to deal with difficult conflicts that arise. As Whitehead said:

> It would . . . be missing the point to think that we need not trouble ourselves about the conflict between science and religion. In an intellectual age there can be no active interest which puts aside all hope of a vision of the harmony of truth. To acquiesce in discrepancy is destructive of candour, and of moral cleanliness.[4]

That is why theology and therapy must be integrated—our deepest natures need such integration. No man can serve two masters. But it

2. L. L. Whyte, *The Unitary Principle in Physics and Biology* (New York: Henry Holt, 1949).

3. Mary P. Follett, *Creative Experience* (New York: Longmans, Green, 1924).

4. Whitehead, *Science*, pp. 184–85.

is not a question in this case of loving the one and hating the other. It is not a question of the truth of one and the falsity of the other. What we seek is a truth, a value, deeper and more inclusive than either. Nor can we be satisfied with our present armed (or at least defensive) and uneasy truce wherein each warns the other to stay in his own domain of specialization. Sometimes a feeble defense is made of such compartmentalization by calling it a "division of labor," but such a division of labor is not genuine, for the laborers are not united by any overarching organic perspective or purpose, as in an organism or family or cooperative factory or economy.

To be sure, there will always be important differences between the work of the minister and that of the psychiatrist. Each has unique insights and resources to bring to the common problems which confront men. But we tend to forget that with their unique and diverse perspectives they focus on *common* problems because they are both concerned with men and women in their struggles for health. They are united because we all live in *one* world, which no theory or technique or institution can put asunder. We all *require* by our very nature a oneness within ourselves and between ourselves and others.

The Way of Integration

Theology and therapy *can* be integrated because they deal with a common problem: What must I do to achieve health? But they *will* be integrated only if, however different, they succeed in giving a common answer to that problem. This means that they must employ a common method. And it turns out that the only method which is susceptible of commonality, of community, as John Dewey has pointed out, is the general method of empirical inquiry and creative communication— the method of science. There is no intrinsic virtue in such a method; it is preferable simply because *it is the only way of synthesizing diverse perspectives into broader truths and richer values.* If a minister and a psychiatrist differ in interpreting the behavior of a given person, and if each has some truth, the only way of improving the total truth and cutting down on the total error is for each to communicate as clearly as he can to the other his own perspective and to subject their perspectives to a common empirical test. If one or the other resorts to claims of supernatural revelation or some other such incommunicable and untestable claim, then even if it be true it cannot get across to be checked and supplemented by the perspectives and experience of the other. Truth does not grow by our getting private propositions which are kept to ourselves. Theology and therapy can be integrated and made communal only by communication and action which are free, deep, and full, and which creatively fund the truths of each.

A science of human health is a study of value. "Value" comes from the Latin *valere*, to be strong or well. Theologians direct their attention to ultimate, creative value—God. But, since only happenings in space and time can be observed directly or inferred and logically analyzed and so communicated, any study of value that purports to be "scientific" and yet deals with nontemporal, nonspatial events which are "supernatural" is a contradiction in terms. Only that theology which employs the methods of observation and rational analysis on concrete events can deal with value and with God. Value and supreme value (God) are facts, or possibilities related to facts, or they are nothing.

This does not mean that God's value is identical with man's. But, unless there is some continuity between the principle of man's health and the principle of God, and unless we can approach unto God's character through man's character, then it is useless to talk about the integration of theology and therapy. God as supreme value is in man and is the principle of man's health, the means of his salvation; but God is not merely confined to man. A scientific theology would thus begin with observation and analysis of man's values and seek to discover an undergirding, creative value more abiding, powerful, and good than any of man's particular values. This would be called God.

Actually, theologians usually begin their studies with the conviction that there is such an ultimate value-fact present in all human values, which is variously described as the source, ground, or totality of all value. In a scientific study they would commence with a rough idea of what this ultimate value is, derived in part from their tradition and in part from their common-sense observation of better and worse human situations in real life or in works of the human imagination. Then, by a careful observation and analysis of the various value-situations of men, they would search to discover if that initial notion or hypothesis concerning the ultimate standard of human good, the norm of health, corresponds to actual fact. They would ask, Is this in reality the creative source of all human good? If not, they would revise it or adopt a different notion and begin anew their empirical search and analysis. The method of Henry N. Wieman illustrates such a method in theological inquiry.

Therapists are probably more inductive. But it is questionable if any psychologist, or any scientist, for that matter, begins his studies without any "preconceptions" whatsoever regarding what is better and what is worse. After all, a therapist, if he is not a charlatan, does want to *improve* the patient. As he deals with diverse patients his sense of contrast is stimulated—the severity of illness will vary—and he begins to develop crude empirical norms of better and worse, of good health and ill health, of value and evil. He refines these by analysis and further observation, and so progressively approaches, whether or not this process is conscious, some more or less stable standards of health, and of what men must do to be made healthy, and of what he as a therapist must do to help make them healthy. The method of Carl Rogers, as made explicit by him, in developing norms and techniques for therapy, seems to me preeminently to illustrate the scientific method for therapy.

I do not mean that all therapists claim to have arrived at a universal norm of health applicable to all personalities in all situations. Indeed, some of them refuse to acknowledge that they deal with "good" and "evil" at all, and some have never consciously formulated those principles which do in fact guide them in their everyday work. But implicit in their work and their writings one may find norms and a good deal of agreement among therapists of diverse schools on what these norms of human health are. Anthropologists like Margaret Mead are suggesting that these norms apply as well to cultures other than our own.

The theologian has less difficulty with the notion that there *is* a universal good for all men. That he usually has acquired through training and study. He believes with Immanuel Kant that a standard of health or norm is useless if it is not universal, since the function of a norm is to guide us through changing situations and changing interpersonal relations. His difficulty is with documentation; he may lack the concrete facts, refined and ordered, whereby to demonstrate his conviction. I think it is for this reason that so many of them, from Plato on, have become supernaturalists, failing to find the good in the world of sights and sounds and smells, the world of vague intuitions and complex processes within and without man.

Regardless of where they begin or what forces impel them, theologian and therapist, so long as they use the scientific method of observation and rational analysis, must ultimately resort to a common body of evidence, the activities of men. The first and last data of all value-theory must be human beings, that goodness which is incarnate in our fellow creatures and which is the inspiration and ultimate appeal of all theory. As Emerson says, "all the religion we have is the ethics of one or another holy person." It is true that, for the perception of health, training and refinement of our innate value-sense is required, in a similar way that training and refinement of certain perceptive capacities are required for a physicist, musician, or statesman.

Some one will ask, What does all this have to do with God? Historically, the term *God* has meant that which creates health, that which saves, that which gives every good and perfect gift. "God" is the name given to that factor present in all experiences accountable as good—or, supremely, that factor common to all cases of healing or all cases of health. Hippocrates long ago pointed out that the task of the physician is to remove obstructions to the healing process, and, in general, physicians today attempt to follow this procedure. Mental therapists are coming to a recognition of the same principle. Both groups are now supplementing this procedure with a positive approach, namely, providing conditions which will facilitate the healing or health-giving process.

What is this health-giving process? Do theologians and therapists agree on its nature? In very general terms, this process is one of progressive integration, or growth. And therapists and theologians, both using methods of observation and analysis, agree on its nature. Thus Carl Rogers, a therapist, says,

> The aim is not to solve one particular problem, but to assist the individual to *grow*, so that he can cope with the present problem and with later problems in a better-integrated fashion. If he can gain enough integration to handle one problem in more independent, more responsible, less confused, better-organized ways, then he will also handle new problems in that manner. . . . This newer approach . . . relies much more heavily on the individual drive toward growth, health, and adjustment. Therapy is not a matter of doing something *to* the individual, or of inducing him to do something about himself. It is instead a matter of freeing him for normal growth and development, of removing obstacles so that he can move forward.[5]

Compare this statement with that of a theologian, Henry Nelson Wieman:

> When good increases, a process of reorganization is going on, generating new meanings, integrating them with the old, endowing each event as it occurs with a wider range of reference, molding the life of a man into a more deeply unified totality of meaning. The wide diversities, varieties, and contrasts of all the parts of a man's life are being progressively transformed into a more richly inclusive whole. The several parts of life are connected in mutual support, vivifying and enhancing one another in the creation of a more inclusive unity of events and possibilities. This process of reorganization is what we shall call the "creative event. . . ." We have identified God with the creative event. . . . One act or course of conduct is better than another if it provides more amply the conditions enabling the creative event to produce. . . .[6]

I interpret these two statements to be saying fundamentally the same thing: that health (the good life) is a continuous and never-end-

5. Carl Rogers, *Counseling and Psychotherapy* (Boston: Houghton Mifflin, 1942), p. 29.

6. Henry N. Wieman, *The Source of Human Good* (Chicago: University of Chicago, 1946), pp. 56, 305, 82.

ing integrating of thoughts, feelings, actions, within individuals and between individuals and groups; that such a creative process, while not in the complete control of man, may be released within us if proper conditions are provided. Beneath these somewhat different terminologies lie common thoughts, and back of them lies a common reality, the reality of healing, growing, creating, the reality designated by the theologian as salvation (when related to man) or as God (when viewed as a power not in man's control).

Some theologians will claim that the discovery of the therapists of modern times is merely a rediscovery of what saints and theologians in ancient times knew intuitively. That may be true. But, as many a volume has shown, theology as a whole has waged (and even now wages) a warfare on science and hence has obstructed the road of progress by claiming the purposes of God to be inscrutable, and all human therapy in the last resort to be futile. W. H. Sheldon has pointed out that theologizing has been a deadly monkey trap because it has failed to protect and employ creatively the biological energy of the human species.[7] The delinquency of theology has been hebephrenic withdrawal into the Word, into word magic, forgetting the real biological needs of human beings. Perhaps modern therapy, insofar as it brings us back to life and the life more abundant, will prove therapeutic for the hebephrenic theology of ancient days.

Therapists, too, can become delinquent (as Sheldon suggests) by moving too far in the direction of unbridled biological expression. We might hope that the double delinquency of theology and therapy at their worst would be combined to check one another in their excesses and produce a dynamic and creative synthesis, theology contributing the concern for the general, universal good, therapy the healthy respect for concrete, human fact, and for efficient technique.

In understanding the relations between theology and therapy we cannot forget that theology belongs to the rational, speculative, Platonic tradition and that therapy is a branch of that empirical, pragmatic, scientific tradition which, as Whitehead has pointed out, is a revolt against rationalism. The modern temper, he says, is a "vehement and passionate interest in the relation of general principles to irreducible and stubborn facts."[8] As progress in the physical and biological sciences has issued from the marriage of general theory and effective technique, so in the field of human values we require for progress the creative synthesis of broad theory and observed fact. It

7. W. H. Sheldon, *Varieties of Delinquent Youth* (New York: Harper and Bros., 1949), pp. 840ff.
8. Whitehead, *Science*, p. 3.

does not now appear that either theology or therapy has come of age for such a union. Yet as one studies the literature of the two fields one may find striking parallels and convergences. Within this century one may see theologians leaning in the direction of therapy for insights into human nature and health, and therapists looking to the religious literature for guidance. There has been mutual modification. But there have also been shallow and half-hearted attempts to effect a peaceful partition of territory between the two, by denying that any genuine, organic relation exists between them, or by refusing the effort to find some common foundation or goal, some common perspective embracing the methods and aims of both, some common theory of value. I have suggested what this common theory of value might be. But what is required is widespread searching and widespread concern for a creative integration of theology and therapy.

Summary

The articles in this section dealt with the therapeutic task and discussed its theoretical foundations as well as the similarities and differences between pastoral and secular counselors. Several approaches to these issues were given.

Although Bonhoeffer was the son of a psychiatrist, this influential theologian attended only in passing to the relationships between therapy as self-understanding and theology as God's self-disclosure. Yet, as Oden observed, Bonhoeffer was concerned that we avoid thinking in terms of two spheres and that we relate Christianity to the real world, i.e., a world come of age. Oden finds in Bonhoeffer ample warrant for a thesis he explicated more fully in *Kerygma and Counseling*, namely, that client-centered therapy includes the conditions of grace regardless of whether or not the therapist acknowledges this to be true.

Tillich asserts that every Christian should participate in the act of counseling because, as priest to the neighbor, it is the task of every Christian to relate the answers of faith to the questions of life. All persons are estranged and all *neurotic* anxiety is grounded in *basic* anxiety as he so pointedly states in *The Courage to Be*. Even secular counselors are human beings who exist within the human "predicament." There is no final healing apart from ultimate answers, according to Tillich.

Peters attempts to distinguish between "pastoral care," "pastoral counseling," "counseling," and "psychotherapy," but notes they are all grounded in a set of values. His concern for the role of the *evan-*

254

gelical pastor is unique among these authors. He sees this role as firmly grounded in the centrality of guilt/forgiveness and the radical self-assurance that comes when the counselee accepts these facts.

Parsons emphasizes the role of inductive, empirical reasoning wherein the values for which people yearn are undergirded by those of God—the supreme value. Parsons terms this approach *scientific* theology and recommends the method of Henry Nelson Wieman as exemplary. Health becomes a creative, created process.

Questions for Dialogue

1. Compare and contrast the approaches of Peters (evangelical theology) and Parsons (scientific theology).
2. How does the contention that counseling is the task of all Christians (Tillich) relate to the uniqueness of pastoral counseling proposed by Peters?
3. Can the covert communication of the Christian understanding of God's grace, as suggested by Oden, be legitimate in light of the need for persons to acknowledge their sin and God's forgiveness as suggested by Peters?
4. In what ways do Tillich's contention that all persons live within the human predicament and Bonhoeffer's contention that we live in a world come of age relate to one another?

Additional Readings

Books

Browning, D. *Atonement and psychotherapy.* Philadelphia: Westminster, 1966.

Doniger, S., ed. *Healing: Human and divine.* New York: Association, 1951.

Sanford, J. A. *Healing and wholeness.* New York: Paulist, 1977.

Tillich, P. J. *The courage to be.* New Haven, Conn.: Yale University, 1952.

Tournier, P. *The healing of persons.* San Francisco: Harper and Row, 1965.

Articles

Fish, S. Is there a doctor in the house? Holistic health takes a Christian turn. *Eternity,* August 1979, 14–20.

Mathison, J. I.; Lewis, B. F.; and Howland, E. S. Healing and wholeness. *Journal of Religion and Health.* 11, no. 2 (1972): 181–91.

Oakland, J. A. Self-actualization and sanctification. *Journal of Psychology and Theology* 2, no. 3 (1974) 202–9.

O'Byrne, M., and Angers, W. P. Jung's concept of self actualization and Teilhard de Chardin's philosophy. *Journal of Religion and Health* 11, no. 3 (1972): 241–51.

Methods
of Therapy

This last section details practical procedures that jointly employ religious and psychological means. These articles are the natural outgrowth of the previous sections which are more theoretical. A variety of approaches are offered. In each case attention is paid to the delicate but serious combination of theological and scientific concerns.

In "Utilization of Christian Beliefs in Psychotherapy," psychiatrist William Wilson reports in case fashion his moderately successful efforts to use explicit Christian ideas in the treatment of emotional disorders. Summarizing these procedures, he states, "It can be clearly stated that development of insight, decathexis of past events and previously held values are an essential part of the Christian psychological system. A dramatic change in the patient's emotional tonus as a result of conversion (James, 1902) can set in operation all of the beneficial events that are considered desirable in insight psychotherapy."

In the essay "God Talk in Psychotherapy," I identify explicit religious verbiage as a viable option in counseling. I pinpoint several differences in the locale where God is presumed to reside and the ways in which the healing dynamic of love is to be expressed. In dealing with *how* God talk is to be used, I conclude ". . . the Environmental, the Confessional, and the Dialogical provide three alternatives . . . they set the stage but do not predetermine *what* God talk will be used. As [John A. T.] Robinson (1963) suggested, there is a need to be not only honest *to* God but honest *about* God. Method and content go together."

Jay Adams, well-known proponent of "Nouthetic" counseling, writes in "The Use of Scriptures in Counseling," ". . . counseling that is truly scriptural is motivated by the Scriptures, (2) founded presuppositionally on the Scriptures, (3) structured by the goals and objectives of the

Scriptures, and (4) developed systematically in terms of the practices and principles modeled and enjoined in the Scriptures." His is a unique and consistent point of view. He suggests that the Christian counselor will use Scripture to the exclusion of other counseling techniques.

The late David Roberts takes quite a different approach from Adams. According to him, religious counseling may involve no explicit use of religious concepts. In fact, he considers much overt use of religion to be just as manipulative as psychiatric sole reliance on behavior. Roberts commends a more implicit reliance on persons getting in touch with basic reality which leads them to seek religious answers. As he states, ". . . I do not believe that such an outlook always takes ignoble forms. It can be defiant and grandiose . . . but at best it issues in tragic stoicism. . . . But I would contrast it with a Christian orientation where these same qualities of love, faith, conscience and freedom are known, at least as potentialities, in our lives . . . this is possible because we live in a universe where reciprocal relations are possible between man and the ground of meaning."

The essay, "Psychotherapy and Catholic Confession," by Valerie Worthen, is a serious attempt to delineate the contrasts and similarities in these two remedial endeavors. An example of her analysis: "First, one could conclude that the two disciplines could never complement one another on an equal basis, since they are based on different presuppositions and, therefore, could not logically come out with the same results . . . confession presupposes man's conscious sin as a cause, the mediating judgment of the priest, and the restituting grace of God. Psychotherapy presupposes the acceptance of sin as a symptom of some larger problem that is unconsciously motivated." However, she concludes that the two have important points in common also.

The final article in this section, "Psychotherapy and Religious Values," is a recent attempt by noted psychologist, Allen Bergin, to make a case for including religion in the counseling task. He states, "Clinical pragmatism and humanistic idealism thus exclude what is one of the largest subideologies, namely, religious or theistic approaches espoused by people who believe in God and try to guide their behavior in terms of their perception of His will . . . the alternative I wish to put forward is a spiritual one. It might be called theistic realism."

The reader can expect to be enlightened regarding the possibilities of including religious techniques in counseling approaches. Although there are vast differences between the suggested approaches and in spite of the fact that inclusion of such approaches is by no means simple, the reader can expect to be stimulated to consider these matters seriously and adopt a viewpoint of his/her own.

Past evidence has indicated that strong religious faith has had therapeutic effects on individuals suffering from a variety of problems. Christian beliefs should be used rather than attacked or ignored in therapy. This paper reports on the treatment of eighteen patients utilizing Christian maneuvers of commitment or rededication, confession (uncovering), forgiveness, and fellowship change to supplement conventional psychiatric methods. Symptomatic relief was obtained in sixteen of the patients when Christian maneuvers were used. Previous therapy had been unsuccessful in fourteen of the cases.

Utilization of Christian Beliefs in Psychotherapy

William P. Wilson

Considerable scientific and anecdotal evidence is available to document a statement that a strong religious faith and the holding of values that pertain to that faith have a beneficial effect on the mental health of an individual (Wilson, 1972). Nevertheless, for various reasons, these individuals do become ill as do persons whose faith is weak or nonexistent and whose values are confused or weakly held. Statements have been made that a strong religious faith is an asset in psychotherapy (Pattison, 1965), that religious experiences and faith can result in instantaneous cure of alcohol, heroin, and other drug addictions, and that depression can be dramatically relieved (*The Psychic Function*, 1968; Lemere, 1953).

Since Christianity can be of benefit to the mental health of both mentally diseased and "normal" individuals, it behooves us to inquire further and ask if we can identify and utilize a "Christian psychology" in treating patients. We hypothesize that such personality resources should be utilized rather than ignored or attacked. This essay is intended to present the results of some preliminary efforts in "Christian psychotherapy."

Reprinted from *Journal of Psychology and Theology* 2, no. 2 (1974): 125–31. Used by permission.

Theoretical

Christianity

A basic concept shared by both psychiatry and Christianity is that man is self-oriented. Christianity argues that self-orientation is "sin" and is therefore wrong. Christianity goes further and says that all of man's problems and therefore his suffering are related to this self-orientation. His unhappiness is a direct outgrowth of his basic selfishness and pridefulness, for if he thinks only of himself, it is only logical that anger, jealousy, sorrow, fear, pain, and shame will occur more readily when he interacts with other people and the environment. Greed, another aspect of man's self-orientation, contributes to his unhappiness. To deal with his unhappiness, Christianity teaches that it is necessary that man "forget himself" and that he relate to others, especially God and Jesus Christ, in love. Love, defined as putting the other person's welfare and best interests above his own (Landis and Landis, 1968), is likely to create a reciprocal relationship and thus bring about joy or love as a response. Specific directions are given as to how to relate to others or deal with one's selfishness in order that the response of love can be a common one. This denial of self results in a change that is called conversion.

Basic to the Christian psychological system is the concept of forgiveness. God always forgives a repentant person, and therefore man must forgive others as well as himself as long as the offender is repentant.

Specific guidelines (or "laws") are carefully outlined for all aspects of life. Birth, marriage, family, work, and death, the common ventures of life, are dealt with in detail (Trueblood, 1949). These guidelines (or "laws") provide the basis for the values that reinforce the self-denial.

Finally, there is mutual reinforcement of these values in a group (the church). "Community" provides an environment where the individual is able to obtain rewards for having forgotten himself and also where he can obtain instruction and encouragement to further his change. If all aspects of the Christian life are practiced, rewards are promised: abundant life on earth and eternal life—a life beyond death.

Psychiatry

In contrast to Christianity, Freudian psychology makes common cause with man's self-orientation. To know oneself is the essence of this system. Self-understanding and the role of the past in determining the responsiveness to the environment is the goal of effective insight psychotherapy. Since the individual is what he is because of what has happened, he can be absolved of some of the responsibility and he is set free to develop new values and patterns of behavior that he (ideally), or more commonly the therapist, considers desirable. Because he has relived his past, he can hopefully decathect these memories, deal with the painful emotions, and reevaluate his childhood experiences in the light of adult reality. All too often, though, the patient can only reevaluate the past in the light of current reality and current popular concepts of reality (Mack and Semrad, 1967). Some call these concepts "fads." Because a superego is considered punishing if it possesses values or guidelines that deny the self-gratification of the ego, an effort is made to cleanse the superego of such values and their cathected "bad" emotions. These "bad" emotions are sorrow, shame, emptiness, and pain. The goal of therapy is therefore to replace these punitive values and emotions with nonpunitive values and no emotion or joy. Psychiatry does not attend to the common ventures of life, but only tries to explain man's behavior in these ventures on the basis of his past.

If we are honest, we have a dilemma. What does man do with a value system which is causing others pain? Can he relate in love if he is oriented to himself? What does he do with his anger and jealousy and greed if it causes "pain" in others? We have no answers to these questions and we are unable to find answers when we search the literature.

At this point we can iterate that Christianity does claim to have answers to the questions asked above. We would therefore ask further whether these answers found in conversion, confession, forgiveness, adoption of new value systems, and the cathexis of the specific emotions of love and joy to these new values have therapeutic usefulness.

Patient Material and Method

The patient material reported here is comprised of four males and sixteen females, seen in the author's private practice at the Duke Medical Center in Durham, North Carolina. Each patient was examined in a standard way and the usual details of psychiatric history, mental status, and physical examination obtained. In each instance we further attempted to determine in as much detail as was possible what the patient's religious life had been. We therefore inquired into the patient's early religious training. To do this we asked whether his family had taken or sent him to church and how often; whether they had taught him to pray individually and/or corporately, whether he was required to read and study the Bible. This information was collected and a decision made as to the intensity of religious training and instruction using a four-point scale from zero to three.

We next inquired as to whether the individual had been converted (or born again), and if so, had he on any occasion rededicated his life to God.

Last, we inquired as to whether the individual had tried to increase his knowledge and understanding of God and his faith, if indeed he had acquired a faith.

With this information we felt that we were able to assess "where the person was" religiously and then determine how we were going to treat him. We all the while considered him as a whole person with a body, mind, and spirit.

In every instance we used conventional psychiatric treatment from the beginning as our primary thrust. Electroshock and drugs were used if we felt that one of these was the treatment most indicated. If psychotherapy was indicated as a primary or secondary treatment, we undertook this—considering the fact that we had one additional goal and that was to increase the patient's conscious contact with God and to "move" him as far as we could in the religious sense. In those patients where electroshock was used, we made little effort to deal with the patient's psychological and spiritual problems until electroshock was discontinued and memory function was grossly improved.

Our Christian psychotherapeutic maneuvers were utilized in this order: salvation or rededication, confession, repentance, forgiveness, teaching or reinforcement of values or behavioral guidelines, and introduction into a selected Christian community. Not all of our patients needed intervention into all aspects of their spiritual life. In most instances those areas that needed the greatest effort were selected for initial intervention. Salvation or rededication, however, was considered essential in all at the beginning.

In every patient we carefully explained our point of view and he was told that he was free to choose between conventional psychiatric care and that which included a spiritual dimension in addition to his conventional psychiatric care. Once a Christian approach was requested, great effort was exercised to focus only on basic Christian beliefs. In no instance did we involve ourselves in debate concerning denominational differences.

Results

As a group the majority of these patients were young or middle-aged females who were married (see Table 1). Most of them were diagnosed as having some emotional disorder. Depression was the most common problem encountered (see Table 2), but all patients,

Table 1

Demographic Data

Sex	Age Range	Mean Age	Marital Status	
16 females	16–61	35	Married	12
4 males			Single	4
			Separated	3
			Widowed	1

including the patient whose primary problem was alcoholism, had some kind of affective symptomatology.

In considering psychotherapeutic intervention, it was determined that the problem to be dealt with was not always the primary problem. Many patients were inaccessible to psychotherapeutic treatment until their symptoms were ameliorated by drugs or EST. Then, we find that the categorizations are different from those used as the diagnostic problem presented by the patient (see Table 3).

In Table 4 it can be seen that only six of the patients were untreated when they were referred. A wide variety of psychotherapeutic treatments had been administered ranging from once in two years to three times a week and from classical psychoanalysis to transactional analysis. Fourteen of the patients had at one time or another received an adequate trial of drugs or EST with no more than transitory improvement. All of this group had been ill for six months or longer and in spite of their treatment, which had extended over an equal or lesser length of time, none had significantly improved.

Religious Life

About one-half of these patients were considered as being persons who had a meaningful relationship with God. Most had grown up in homes where there was moderate to minimal early religious training, but the majority were familiar with the fundamental concepts of Christianity (see Table 5). Some had very traumatic childhoods ranging from experiences of incestuous concubinage to continuous threats of separation of parents or separation to complete rejection by one or

Table 2

Diagnostic Categorization

Psychotic Depressive Reaction		3
Manic Depression { Depression		2
{ Mania		1
Neurasthenic Neurosis		2
Phobic Neurosis		3
Depressive Neurosis		8
Alcoholism		1

Table 3

Problem for Psychotherapeutic
Intervention

Depression	7
Emptiness	2
Anger	5
Fear and phobias	3
Loss of loved ones	1
Alcoholism	1
To obtain cooperation in taking medications	1

both parents. Alcoholism of one or both parents was a common problem. One or both parents of 50 percent of the patients was a disturbed person, rarely having received professional help. Eleven of the twenty patients who were treated had had a conversion experience sometime in their life. For most, this was a meaningful and lasting experience that had served as an impetus to work out their problems and come to some solution of these problems. Only one individual had rededicated her life in an effort to obtain relief from the depression she felt. This maneuver was unsuccessful because of her overwhelming fear.

Only one-half of the patients had been able to obtain adequate teaching after their salvation. In most instances this teaching was not of the variety that was conducive to personal growth. This was true irrespective of the patient's denominational ties.

Finally only one-third of the patients had availed themselves of the opportunity for fellowship. These individuals usually did so outside of their home church. The two neo-Pentecostals in the group were most constant in their fellowship, but others were active in Christian Women's Clubs, Campus Crusade, Inter-Varsity, and independent Bible study groups. In most instances Sunday school and other church activities were secondary resources. The neo-Pentecostals were considered separately here because of the content of their fellowship. In both instances there was overemphasis on demonology and the experience of glossolalia.

Table 4

Previous Unsuccessful Therapy

Psychotherapy (alone)	8
Drugs (alone)	4
EST (alone)	1
Psychotherapy (with drugs)	8
EST (with drugs)	2
No treatment	6

Table 5

Religious Life Prior to Illness and
Treatment

A. Early Religious Training	
1. Intensive	3
2. Moderate	7
3. Minimal	7
4. None	3
B. Salvation	
1. No salvation	9
2. Salvation	11
3. Rededicated after salvation	1
C. Growth after Salvation	
1. Good	8
2. Fair	1
3. Neo-Pentecostal	2
4. Does not apply	9
D. Fellowship	
1. Constant	7
2. Regular	3
3. Occasional	2
4. None	8

Therapeutic Maneuvers

In planning therapy with these patients, we began with the assumption that salvation was the most therapeutic event in the Christian's life and that it was a *sine qua non* to any other effort. In eight cases, this was not deemed necessary and we moved on to other avenues of approach. In several patients a definite commitment to the self-denial and obedience to the behavioral and psychological guidelines of Christianity was made. Two patients refused and we made no further reference to the Christian point of view in their therapy unless they brought the matter up themselves. One of these two patients continues to struggle with her spiritual life although she is markedly improved (see Table 6).

After commitment, confession, or uncovering, was undertaken using conventional psychotherapeutic techniques. Here every effort was made in seventeen patients to elicit all of the memories that were part of the patient's record of wrongs held in relation to others as well as to himself. When these were elicited and the offenders identified, an effort was made to get the patients to forgive each and every person who had offended him. As mentioned above, the patient also had to forgive himself.

In eight instances some resource was found in the patient's immediate environment for him to increase his sense of "community" and to learn more through the experience of others.

Table 6

Therapeutic Maneuvers

A.	Commitment	
	1. Made	7
	2. Not Necessary	8
	3. Rededications	3
	4. Commitment Refused	2
B.	Confession (Uncovering)	
	1. Yes	17
	2. Not Necessary	2
	3. Refused	1
C.	Forgiveness	
	1. Yes	17
	2. Not Necessary	1
	3. Refused	1
	4. Unable	1
D.	Fellowship Change	
	1. Not Necessary	10
	2. Yes	8
	3. Refused	2

Discussion

Descriptively the converted individual reverts to a loving relationship with the parents of his childhood, whom he had long since abandoned, and with their representatives in the religious world. There is the illusion of reconciliation and rededication to the renewed love. There also is the conviction of being almost literally reborn. While this pattern seems to be fairly constant we do not yet know why it occurs so seldom or how to evoke it for therapeutic purposes (1968, p. 679).

This statement quoted from GAP Report #67 is important when we considered the data presented here. The descriptive dynamism cannot be considered as adequate or correct, especially the statement concerning illusion; for if the individual sees "himself" as reconciled, he most often is and thus this is not an illusion (Wilson, 1972; James, 1902; Pratt, 1970). It is the last part of that statement that is most in error. We do have the ability to elicit this phenomenon for therapeutic process, but it is nevertheless the greatest resource available in treatment since it provides a new affective state. The patient is relieved of his sorrow and shame and thus his guilt. He may no longer be fearful since he is reassured that he is forgiven and will not be punished or harmed. He "knows" that all of the events of the past which are causing him painful emotions are forgiven and no matter how bad he has been, he will be accepted by others. He is reassured by Jesus' acceptance of prostitutes, tax collectors, all kinds of criminals, and other "sinners." He has been cleansed, thus he can decathect his past memories as does the patient in more convention psychotherapy.

Confession, or uncovering, of his repressed memories is facilitated by conversion. He no longer has to repress these memories out of fear since he has massively decathected them even before they reach awareness. The pain they cause is ameliorated on reaching awareness since he knows he will not be condemned. Specific statements in the Bible will constantly reinforce his beliefs as they relate to his confession of various conflictual memories.

Sharing of his problems in the therapeutic situation and in his community reinforces the decathexis of these memories and facilitates his deconditioning. Finally as he learns more through a systematic study, he is given specific guidelines to deal with painful emotions as they are elicited and thus prevent the development of new conflicts. Because he is told that his life should have less pain, he constantly searches to ascertain the origin of his pain and "do something" about it.

Because he is rewarded with acceptance and love, by both his peers and by a loving God, the patient strives to maintain his psychologically pleasurable state by doing the right things, by being self-less and self-denying. He thus should and does become a loving person by inhibiting his usual negative responses to the environment.

On the basis of the foregoing data and discussion, it would seem that utilization of basic Christian beliefs in psychotherapy can facilitate psychotherapy. It can be clearly stated that development of insight, decathexis of past events, and previously held values are an essential part of the Christian psychological system. A dramatic change in the patient's emotional tonus as a result of conversion (James, 1902) can set in operation all of the beneficial events that are considered desirable in insight psychotherapy. Christianity goes further in that once decathected values are recognized and reevaluated, they may be replaced by values which provide the patient with new conditioning responses that are pleasurable and in his eyes more desirable than those previously experienced. These facilitate the personality change and provide a continuing motivation to remain changed.

Conclusions

Twenty patients were treated psychotherapeutically using basic Christian maneuvers to supplement conventional psychiatric treatment. It was observed that symptomatic relief was obtained in sixteen

Table 7

Outcome

Treatment Facilitated or Successful	
Yes	16
No	3
Questionable	1

of the eighteen patients so treated (see Table 7). Previous therapy in fourteen of the patients had been unsuccessful. It is concluded that further investigation of the use of Christian therapeutic insights is warranted.

References

James, W. 1902. *Varieties of religious experience: A study in human nature.* New York: Longmans, Green.

Landis, J. T., and Landis, M. C. 1968. *Building a successful marriage.* Englewood Cliffs, N.J.: Prentice-Hall.

Lemere, F. 1953. What happens to alcoholics? *American Journal of Psychiatry* 109: 674.

Mack, J. E., and Semrad, E. V. 1967. Classical psychoanalysis. In *Comprehensive textbook of psychiatry,* edited by A. M. Freedman and H. I. Kaplan. Baltimore: Williams and Wilkins.

Pattison, E. M. 1965. Social and psychological aspects of religion in psychotherapy. *The Journal of Nervous and Mental Disease* 141: 586–97.

Pratt, J. B. 1970. *The psychology of religious belief.* New York: Macmillan.

Committee on Psychiatry and Religion, 1968. Group for the Advancement of Psychiatry. *The psychic function of religion in mental illness.* Gap Report #67, vol. 6. New York.

Trueblood, E. 1949. *Common ventures of life.* New York: Harper and Row.

Wilson, W. P. 1972. Mental health benefits of religious salvation. *Diseases of the Nervous System* 33: 382–86.

This essay is concerned with whether, how, and when to use God talk in psychotherapy. Psychotherapy is defined as planned change based on value assumptions about the nature of the good life. God talk is presented as a set of values based on the presumption of a divine reality and the principle of love. As such it is considered one of the viable value systems for psychotherapy. Distinctions are made among several types of God talk and among educative, normative, and coercive strategies of change. Finally, the environmental, the confessional, and the dialogical options for using God talk in the psychotherapeutic task are discussed.

God Talk in Psychotherapy

H. Newton Malony

This essay will be concerned with whether, how, and when to use "God talk" in psychotherapy.

Initially a definition of terms is in order.

Psychotherapy

"Psychotherapy" can be defined as planned change in which a person (called a therapist) helps another person (called a client) more effectively to cope with problems of living. This grounds the psychotherapeutic task firmly in the realm of adjustment rather than in the realm of disease. As Szasz (1961) has suggested, psychotherapy presumes the essential problem to be in the interaction of the person with the world rather than in the interaction of the person with his/her physical body. Mental illness is presumed to be a social—not a somatic—problem.

Szasz asserts that the psychotherapist is the agent of society in general and the legal system in particular. In both diagnosis and treatment the psychotherapist's goals are adequacy and achievement within a culture.

A paper read at the annual meeting of the American Psychological Association, New York, New York, September, 1979.

269

And it is well known that culture is culture—nothing more, nothing less. Customs or laws, while they may seem absolutes, are, in fact, agreed-upon ways of behaving that work for persons at a time and in a place.

Thus the psychotherapist is the handmaiden or representative of a set of functional values whether he/she likes it or not—even if those values be those of a subculture within the larger society. "Mental health" is to cope with frustration and function adequately within an environment that both receives one's behavior and responds positively with desirable goods and services. There is no such thing as health without society.

Therefore psychotherapy always espouses a set of values. The dialogue between the adjustment theorists and the proponents of client-centered individualism in the 1950s was a false battle. In the final analysis all psychotherapy is directed toward adjustment in the name of a set of values the therapist presumes to be optimal for the client.

This has led many to conceive of psychotherapy as preeminently the imparting of "wisdom"—i.e., sharing a view of the good life. As Perry London (1964) suggests, "Psychotherapy is a moralistic as well as scientific undertaking . . ." (p. v). Taking this assumption one step further, it could be said that the psychotherapist functions more like a clergyman than a physician (cf. London, p. 3). This means all psychotherapists are advocates of a certain view of life and reality. They are evangelists whether or not they intend to be. The issue, therefore, is not "whether" but "which." Which set of values provides the basis for a given psychotherapy? This is the question and it leads us to a discussion of God talk.

God Talk

"God talk" is that set of values which presumes that *the* way to live is evidenced through what persons have discovered about or what has been revealed to them by a transcendent reality called "God." In the Judeo-Christian tradition, which will be used as exemplary in this discussion, there is the central notion that "love" is the primary force which guides the good life and that this love has been made known by the acts of God in creation, election, covenant, and sacrifice as depicted in the Old and New Testaments. Further, there is the affirmation that this principle of love is preeminently seen in the eighth-century prophets and in Jesus of Nazareth. To speak about this truth (i.e., love) and to assume that the good life requires faith in God who reveals it (i.e., love)—this is God talk.

This Judeo-Christian idea that love is the key to life stands in modern Western culture in contrast to the classical Greek notion that knowledge, not love, is the primary ingredient of the good life. From this alternative viewpoint, "knowledge" is that which will dispel ignorance and reason and can guide persons toward effectiveness in their dealings with others.

These values, love and knowledge, have provided the contemporary world of mental health with basic alternatives. On the one hand there is the choice of love as represented by St. Augustine and on the other hand there is knowledge as represented by Socrates. Most proponents of psychotherapeutic systems, secular or sacred, have chosen one or the other as a basic paradigm. For example, it could be said that Transactional Analysis has chosen love, Rational Emotive Therapy has chosen knowledge, and Reality Therapy has attempted a combination of both.

In passing it could be said that, with the above distinction in mind, it is not surprising that Ellis should be so opposed to religion. He suggests that when "God talk" arises in therapy it should not be accepted or understood. Instead it should be challenged and discarded as counterproductive to mental health. Perhaps, however, his opposition is not so much to the talk about God as it is to the presumption about love. For Ellis, knowledge, not love, is the way to the good life. And knowledge can be discovered—it does not need to be disclosed by a suprahuman deity!

As indicated there are two components to God talk—i.e., the principle of love and the person of God. A delineation of the several options for locating these components is helpful in determining what kind of God talk is being presented. Figure 1 depicts four possibilities for consideration. The options vary in the degree to which a personal God is postulated, the locale of the experience of love, and the extent to which the principle of love is to be discovered by trial and error or disclosed by revelation.

Option 1 (God = above, love = something God does, i.e., forgive) presumes an entirely independent existence for the Deity and a location of love in the forgiveness of that Deity for sinful acts. Option 2 (God = out there, love = something we do, i.e., be just) presumes the existence of the Deity to be in historical interaction with the world, and love therefore is located in the interrelationships of persons. Option 3 (God = within, love = something we do for ourselves) presumes the Deity to be some unique aspect of the individual himself/herself, and love is thus living in terms of this personal potential divinity. Finally, option 4 (God = beneath, love = being in harmony with the real) presumes the Deity to be synonymous with a principle

Figure 1

Possible Options for God-Talk Components

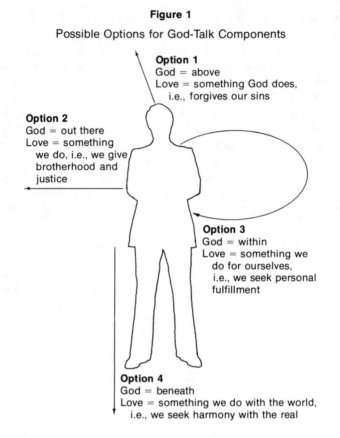

Option 1
God = above
Love = something God does,
    i.e., forgives our sins

Option 2
God = out there
Love = something
    we do, i.e., we give
    brotherhood and
    justice

Option 3
God = within
Love = something we
    do for ourselves,
    i.e., we seek personal
    fulfillment

Option 4
God = beneath
Love = something we do with the world,
    i.e., we seek harmony with the real

underlying all things, and love becomes living in harmony with this inner dynamic.

Although it would seem as if the continuum of supranaturalism ran from options 1 to 4, the various combinations of transcendence, revelation, and expression are complex indeed. For example, although the theologian Paul Tillich suggests (in option 4 fashion) that "God does not exist—He is," Tillich nevertheless affirms the critical importance of revelation in his insistence that the answers to finite existence cannot come from within the situation. The essential need is to transcend the situation and accept, by faith, love which is freely given yet is at the same time the "ground of being." Tillich, of course, uses only one example of the numerous combinations of God talk that are extant. It is therefore necessary to ask the question "What God talk?" before finally judging its efficacy in psychotherapy or any other endeavor. It goes without saying that even within the God-talk circle differing values are implied by virtue of the several options noted above.

Nevertheless, God talk, as a basic value assumption about life, has as much place as any other set of values in providing a basis for the psychotherapeutic task if one presumes, as heretofore detailed, that psychotherapy is essentially the sharing of wisdom about how to live. Thus the question of whether God talk is legitimate in psychotherapy can be answered in the affirmative. It is indeed a valid option. However, to say that it is an appropriate alternative is not automatically to answer the question "How?" or "When?" It cannot be presumed that any values, much less those denoted by God talk, can simplistically be communicated best by explicit quotations of propositions or conclusions. Having a set of basic values is one thing. Influencing someone else is another.

How Is God Talk to Be Used in Psychotherapy?

Psychotherapy is an example of planned change. As such it is not primarily a haphazard or an intuitive task. Because it is based on presumptions about the good life, it intentionally seeks to guide clients toward those functional values. Persuasion and influence are the goals. Technique is the means.

Bennis, Benne, and Chin (1969) have concluded that there are three basic strategies in any effort of planned change. They are the educative, the normative, and the coercive strategies. Educative change focuses on the communication of new ideas and presumes that information will be accepted and acted on. Insight therapies utilize this model of change. Normative change focuses on reflection and reexperiencing. It presumes that good feelings will lead to new behavior. Gestalt therapies utilize this model of change. Coercive change focuses on reinforcement and punishment. It presumes that trial and error will lead to the forceful shaping of behavior regardless of whether one thinks it is logical or it feels good. Behavior therapies are based on this model of change.

Figure 2 summarizes Bennis, Benne, and Chin's conclusions about the rapidity and duration of change resulting from these three strategies.

It can be assumed that the twin goals of any therapy are mental healing that occurs as fast as possible and that lasts as long as possible, hence the twin concerns of rapidity and duration. In reference to God talk, presuming it is a viable optional value base for psychotherapy, the question would therefore be, "How is it best utilized? Educatively, normatively, or coercively?"

Seemingly the quickest change would result from forceful direct confrontation of the client's thought patterns and explicit insistence

Figure 2

Rapidity and Duration of Change as
a Function of Type of Strategy

	Change Strategy		
	Educative	Normative	Coercive
Rapidity (3 = quickest change)	2	1	3
Duration (3 = longest change)	2	3	1

that the God-Love point of view was the only viable option if one would be healthy. Extant therapies such as the Integrity therapy of Hobart Mowrer (1961) and the Nouthetic Counseling of Jay Adams (1970) illustrate this method. These might be labeled Religious Rational Emotive therapies. However, the problem is that such methods do not last, if Bennis, Benne, and Chin are correct.

The next most rapid change would probably result from an educative approach in which a persuasive reasonable effort is made to convince the client of the legitimacy of the God-Love model either by didactic interpretation or by therapist sharing in a modeling manner. Christian Existential Analysis (cf. Tweedie, 1963) and Crabb's Biblical Counseling (1977) are examples of this approach. These might be labeled Religious Insight therapies. They have the disadvantage of not being as rapid, but they last longer than the coercive methods, according to Bennis, Benne, and Chin.

The last option, the normative, would be largely inductive and experiential. The presumption here would be that the most lasting changes result from reflection on experience in which the client's sense is that he/she has been deeply moved and emotionally affected. God talk here is implicit, after the fact, or indirect. It is never imposed but is inferred. Tillich's suggestions about ontological therapy and the conclusions of Oden et al. (1974) that the client-centered therapeutic conditions of empathy, warmth, and congruence are the concrete expressions of God as evidenced in Christ's incarnation are examples of this approach. Although the slowest of the alternatives, this approach has the potential for having the most lasting impact, if Bennis, Benne, and Chin are correct.

As previously noted the question of how to utilize God talk in psychotherapy is not unrelated to what type of God talk is being used. Another dimension of the problem pertains to whether the language used should be explicit or implicit. In words, should God talk be overt or covert?

An extreme example of overt, explicit God talk was the counselor who said after three minutes into the first interview with a client, "I have seen many situations just like yours; I know your problem—what you need is the Lord, Jesus Christ." At the opposite extreme was the client who heard his therapist give a talk at a church and said in the next session, "What you said there made therapy much clearer. Why didn't you tell me those things about God in our session?"

These examples pose the issues. They are integral to a discussion of therapy at two junctures: (1) symptom relief, and (2) interpretation. Again and again, clients seek therapy because of painful symptoms and end therapy with minimal release of their discomfort. They seem content with reaching penultimate goals and often resist thinking of their lives in terms of ultimate, or underlying, values. Symptom relief seems sufficient. Further, they seem to resist any reversal of the process wherein ultimate values are discussed first and symptoms are considered later. The client exposed to the counselor's diagnosis of her "need for the Lord, Jesus Christ," reported great anger and a deep sense of being misunderstood.

However, if, as some theorists (cf. Tillich) have suggested, "All neurotic anxiety is at heart basic anxiety," and if all symptoms are indicative of a value crisis, then the question of interpretation cannot be ignored. As the early research on therapeutic outcome suggested, what is learned in psychotherapy is a language or a way of talking about one's life. How is this language, or value system, best communicated?

Eric Berne (1961) faults most therapists for doing little to help others and spending time in case conferences talking about it in technical jargon. He calls for "no jazz" (fancy words) in therapy. But it is interesting to note that Transactional Analysis, more than almost any other system, has developed an elaborate array of terms to be learned by the client. Berne maintains that the language of therapy must be simplified in order that the client may be fully aware what the therapist is talking about.

Three options in the matter of understandable counseling terms have been suggested. They are the environmental, the confessional, and the dialogical.

Environmental God Talk

The environmental option suggests that the conditions of good psychotherapy provide the situation in which God's action is made real. Thus God is implicit and integral to the therapeutic task. Overt talk about the God factor in psychotherapeutic events is superfluous because

God is there apart from and often in spite of talk about Him. To the degree that empathic understanding, therapeutic congruence, acceptance, permissiveness, and unconditional positive regard exist in the therapeutic hour there God is present whether or not His name is mentioned, whether or not the therapist believes it to be true. Psychotherapy is regarded as under the "analogy of faith" (Oden, 1966, p. 48). This position begins with the assumption that God (i.e., Jesus Christ) is acting in the world and that natural relationships, such as psychotherapy, can be viewed from the vantage point of this divine activity. Because it emphasizes the conditions in which healing takes place and the behavior of the therapist which can simulate or mediate divine activity whether or not the therapist knows it, this view can be termed the "environmental" option.

T. C. Oden has explicated this point of view most lucidly in his volume *Kerygma and Counseling: Toward a Covenant Ontology for Secular Psychotherapy* (1966). He includes a chart of theological terms to be correlated with the therapeutic conditions delineated by client-centered theorists.

He concludes that where the empathic therapist descends into the depths with the client there God, who emptied Himself in Christ, is present. Also, where the therapist participates in the estrangement of the client from himself/herself without losing his/her self-identity, there God, who became fully human in Christ but continued to be God, is present. Further, where the therapist affirms the person in the midst of the sickness, there the forgiveness and radical acceptance of God is present. In addition, where the client permits new freedom there the grace of God is present as a gift. Finally, where warm caring for the client is pervasively communicated there the freeing agape love of God is present.

The strategic ingredient of this environmental option is the realization that God talk is not essential for its actualization. It has been called the position of the "incognito Christ" in that explicit mention

Figure 3

Theological, Therapeutic, and Healing Terms

God's Activity (Revelation)	Therapist's Actions (Clarification)	Individual Response (Growth toward Authenticity)
Incarnation	Empathic Understanding	Increased Self-Understanding
Divine Congruence	Therapeutic Congruence	Increased Self-Identity
Forgiveness	Acceptance	Increased Self-Acceptance
Grace	Permissiveness	Increased Self-Direction
Divine Love	Unconditional Positive Regard	Increased Love of Others

of God's name or presence is not necessary. As Oden says, "Clearly the love of God does not need to be verbally expressed in order to be present" (p. 49).

Confessional God Talk

The second option, the confessional point of view, can be contrasted with a professional alternative. Those who profess tend to state their assumptions at the beginning of the process and, in the case under consideration, introduce God talk into therapy throughout the encounter. For example, a professing point of view might explicitly identify the aforementioned therapeutic conditions as godly, might state clearly the goals of therapy in theological terms, and might model resolution of personal problems by ready reference to God's help or guidance. The confessional option, however, assumes these realities but points to them after the fact and only when queried. It presumes that God does not need to be labeled to be present—just as Oden noted. It also presumes, however, that there is a valid purpose for language which provides categories for organizing reality. While good therapy can occur without explicit God talk, the best therapy occurs with it.

The word *confessional* in this alternative refers to the timing of the God talk, i.e., toward the end rather than at the beginning of therapy. Confessing means to admit to or point to or interpret the reality underneath the experience. However, this viewpoint considers it crucial that the labeling come after the experience, not before. God talk thus becomes the "Ah-ha" that denotes the insight which gives meaning to the therapeutic experience. It thus presumes that insight *does* heal.

Confessional God talk occurs best when the therapist is asked about the meaning of the therapeutic experience. These client questions are familiar to most therapists and run the gamut from "What happened to me?" to "This has been so different from other relationships, how do you explain that?" to "Tell me, how do you handle stress in your life?" At this point, the confessional approach does not turn the question into a question (i.e., What do you think?) but instead "confesses" what is going on from a theological perspective. This has been called the "do and tell" approach. You do therapy first and talk about it later. Thus God talk becomes explicit and specific. There is nothing mechanical about this, however. At its most intuitive point, it is a delicate process of sharing the ultimate context in which therapy and growth occur in both the client and the counselor. Although it labels, interprets, and describes, it does so in a manner that avoids coercion and encourages exploration.

In another context I have written this description of the process: "I have found that sharing or disclosing myself to others in the midst of their struggling has been a most productive means of change in them and in me. The what of what I share is the Christian faith and hope. But sharing is much more than content. Most important, I share myself as a faithing person, i.e., a person with commitment yet with tentative answers, i.e., a person who himself is in the process. I share myself as a person who self-consciously stands in the long tradition of those who accepted the meaning of their life and destiny as coming from God in Christ. I share myself as one who remains open to further elaboration of this faith as it comes from those who also struggle to find themselves" (Malony, 1970, p. 6).

Dialogical God Talk

Finally there is the dialogical option. As opposed to the implicit approach of the environmental alternative and explicit approach of the confessional, the dialogical method of God talk in psychotherapy uses the indirect procedure. In a sense it combines the assumptions of the environmental with the techniques of the confessional option. It affirms the depth analogy between human events and the action of God, but it retains an emphasis on the need for symbolic labeling in order that persons may encounter meaning in their experience. Nevertheless, the dialogical viewpoint is not as confident as the confessional that the use of explicit God talk will truly communicate the reality underlying overtly religious language. In our culture where religious language is so pervasive, God talk may lead to cognitive acceptance without depth understanding.

Further, the dialogical method presumes that the importance of God talk may lie in the midst of the process rather than at the end as the confessional position asserts. Personal anxiety, for example, may need to be set within the context of basic anxiety about selfhood or being, as Tillich termed it, in order that healing or courage may become possible. It is not just an after-the-fact addendum but a dynamic essential to hear of a God who accepts us just as we are.

The dialogue in the dialogical approach is the interaction of the pain and dilemmas brought to therapy by the client and their deeper context in the estrangement of the person from the center (or truth) of his/her existence. The goal of therapy, therefore, becomes one of gentle contextualization of the struggle of the client so that uncovering the depth meaning of a specific event becomes probable and the reception of the saving truth about God becomes possible.

The words *saving truth* are used intentionally here. The functional nature of God talk is thereby emphasized. God talk for belief's sake is only secondary to God talk for faith's sake. *Faith* is a term which implies trust and reliance. It also implies a change of life characterized by deep self-understanding and courage. As Becker (1973) suggests, psychotherapists do a great disservice to clients in suggesting that therapy can do away with finitude or prevent death. Anxiety is always the lot of persons because of the nature of existence. However, despair is not a necessary outcome of anxiety, as Sellers (1961) notes. The Christian faith offers another alternative. It is this option to which the dialogical approach points indirectly. There can be the courage (cf. Tillich, 1951) which comes from plumbing the depths of neurotic anxieties, from abandoning defensive or technological maneuvers to ward off fear, and from accepting God as the foundation of life and presence which never rejects us. The communication of these realities is the dialogical option for God talk in psychotherapy.

Thus these options, the environmental, the confessional, and the dialogical, provide three alternatives for using God talk in psychotherapy. It should be noted that they set the stage but do not predetermine what God talk will be used. As indicated earlier, the kind of God talk is just as crucial as the way it is used. As Robinson (1963) has suggested, there is a need to be not only honest *to* God but honest *about* God. Method and content go together.

Summary

This essay has been concerned with whether, how, and when to use God talk in psychotherapy. Psychotherapy was defined as planned change based on value assumptions about the nature of the good life. God talk was presented as a set of values based on the presumption of a divine reality and the principle of love. As such it was considered one of the viable value systems for psychotherapy. Distinctions were made between several types of God talk and between educative, normative, and coercive strategies of change. Finally, the environmental, the confessional, and the dialogical options for using God talk in the psychotherapeutic task were discussed.

References

Adams, J. 1970. *Competent to counsel.* Grand Rapids: Baker.

Becker, E. 1973. *The denial of death.* New York: Free.

Bennis, W. G.; Benne, K. D.; and Chin, R. 1969. *The planning of change.* 2d ed. New York: Holt, Rinehart, and Winston.

Berne, E. 1961. *Transactional analysis in psychotherapy.* New York: Grove.

Crabb, L. 1977. *Effective biblical counseling.* Grand Rapids: Zondervan.

Ellis, A. *The case against religion.* New York: Institute for Rational Living, n.d. Sound recording.

London, P. 1964. *The modes and morals of psychotherapy.* New York: Holt, Rinehart, and Winston.

Malony, H. N. 1970. Hope is what I'm doing. Fuller Theological Seminary, Pasadena, California. Mimeo.

Mowrer, O. H. 1961. *The crisis in psychiatry and religion.* Princeton, N.J.: Van Nostrand.

Niebuhr, H. R. 1951. *Christ and culture.* New York: Harper and Row.

Oden, T. C. 1966. *Kerygma and counseling: Toward a covenant ontology for secular psychotherapy.* Philadelphia: Westminster.

Oden, T. C.; Warren, N. C.; Mulholland, K. B.; Schoonhoven, C. R.; Kraft, C. H.; and Walker, W. 1974. *After therapy what? Lay therapeutic resources in religious perspective.* Springfield, Ill.: Charles C. Thomas.

Robinson, J. A. T. 1963. *Honest to God.* Philadelphia: Westminster.

Sellers, J. E. 1961. *The outsider and the Word of God.* New York: Abingdon.

Szasz, T. 1961. *The myth of mental illness.* New York: Harper and Row.

Tillich, P. 1952. *The courage to be.* New Haven, Conn.: Yale University.

There is a common conviction among conservative, evangelical persons that the Bible should have a central place in counseling. It is a must, not an option. The counselor's counselor is the Holy Spirit who works through the use of Scripture. God has assigned the role of counselor to ministers and has provided the Bible as a guidebook in this calling. All problems the counselor will face can be solved by using a biblical plan of action. Christian counselors use the Bible to give judgment and hope to persons. This requires courage and commitment on the part of the counselor.

Christian Counseling Is Scriptural

Jay E. Adams

You Must Use the Scriptures in Counseling

I do not think that I need to labor this point at Dallas Seminary. I am sure that the reason I was invited to deliver these lectures in the first place was because of our common conviction about this vital imperative.[1] Therefore, since I think that I can safely assume that we are in basic agreement about this, since I have argued the issue elsewhere in print,[2] and since I am certain that your interest lies more in questions growing out of problems connected with the ways and means of using the Scriptures in counseling, I shall quickly move beyond this point. But before I do, perhaps a word or two would be in order.

You Must Have Conviction, Courage, and a Steady Determination to Use the Scriptures in Counseling

First, you may think that it will be easy to graduate from this school, take up your work in a conservative pastorate, and, as a part of your

Reprinted from *The Use of the Scriptures in Counseling* (Grand Rapids: Baker, 1975), pp. 1–16. The first eight chapters of this book were given as the W. H. Griffith Thomas Memorial Lectures at Dallas Theological Seminary, November 6–9, 1973. Subsequently they were published in the four issues of *Bibliotheca Sacra* during the year 1974. They have been revised and additional chapters have been included for use in this volume. The entire book is reprinted in *Lectures on Counseling* (Grand Rapids: Baker, 1978). Used by permission.
  1. I have retained much of the original lecture flavor in these chapters.
  2. *The Christian Counselor's Manual* (Grand Rapids: Baker, 1973), pp. 92–97.

effort there, begin to do biblical counseling. Please believe me when I say that it will not be that simple. The pressures exerted against a ministry of biblical counseling are great, as you will discover all too soon. For one thing, when you begin to counsel biblically some counselees will rebel. They will protest that you are being unduly hard on them, and will demand an easier way out. After all, scriptural counsel is often *hard*. Sin creates no *easy* problems; they are all so difficult that it took nothing less than the death of Christ to meet them. Untangling men from the webs of sin can be a quite painful process. The hard (but needed) directions that you will give to others from God's Word about repentance, confession of sin, reconciliation with one's brother, and so on, will not sit right with those who want to remove the miseries caused by sin without dealing with the sin itself. Though men want it, you must tell them that there is no such instant holiness.

Second, because sinners (and never forget that *Christians* are sinners, too) always want to do things the *easy way*,[3] they often will insist on bypassing the hard work of determining from the Scriptures what God's solutions to their problems may be. Instead, they will run to faith healers, exorcists, and those who claim to receive extrabiblical guidance or revelation for quick answers; they will plead experience as the interpreter of the Scriptures[4] or will try to use the Bible as a talisman from which to extract magical answers. For instance, more than once parents will appear for counseling dragging their rebellious teenager, whom they have failed to discipline for the past seventeen years, and say (in effect), "OK, do it to him." They expect the counselor to put two feathers in his hair, do a short rain dance, wave the Bible over the boy's head seven times, and pronounce him "cured." Such people are not happy when they learn that they may have to spend from six to eight weeks establishing Christian communication and developing biblical relationships with their son. They wanted a medicine man, not a Christian counselor. To resist these tendencies and instead hold out for careful exegesis and application will not always be easy.

Third, you will find too that even in the midst of the present disillusionments with it, many Americans still worship science—and science falsely so-called. How else could B. F. Skinner, who pontificates that man is merely an animal, and that the world's problems can be solved by scientific retraining, command such a large hearing today? Members of your congregation, elders, deacons, and fellow ministers (not

---

3. That is one major reason people get into trouble in the first place and find it necessary to seek counseling.

4. A very prevalent problem in our irrational day.

to speak of Christians who are psychiatrists and psychologists) may turn on the pressure and try to dissuade you from any resolute determination to make your counseling wholly scriptural. They may insist that you cannot use the Bible as a textbook for counseling, try to shame you into thinking that seminary has inadequately trained you for the work, tempt you to buy all sorts of shiny psychological wares to use as adjuncts to the Bible, and generally demand that you abandon what they may imply or openly state to be an arrogant, insular, and hopelessly inadequate basis for counseling. They may even warn and threaten, as they caricature the biblical method: "Think of the harm that you may do by simply handing out Bible verses like prescriptions and pills."

All these—and a dozen more—pressures will be exerted upon you to give up any idea of a scripturally founded and functioning system of counseling. Combined with personal doubts that may arise during times of discouragement, these pressures can be greater than you now may think.

What then can be done to meet and to resist effectively all such pressures? There is but one answer: during periods of pressure look to the Scriptures for their help in doing this too. The counselor's Counselor is the Holy Spirit, speaking by His Word. All of which leads us to an examination of the important question:

What Does Scriptural Counseling Involve?

Your encouragement and assurance will come from an understanding of this matter. The answer to the question is that counseling that is truly scriptural is (1) motivated by the Scriptures, (2) founded presuppositionally upon the Scriptures, (3) structured by the goals and objectives of the Scriptures, and (4) developed systematically in terms of the practices and principles modeled and enjoined in the Scriptures. To put it simply, scriptural counseling is counseling that is *wholly* scriptural. The Christian counselor uses the Scriptures as the sole guide for both counselor and counselee. He rejects eclecticism. He refuses to mix man's ideas with God's. Like every faithful preacher of the Word, he acknowledges the Scriptures to be the only source of divine authority and, therefore, judges all other matters by the teaching of the Scriptures.

In short, such counseling takes the Scriptures seriously when they say that they are able to make the man of God[5] "adequate," and equip

5. In the pastorals this designation, picked up from the Old Testament, is used for the Christian minister. Cf. I Tim. 6:1. See also Deut. 33:1; Josh. 14:6; I Sam. 9:6; I Kings 17:18, 24; II Kings 1:10, 12; 4:7; 5:8.

him for "every good work."[6] In the passage from which those words come, Paul piled words and phrases upon one another to convey the idea of *complete adequacy*: the Scriptures no: only make the Christian minister "adequate" for his work, but, as Paul put it, "entirely equip him for it." Not only do they thoroughly anticipate and show him how to meet all possible pastoral counseling situations, but by doing so they make him adequate (Paul insisted) "for *every*"—not just for some but—"*every* good work" that his office requires of him. Because the minister, *par excellence*, must counsel as part of his life calling,[7] he knows, therefore, that God's written Word will adequately equip him for this phase of ministerial work. While all sorts of other resources may be useful illustratively and in other secondary ways, the basic principles for the practice of counseling are *all* given in the Bible. Counseling that relies upon these principles is scriptural. This leads us to the main matter before us:

The Use of the Scriptures in Counseling

The Scriptures are the counselor's textbook for counseling

Like his Lord—who was the wonderful Counselor predicted by Isaiah—the counselor will find that all that he needs for the work of counseling is in the Bible. Jesus Christ needed no other text to become the world's only perfect Counselor. He was that because He used the Scriptures more fully than anyone else either before or since. His counsel was perfect because it was *wholly* scriptural in the absolute sense of those words. The minister who engages in scriptural counseling, like Him, believes that because the Holy Spirit inspired the Book for that purpose, the Bible *must* be used in counseling.

Arguments that one does not use the Bible as a textbook for architecture or for mechanical drawing beg the question. If God has assigned the task of nouthetic confrontation to ministers as part of their life calling[8] and He has given the Scriptures to them to equip them fully for this life calling, then it follows that the Scriptures, while treating other matters as well, adequately furnish all that ministers need to counsel. Remember, the Scriptures do not purport to give shipbuilders or architects or electrical engineers detailed information for pursuing their arts, but they *do* claim to equip ministers adequately for theirs.

---

6. II Tim. 3:17.

7. For the argumentation behind this assertion see *Competent to Counsel* (Grand Rapids: Baker, 1970), pp. 42ff., and *The Christian Counselor's Manual*, pp. 93–95.

8. See argumentation for this in *Competent to Counsel*, pp. 42ff.; *The Christian Counselor's Manual*, pp. 93–95.

Indeed, where else may one turn to obtain the precise data needed to meet the two major issues in counseling: namely, the problem of how to love God and the problem of how to love one's neighbor? After all, we spend little time discussing counselee problems about things; it is in relationships with God and with other persons that counseling problems develop. The Scriptures, in *focusing* upon these two questions, provide "all things" pertaining to and necessary for "life and godliness." With Martyn Lloyd-Jones, the Christian counselor affirms, "Every conceivable view of life and of men is invariably dealt with somewhere or another in the Scriptures."[9] When it comes to counseling, then, eclecticism is not an option. The issue resolves itself quite simply into this: if a principle is new to or different from those that are advocated in the Scriptures, it is wrong; if it is not, it is unnecessary.

It is at this point that so many of the self-styled professionals balk. They want the Bible in part, but not *solely*, as the basis for their counseling. Yet, just because of the fundamental nature of the question, it is right here that one makes the most vital decision about counseling; it is here that he decides whether his counseling will be wholly scriptural (and, therefore, Christian), or whether it will be something else.

The Scriptures tell the counselor all that he needs to know about God, his neighbor, himself, and the relationships between these

They speak of man's nature, as a creature who bears God's image and likeness, his basic problem (sin), and God's solution in Christ. They tell him what counseling should be, provide the content (i.e., the counsel) for it, detail the qualifications required of those who do it, and govern and regulate the methodology that may be used in it. What more is needed? Apart from the Bible, who else has such information?

You Must See Scriptural Counseling Alone as Adequate to Meet Man's Problems

All right, we have generalized enough. *How* does this all come out in the wash? *What* does scriptural counseling mean in concrete contexts? Let us conclude this article with some examples of scriptural counseling that will serve to point up more vividly what I have been saying.

Start with the most difficult counseling problem of all: death. To be more specific, let us ask who best counsels a grief-stricken widow following the death of her husband? Who is adequate for this task? Is the psychiatrist? The clinical psychologist? You know that he is not; and

9. Martyn Lloyd-Jones, *Truth Unchanged, Unchanging* (New York, 1955), p. 16.

so does he. Quite seriously, what does he have to offer? On the other
hand, are you competent? Armed with God's scriptural promises, you
know that you are adequate. You know that among God's children you
can (as Paul put it) "comfort one another" with God's words (I Thess.
4:18); you know that God has said that the scriptural data in
I Thessalonians 4 will act as an anchor for the believer to keep his
grief from drifting into despair, and that they will moderate that grief
by balancing it with hope, so that in the end, through scriptural counsel the widow is enabled to sorrow in a way different from others
"who have no hope" (I Thess. 4:13).[10] And to the surviving one who
does not know Christ, in that hour the only word that can make any
real difference is the redemptive word of the gospel, by which, in God's
providence, the Christian counselor may be used to bring eternal life
to her out of the occasion of death. If the Christian counselor can
handle the most serious counseling problem adequately, there should
be reason to suppose that he can handle others that pose less difficulty
too.

"Not fair," I can almost *hear* someone say. "You've stacked the deck
in your favor; everyone knows that death (at least until recently) has
been the peculiar province of pastors." While I do not think that it is
at all unfair to begin with life's most difficult counseling problem,
since it so clearly points up the contrast between psychiatric inadequacy and scriptural provision, and since it so pointedly shows who
it is that really is engaged in "depth counseling," and who on the other
hand has but thin soup to offer, I am, nevertheless, quite willing to
leave the matter right here and take up a different one.

What about a marriage that has been strained to its breaking point?
Two people, let us say two *Christians*, fighting and arguing sit before
a non-Christian counselor. As they spit out acrimonious words of bitterness and discouragement and declare that there is "nothing left" to
their marriage, that they "loathe rather than love" one another, what
does the unbelieving counselor have to offer? In this day of unparalleled marital failure, on what thin thread can he hang hope? From
what source can he promise change? By what authority can he insist
upon reconciliation (indeed, does he even believe reconciliation to be
possible, or desirable)? Is he adequate?

The scriptural counselor, in contrast, is able to meet the situation
adequately. He says (in effect) with the full authority of God, "Since
the information that you have given me indicates that you have no

10. Cf. Jay Adams, *Shepherding God's Flock* (Nutley, N.J.: Presbyterian & Reformed,
1974), vol. 1, Appendix A, pp. 135–56, for a fuller discussion of grief as a counseling
opportunity.

scriptural warrant for dissolving this marriage, there is but one course open to you: repentance and reconciliation followed by the building of an entirely new relationship that is pleasing to God." In contrast to the non-Christian, because he does not speak out of his own authority, the scriptural counselor speaks with confidence, knowing the goal and how to reach it. "Happily," he continues, "the Scriptures contain all of the information that you need to make these changes a reality, and—what is more—the Holy Spirit, who provided these instructions, promises also to give the strength to follow them, to all Christians who sincerely wish to do so and who step out in obedience by faith."

After detailing some of the many hopeful biblical specifics about such change (I shall not do so here as I have already done this elsewhere),[11] confidently he can encourage and persuade them: "If you mean business with God, even though your marriage presently is in a desperate condition, within a few weeks you can have instead a marriage that sings! Indeed, there is no reason why the first steps toward God's dramatic change cannot be taken *this week*, beginning *today*. What do you say?"

I ask you, *who* is adequate for such things? The answer: Christian counselors who use the Scriptures *authoritatively* to give *hope* through God's *promises* and *concrete instruction*—and no one else.

It is precisely because the will of God is made known authoritatively in these divinely inspired writings that the Christian may counsel with confidence. He does not need to guess about homosexuality or drunkenness, for instance, nor does he need to wait for the latest (changeable) scientific pronouncements to discover whether these human deviations stem from sickness or from learned behavior. God has spoken and clearly declared both to be *sins*. Therein lies hope. God has not promised to cure every illness, He has said nothing about changing genetic structures, but in Christ He has provided freedom from every *sin*. Together with a long string of similar difficulties, God has shown that those who trust Christ not only can be forgiven and cleansed, but also can fully overcome both of these sins. He says to converted Corinthians, using the past tense, "Such *were* some of you; but you were washed, but you were sanctified" (I Cor. 6:11).

Absolute authority, Christ's commandments and precise pronouncements, are all but universally decried as restrictive and evil by those who eject the Scriptures from counseling. They make no distinction between authority and authoritarianism. Unwittingly thereby they jettison the basis for all hope, both for themselves and for their counselees.

When God authoritatively directs His children to forsake any sin or

11. *Competent to Counsel*, pp. 231ff.; *The Christian Counselor's Manual*, pp. 161–216.

to follow any path of righteousness, the Christian may take hope. For apart from authoritative directions all is in flux, nothing is certain—there is no foundation for hope. Although his first reaction may be dismay when he recognizes how far his present life patterns have veered from God's way, upon repentance and further reflection the counselee should realize that whenever the heavenly Father requires anything of His children, He always provides instruction and power to meet those requirements. That means, for example, that when He says that we must "walk no longer as the Gentiles walk" (Eph. 4:17), in Christ God will *enable* us to walk differently. Every directive of God—no matter how far short of it that we may come at the moment—serves to provide a solid foundation for the Christian's hope. Both counselor and counselee, therefore, may take heart in scriptural counseling for the very reason that it is authoritative.

"Still," you protest, "marriage counseling, like counseling the grief stricken, is not quite the same thing as dealing with those who are depressed, or those who exhibit bizarre behavior. What of the use of the Scriptures in those cases?"[12] Fair enough; let us consider another example. Fred's behavior, over a period of several years, at times became so bizarre that he was jailed, sent to two mental institutions, received a series of shock treatments, was placed on heavy medications, and was subjected to intensive psychotherapy and various psychiatric treatments; all to no avail. When he came for scriptural counseling, it was as a last resort. But after six sessions his problem was solved. He has been leading a successful life as a productive Christian for over two years.

What made the difference? Biblical convictions. Since no evidence of organic damage or malfunction had been discovered during extensive medical tests, the Christian counselor rightly assumed that the roots of the problem were likely to be imbedded in the soil of sin. With that conviction he set to work.

His goal was not to treat symptoms (as had been done previously by those who administered shock treatments and by those who prescribed medication), nor was he intent upon discovering who had maltreated Fred in the past (as were others who had spent long hours dredging up all manner of parental and societal abuses in hopes of freeing the poor "victim" of a "tyrannical superego"). Nor did the biblical counselor focus upon feelings (as a third group of counselors had when they spent months attempting, by reflecting his emotional responses, to draw solutions out of his own storehouse of resources).

12. Cf. Jay Adams, "A Christian View of Schizophrenia," in *The Construction of Madness*, ed. Peter Magaro (Elmsford, N.Y.: Pergamon, 1975).

What did he do? Simply this: he set out in search of sin or sins that he supposed were at the bottom of the difficulty. A few weeks later, through proper questioning, he discovered that Fred had been sinning against his body, the temple of the Holy Spirit, by failing to get adequate sleep. Every effect of LSD or other hallucinogenic drugs may be caused by significant sleep loss (an important fact for seminary students and faculty to remember during exam periods, incidentally). Fred's bizarre behavior always followed periods of sleep loss. Fred was convicted of his sin against God and, following forgiveness, was placed on a carefully monitored sleep regime, his daily schedule was revised according to biblical life priorities, and the problem was erased.

How did the counselor know to do this? Well, he went in search of sin because he believed the Bible. The Bible knows only two categories of causes for bizarre behavior: (1) organic causes, and (2) nonorganic causes. Organic factors may be hereditary or later acquired through accident, toxic destruction of brain cells, etc. Some—but not all— organic problems may be due to the sin of the individual (e.g., drug abuse may impair normal bodily functioning). On the other hand, all nonorganic problems are represented in the Scriptures as stemming from the counselee's sin. There is no third, neutral category or sub-category that allows for nonorganic difficulties for which the counselee may not be held personally responsible. On the basis of these biblical presuppositions, the Christian counselor began his search.

It is important to note that the Freudians and Rogerians who treated Fred also did so *on the basis of their presuppositions*. The former presupposed that Fred's problem stemmed from past malsocialization; the latter, from failure to actualize his full potential. If Fred had been treated by a Skinnerian behaviorist, he too would have dealt with him on the basis of his conviction that man is only an animal and that a new set of environmental contingencies (or learning conditions) must be substituted for the previous ones which had brought about the undesirable behavior.

Every counselor, then, comes into counseling with presuppositions. These presuppositions pertain to all of the fundamental questions of life—its purpose (or lack of it), its problems, their solutions, the nature of man, and the relationships which he sustains to others and to his world. Most important, every one of those presuppositions, wittingly or unwittingly, either includes or excludes God the Father, the Son, and the Holy Spirit. If, then, counseling begins with such presuppositions, how vital to begin with the right ones! And these are found only in the Scriptures.

Each counselor finds what he is searching for. The Freudian looks for others who "did it to him," and since parents, educators, and even preachers and Sunday-school teachers are sinners, he has little trouble finding many persons who have wronged the counselee. The Rogerian looks for insights from within the counselee that may be drawn out from a fully prepackaged supply of potential resources upon which the counselee has failed to rely. Since no sinful counselee lives up to his full potential, Rogerians may elicit some such insights. The Skinnerian looks for environmental changes that must be made in order to reshape his behavior. He will find much in the environment that needs to be altered. But, notice, not one of them looks for sin. Indeed, if he discovers it by accident, he renames it. Instead, the sin becomes an "emotional problem" or "immaturity" or "insecurity" or a "neurosis" or "mental illness" or something else that better fits the system built upon his unbiblical presuppositions.

Reinterpreting sin redirects one from real solutions involving regeneration, forgiveness, sanctification, etc., to some lesser inadequate remedy that never can satisfy the radical needs of condemned and corrupted man which took nothing less than the death of the Son of God to meet. Only scriptural counseling, grounded upon scriptural presuppositions, can do that.

Because of these facts, you must "be steadfast, immovable, always abounding in the work of the Lord, knowing that your labor is not in vain in the Lord" (I Cor. 15:58). When you counsel, it should be with hope, with expectation that since it is scriptural your efforts will not be in vain. If your counseling labors are done "in the Lord," that is, in obedience to His Word and in reliance upon His power, then they will issue in the Lord's results, in the Lord's time, and in the Lord's way.

No other counselor has such assurance. At best, he knows that he has opted for some system (or eclectic amalgam from various systems) over against others. For a number of reasons this proves most dissatisfying. If he is a Freudian, he knows that more than half of the psychiatric world itself has abandoned his position and that vigorous attacks built upon strong arguments have been mounted against his views. Only the most arrogant psychiatrist today could be wholly "sold" on psychoanalysis if he has stood in full face of the prevailing winds. Moreover, look at the plethora of psychoanalytic cults, offshoots, and isms from which he must choose. Which sort of psychoanalysis will you have: classical Freudianism, neo-Freudianism, dynamic Freudianism, or what? Each of these differs from the next, not as conservative churches or denominations who agree on the fundamentals, but as widely as Orthodox Presbyterians and the Church of Rome. When one begins to branch out beyond the avowedly psychoanalytic schools to the existentialists, the Rogerians, the Behaviorists, the Transactional Analysts, the many sorts of group therapists, the Crisis Interventionists, the Rational Therapists, the Reality Therapists, the Radical Therapists, the Primal Screamers, the followers of Laing, and so on and on and on, he begins to see that confusion reigns.

And unlike the Christian counselor, the rest have no standard, no way to know and no way to be sure who is right. What a difference it makes to have the authoritative Word of God!

The unbelieving counselor, seated in his plush, expensive furniture, surrounded by hundreds of books on psychology and psychiatry, with every word may seem to exude an outward confidence and certainty that one might have thought originated on Mount Olympus. Yet, unless he is incredibly naive, unless the volumes on his shelves are there for impression alone, he knows that every statement, that every judgment, that every decision that he makes in counseling is challenged and countered by scores of authors from an equal number of viewpoints. Psychiatric jargon or prestige, which may be heavily plastered over inner insecurities, ought never to be equated with psychiatric knowledge or wisdom.[13]

The truth of the matter is that the Christian counselor who determines by the grace of God to know and use the Scriptures in his counseling is the only one who can ever have a solid basis for what he says and does. While there may be any number of issues about which he has not yet come to a fully biblical understanding, nevertheless, because he has the Scriptures, on all of the fundamental questions of life he not only knows but is fully assured of the truth and of the will of God.

Let no one, therefore, tell you that the scriptural counselor is inadequate and that he must take a back seat while learning from his pagan counterpart. The opposite is true, and it is about time that Christian counselors began to make the fact known.

In closing, I cannot help but think of the psalmist when he wrote, "I have more insight than all my teachers, for your testimonies are my meditation" (Ps. 119:99). To those of you who believe this, let your prayer, together with him, be:

Sustain me according to your Word that I may live; and do not let me be put to shame because of my hope (Ps. 119:116).

13. For interesting comments on this subject, see David S. Viscott, *The Making of a Psychiatrist* (New York: Arbor House, 1972), pp. 24–25, 84.

*There is a paradox in counseling. Often religious counselors use
religion manipulatively while atheistic counselors operate as channels
of healing love which is dependent on a divine source. There are distinct differences in an "orientation to manipulation" and an
"orientation to communion." The latter incorporates a sensitivity to
the uniqueness of each aspect of human life and sees each level of
existence as a potential medium wherein persons can become aware of
the eternal ground of all being. Morality is a term which refers less to
actions than to awareness of this dimension of life. Conscience is
the impetus to live in this depth dimension. This is what it means to
counsel religiously.*

When Is Counseling or Psychotherapy Religious?

David E. Roberts

Several of the topics which have been discussed today involve
semantic difficulties, and I am sure that we would get into a rather
extensive tangle over definitions if I discussed precisely the topic that
has been assigned for this evening, namely, "When are counseling and
psychotherapy religious?" I doubt whether you would be interested in
a series of definitions which strove merely for conceptual clarity. So
I will spend just a moment or two on the topic exactly as worded, and
then pass on to an aspect of the problem which seems to me to be of
primary importance.

All of us would agree that there are ways of defining religion that
throw no light upon what is really going on in a counseling process.
If one defines the presence of religious factors in terms of some kind
of church affiliation, or the use of given theological concepts of biblical
terminology, certain aspects of religious belief and practice can be
isolated by such means. But obviously this throws no light on whether

Paper delivered at the National Conference on Clinical Pastoral Training, Boston,
October, 1951.

Reprinted from *Journal of Pastoral Care* 5, no. 4 (1951):15–22. Used by permission.

the kind of counseling that a religious person is carrying on is thera-
peutically sound, or sound in a fully Christian sense. The most dreadful
invasions of human dignity and human rights can be carried on under
the aegis of an official relationship within the church, e.g., that of a
pastor to his parishioner; and the theological language and concepts
employed may be impeccable throughout; but it is bad counseling.

Similarly, if one tries to isolate what is meant by the unreligious or
the irreligious or the secular, and even succeeds in doing so, that *may*
throw a little light on whether the counseling carried on under such
auspices was good or bad. As we all know, many therapists who regard
themselves as atheists, and certainly are not Christian in any strict
sense, nevertheless are able to incorporate into their relations with
patients certain qualities which we in the Christian tradition would
want to affirm. And we would want to say that the therapist, even
though he rejects such language, is actually operating as a channel of
healing love, the ultimate source of which is divine.

Therefore I should like to restate the issue in a fashion which gets
at what is really crucial for our purposes. I wish to do this by means
of a contrast that may not be more defensible than the contrasts I
have just rejected. But at least it is useful to me, and I hope it will be
to you. It is a contrast between a *manipulative orientation* and an *orientation of communion.* I do not want to represent this as an absolute
either-or, however. Both methods may have something to contribute.
The central question is whether the former is subordinated to the
latter.

Let me illustrate the manipulative orientation, first from the side
of psychiatry and then from the side of religion. The scientist and
medical doctor may have a natural concern to concentrate on what is
objectively verifiable, on what is quantitative and measurable. This
may lead him into the assumption (and the feelings that go with it)
that his primary task is to learn the laws which operate through natural and human processes, so that by means of his knowledge he can
direct and control these processes. Thus he can most dependably promote results which are gratifying in terms of a better adjustment to
the community, or in terms of a greater sense of happiness and satisfaction in the life of an individual, or both. I see no danger in this
attitude of mind as long as the kind of knowledge that is available to
us through the natural and social sciences and through medical
resources is regarded, so far as therapy is concerned, merely as an
instrument, subordinated to the service of something else. That "something else" I have referred to as communion, and I'll come back to it
in a moment.

Let us now look at the manipulative orientation from the religious side. It is quite possible to have a conception of God which in fact reflects a manipulative attitude toward the human race (including oneself), whether this fact gets verbalized theologically or not. God, as so conceived, overrides and abrogates freedom; and the man who believes in God in this way *wants* this to be the case. His religion is an "escape from freedom," and, I repeat, no matter how he verbalizes it. By various theological devices that some of us are familiar with, it is always possible to assert that one does not deny freedom and responsibility while nevertheless holding to an attitude toward God that is utterly incompatible with them. A pastor or any other religious person may take a manipulative attitude toward those who come to him for help, or indeed toward all those with whom he enters into interpersonal relations. Frequently, in such instances, the inner motivation is associated with a sense of rightness which stems from the claim that everything is being done in the name and for the sake of God. Since the religious person can point to an authority beyond himself, he feels that it is the power of God which is at work instead of his own human power-motives. Therefore his cause is righteous, and he manipulates other people with a clear conscience. I doubt whether this sort of playing God can be isolated and identified only in a direct person-to-person relationship, i.e., dynamically.

Thus far I have tried to illustrate two types of the manipulative approach. The first stems from objective scientific knowledge. The second stems from religious authority. I admit that both types can be used in maintaining social order and moral standards. They can take forms less repellent than those I have cited. And they may even play, at times, an indispensable role so long as they are subordinate to communion.

The attitude of communion, as I want to characterize it, implies a sensitivity to the uniqueness, not only of each person, but of every aspect of being. The contrast between manipulation and communion is not strictly parallel to the contrast between things and persons; for it is meaningful to talk about communion with subhuman nature. "To him who in the love of nature holds communion with her visible forms, she speaks a various language." A horticulturist may approach a tree with the aim of identifying and classifying it; he may be interested in learning about it only for the sake of the results he can thereby produce. Contrast an artist's approach to the same tree where he is interested in the uniqueness, the peculiar *thisness* of the tree as an organic whole, and where any concern he may have about the painting he may produce is entirely subordinate to and derivative from the quality of his communion with the tree. Needless to say, these two approaches are not necessarily mutually exclusive. They may be combined in one person who is both a horticulturist and an artist; and each approach may enrich the other. But if the manipulative orientation is the only one employed, it is bound to miss certain salient aspects of the reality of the tree. When I speak of communion, I am not suggesting that the tree is animistically capable of reciprocating the artist's interest. But I do believe that everything we encounter in the world, from grains of sand to human beings, can be dealt with in either of the two ways I have been describing. The first attitude, if it is our only one, means that we look upon nature and human beings as objects to be controlled or directed by devising certain conditions. The second attitude makes it possible for us to regard every item and every level of existence as potentially a medium whereby we are made aware of our relationship to the ground of all being, with which we are in reciprocal communion. It makes a vast difference whether we regard grains of sand, trees, and people as events in a process that is basically blind and heedless so far as values are concerned, or whether we regard all events as grounded in a reality with whom we can have personal commerce. My statement may seem abstract; yet it is essential to introduce it as part of our fundamental distinction. Only so are we able to pass on to a consideration of what is probably the basic point of disagreement within this group.

Before discussing this basic disagreement, however, let us examine some of the terms which have been used in preceding discussions. Let us contemplate these terms now in the light of the distinction between manipulation and communion. Take the word *morality*. There are at least two ways of using this word. The first connotes a sort of pressure exerted upon the individual to conform, even at the cost of repressing resistances within himself. It means knuckling under to some pattern which is regarded as indispensable for the maintenance of social order. For some children and adolescents, I am sure, it can even mean simply knuckling under to people who like to see you have to knuckle under. An enormous amount that goes by the name of "morality" has this sort of sadism behind it, and is motivated by a covert desire to put a straitjacket upon human impulses. Both conformity to and rebellion against "morality" of this kind are frequently compulsive.

The second meaning of the word *morality* should somehow be recovered for a constructive use. It is encountered at a point where any psychiatrist or pastor who knows his business will take an attitude that helps an individual to verbalize, and to express by other means, whatever attitudes and feelings are operating in him. This counseling relationship has a "moral" aim. And the kind of permissiveness which enters into it, and is so often called "immoral," is an indispensable precondition to the fulfillment of this aim. What, then, is the sort of morality which is the goal of counseling? It goes hand in hand with the kind of character structure which can make value discriminations on the basis of adequate awareness of one's own depths. This is the only type of person with whom moral values are really safe anyway, namely, a person who can sustain spontaneously what through experience and suffering he has been led to affirm for himself and for others. He acts in a given way not because any tyrant, celestial or earthly, is going to punish him if he does otherwise, but because his action is the most adequate available expression of his own integrity. It springs from a hard-won unity of character that he does not want to violate, and that he does not have to strain not to violate. This is the kind of man you can trust. You can send him out into a community and he will be a creative ethical force because he has a living, growing approach to persons and to moral problems in his heart, instead of a set of rigid, abstract rules in his head.

This leads us to another word which has been mentioned frequently in our previous discussions, the word *conscience*. Here we encounter a similar ambiguity, and the ambiguity once again reflects the contrast between manipulation and communion. Perhaps the point is clear enough if we simply draw a distinction between a condemning and an emancipating conscience. The way we are manipulated and coerced through condemnation which comes from others and from within the self is obvious. But perhaps what I mean by an emancipating conscience is not equally obvious. Primarily I have in mind the release of energy, hope, and resolve which can occur when a counseling process, or any other circumstances which have resulted in a deepening of insight, make possible an understanding (not a condonation) of one's own failures. The emancipation comes at a point where one is able to draw up a realistic appraisal of what he can expect of himself, and finds that this may be the first step toward inaugurating a process of growth whereby many past failures need no longer be repeated. "Conscience" in this sense includes what Erich Fromm refers to as man's listening to his own voice; but I think it goes beyond that. It includes also the anticipation, the breakthrough, of what Karen Horney (in *Neurosis and Human Growth*) calls "the true self" as contrasted with "the empirical self." But from time immemorial men have characterized this "voice," though speaking *in* us, as coming from beyond ourselves. And unless conscience can have in it this word of allurement, this word of promise, it becomes a source of deepening paralysis.

The words *responsibility* and *freedom* are closely related to those we have been considering. In connection with them I have only one thing to add. This involves a paradox. It is this. An individual begins to move toward increased responsibility and freedom at the point where he recognizes his bondage to involuntary and unconscious factors. In my own experience, a person gets light on his own compulsions only when he relinquishes the assumption that he possesses "free-will" as indeterminism defines it. This is closely related to what I have said about manipulation. For the theory of indeterminism assumes that there is some aspect or center of the self, way back inside, which is not touched by influences of bodily, psychological, and social conditioning. It assumes that I always can turn myself this way or that if I just make up my mind to. The alcoholic provides an extreme illustration when he says, "I can always leave it alone if I really want to." And I suggest that it is not until an individual has "hit the bottom," not only in the alcoholic's sense of the word, but in connection with any neurotic pattern, so as to register deeply his full involvement in his own conditioning, that a change begins to take place. Sometimes the patient does a "double take," and every counselor here has seen it happen. Finally he says "My God, I *am* trapped." He has been saying it before in dozens of ways, but he has never really meant it before. This is the point at which increase in responsibility begins because an increase in self-awareness has taken place. Notice that this is communion. It is communion with its own depths. And it is communion— completely honest confession—with another person. I would characterize the process as far as it goes forward primarily as one of "letting go." Alternatively, what I have in mind could be described as an ability to "take in" what comes to us from life and from our own depths, instead of trying to impose an insistent pattern of interpretation upon it or trying to hold our awareness within the limits of what we like to think of ourselves. At this point I do not care much whether you choose psychiatric or Christian language, although personally I see the implications of what I have described in a theological context. I see in such happenings the mysterious interweaving of grace and freedom, where God (or, if you prefer, "reality") outflanks our resistances without destroying our freedom. Indeed, instead of destroying our freedom, we may be led by such an experience to a higher level of freedom. But notice that we cannot do so without a realistic prior awareness of bondage.

The main thing I am sure of is that only "letting go" enables us to say "Yes" to our own suffering, our own finitude, our own past evildoing; enables us to say "Yes" to what our parents did to us before we were able to defend ourselves. And by this "Yes" we do not mean that what has happened was not harmful or tragic. But we do give expression to a deep, inner self-acceptance at the point where something can begin to work through us which had been blocked off before. "Letting go" means, not "capitulation," but *pistis*, "trust," in the New Testament sense.

The last term I am going to mention is *love*. We have heard it said here that the primary obligation and responsibility of counselors, psychiatrists, and pastors is to love the patient and the parishioner. Who could deny this? But here the contrast between manipulation and communion strikes home with full force. There is an aspect of love which always falls outside the confines of anything we can plan, control, or pump up by an effort of will. We can obtain objective knowledge of the conditions that tend to foster or to inhibit the availability of love, whatever we mean by the term. (It is also very ambiguous; but I cannot take the time to go into distinctions between *Eros* and *Agape*.) I do not want to deprecate what can thus be learned through objective knowledge. But I do want to differentiate as sharply as possible between having objective knowledge about it, and having it. And I want to differentiate between the determination to try like hell to be a good therapist or a good pastor, and being one. This seems to me to illustrate again, as we saw in connection with freedom and responsibility, that creativity is at least as much a gift as it is an autonomous accomplishment. Think once again of the artist. But think also of how you want to describe what happens when, in a counseling relationship, you stop viewing the other person in the light of what you have learned from books, classes, or any other way. You stop viewing him as an external entity. He is by no means a conglomeration of functions which illustrate the principles of psychiatry or of pastoral care. No, you are face to face with the unique *thisness* of another person who is "over against" you, and yet with whom you are "one." In such a situation you find yourself (without conscious planning, although using every bit of previously acquired technical knowledge and skill) "in the groove" in terms of the interchange of feeling, rapport, understanding, and insight. I submit that what occurs *between* the two persons is a gift; it is not something which either produces autonomously. This is why counseling is an art. The artist, when he feels that he is "getting it right" in a painting or a poem, knows that he is doing it, certainly; but he also knows that something is being done through him.

I cannot pursue the many theoretical issues which arise in connection with what I have said. And my interest in how religion and psychotherapy may be related does not take a primarily theoretical form. For I am convinced that the ominous problems which our age confronts must take precedence over polite discussion of the relationship between disciplines. Our job is to find some working unanimity of motivation so that we can implement what we already have, even though we may never fully understand it. The creativity and freedom we all talk about are so acutely threatened that we must avail our-selves of every human resource in resisting and trying to break through the patterns which are very rapidly choking us.

The history of religion can throw light upon our present situation. Most people in past ages lived at the level of "the letter" and "the law." They got along reasonably well at that level because they were living in cultures which possessed some measure of organic unity, usually furnished by religion. The prophet, the mystic, and the Savior threaten such collective stabilities, and institutionalized religion has never known quite what to do with these figures; but it has found ways of draining off some of the dangerous energy until a new sort of stability could be established. The great pioneers of religion have been disruptive figures from the standpoint of social order, because they have always pressed for integration at a higher level.

Part of our present dilemma, so far as it is religious, stems from the fact that most human beings now have to encounter their own depths without environing support, guidance, and cushioning of social sta-bilities and institutional religion which can be taken for granted. They have to face the pressure to integrate at a higher level; but they do not possess the lonely strength of the prophet, the mystic, the Savior. This is one of the reasons that, on a mass scale, people are asking (whether they put it into words or not) whether there is any essential meaning to life. They know that life can have provisional, transitory meanings, many of which are very precious and eminently worth working for. But this awareness of provisional meaning does not silence the haunting query about ultimate meaning. If, broadly speaking, the past has found various ways of fusing cultural and eternal meanings together into a sort of workable compromise, our age has seen these two split apart; and since the eternal meaning has vanished, the cul-tural meanings have lost their core.

This brings us, finally, to the major dispute between members of this audience. For our present situation poses in a radical fashion the question as to whether God is real. This is not a question which can be answered by means of slick formulae. That is why I said earlier that the use of theological concepts guarantees little concerning the inner quality of a counseling relationship—or a religious relationship, for that matter. It may give some people a feeling of comfort when they hear the word. "That man is saying 'God', so his ideas must be all right." It may give other people a feeling of hostility and suspicion. Neither reaction is of essential significance. We get at the real issue only when we find out what is being resisted or accepted. (When I examine what Erich Fromm is rejecting when he uses the word *God*,

I want to reject it too. Who would not be against this nasty old tyrant who, like the most threatening forms of social oppression, is always trying to demand blind obedience? It is quite right to reject *this* meaning of the word *God.*)

But when contemporary man, in the midst of a situation where religious stabilities are largely shattered, asks in a radical way whether his life is "meaningful," he is asking the question about God, regardless of the words he uses. We know that some men are driven, in their search for security, into forms of authoritarianism which engulf them as marionettes. But wherever men have not completely relinquished their own capacity to grow and to fight their way through to an answer to the mystery of life's meaning, they must take the load of insecurity onto themselves.

Neither psychotherapy nor religion can meet the deepest levels of their need if the former can offer only a rootless autonomy and the latter can offer only an individualistic faith. As I read the literature even of the most progressive psychotherapists today, I am impressed by the fact that, as one might expect, they too reflect the sickness of our age. The best they have to offer is a rootless autonomy. For example, they are compelled, by reason of intellectual integrity, to conceive of faith, love, conscience, and freedom as projections into a cosmic void. Man is a freak; his distinctive endowments are accidents of emergent evolution; and the only thing we can do is to strive to build cooperatively an order of life on which *we* bestow the meaning. There is no superhuman ground of meeting. Therefore man's dignity does not rest upon something *given* (a gift of creation and grace) which provides the context for our efforts and our accomplishments and our relative moral notions. In short, there is no value higher than man for him to worship. Now I do not believe that such an outlook always takes ignoble forms. It can be defiant and grandiose (or even complacent); but at its best it issues in a tragic stoicism. If this be the only honest answer, it is a noble one. But I would contrast it with a Christian orientation where these same qualities of love, faith, conscience, and freedom are known, at least as potentialities, in our own lives. They are distinctly human characteristics, ours to embody through self-affirmation. But this is possible only because we live in a universe where reciprocal relations are possible between man and the ground of meaning. The orientation which I have described as "communion" *can* be carried forward apart from any conscious faith in God; but when this is the case, it lacks the setting which makes of communion the ultimate clue to the reality of nature, and personality, and history, and culture. It lacks the setting wherein human creativity and inner transformation are a response, not merely to "oneself," but to a call, an offer, and a sacrificial gift. It lacks the setting whereby, when we break through the relative and often tyrannical patterns of our environing society, we are enabled to enter into a *community* which signifies "integration at a higher level."

The alienation of therapeutic psychology from religious values is described and contrasted with a growing professional and public interest in religious experience and commitment. Six theses that have the purpose of broadening clinical psychology's scope to include religion more systematically in theories, research, and techniques, especially as they bear on personality and psychotherapy, are presented and documented. The theses include a contrast between dominant mental health ideologies, defined as clinical pragmatism and humanistic idealism, and theistic realism, which is a proposed alternative viewpoint. The values of clinicians are identified and shown to be discrepant from those of many clients. Greater openness is encouraged. It is argued that until the theistic belief systems of a large percentage of the population are sincerely considered and conceptually integrated into our work, we are unlikely to be fully effective professionals.

Psychotherapy and Religious Values

Allen E. Bergin

The importance of values, particularly religious ones, has recently become a more salient issue in psychology. The pendulum is swinging away from the naturalism, agnosticism, and humanism that have dominated the field for most of this century. There are more reasons for this than can be documented here, but a sampling illustrates the point:

1. Science has lost its authority as the dominating source of truth it once was. This change is both reflected in and stimulated by analyses that reveal science to be an intuitive and value-laden cultural form (Kuhn, 1970; Polanyi, 1962). The ecological, social, and political consequences of science and technology are no longer necessarily viewed as progress. Although a belief in the value of the scientific method appropriately persists, there is widespread disillusionment with the way it has been used and a loss of faith in it as the cure for human ills.

Bergin, Allen E. Psychotherapy and religious values. *Journal of Consulting and Clinical Psychology* 48 (1980):95–105. Copyright 1980 by the American Psychological Association. Reprinted by the permission of the publisher and author.

2. Psychology in particular has been dealt blows to its status as a source of authority for human action because of its obsession with "methodolatry" (Bakan, 1972), its limited effectiveness in producing practical results, its conceptual incoherence, and its alienation from the mainstreams of the culture (Campbell, 1975; Hogan, 1979).

During a long period of religious indifference in Western civilization, the behavioral sciences rose to a crest of prominence as a potential alternative source of answers to basic life questions (London, 1964). Enrollments in psychology classes reached an unparalleled peak, but our promises were defeated by our premises. A psychology dominated by mechanistic thought and ethical naturalism has proved insufficient, and interest is declining. A corollary of this trend is the series of searing professional critiques of the assumptions on which the field rests (Braginsky and Braginsky, 1974; Collins, 1977; Kitchener, 1980; Myers, 1978).

3. Modern times have spawned anxiety, alienation, violence, selfishness (Kanfer, 1979), and depression (Klerman, 1979); but the human spirit appears irrepressible. People want something more. The spiritual and social failures of many organized religious systems have been followed by the failures of nonreligious approaches. This seems to have stimulated renewed hope in spiritual phenomena. Some of this, as manifested in the proliferation of cults, magic, superstitions, coercive practices, and emotionalism, indicates the negative possibilities in the trend; but the rising prominence of thoughtful and rigorous attempts to restore a spiritual perspective to analyses of personality, the human condition, and even science itself represents the positive possibilities (Collins, 1977; Myers, 1978; Tart, 1977).

4. Psychologists are being influenced by the forces of this developing zeitgeist and are part of it. The emergence of studies of consciousness and cognition, which grew out of disillusionment with mechanistic behaviorism and the growth of humanistic psychology, has set the stage for a new examination of the possibility that presently unobservable realities—namely, spiritual forces—are at work in human behavior.

Rogers (1973) posed this radical development as follows:

> There may be a few who will dare to investigate the possibility that there is a lawful reality which is not open to our five senses; a reality in which present, past, and future are intermingled, in which space is not a barrier and time has disappeared. . . . It is one of the most exciting challenges posed to psychology (p. 386).

Although there has always been a keen interest in such matters among a minority of thinkers and practitioners (Allport, 1950; James,

1902; Jung, 1958; the pastoral counseling field, etc.), they have not substantially influenced mainstream psychology. But the present phenomenon has all the aspects of a broad-based movement with a building momentum. This is indicated by an explosion of rigorous transcendental meditation research, the organization and rapid growth of the American Psychological Association's Division 36 (Psychologists Interested in Religious Issues, which sponsored nearly seventy papers at the 1979 national convention), the publication of new journals with overtly spiritual contents, such as the *Journal of Judaism and Psychology* and the *Journal of Theology and Psychology*, and the emergence of new specialized, religious professional foci, such as the Association of Mormon Counselors and Psychotherapists, the Christian Association for Psychological Studies, and so on.

These developments build in part on the long-standing but insufficiently recognized work in the psychology of religion represented by various organizations (e.g., Society for the Scientific Study of Religion, American Catholic Psychological Association), journals (e.g., *Review of Religious Research*), and individuals like Clark, Dittes, Spilka, Strunk, and others (cf. Feifel, 1958; Malony, 1977; Strommen, 1971); however, the newer positions are more explicitly proreligious and are not deferent to mainstream psychology.

The trend is therefore also manifested by the publication of straightforward religious psychologies by academicians such as Jeeves (1976), Collins (1977), Peck (1978), Vitz (1977), and Myers (1978), and by more wide-open values analyses (Feinstein, 1979; Frank, 1977). Even textbooks are slowly beginning to introduce these formerly taboo considerations. In previous years basic psychology texts rarely mentioned religious phenomena, as though the psychology and sociology of religion literature did not exist. But the new edition of the leading introductory text (Hilgard, Atkinson, and Atkinson, 1979) contains a small section called "The Miraculous." Although the subject is still interpreted naturalistically, its inclusion does mark a change in response to changing views.

Values and Psychotherapy

These shifting conceptual orientations are especially manifest in the field of psychotherapy, in which the value of therapy and the values that prevade its processes have become topics of scrutiny by both professionals (Lowe, 1976; Smith, Glass, and Miller, 1980; Szasz, 1978) and the public (Gross, 1978).

In what follows, these issues are analyzed, as they pertain to spiritual values, in terms of six theses.

Thesis 1: Values are an inevitable and pervasive part of psychotherapy.
As an applied field, psychotherapy is directed toward practical goals
that are selected in value terms. It is even necessary when establishing
criteria for measuring therapeutic change to decide, on a value basis,
what changes are desirable. This necessarily requires a philosophy of
human nature that guides the selection of measurements and the setting of priorities regarding change. Strupp, Hadley, and Gomes-
Schwartz (1977) argued that there are at least three possibly divergent
value systems at play in such decisions—those of the client, the clinician, and the community at large. They stated that though there is
no consensus regarding conceptions of mental health, a judgment must
always be made in relation to some implicit or explicit standard,
which presupposes a definition of what is better or worse. They asked
that we consider the following:

> If, following psychotherapy, a patient manifests increased self-assertion
> coupled with abrasiveness, is this good or a poor therapy outcome? . . .
> If . . . a patient obtains a divorce, is this to be regarded as a desirable or
> an undesirable change? A patient may turn from homosexuality to het-
> erosexuality or he may become more accepting of either; an ambitious,
> striving person may abandon previously valued goals and become more
> placid (e.g., in primal therapy). How are such changes to be evaluated?
> (pp. 92–93).

Equally important is the fact that

> in increasing number, patients enter psychotherapy not for the cure of
> traditional "symptoms" but (at least ostensibly) for the purpose of find-
> ing meaning in their lives, for actualizing themselves, or for maximizing
> their potential (p. 93).

Consequently, "every aspect of psychotherapy presupposes some
implicit moral doctrine" (London, 1964, p. 6). Lowe's (1976) treatise
on value orientations in counseling and psychotherapy reveals with
painstaking clarity the philosophical choices on which the widely
divergent approaches to intervention hinge. He argued cogently that
everything from behavioral technology to community consultation is
intricately interwoven with secularized moral systems, and he supported London's (1964) thesis that psychotherapists constitute a secular
priesthood that purports to establish standards of good living.

Techniques are thus a means for mediating the value influence
intended by the therapist. It is inevitable that the therapist be such a
moral agent. The danger is in ignoring the reality that we do this, for
then patient, therapist, and community neither agree on goals nor
efficiently work toward them. A correlated danger is that therapists,

as secular moralists, may promote changes not valued by the client or the community, and in this sense, if there is not some consensus and openness about what is being done, the therapists may be unethical or subversive.

The impossibility of a value-free therapy is demonstrated by certain data. I allude to just one of many illustrations that might be cited. Carl Rogers personally values the freedom of the individual and attempts to promote the free expression of each client. However, two independent studies done a decade apart (Murray, 1956; Truax, 1966) showed that Carl Rogers systematically rewarded and punished expressions that he liked and did not like in the verbal behavior of clients. His values significantly regulated the structure and content of therapeutic sessions as well as their outcomes (cf. Bergin, 1971). If a person who intends to be nondirective cannot be, then it is likely that the rest of us cannot either.

Similarly, when we do research with so-called objective criteria, we select them in terms of subjective value judgments, which is one reason we have so much difficulty in agreeing on the results of psychotherapy outcome studies. If neither practitioners nor researchers can be nondirective, then they must accept certain realities about the influence they have. A value-free approach is impossible.

Thesis 2: Not only do theories, techniques, and criteria reveal pervasive value judgments, but outcome data comparing the effects of diverse techniques show that nontechnical, value-laden factors pervade professional change processes. Comparative studies reveal few differences across techniques, thus suggesting that nontechnical or personal variables account for much of the change. Smith et al. (1980), in analyzing 475 outcome studies, were able to attribute only a small percentage of outcome variance to technique factors. Among these 475 studies were many that included supposedly technical behavior therapy procedures. The lack of technique differences thrusts value questions upon us because change appears to be a function of common human interactions, including personal and belief factors—the so-called nonspecific or common ingredients that cut across therapies and that may be the core of therapeutic change (Bergin and Lambert, 1978; Frank, 1961, 1973).

Thesis 3: Two broad classes of values are dominant in the mental health professions. Both exclude religious values, and both establish goals for change that frequently clash with theistic systems of belief. The first of these can be called clinical pragmatism. Clinical pragmatism is espoused particularly by psychiatrists, nurses, behavior therapists, and public agencies. It consists of straightforward implementation of the values of the dominant social system. In other words, the clinical operation functions within the system. It does not ordinarily question the system, but tries to make the system work. It is centered, then, on diminishing pathologies or disturbances, as defined by the clinician as an agent of the culture. This means adherence to such objectives as reducing anxiety, relieving depression, resolving guilt, suppressing deviation, controlling bizarreness, smoothing conflict, diluting obsessiveness, and so forth. The medical origins of this system are clear. It is pathology oriented. Health is defined as the absence of pathology. Pathology is that which disturbs the person or those in the environment. The clinician then forms an alliance with the person and society to eliminate the disturbing behavior.

The second major value system can be called humanistic idealism. It is espoused particularly by clinicians with interests in philosophy and social reform such as Erich Fromm, Carl Rogers, Rollo May, and various group and community interventionists. Vaughan's (1971) study of this approach identified quantifiable themes that define the goals of positive change within this frame of reference. They are flexibility and self-exploration; independence; active goal orientation with self-actualization as a core goal; human dignity and self-worth; interpersonal involvement; truth and honesty; happiness; and a frame of orientation or philosophy by which one guides one's life. This is different from clinical pragmatism in that it appeals to idealists, reformers, creative persons, and sophisticated clients who have significant ego strength. It is less practical, less conforming, and harder to measure than clinical pathology themes because it addresses more directly broad issues such as what is good and how life should be lived. It embraces a social value agenda and is often critical of traditional systems of religious values that influence child rearing, social standards, and, ultimately, criteria of positive therapeutic change. Its influence is more prevalent in private therapy, universities, and independent clinical centers or research institutes, and among theologians and clinicians who espouse spiritual humanism (Fromm, 1950).

Though clinical pragmatism and humanistic idealism have appropriate places as guiding structures for clinical intervention and though I personally endorse much of their content, they are not sufficient to cover the spectrum of values pertinent to human beings and the frameworks within which they function. Noticeably absent are theistically based values.

Pragmatic and humanistic views manifest a relative indifference to God, the relationship of human beings to God, and the possibility that spiritual factors influence behavior. A survey of the leading reference sources in the clinical field reveals little literature on such subjects, except for naturalistic accounts. An examination of thirty introductory psychology texts turned up no references to the possible reality of spiritual factors. Most did not have the words *God* or *religion* in their indexes.

Psychological writers have a tendency to censor or taboo in a casual and sometimes arrogant way something that is sensitive and precious to most human beings (Campbell, 1975).

As Robert Hogan, new section editor of the *Journal of Personality and Social Psychology*, stated in a recent *APA Monitor* interview,

> Religion is the most important social force in the history of man. . . . But in psychology, anyone who gets involved in or tries to talk in an analytic, careful way about religion is immediately branded a meathead; a mystic; an intuitive, touchy-feely sort of moron (1979, p. 4).

Clinical pragmatism and humanistic idealism thus exclude what is one of the largest subideologies, namely, religious or theistic approaches espoused by people who believe in God and try to guide their behavior in terms of their perception of His will.

Other alternatives are thus needed. Just as psychotherapy has been enhanced by the adoption of multiple techniques, so also in the values realm, our frameworks can be improved by the use of additional perspectives.

The alternative I wish to put forward is a spiritual one. It might be called theistic realism. I propose to show that this alternative is necessary for ethical and effective help among religious people, who constitute 30% to 90% of the U.S. population (more than 90% expressed belief, while about 30% expressed strong conviction about their belief— American Institute of Public Opinion, 1978). I also argue that the values on which this alternative is based are important ingredients in reforming and rejuvenating our society. Pragmatic and humanistic values alone, although they have substantial virtues, are often part of the problem of our deteriorating society.

What are the alternative values? The first and most important axiom is that God exists, that human beings are the creations of God, and that there are unseen spiritual processes by which the link between God and humanity is maintained. As stated in the Book of Job (32:8), "There is a spirit in man and the inspiration of the Almighty giveth them understanding." This approach, beginning with faith in God, assumes that spiritual conviction gives values an added power to influence life.

With respect to such belief, Max Born, the physicist, said, "There are two objectionable kinds of believers. Those who believe the incredible and those who believe that belief must be discarded in favor of the scientific method" (cited in Menninger, 1963, p. 374). I stand in opposition to placing the scientific method in the place of God, an attitude akin to Bakan's (1972) notion of "methodolatry" that has become common in our culture.

Abraham Maslow, though viewed as a humanist, expressed concepts in harmony with the views presented here. He said, "It looks as if there is a single, ultimate value for mankind—a far goal toward which men strive" (cited in Goble, 1971, p. 92). He believed that to study human behavior means never to ignore concepts of right and wrong:

> If behavioral scientists are to solve human problems, the question of right and wrong behavior is essential. It is the very essence of behavioral science. Psychologists who advocate moral and cultural relativism are not coming to grips with the real problem. Too many behavioral scientists have rejected not only the methods of religion but the values as well (Maslow, cited in Goble, 1971, p. 92).

To quote further, "Instead of cultural relativity, I am implying that there are basic underlying human standards that are cross cultural" (Maslow, cited in Goble, 1971, p. 92). Maslow advocated the notion of a synergistic culture in which the values of the group make demands on the individual that are self-fulfilling. The values of such a culture are considered transcendent and not relative.

Maslow's views are consistent with the notion that there are laws of human behavior. If such laws exist, they do not sustain notions of ethical relativism. Kitchener (1980) has shown, for example, that behavioristic, evolutionary, and naturalistic ethical concepts are not relativistic (cf. Bergin, 1980). He makes the important point that ethical relativism is not a logical derivative of cultural relativism. Such views are consistent with the axiom of theistic systems that human growth is regulated by moral principles comparable in exactness with physical laws. The possible lawfulness of these moral traditions has been argued persuasively by Campbell (1975). Some comparative religionists[1] and anthropologists (Gusdorf, 1976) also recognize common religious value themes across dominant world cultures. Palmer in particular has stated that 80% of the world population adheres to common value themes consistent with the theses argued here (cf. Bergin, 1980). Conceivably, these moral themes reflect something lawful in human behavior.

In light of the foregoing, it is possible to draw contrasts between theistic and clinical humanistic values as they pertain to personality and change. These are my own constructions based on clinical and

1. E.g., S. Palmer, personal communication, April 1977.

religious experience and are not intended to support organized religion in general. History demonstrates that religions and religious values can be destructive, just as psychotherapy can be if not properly practiced. I therefore am not endorsing all religion. I am simply extracting from religious traditions prominent themes I hypothesize may be positive additions to clinical thinking. These are depicted in Table 1 alongside the contrasting views.

It should be noted that the theistic values do not come ex nihilo, but are consistent with a substantial psychological literature concerning responsibility (Glasser, 1965; Menninger, 1973), moral agency (Rychlak, 1979), guilt (Mowrer, 1961, 1967), and self-transcendence (Frankl).[2]

Table 1

Theistic Versus Clinical and Humanistic Values

Theistic	Clinical-Humanistic
God is supreme. Humility, acceptance of (divine) authority, and obedience (to the will of God) are virtues.	Humans are supreme. The self is aggrandized. Autonomy and rejection of external authority are virtues.
Personal identity is eternal and derived from the divine. Relationship with God defines self-worth.	Identity is ephemeral and mortal. Relationships with others define self-worth.
Self-control in terms of absolute values. Strict morality. Universal ethics.	Self-expression in terms of relative values. Flexible morality. Situation ethics.
Love, affection, and self-transcendence are primary. Service and self-sacrifice are central to personal growth.	Personal needs and self-actualization are primary. Self-satisfaction is central to personal growth.
Committed to marriage, fidelity, and loyalty. Emphasis on procreation and family life as integrative factors.	Open marriage or no marriage. Emphasis on self-gratification or recreational sex without long-term responsibilities.
Personal responsibility for own harmful actions and changes in them. Acceptance of guilt, suffering, and contrition as keys to change. Restitution for harmful effects.	Others are responsible for our problems and changes. Minimizing guilt and relieving suffering before experiencing its meaning. Apology for harmful effects.
Forgiveness of others who cause distress (including parents) completes the therapeutic restoration of self.	Acceptance and expression of accusatory feelings are sufficient.
Knowledge by faith and self-effort. Meaning and purpose derived from spiritual insight. Intellectual knowledge inseparable from the emotional and spiritual. Ecology of knowledge.	Knowledge by self-effort alone. Meaning and purpose derived from reason and intellect. Intellectual knowledge for itself. Isolation of the mind from the rest of life.

2. Honors seminar lecture, Brigham Young University, November 3, 1978.

The comparisons outlined in the table highlight differences for the sake of making the point. It is taken for granted, however, that there are also domains of significant agreement, such as many of the humanistic values outlined by Vaughan (1971) that are fundamental to personal growth. Fromm's brilliant essays on love (1956) and independence (1947), for example, illustrate value themes that must be given prominence in any comprehensive system. The point of difference is their relative position or emphasis in the values hierarchy. Mutual commitment to fundamental human rights is also assumed, for example, to those rights pertaining to life, liberty, and the pursuit of happiness specified in the Declaration of Independence. Both theistic and atheistic totalitarianism deprive people of the basic freedoms necessary to fully implement any of the value systems outlined here; therefore clinical humanists, pragmatists, and theists all reject coercion and value freedom of choice. This basic common premise is a uniting thesis. Without it, theories of mental health would have little meaning.

Substantial harmony can thus be achieved among the views outlined, but there is a tendency for clinical pragmatism and humanistic idealism to exclude the theistic position. On the other hand, religionists have tended to be unempirical and need to adopt the value of rigorous empiricism advocated by humanists and pragmatists. My view then would be to posit what each tradition can learn from the other rather than to create an artificial battle in which one side purports to win and the other to lose. Thus, the religion-based hypotheses stated later in Thesis 6 are an open invitation to think about and test these ideas.

Thesis 4: There is a significant contrast between the values of mental health professionals and those of a large proportion of clients. Whether or not one agrees with the values I have described above, one must admit that they are commonplace. Therapists therefore need to take into account possible discrepancies between their values and those of the average client. Four studies document this point. Lilienfeld (1966) found at the Metropolitan Hospital in New York City large discrepancies between the values of the mental health staff members and their clients, who were largely of Puerto Rican, Catholic background. With respect to topics like sex, aggression, and authority, the differences were dramatic. For example, in reply to one statement, "Some sex before marriage is good," all nineteen mental health professionals agreed but only half the patients agreed. Vaughan (1971), in his study of various samples of patients, students, and professionals in the Philadelphia area, found discrepancies similar to those Lilienfeld obtained. Henry, Sims, and Spray (1971), in their study of several thousand psychotherapists in New York, Chicago, and Los Angeles, found the values of therapists to be religiously liberal relative to those of the population at large. Ragan, Malony, and Beit-Hallahmi[3] reported that of a random sample of psychologists from the American Psychological Association, 50 percent believed in God. This is about 40 percent lower than the population at large, though higher than one would expect on the basis of the impression created in the literature and at convention presentations. This study also indicated that 10 percent of the psychologists held positions in their various congregations, which also indicates more involvement than is predictable from the public statements of psychologists. Nevertheless, the main findings show that the beliefs of mental health professionals are not very harmonious with those of the subcultures with which they deal, especially as they pertain to definitions of moral behavior and the relevance of moral behavior to societal integration, familial functioning, prevention of pathology, and development of the self.

Thesis 5: In light of the foregoing, it would be honest and ethical to acknowledge that we are implementing our own value systems via our professional work and to be more explicit about what we believe while also respecting the value systems of others. If values are pervasive, if our values tend to be on the whole discrepant from those of the community or the client community or the client population, it would be ethical to publicize where we stand. Then people would have a better choice of what they want to get into, and we would avoid deception.

Hans Strupp and I (Bergin and Strupp, 1972) had an interesting conversation with Carl Rogers on this subject in La Jolla [California] a few years ago, in which Carl said,

> Yes, it is true, psychotherapy is subversive. I don't really mean it to be, but some people get involved with me who don't know what they are getting into. Therapy theories and techniques promote a new model of man contrary to that which has been traditionally acceptable (paraphrase cited in Bergin and Strupp, 1972, pp. 318–19).

Sometimes, as professionals, we follow the leaders of our profession or our graduate professors in assuming that what we are doing is professional, without recognizing that we are purveying under the guise of professionalism and science our own personal value systems (Smith, 1961), whether the system be psychodynamic, behavioral, humanistic, cognitive, or whatever.

3. Psychologists and religion: Professional factors related to personal religiosity. Paper presented at the meeting of the American Psychological Association, Washington, D.C., September 1976.

During my graduate and postdoctoral training, I had the fortunate experience of working with several leaders in psychology, such as Albert Bandura, Carl Rogers, and Robert Sears. (Later, I had opportunities for substantial discussions with Joseph Wolpe, B. F. Skinner, and many others.) These were good experiences with great men for whom I continue to have deep respect and warmth; but I gradually found our views on values issues to be quite different. I had expected their work to be "objective" science, but it became clear that these leaders' research, theories, and techniques were implicit expressions of humanistic and naturalistic belief systems that dominated both psychology and American universities generally. Since their professional work was an expression of such views, I felt constrained from full expression of my values by their assumptions or faiths and the prevailing, sometimes coercive, ideologies of secular universities.

Like others, I too have not always overtly harmonized my values and professional work. By now exercising the right to integrate religious themes into mainstream clinical theory, research, and practice, I hope to achieve this. By being explicit about what I value and how it articulates with a professional role, I hope to avoid unknowingly drawing clients or students into my system. I hope that, together, many of us will succeed in demonstrating how this can be healthy and fruitful.

If we are unable to face our own values openly, it means we are unable to face ourselves, which violates a primary principle of professional conduct in our field. Since we expect our clients to examine their preceptions and value constructs, we ought to do likewise. The result will be improved capacity to understand and help people, because self-deceptions and role playing will decrease and personal congruence will increase.

Thesis 6: It is our obligation as professionals to translate what we perceive and value intuitively into something that can be openly tested and evaluated. I do not expect anyone to accept my values simply because I have asserted them. I only ask that we accept the notion that our values arise out of a personal milieu of experience and private intuition or inspiration. Since they are personal and subjective and are shaped by the culture with which we are most familiar, they should influence professional work only to the extent that we can openly justify them. As a general standard, I would advocate that we (a) examine our values within our idiosyncratic personal milieus; (b) acknowledge that our value commitments are subjective; (c) be clear; (d) be open; (e) state the values in a professional context without fear, as hypotheses for testing and common consideration by the pluralistic groups with which we work; and (f) subject them to test, criticism, and verification.

On this basis, I would like to offer a few testable hypotheses.[4] These are some of the possibilities that derive from my personal experience.

1. Religious communities that provide the combination of a viable belief structure and a network of loving, emotional support should manifest lower rates of emotional and social pathology and physical disease. To some extent this can already be documented (cf. Lynch, 1977).

2. Those who endorse high standards of impulse control (or strict moral standards) have lower than average rates of alcoholism, addiction, divorce, emotional instability, and associated interpersonal difficulties. For example, Masters and Johnson (1975, p. 185) found that "swingers" at a one-year follow-up had reduced their sexual activity and had stopped swinging. They apparently found that low impulse control increased the subjects' problems, and all but one couple said they were looking for an improved sense of social and personal security.

3. Disturbances in clinical cases will diminish as these individuals are encouraged to adopt forgiving attitudes toward parents and others who may have had a part in the development of their symptoms.

4. Infidelity or disloyalty to any interpersonal commitment, especially marriage, leads to harmful consequences—both interpersonally and intrapsychically.

5. Teaching clients love, commitment, service, and sacrifice for others will help heal interpersonal difficulties and reduce intrapsychic distress.

6. Improving male commitment, caring, and responsibility in families will reduce marital and familial conflict and associated psychological disorders. A correlated hypothesis is that father and husband absence, aloofness, disinterest, rejection, and abuse are major factors and possibly *the* major factors in familial and interpersonal disorganization. This is based on the assumption that the divine laws of love, nurturance, and self-sacrifice apply as much to men as to women but that men have traditionally ignored them more than women.

7. A good marriage and family life constitute a psychologically and socially benevolent state. As the percentage of persons in a community who live in such circumstances increases, social pathologies will decrease and vice versa.

4. Hypotheses like these have been tested, with ambiguous results (Argyle & Beit-Hallahmi, 1975). The reasons for the ambiguous results are analyzed in a forthcoming paper by our research group.

8. Properly understood, personal suffering can increase one's compassion and potential for helping others.

9. The kinds of values described herein have social consequences. There is a social ecology, and the viability of this social ecology varies as a function of personal conviction, morality, and the quality of the social support network in which we exist. If one considers the 50 billion dollars a year we spend on social disorders like venereal disease, alcoholism, drug abuse, and so on, these are major symptoms or social problems. Their roots, I assume, lie in values, personal conduct, morality, and social philosophy. There are some eloquent spokesmen in favor of this point (Campbell, 1975; Lasch, 1978; and others). I quote only one, Alexander Solzhenitsyn, who said,

A fact which cannot be disputed is the weakening of human personality in the West while in the East it has become firmer and stronger. How did the West decline? . . . I am referring to the calamity of an autonomous, irreligious, humanistic consciousness. It has made man the measure of all things on earth. . . . Is it true that man is above everything? Is there no superior spirit above him? Is it right that man's life . . . should be ruled by material expansion above all? . . . The world . . . has reached a major watershed in history. . . . It will demand from us a spiritual blaze, we shall have to rise to a new height of vision . . . where . . . our spiritual being will not be trampled upon as in the Modern Era (Solzhenitysyn, 1978, pp. 681–84)

Conclusion

Although numerous points of practical contact can be made between religious and other value approaches, it is my view that the religious ones offer a distinctive challenge to our theories, inquiries, and clinical methods. This challenge has not fully been understood or dealt with.

Religion is at the fringe of clinical psychology when it should be at the center. Value questions pervade the field, but discussion of them is dominated by viewpoints that are alien to the religious subcultures of most of the people whose behavior we try to explain and influence. Basic conflicts between value systems of clinical professionals, clients, and the public are dealt with unsystematically or not at all. Too often, we opt for the comforting role of experts applying technologies and obscure our role as moral agents, yet our code of ethics declares that we should show a "sensible regard for the social codes and moral expectations of the community" (American Psychological Association, 1972, p. 2).

I realize that there are difficulties in applying the notion of a particular spiritual value perspective in a pluralistic and secular society.

I think it should be done on the basis of some evidence that supports doing it as opposed to the basis of the current format, which is to implement one's values without the benefit of either a public declaration or an effort to gather data on the consequences of doing so.

It is my hope that the theses I have proposed will be contemplated with deliberation and not emotional dismissal. They have been presented in sincerity, with passion tempered by reason, and with a hope that our profession will become more comprehensive and effective in its capacity to help all of the human family.

References

Allport, G. W. 1950. *The individual and his religion: A psychological interpretation.* New York: Macmillan.

American Institute of Public Opinion. 1978. Religion in America, 1977–78. *Gallup Opinion Index* Report #145. Princeton, N.J.: Author.

American Psychological Association. 1972. *Ethical standards of psychologists.* Washington, D.C.: Author.

Argyle, M., and Beit-Hallahmi, B. 1975. *The social psychology of religion.* London: Routledge and Kegan Paul.

Bakan, C. 1972. Interview. In *Changing frontiers in the science of psychotherapy*, edited by A. E. Bergin and H. H. Strupp. Chicago: Aldine.

Bergin, A. E. 1971. Carl Rogers' contribution to a fully functioning psychology. In *Creative developments in psychotherapy*, vol. 1, edited by A. R. Mahrer and L. Pearson. Cleveland: Case Western Reserve University.

———. 1980. Behavior therapy and ethical relativism: Time for clarity. *Journal of Consulting and Clinical Psychology* 48:11–13.

———. 1981. Conceptual basis for a religious approach to psychotherapy. In *Psychology and ideology*, vol. 3, edited by K. S. Larsen. Monmouth, Oreg.: Institute for Theoretical History.

Bergin, A. E., and Lambert, M. J. 1978. The evaluation of therapeutic outcomes. In *Handbook of psychotherapy and behavioral change*, edited by S. L. Garfield and A. E. Bergin. 2d ed. New York: Wiley.

Bergin, A. E., and Strupp, H. H. 1972. *Changing frontiers in the science of psychotherapy.* Chicago: Aldine.

Braginsky, D., and Braginsky, B. 1974. *Mainstream psychology: A critique.* New York: Holt, Rinehart, and Winston.

Campbell, D. T. 1975. On the conflicts between biological and social evolution and between psychology and moral tradition. *American Psychologist* 30:1103–20.

Collins, G. R. 1977. *The rebuilding of psychology: An integration of psychology and Christianity.* Wheaton, Ill.: Tyndale House.

Feifel, H. 1958. Symposium on relationships between religion and mental health. *American Psychologist* 13:565–79.

Feinstein, A. D. 1979. Personal mythology as a paradigm for a holistic psychology. *American Journal of Orthopsychiatry* 49:198–217.

Frank, J. D. 1961. *Persuasion and healing.* Baltimore: Md.: Johns Hopkins University.

————. 1973. *Persuasion and healing.* 2d ed. Baltimore, Md.: Johns Hopkins University.

————. 1977. Nature and functions of belief systems: Humanism and transcendental religion. *American Psychologist* 32:555–59.

Fromm, E. 1947. *Man for himself.* New York: Rinehart.

————. 1950. *Psychoanalysis and religion.* New Haven, Conn.: Yale University.

————. 1956. *The art of loving.* New York: Harper and Row.

Glasser, W. 1965. *Reality therapy.* New York: Harper and Row.

Goble, F. G. 1971. *The third force: The psychology of Abraham Maslow.* New York: Pocket Books.

Gross, M. L. 1978. *The psychological society.* New York: Random House.

Gusdorf, G. P. 1976. Philosophical anthropology. *Encyclopedia Britannica* 1:976–85.

Henry, W. E., Sims, J. H., and Spray, S. L. 1971. *The fifth profession: Becoming a psychotherapist.* San Francisco: Jossey-Bass.

Hilgard, E. R., Atkinson, R. L., and Atkinson, R. C. 1979. *Introduction to psychology.* 7th ed. New York: Harcourt Brace Jovanovich.

Hogan, R. 1979. Interview. *APA Monitor,* April, 4–5.

James, W. 1902. *The varieties of religious experience.* Garden City, N.Y.: Doubleday.

Jeeves, M. A. 1976. *Psychology and Christianity: The view both ways.* Leicester, England: Inter-Varsity.

Jung, C. G. 1958. *The collected works, vol. 11: Psychology and religion: West and East.* New York: Pantheon Books.

Kanfer, F. H. 1979. Personal control, social control, and altruism: Can society survive the age of individualism? *American Psychologist* 34:231–39.

Kitchener, R. F. 1980. Ethical relativism and behavior therapy. *Journal of Consulting and Clinical Psychology* 48:1–7.

Klerman, G. L. 1979. The age of melancholy? *Psychology Today,* April, 36–42, 88–90.

Kuhn, T. S. 1970. *The structure of scientific revolutions.* 2d ed. Chicago: University of Chicago.

Lasch, C. 1978. *The culture of narcissism.* New York: Norton.

Lilienfeld, D. M. 1966. The relationship between mental health information and moral values of lower class psychiatric clinic patients and psychiatric evaluation and disposition (Ph.D. diss., Columbia University, 1965). *Dissertation Abstracts* 27:610B–611B. (University Microfilms No. 66–6941.)

London, P. 1964. *The modes and morals of psychotherapy.* New York: Holt, Rinehart, and Winston.

Lowe, C. M. 1976. *Value orientations in counseling and psychotherapy: The meanings of mental health.* 2d ed. Cranston, R.I.: Carroll.

Lynch, J. J. 1977. *The broken heart: The medical consequences of loneliness.* New York: Basic Books.

Malony, H. N., ed. 1977. *Current perspectives in the psychology of religion.* Grand Rapids: Eerdmans.

Masters, W. H., and Johnson, V. E. 1975. *The pleasure bond.* New York: Bantam Books.

Menninger, K. 1963. *The vital balance: The life process in mental health and illness.* New York: Viking.

————. 1973. *Whatever became of sin?* New York: Hawthorn Books.

Mowrer, O. H. 1961. *The crisis in psychiatry and religion.* Princeton, N.J.: Van Nostrand.

Mowrer, O. H., ed. 1967. *Morality and mental health.* Chicago: Rand McNally.

Murray, E. J. 1956. A content-analysis method for studying psychotherapy. *Psychological Monographs* 70, 13 (Whole no. 420).

Myers, D. G. 1978. *The human puzzle: Psychological research and Christian belief.* New York: Harper and Row.

Peck, M. S. 1978. *The road less traveled: A new psychology of love, traditional values, and spiritual growth.* New York: Simon and Schuster.

Polanyi, M. 1962. *Personal knowledge: Towards a post-critical philosophy.* Chicago: University of Chicago.

Rogers, C. R. 1973. Some new challenges. *American Psychologist* 28:379–87.

Rychlak, J. F. 1979. *Discovering free will and personal responsibility.* New York: Oxford University.

Smith, M. B. 1961. "Mental health" reconsidered: A special case of the problem of values in psychology. *American Psychologist* 16:299–306.

Smith, M. L., Glass, G. V., and Miller, T. I. 1980. *The benefits of psychotherapy.* Baltimore, Md.: Johns Hopkins University.

Solzhenitsyn, A. 1978. A world split apart: The world demands from us a spiritual blaze. *Vital Speeches of the Day* 45:678–84.

Strommen, M. P. 1971. *Research on religious development: A comprehensive handbook.* New York: Hawthorn Books.

Strupp, H. H., Hadley, S. W., and Gomes-Schwartz, B. 1977. *Psychotherapy for better or worse: The problem of negative effects.* New York: Aronson.

Szasz, T. S. 1978. *The myth of psychotherapy: Mental healing as religion, rhetoric, and repression.* Garden City, N.Y.: Doubleday.

Tart, C. 1977. *Transpersonal psychologies.* New York: Harper and Row.

Truax, C. B. 1966. Reinforcement and nonreinforcement in Rogerian psychotherapy. *Journal of Abnormal Psychology* 71:1–9.

Vaughan, J. L. 1971. Measurement and analysis of values pertaining to psychotherapy and mental health (Ph.D. diss., Columbia University, 1971). *Dissertation Abstracts International* 32:3655B–3656B. (University Microfilms No. 72–1394.)

Vitz, P. C. 1977. *Psychology as religion: The cult of self-worship.* Grand Rapids: Eerdmans.

Religious and secular counselors have often differentiated their roles in terms of whether or not the presenting problem was overtly religious. In spite of these distinctions, there are many similarities between confession and psychotherapy. Both deal with human experience. While confession offers absolution from the guilt of sin and psychotherapy offers release from self-destructive behaviors, both promise hope and healing. Their procedures have many commonalities. They take human evil and problems seriously and they are willing to plan life in terms of new beginnings.

Psychotherapy and Catholic Confession

Valerie Worthen

The problem of easing human anguish and guilt most often falls upon two categories of individuals—psychotherapists and the clergy. As the problems present themselves in increasing proportion and complexity, both psychotherapists and clergymen are forced to examine their calling a little more closely. How does the role of the psychotherapist differ, for example, from that of the priest hearing confession in terms of guiding the individual who comes to him with a pressing problem that has instilled much guilt? Carl Jung was perhaps among the first to examine critically the suppositions of Catholic confession and psychotherapy. His article, "Psychotherapy and the Clergy,"[1] represented a composite of positive values of both disciplines. He concludes that:

1. The Catholic church possesses a rich instrument (in the form of confession) that can be utilized as a ready-made pastoral technique.

2. The Catholic form of penance serves as a source for immediate release of tension, however temporary.

Reprinted from *Journal of Religion and Health* 13, no. 4 (1974):275–84. Copyright 1974 by Human Sciences Press, 72 Fifth Avenue, New York, N.Y. 10011. Used by permission.

1. C. G. Jung, "Psychotherapy and Religion," in *Psychology and Religion* (Princeton, N.J.: Princeton University, 1952).

3. The Catholic church is rich in symbolism that appeals to the unconscious mind and thereby makes it more accessible.

4. Psychotherapy involves no direct condemnation for any "bad behavior."

5. Psychotherapy is more objective and easier to handle because of its comparative simplicity and lack of ritualism.

6. Psychotherapy can speak to almost every person on some level of other (in contrast to confession, which, as an activity, actually speaks to a few willing people).

There remains, however, the problem as to how the two disciplines are truly comparable in terms of contributing to one another. Psychotherapists struggle under the light of recent research that reveals that many of their clients could have progressed effectively without their therapists. In a similar light, the priests struggle under the laymen's constant demands for the church to help them find meaning in life.

Bringing together the potentialities of psychotherapy and confession to produce a possibly more dynamic approach seems to be an insurmountable problem. An even more critical problem is the necessary understanding of those Catholics who choose to use both methods—for it requires that the psychotherapist have full knowledge of the Catholic history out of which the client speaks, and that the priest have sufficient knowledge of the therapeutic process so that he may guide the client toward the "wholeness" that both Christianity and psychotherapy strive to achieve.

The basic questions to be asked are: 1) What are confession and psychotherapy? 2) How is confession comparable to psychotherapy? 3) Can the two be resolved into one, more efficient, method?

Definitions of Psychotherapy and Confession

Confession is said to be "the accusation that a man makes of his own sins to a priest, with a view to necessary absolution."[2] Confession, or more correctly, the sacrament of penance, is sought when man has made an offense against God, or, in other words, when he has denied love of God. Confession is then seen as a necessary condition for receiving the forgiveness of God (I John 1:8ff.) and represents the necessary link between that sin and forgiveness.

Originally the Jews set aside a special day in which confessions were made to the person against whom the sin had been committed and from whom the offender desired and needed to receive forgiveness. Jesus emphasized this tradition, and Catholic doctrine that came into

2. J. M. T. Barton, *Penance and Absolution* (New York: Hawthorn Books, 1961), p. 65.

full bloom in the sixth century expanded and clarified the sacrament. Stott clarifies the sacrament of confession by basing its source and continuance on the doctrine of Catholic priesthood itself. He writes,

> This is still the official teaching of the Roman Catholic Church, which (it is important to grasp) rests on their doctrine of the priesthood. Their view of confession arises and depends on their view of absolution. According to Ludwig Ott's book *Fundamentals of Catholic Dogma*, the argument runs like this: when Jesus was on earth He forgave sins, Mr. 2:5f.; Lk. 7:4f. (p. 419). This very same power to forgive sins He bestowed "on the Apostles and on their legitimate successors" (p. 417) who are not "all the faithful indiscriminately, but only . . . the members of the hierarchy" (p. 439)—that is, Catholic priests. He promised it to them in His words about the keys of the kingdom and about binding and loosing, both of which include "the power to forgive sins" (p. 410) and then actually transferred it to them "on the evening of the day of the Resurrection" when He said to them "As the Father hath sent me, I also send you . . .; whose sins you shall forgive, they are forgiven them; and whose sins you shall retain, they are retained" (p. 410ff). This "power to forgive sins involves not merely the power of preaching the gospel of the forgiveness of sins as the Reformers interpreted it, but also the full power of really remitting sins" (p. 417). Again, "the Church firmly insists that the power of absolution is a true and real power of absolution, by which sins committed against God are immediately remitted. The Proof derives from John 20:23. According to the words of Jesus, the act of the remission of sins, performed by the apostles and by their successors, has the effect that sins are remitted by God. There is a causal connection between the active remitting and the passive being remitted" (p. 422). Priestly absolution "does not merely indicate forgiveness of sins, but also effects it" (p. 436).[3]

The deep meaning by which this sacrament is carried out is, therefore, understandable. The priest plays the important role of mediator between the sinner and God and acts in a jurisdictional capacity—penance implying a penalty imposed by the priest for a committed unconscious sin.

The sacrament of penance involves a threefold process. First is that of contrition or the sinner's acknowledgment of his grief or hatred of the committed sin with a strong resolve not to repeat it if at all possible. Second, the confession proper is heard by the priest. And third is the element of satisfaction or the "willing acceptance or performance of some task imposed as compensation and as a token of good faith and willingness to accept the penal consequences of sin."[4]

In comparison, psychotherapy is the process by which emotional

3. J. R. W. Stott, *Confess Your Sins* (Waco, Tex.: Word, 1974). Used by permission.
4. V. White, *God and the Unconscious* (New York: World, 1952), p. 182.

and mental disorders are alleviated as a result of recalling material from the unconscious. Maher states that "psychotherapy" as defined by the American Psychological Association is " 'a process involving interpersonal relationships between a therapist and one or more patients or clients by which the former employs psychological methods based on systematic knowledge of the human personality in attempting to improve the mental health of the latter.' "[5] The key phrase in this definition is "interpersonal relationships"; the process of psychotherapy involves confrontation on a one-to-one basis, the same element that exists in Catholic confession. Here, however, conscious recall is stressed only in the beginning stages of therapy with the ultimate goal being that of recalling unconscious motivating material. The means by which the unconscious motivating material is laid bare are diverse and varied. Yet the ultimate goal, that of improving the mental health to maximum efficiency, is the same regardless of how the problem is approached. Psychotherapy is based not only on the principle that "something is wrong in my life," as is also found in confession, but also on the fact that "much of what is wrong lies beneath hidden motivation."

Before proceeding to examine these two disciplines more closely, I wish to make an abbreviated comment or two on the definition and dynamics of "sin" as viewed by the psychotherapist and the priest-confessor.

Thurian states that

> the Church recognizes, in fact, that *sin—which is essentially a revolt against God* [my italics], that is to say a lack of love for him and for what he has created—brings in its train a whole series of psychological and even physical consequences.... Within its own limits psychoanalysis, whether practiced by a Christian or an agnostic, is not called upon to consider the theological or metaphysical causes of what we call sin.[6]

It can be further pointed out that psychotherapy seldom goes beyond the consideration of sin as an act that is looked upon by society as morally wrong or damaging to the patient and his contacts. Indeed, some psychotherapists even go so far as to encourage "sin" if it will ultimately benefit the total growth of the person (e.g., such as having premarital intercourse to overcome childhood fears of sex). White says,

> For all this is not of course to say that no good and no integration can come as an indirect consequence of sin, of willing and doing evil. Indi-

5. B. A. Maher, *Principles of Psychotherapy: An Experimental Approach* (New York: McGraw-Hill, 1966).

6. M. Thurian, *Confession* (London: SCM, 1958), pp. 80–81.

rect, because directly and in itself sin is wholly destructive of good and of integration. But indirectly, good can and has come of it ever since the felix culpa (the "happy fault") of Adam, the certe necessarium peccatum (the "truly necessary sin" of Adam). Where sin abounds, there does grace the more abound; though we may not sin *that* grace may abound. The neurotic, all too often, is unable to sin freely: his very repressions and fears of the "shadow" prevent it, and the same fear can produce an equally compulsive and largely spurious "goodness." Just for this reason, the Christian Gospel and the rites of the Church have no real meaning for him, for they presuppose the experience of sin and the power to respond to them freely. The actual experience of having sinned may (as, according to the Epistle to the Romans, it did for the whole Gentile and Hebrew worlds) enable him to appreciate his need for faith and the healing Christ. But sin remains sin, and the end does not justify the means. Psychotherapists who assure their patients that their sins are no sins, because of the benefits to their health which may come from them, are not only transgressing their professional competence; they are encouraging the accompanying guilt-sense to be repressed into unconsciousness, and hence, likely to form another, and even more intractable "shadow."[7]

It would appear that the priests and psychotherapists have two completely different approaches. Yet a closer look might suggest otherwise. For the priest, sin is a turning away from God's love and a corresponding lack of love for Him. It is both an intensely personal conflict between "I" and God, but also a conflict between "I" and community. While the word *sin* would rarely be used by psychotherapists, the conflict of any one individual is ultimately "I" and community. For psychotherapy the often missing link here is the conflict between "I" and Him.

This does not, however, destroy any commonality between the two views of sin, for one important element is clear. Whether one is speaking of sin in terms of turning from God, or in terms of a break from society's moralities or the development of conflicts, both views are firmly based on the notion of egocentrism—the turning from Him and from the community to the selfish "I." In this respect both the psychotherapist and the priest look upon sin as corruptive. It is crucial to the Catholic view of sin and to the psychotherapeutic view that conscious sin or shortcomings not only produce pathological attitudes for the person involved, but ultimately adversely affect the peace and joy of the community at large. Thurian states, "Not only has it [sin] psychological consequences which shed abroad some degree of disorder and suffering; any sin, however secret, since it is a sin of a member of the body, is a drag on the Church because it causes a

7. V. White, *Soul and Psyche* (New York: Harper and Bros., 1960), p. 164. Used with permission of Harper and Row.

rupture in her relationship with God."[8] The same is true of the conflict of psychopathology as viewed by the therapist. Egocentrism has a negative effect on the "I" and on the community.

The subtleties of the topic of sin are many and are further compounded by the fact that man is none too eager to express the guilt behind sin and so consistently covers up his tracks and sidesteps sin by stating that 1) it is morbid to concentrate on sin; 2) man is perfection, since he was created in the image of God; or 3) man was meant to hide his sins or guilt in the same manner that Adam hid from God after the fall. Or man can attempt to avoid sin altogether and lead a truly neurotic life lacking any form of unity.

> It is possible, no doubt, to be afraid of God's punishments in such a way that sin is avoided simply because of the penalties attaching to it, so that the sinner remains with all the will and the desires of sin, if only he could escape from the consequences. This, as most people would admit, is a wholly unworthy state of mind, and is not the sort of fear that the Council would accept as sufficient for true sorrow.[9]

Understandably, even as psychotherapists and priests try to struggle with the apparent similarities of their disciplines, the confusion deepens when one tries to tease out the implications, motivations, and defense of sin.

Confession vs. Psychotherapy: A Comparison

Of prime consideration is the attitude by which one approaches the problems of the client or penitent. Belgum writes,

> The role in which a person perceives himself will greatly influence how he reacts to his situation in life. For example, two roommates in a hospital are incapacitated by a physical or mental illness. One considers himself the victim of an impersonal disease over which he has little or no control; the other views himself as a sinner who is receiving just reward for his evil life. Such a basic difference in viewpoint has profound implications for diagnosis of the disease, responsibility for the cure, type of therapy to be used, the locus of the problem, as well as for the question of one's philosophy of life.[10]

What, specifically, are the "contemporary" comparisons in viewpoint established by these two professions that deal with this issue?

8. Thurian, *Confession*, p. 43.
9. Barton, *Penance and Absolution*, p. 58.
10. D. Belgum, *Guilt: Where Religion and Psychology Meet* (Englewood Cliffs, N.J.: Prentice-Hall, 1963), p. 48.

1) Although the basic aim of psychotherapy is to aid the individual to function better in his environment, therapy is, for the most part, individualistically oriented. The community is seldom involved in the process of therapy. The very nature of psychotherapy implies that man can "determine" his fate. Confession presupposes that a transgression is not only against God, but is performed in a manner that necessarily affects all others in the community. Restoration with the community and the grace of God are necessarily "predetermined" by God's own free will to impart grace and reassurance.

2) Psychotherapists do not have a universal format of procedures to follow such as the Catholics have. The sacrament of penance is based on an almost universally accepted procedure; a penitent entering the confessional in almost any country can be assured of the same basic procedure.

3) The priest-confessor views sin as a weak human act that lacks the ultimate goodness—that of striving to attain conformity with the divine mind. Sin is the *cause* of the unhappiness. The psychotherapist often views sin or egocentrism as the end *result* of an involuntary process contrary to the individual's will. It is more a question of something that happens to the client (i.e., puts him in a bad position that forces him toward egocentricism), rather than something he succumbs to himself.

4) It is often stated that confession deals with the evils of human freedom while psychotherapy deals with the results of human compulsion. Contrary to this statement, however, there is really no difference between the confessing individual who is fighting problems of human freedom and the neurotic individual who must necessarily deal with the choice of freedom, too. It can be just as vicious and evil not to choose as to choose.

5) The sacrament of penance is called upon to deal with *willful* misdeeds and thoughts while psychotherapy most often sees itself dealing with dynamics of unconscious motivation.

6) The "confessing act" in psychotherapy and confession differs in content. The psychotherapist is not normally concerned with the confession of a moral offense, but rather looks for causes of the problem. The Catholic confession requires the priest to act as a judge of subjective moral rightness or wrongness.

7) While the sacrament of penance was not ordained to cure, it may help prevent problems if the individual keeps a continual open heart in speaking to his confessor. Similarly, psychotherapy, while not ordained to forgive sins, does much to free the individual from those compulsions that make sin, and repentance of sin, difficult.

8) Sheerin states: "It is not enough simply to remember that you

did such and such a wrong act. The core of the sin is in the intention and unless you had a sinful intention, the external act was not a sin."[11] The intention, or egocentrism, is equated to the conscious cause of the problem. Psychotherapy also endorses the view of the intention (i.e., motivation) of the external act as a result rather than as a cause. The sin, i.e., egocentrism, is a result of the individual's inability to cope effectively with outside influences.

These issues are further complicated by the general disagreement within the church itself as to the involvement of the priest in the confessing individual's life and the disagreement among psychotherapists as to the use of techniques and the inclusion of the religious aspect in the life of the patient.

With regard to the first of these disagreements, it is admittedly difficult for the priests to separate the sacrament from personal counseling. Most admit that confession should first be an encounter in the mystery of Christ's redemption. Moralizing and intervention on the psychological level should follow second, if at all. The younger priests who have more education in psychological dynamics tend to concentrate more on this secondary level. Snoeck points out that this is an error on their part since "much harm has been caused by prematurely drawing a person's attention to those elements of his unconscious with which he had contented himself to live, even if in an unhealthy way."[12] Elaborating on this point, he writes,

> Neither should the examination of the conscience inquire into the hidden structures which influence our lives without our will. This examination is not a consideration of depth psychology in which one traces all the concomitants that had some bearing upon the sinful decision of our acts. Such concomitants as instincts, endogenic drives, fixations, inhibitions, the devious ways of uncontrolled and uncontrollable orientations of sentiment, which run through the obscurity of the subconscious, are things over which the conscious will has no power and of which the healthy intellect knows nothing.[13]

He further concludes,

> Man has, generally, little or no control over his life of emotions and sentiment. They are passive phenomena usually accompanying man's efforts and strivings. Only over his external will does man have direct control, and it is in this that his freedom consists. Therefore, if it is a

11. J. B. Sheerin, *The Sacrament of Freedom: A Book in Confession* (Milwaukee: Bruce, 1961).
12. A. Snoeck, *Confession and Pastoral Psychology* (Westminster, Md.: Newman, 1961), p. 10.
13. Ibid., p. 18.

matter of contrition insofar as it should be stirred up by the penitent himself, this must be fundamentally in the will and not in the emotions over which man has no control.[14]

There can be no doubt at this point that Snoeck represents the more dogmatic of the Catholic priests. He and many others vouch for a belief that a difference exists between moral and emotional problems; emotional problems must be dealt with outside of the confessional.

Haring represents the other side of the above view and suggests that a broader background is necessary for the priest-confessor.

There is a definite need for the priest to study psychology and sociology if he is to be an effective guide in the direction of penitents. Psychology will make him aware of the frustrations, conflicts and maladjustments prevalent in this day and age. Sociology will reveal the impact of the environment on the people. Both will serve to bridle his impulse at times to say: "You have to do this and if you don't obey, you're showing your bad will."

Finally, there seems to be a need for some sort of common pastoral planning which, perhaps, could be achieved through Episcopal Conferences. One of the aims of the Conferences could be to try to reduce the inconsistencies of practice that people meet within the confessional. It is not uncommon to hear people themselves complaining that Father So-and-So says that this is perfectly all right whereas Father Such-and-Such finds it objectionable and wrong. Inconsistencies of this nature tend to make people suspect that perhaps the priest in the confessional does not represent the Church. These people do not understand that there are areas in theology that are open to different opinions. However, each priest should seek to explain as clearly as possible the doctrine of the Church and then let his penitent see that his counsel is based on an interpretation of that doctrine.[15]

The problem of what confession truly involves is, as yet, unclear even to the clergy of the church, particularly with regard to the extent of involvement into the personal problems of the sinner.

Similarly, disagreements exist within the psychotherapeutic discipline. Not only is there dissension concerning the various types of psychotherapy and their means to ultimate mental health, but there is continuous disagreement concerning the inclusion of religion in psychotherapeutic pursuits. Because psychology vies for respectability with the other scientific disciplines such as medicine, physics, and biology, it often implies that the apparent subjective topic of religion be omitted. Menninger, quoting a speech by David McClellan, writes,

14. Ibid., p. 30.
15. B. Haring, *Shalom: Peace* (New York: Farrar, Straus, and Giroux, 1967), pp. 48–49.

"Speaking publicly about religious matters presents many difficulties for a behavioral scientist today. To admit to a religious point of view, to some personal commitment, is to violate the most fundamental rule governing the behavior of a scientist—namely, to be objective. Personal bias serves only to distort the search for truth. So it is part of the professional role of the scientist, particularly if he is interested in human affairs, to keep himself free from entangling commitments, to remain in a state of suspended judgment so far as many of life's most serious issues are concerned.

"And most of my colleagues live up to their professional role with great strictness so far as religion, and in particular Christianity, is concerned. I can hardly think of a psychologist, sociologist or anthropologist of my generation who would admit publicly or privately to a religious commitment of any kind. . . ."[16]

Menninger continues:

This, I think, is a startling statement and one I find a little difficult to accept literally. I myself know quite a number of psychiatrists and psychologists who "admit" both privately and publicly of religious commitments.[17]

Psychology is at present finding the dissension quite strong on both issues—a fact that further complicates the comparative study of confession in psychotherapy and religion.

A Potential Resolution

The history and background of psychotherapy and Catholic confession share many similarities and conflicts. Both include as a goal (or one of several goals) the healthy restitution to community life once sin or egocentrism is redirected or eliminated.

Psychopathology not only hampers man's attempt to eliminate egocentrism and attain wholeness in life; psychopathology also hampers man's ability to acknowledge his real guilt before God in true contrition. In counteracting these unhealthy tendencies, successful psychotherapy attempts to give freedom to the inner man and enables him to respond fully to his environment in a wholly integrated, realistic manner. The church sees as its function the mediation between God and man: the Holy Spirit seeks through the sacrament of penance to order the whole of man's physical, psychological, and spiritual life,

16. K. Menninger, *The Common Enemy*, in *Personaltiy and Religion: The Role of Religion in Personality Development*, ed. W. A. Sadler, Jr. (New York: Harper and Row, 1970), p. 234.
17. Ibid.

i.e., coming to internal truth before God and before the community. Snoeck comments that "while psychotherapy tries to integrate personal structures, spiritual direction tries to enable a person to find his calling and to fulfill his personal response to that calling."[18]

Belgum, speaking from a Lutheran background, suggests three steps or "prescriptions" necessary for man to break away from his egocentrism, which includes sin, hypocrisy, and pride. The essential elements for a functional confession include the confession itself, amendment, and repentance.[19]

Amendment, or constructive change, suggests the usefulness or light that psychology might shed on the total adjustment toward the ultimate wholeness of man.

A pattern is beginning to emerge at this point—one that might suggest that psychotherapy and Catholic confession can work in an integrative way toward individual understanding and truth. Psychotherapy can aid the individual to psychological freedom to respond to the environment. Confession (the next level above psychotherapy) can aid the individual in spiritual freedom to respond to the environment and, more importantly, to God. These separate functions of psychotherapy and confession can work on a progression toward the goal of being oneself in truth before God, i.e., wholly integrated psychologically and spiritually.

The working reality of the foregoing discussion can be found 1) in the *integrative* attempts of psychology and religion to come together on what appears at first glance to be uncommon grounds, and 2) in church consultation services in which a therapist can work from within the church setting to aid the individual's total growth and in the growth of the community of the church itself.

Conclusion

Two seemingly different conclusions can be drawn from the preceding presentation concerning the compatibility of psychotherapy and Catholic confession.

First, one could conclude that the two disciplines could never complement one another on an equal basis, since they are based on different presuppositions and, therefore, could not logically come out with the same results. For example, confession presupposes man's conscious sin as a cause, the mediating judgment of the priest, and the restituting grace of God. Psychotherapy presupposes the acceptance of sin as a

18. Snoeck, *Confession and Pastoral Psychology*, p. 59.
19. Belgum, *Guilt*, p. 120.

symptom of some larger problem that is unconsciously motivated. No judgment is involved, and the restituting power depends on the individual's power to pull himself up by the bootstraps and accept himself.

The very fact, however, that psychotherapy and Catholic confession deal with the same problems—guilt, anger, hostility, loneliness, jealousy, and so on—would support the conclusion that despite theoretical approaches, these two disciplines share commonality and could meet on a point of common interest if psychotherapy viewed itself as "part of" a total restoration process of man toward truth. This is even more critical to those Catholic individuals who utilize both psychotherapy and confession to order their lives.

Summary

The articles in this section dealt with "hands-on" or practical methods whereby theology and psychology could be combined in counseling. They are the culmination of the theoretical articles which preceded them in the foregoing sections and represent numerous efforts in recent years to integrate religious values into therapeutic procedures.

Wilson's essay reports successful treatment of persons who came from Christian backgrounds. He used salvation or rededication, confession, repentance, forgiveness, teaching or reinforcement of values or behavioral guidelines, and introduction into a selected Christian community. He related the treatment results to the Group for the Advancement of Psychiatry's report on the psychic function of religion in mental illness.

My article was concerned with whether, how, and when to use explicit religious language in psychotherapy. Religion includes presumption about the transempirical reality in whose presence people live plus a set of prescriptions about how persons should treat each other. Recommendations for including such ideas in therapeutic technique were given.

Adams, of all the authors included in this section, was the most adamant about *whether* or not to use religious ideas. In fact, he subsumes all mental illness under the rubric of spiritual sickness and suggests that Christian counselors should rely solely on the Bible for guidance in dealing with troubled people. Scriptures provide the only solid base for counsel in a world deluged with many alternative psychological systems, according to Adams.

Roberts is more inclined to see religious dimensions in a depth understanding of the human predicament. Although he would not disagree with the content of Adam's biblical answers, he would suggest these answers would fall on deaf ears if persons had not experienced the despair to which faith came as the answer. Furthermore, he contends that the answer is written in the created order itself in addition to the record of redemption recorded in the Bible.

The article by Bergin is a bold call by a psychotherapeutic researcher for the inclusion of religion as a resource in counseling—especially with the large majority of Americans who claim to believe in God. To ignore such a life dimension is tantamount to not utilizing an obvious positive resource and could be labeled unprofessional behavior, particularly since it has been demonstrated that religious belief is not necessarily related to emotional disturbance.

Worthen's article is a unique comparison of modern psychotherapy with one of the the most ancient counseling techniques known, namely, the Catholic confessional. Although it would seem as if psychotherapy was primarily concerned with helping the individual function in his/her environment while confession was concerned with a person's relationship to God, the two are not as disparate as might initially seem. Confession has a practical dimension and psychotherapy has a valuative dimension.

Questions for Dialogue

1. Contrast and compare:
   —Adams and Roberts
   —Wilson and Malony
2. To what extent do you affirm the use of *explicit* religious language in counseling. Why?
3. How valid is the argument offered by Bergin that since most people are religious, religion should be used in psychotherapy. Support your answer with comments about the function of religion in life.
4. Should psychotherapy that uses religion be called by another name, such as "confession"? Or is all therapy alike—whether or not this is admitted to be true?

Additional Readings

Books

Browning, D. *The moral context of pastoral care.* Philadelphia: Westminster, 1976.

Clinebell, H. *Growth counseling: Hope centered methods of actualizing whole-ness.* Nashville: Abingdon, 1979.

Curran, C. A. *Religious values in counseling and psychotherapy.* New York: Sheed and Ward, 1969.

Leslie, R. C. *Jesus and logotherapy.* Nashville: Abingdon, 1965.

London, P. *The modes and morals of psychotherapy.* New York: Holt, Rinehart, and Winston, 1964.

Oden, T. C. *After therapy what? Lay therapeutic resources in religious perspective.* Springfield, Ill.: Charles C. Thomas, 1974.

————. *Contemporary theology and psychotherapy.* Philadelphia: Westminster, 1967.

Articles

Bufford, R. K. God and behavior mod: Some thoughts concerning the relationship between biblical principles and behavior modification. *Journal of Psychology and Theology* 5, no. 1 (1979):13–22.

Farnsworth, K. E. Embodied integration. *Journal of Psychology and Theology* 2, no. 2 (1974):116–24.

Knight, J. A. The minister as healer, the healer as minister. *Journal of Religion and Health* 21, no. 2 (1982):100–114.

Lee, R. R. Totemic therapy. *Journal of Religion and Health* 10, no. 1 (1979):21–28.

Madden, J. T. The meaning of value systems in pastoral counseling. *Journal of Religion and Health* 14, no. 2 (1975):96–99.

Oakland, J. A., North, J. A., Camerilli, R., Stenberg, B., Venable, G. D., and Bowers, K. W. An analysis and critique of Jay Adam's theory of counseling. *Journal of the American Scientific Affiliation* 28, no. 3 (1976):101–9.

Index of Authors

335

Index of Subjects

Index of Scripture

342